D1374610

THOMAS HARDY AND THE SURVIVALS OF TIME

For my mother and father

Thomas Hardy and the Survivals of Time

ANDREW RADFORD
University of Durham, UK

ASHGATE

3

Andrew Radford has asserted his moral right under the Copyright, Designs and Patents
Act, 1988, to be identified as the author of this work.

Published by
Ashgate Publishing Limited
Gower House
Croft Road
Aldershot
Hampshire GU11 3HR
England

Ashgate Publishing Company
Suite 420
101 Cherry Street
Burlington, VT 05401-4405
USA

Ashgate website: http://www.ashgate.com

British Library Cataloguing in Publication Data
Radford, Andrew
    Thomas Hardy and the survivals of time. - (The nineteenth
    century)
    1. Hardy, Thomas, 1840-1928 - Criticism and interpretation
    I. Title
    823.8

Library of Congress Cataloging-in-Publication Data
Radford, Andrew D., 1972-
        Thomas Hardy and the survivals of time / Andrew D. Radford.
            p. cm. -- (The nineteenth century series)
        Includes bibliographical references and index.
        ISBN 0-7546-0778-X (alk. paper)
        1. Hardy, Thomas, 1840-1928--Knowledge--History. 2. Literature and
    anthropology--England--History--19th century. 3. Literature and
    history--England--History--19th century. 4. Hardy, Thomas,
    1840-1928--Knowledge--Archaeology. 5. Hardy, Thomas, 1840-1928--Fictional
    works. 6. Wessex (England)--In literature. 7. Wessex (England)--Antiquities.
    8. Antiquities in literature. 9. Paganism in literature. 10. History in literature. I. Title.
    II. Nineteenth century (Aldershot, England)

PR4757.H5 R33 2002
823'.8--dc21

2002032675

ISBN 0 7546 0778 X

Printed and bound in Great Britain by MPG Books Ltd, Bodmin, Cornwall

Contents

The Nineteenth Century Series
General Editors' Preface

The aim of the series is to reflect, develop and extend the great burgeoning of interest in the nineteenth century that has been an inevitable feature of recent years, as that former epoch has come more sharply into focus as a locus for our understanding not only of the past but of the contours of our modernity. It centres primarily upon major authors and subjects within Romantic and Victorian literature. It also includes studies of other British writers and issues, where these are matters of current debate: for example, biography and autobiography, journalism, periodical literature, travel writing, book production, gender and non-canonical writing. We are dedicated principally to publishing original monographs and symposia; our policy is to embrace a broad scope in chronology, approach and range of concern, and both to recognize and cut innovatively across such parameters as those suggested by the designations 'Romantic' and 'Victorian'. We welcome new ideas and theories, while valuing traditional scholarship. It is hoped that the world which predates yet so forcibly predicts and engages our own will emerge in parts, in the wider sweep, and in the lively streams of disputation and change that are so manifest an aspect of its intellectual, artistic and social landscape.

Vincent Newey
Joanne Shattock

University of Leicester

Acknowledgements

In researching and writing this book I have received the invaluable assistance of many people. First and foremost, I would like to thank my academic supervisors R. C. Hood and A. D. Moody, to whom my debt is immense. For richly informed advice and unfailing encouragement I also thank John Clarke, Brian Donnelly, Ben Harker, Anthony Leyland, Mark Sandy and Veyin Tee. Paul Whillis at the University of Durham IT Centre provided crucial help in the preparation of camera-ready copy. Special thanks also go to Erika Gaffney and the external readers at Ashgate for many incisive comments and suggestions.

This study was initially made possible financially by the British Academy, to whom I am extremely grateful.

For kind permission to reprint the substance of articles on Hardy I am indebted to G. Stevens Cox, Rosemarie Morgan and Ward Hellstrom. An early version of Chapter 2 was published as 'The Victorian Dilettante and the Discoveries of Time in *A Pair of Blue Eyes*' in *The Thomas Hardy Yearbook* 33, ed. G. Stevens Cox (Guernsey: The White Cottage, Toucan Press, 2002), 5-19. An early version of Chapter 4 appeared as 'The Excavating Consciousness in Hardy's *Two on a Tower*' in *The Thomas Hardy Review*, Vol. 4, ed. Rosemarie Morgan (New Haven, Conn.: The Hardy Association Press, 2002), pp. 141-7. An early version of Chapter 5 appeared as 'The Unmanned Fertility Figure in Hardy's *The Woodlanders* (1887)', in *The Victorian Newsletter* 99, ed. Ward Hellstrom (Spring 2001), 24-32.

Chapter 1

Introduction

In the far north-east sky he could see between the pillars a level streak of light. The uniform concavity of black cloud was lifting bodily like the lid of a pot, letting in at the earth's edge the coming day, against which the towering monoliths and trilithons began to be blackly defined.

'Did they sacrifice to God here?' asked she.

'No,' said he.

'Who to?'

'I believe to the sun. That lofty stone set away by itself is in the direction of the sun, which will presently rise behind it.'[1]

Tess Durbeyfield and Angel Clare find themselves in the 'heathen temple' of Stonehenge, eight miles north of Salisbury, in the penultimate chapter of *Tess of the d'Urbervilles* (1891). It is one of the best known and perhaps least fully appreciated episodes in Hardy's fictions. He captures the hushed sanctity of entering a site around which a mass of legends has grown; among them was one that sacrifices were made here to a sun-god who demanded blood to perpetuate his life-giving abilities (*Tess* 379). The idea of a fertility ritual is difficult to reconcile with the scene Hardy presents: he does not simply evoke the desolate spirit of place – its wild treeless isolation, the wind playing eerily upon the pillars like a gigantic harp, the huge mass of the stones silhouetted against the sky – but he also has Tess fling herself with exhausted relief on the Stone of Sacrifice. Although it is unlikely that this ancient monument was ever a Druid temple,[2] or that human beings were killed on any of the large, flat stones, it is a belief which Hardy exploits with great imaginative power to show the continuing existence of the past as a mythically relevant force in the present. After her lonely wanderings across the face of Wessex, Tess becomes the sacrificial

---

[1] Thomas Hardy, *Tess of the d'Urbervilles*, ed. Juliet Grindle and Simon Gatrell (Oxford: The World's Classics, 1988), p. 380. Hereafter referred to as *Tess*.

[2] It was William Stukeley who, according to an 1860 reviewer, 'with a vast display of learning, but with a sad want of logic, strove to prove that Stonehenge was a temple of the British Druids...The Druidical theory of Dr. Stukeley has become a part of our stock-belief'. See Anon., 'Stonehenge', *Quarterly Review* 108 (1860), 202, 204.

victim of uncomprehending social laws in a place that may have witnessed countless deaths with the same blank impassivity.[3]

In this Wessex temple 'older than the centuries', Tess feels strangely 'at home'. At Talbothays, Angel thinks of her as a heathen, and her remote ancestor is called Pagan d'Urberville, a name which gives two different indices: d'Urberville, the illustrious Norman family who came to Britain with William the Conqueror; and the Latin *paganus*, a rustic or peasant and more commonly one who practises a primitive form of religion. In the fabric of Tess's deepest being, rather than in her conscious awareness, are woven traces of ancient worship:

> ...women whose chief companions are the forms and forces of outdoor Nature retain in their souls far more of the Pagan fantasy of their remote forefathers than of the systematized religion taught their race at a later date. (*Tess* 109)

In Hardy's scheme, the pagan Stonehenge is 'the hub of olden Wessex',[4] and represents an order based not on Providence but on death. And death here is not the exacting but precious pledge of new life for the community. Something of society's guilt may be expiated by Tess's 'sacrifice' amid the elemental grandeur of this location, but the vitality she embodies can never be revived. At first sight Hardy's sense of occasion seems unmitigatedly bleak.

The ageless enigma of Stonehenge has fascinated many creative writers over the centuries. A field monument visible to all, it is a cultural fossil of prehistoric times and an arresting part of the present-day landscape. The retrospective curiosity that asks how we arrived at a certain place at a certain stage of evolution is perennial, for man is a historical animal with a deep sense of heritage. This heritage has a strong surviving component in the British landscape; it is very much with us, immediate and accessible if often challenging in the signals it emits. So the medieval 'historian' Geoffrey of Monmouth furnished an account of Stonehenge which relied mainly on whimsical imaginings,[5] whilst to the Elizabethan poet Samuel

---

[3] See Nicola Harris, 'An Impure Woman: The Tragic Paradox and Tess as Totem', *Thomas Hardy Yearbook* 26 (1998), 18-21.

[4] The quotation is taken from an interview reported in the *Daily Chronicle*, August 24, 1899, p. 3 in which Hardy talks about Stonehenge. This interview, 'Shall Stonehenge Go?', is reprinted in Harold Orel (ed.), *Thomas Hardy's Personal Writings: Prefaces, Literary Opinions, Reminiscences* (London: Macmillan, 1967), pp. 196-201. Hereafter referred to as *Personal Writings*.

[5] Geoffrey of Monmouth, *The History of the Kings of Britain*, trans. with introd. Lewis Thorpe (Harmondsworth, Middlesex: Penguin, 1966). Geoffrey's *History*, a prose epic

Daniel it remained an awesome and unfathomable mystery.[6] Wordsworth, in *The Prelude* (1850), allows a romantic play of fancy around this relic of a long-forgotten past state of things and records an antiquarian reverie during a walk over Salisbury Plain.

> Time with his retinue of ages fled
> Backwards, nor checked his flight until I saw
> Our dim ancestral past in vision clear.
> (ll. 318-20)[7]

He sees with his inner eye 'A single Briton clothed in wolf-skin vest,/With shield and stone-axe, stride across the wold' and conjures up the holy mystery of sacrificial death on an altar 'fed/With living men'.

What separates Hardy's evocation of Stonehenge from earlier portrayals is his bold use of this ancient remnant as an opportunity imaginatively to revisit several different bygone periods and to contrive that the modern moment is seen in relation to them, the resulting experience being enriched or qualified by scientific and especially anthropological discoveries. It would be a mistake to assume that his presentation of Tess at Stonehenge is monocular. The image of Tess lying on the altar, her breathing 'like that of a lesser creature than a woman', evokes a time of heliolatry and the retributive sacrificial suffering of a primeval ceremony. But Hardy introduces historical and cultural perspectives that complicate the sense of occasion, and in doing so he takes the opportunity to manipulate tone in a sharply unsettling way. At sunrise when Tess wakes, the deputies surrounding her seem as if they are wearing ritual masks. Hardy invokes, perhaps reinvents to invoke, the *artifice* of ancient Greek tragedy through an ominous chiaroscuro effect: 'in the growing light, their faces and hands...were silvered, the remainder of their figures black'; and in the novel's final chapter he famously refers to the 'President of the Immortals', a secular version of the Aeschylean god. Tess's arrest by the deputies has been lambasted for theatricality, and

---

which became a source book for the later writings of others, tells how giants transported Stonehenge 'from the remotest confines of Africa', and set them up on Mount Killarus in Ireland. The wizard Merlin suggested moving it to Mount Ambrius, near Salisbury, as the new national memorial.

[6] See Samuel Daniel's *Musophilus* (1599), a verse dialogue in six- and eight-lined stanzas. He views the temple as a chastening example of our failure to penetrate the profound riddle of how prehistoric man interpreted the cosmic reality in which he was immersed (ll. 337-49). In *'Poems' and 'A Defence of Ryme'*, ed. Arthur Colby Sprague (Chicago and London: University of Chicago Press, 1965), pp. 78-9.

[7] William Wordsworth, *The Prelude: A Parallel Text*, ed. J. C. Maxwell (Harmondsworth, Middlesex: Penguin, 1986), p. 507.

indeed it is blatantly and unapologetically 'staged'. Yet the staginess is a deliberate ploy, for Hardy impishly – or even sardonically imbues this episode with more than a hint of Wagnerian grandiosity too. Whilst at the other extreme of 'theatricality', the disquieting image of the black cloud in the skies above Stonehenge 'lifting bodily like the lid of a pot' conveys a spirit of grim foreboding in an image which suggests a naive stage prop of antique melodrama (a cauldron) or domestic comedy (a cooking pot). Hardy has artfully made sure that there is more to this cruel episode than meets the single eye.

Throughout his literary career, Hardy broods over the landmarks of local topography because they are crusted with ancestral imprints and open up fresh possibilities for his art. He wonders if the resonant meaning these imposing structures possessed for the people who shaped them might be recoverable and so stimulate or enhance late-Victorian life, and he employs occasions of anthropological significance to question the value of and the need for historical continuity. If the Stonehenge episode derails glib critical readings, it quite clearly comes at a point in his writing when he could no longer entertain such vestiges as possible tokens of some exacting but positive order which enabled our primeval forebears to establish kinship, a living bond between themselves and their gods, a rewarding future for their community.

Hardy's discovery through the Stonehenge site of an irretrievable sense of deathliness in the social and personal worlds clashed radically with the rapt conviction of the many Victorian sages and anthropologists, Hegel, Comte and Spencer included – all thinkers whose work Hardy carefully read – who were driven by a staunch belief in the perfectibility of man, postulated constant historical advance, and saw the evolution of human society as one of progressive enlightenment. Hardy's friend, the folklorist and rationalist propagandist Edward Clodd, enthused: 'The early history of man shows us how wonderful his progress has been when we compare the Age of Stone with our present happy lot'.[8] James A. Farrer, in his popular study *Primitive Manners and Customs* (1879), reflected this mood of smug assurance:

> The history of humanity has been a rise, not a fall, not a degradation
> from completeness to imperfection, but a constantly accelerating
> progress from savagery to culture; that, in short, the iron age of the
> world belongs to the past, its golden one to the future.[9]

---

[8]   Edward Clodd, *The Childhood of the World. A Simple Account of Man in Early Times* (London and New York: Macmillan, 1873), p. 50.
[9]   James A. Farrer, *Primitive Manners and Customs* (London: Chatto & Windus, 1879), pp. 314-15.

But Hardy implies that there may be little separating the rites enacted in the temple of primitive blood sacrifice and the atrocities committed at Wintoncester gaol, where Tess is executed in the final chapter. We note continuity of a kind, but it does not reveal man's 'glorious destiny of never-ending advancement'.[10] He sees instead 'the essentially cruel heartlessness of Paganism'[11] repeating itself in the modern re-enactment. This 'find' is in striking contrast to the complacent arguments of those scholars who treated European culture as the capstone of human achievement, and who promoted the idea of progress as logically natural, universal and inevitable.

In general, the more flexibility and scope Hardy allowed himself for time-voyaging, the more likely he was to find irrefutable evidence of the absolute destructiveness of history. And yet, in deciding against the physical, visible remains of the past as stumbling blocks rather than precious signposts, Hardy nevertheless invests Tess's capture amid the pillars of Stonehenge with a pungency and élan that energize this mute monument of forgotten faiths. At a personal level, Hardy's disturbing 'excavations' made in the Stonehenge scene gratifies his own idiosyncratic sense of imaginative excitement. He locates a counterforce to his stricken sense of social and historical severance in an art that involves irony, incongruous juxtaposition and 'black' humour to promote unusual angles of vision. This raises the question of whether the art with which he invests his backward-looking impulse is merely self-indulgent or whether it has public purpose, for the Hardy whose eccentricities of tone and narrative tactic are so oddly enabled and stimulated by the fossil fragments of a lost yesterday is the same figure who in *The Woodlanders*, *Tess* and *Jude* projects himself as very socially-conscious, an aggressively public champion of enlightened liberation against power and privilege.

Hardy's quarrying of disparate bygone moments during the Stonehenge scene with a mixture of solemn intensity and playful wit epitomizes the eclectic spirit and strategy of a novel absorbed by multiple time-schemes. Indeed, the whole countryside in *Tess* is symbolic of an infinitely stratified sense of place. Not only does he uncover and explore a bedrock of primeval perception, but he traverses more local and immediate historical terrain. *Tess* is also a trenchant account of landed gentry d'Urbervilles atrophying over several centuries into squalid and feckless Durbeyfields. From the highborn ancestral past of the d'Urbervilles, we glimpse through Tess's mother, Joan, another stratum of historical experience, that of the Wessex peasantry – a modern evolved form of the 'timeless' rural folk who

---

[10] [J. Phillips], 'Review of *Geological Evidences of the Antiquity of Man* by Charles Lyell', *Quarterly Review* 114 (1863), 415.
[11] Anon., 'Primitive Man: Tylor and Lubbock', *Quarterly Review* 137 (July 1874), 70.

populated the region long before the aristocratic families arrived. Joan Durbeyfield possesses a *Compleat Fortune-Teller*,[12] and a 'fast-perishing lumber of superstitions, folklore, dialect and orally transmitted ballads' (*Tess* 27). Although some of her mother's vibrant folk-culture and superstitious fears rubs off on her daughter, Tess is instructed by a more recent epoch, that of Victorian 'Standard' education, which, as Hardy writes in his Preface to the *Selected Poems of William Barnes*, has 'gone on with its silent and inevitable effacements, reducing the speech of this country to uniformity, and obliterating every year many a fine old local word'.[13] In Tess, an advanced style of education has erased dialectal crudities and parochial narrowness, infecting her with the 'ache of modernism', a moral conscience which stops her participating fully in the peasant customs that have maintained her mother's social group for centuries.[14]

In all his novels Hardy exposes many layers of past experience, covering an extraordinary range of time. R. J. Wright observes that Hardy had 'a lifelong fascination with history' and 'the range of [his] historical reference is very wide...He read history as any educated man read it in Victorian England. Thucydides, Clarendon, Gibbon, Motley, were all in his library, and all were cherished'.[15] Hardy was also drawn to evolutionary anthropology and comparative religion, as attested by his understanding of Sir James George Frazer's *The Golden Bough* (1890). The boy Hardy received a copy of Dryden's *Virgil* from his mother and he continued to study classical literature throughout his life.[16] The Middle Ages attracted the architect in him because they created the most imposing buildings. Coupled with these interests is an antiquarian attachment to village superstitions, local lore and the annals of his birthplace. One of his favourite books was John Hutchins's *The History and Antiquities of the County of Dorset*, referred to mischievously as 'the excellent county history' in his Napoleonic romance, *The Trumpet-Major* (1880).[17] A copy

---

[12] Ruth Firor explains that this volume, along with the *Universal Fortune-Teller*, was 'still very popular in England within the past century'. See *Folkways in Thomas Hardy* (Philadelphia: University of Pennsylvania Press, 1931), p. 99.

[13] Thomas Hardy, *Personal Writings*, p. 76.

[14] Tess has 'passed the sixth standard in the National school' (*Tess* 26). The National Society for Promoting the Education of the Poor in the Principles of the Established Church in England and Wales first founded schools in 1811. The first National school came to Dorset in 1812.

[15] R. J. Wright, *Thomas Hardy and History* (London: Macmillan, 1974), pp. 1, 7.

[16] Hardy was well read in Aeschylean tragedy, Virgil, Horace and Ovid.

[17] Thomas Hardy, *The Trumpet-Major, and Robert his Brother*, ed. with introd. Roger Ebbatson (Harmondsworth, Middlesex: Penguin, 1987), p. 95.

of the third edition (4 vols., London, 1861-73) was in Hardy's Max Gate library. Hutchins, in his Preface to the First Edition (June 1, 1773), saw his 'native County of Dorset' as an major focus for antiquarian research: 'the advantages of its situation, fertility of its soil, rare productions, the many remains of antiquity with which it abounds...well deserves an Historian'.[18] There is an element of Hutchins's wild eclecticism – not restricting himself to one specific type of source material but dextrously combining literary and material evidences of bygone times – in Hardy's use of the past.

Tess of the d'Urbervilles, given its ambitiousness in embracing moments of the remotest antiquity in addition to more parochial and current events, can be read as the crowning imaginative assimilation and recreation of the 'proceedings' of the new sciences of humankind that evolved during the Victorian age. Hardy's contemporaries were indefatigable explorers through time. His era witnessed an immense range of literal and figurative excavations and discoveries – as in geology, which became the foremost science in the first half of the nineteenth century, fixing 'the attention and the gratitude of a daily and hourly widening circle of intelligent readers'.[19] Samuel Daniel's awed perception in *Musophilus* that we could never decode the cryptic riddle of the standing stones, and indeed Lord Byron's bemused curiosity in a later epoch ('The Druid's groves are gone so much the better:/Stonehenge is not – but what the devil is it?') was not shared by the Victorian scientific priesthood.[20] There was an unprecedented desire imaginatively and practically to revisit neglected epochs and dispel their perplexities. 'Hardly any branch of inquiry,' according to a reviewer of E. B. Tylor's *Primitive Culture* (1871), 'has...within the last few years, made more rapid strides than that which has man, his origin, antiquity, and history, his advancements and retrogressions...for its object'.[21] Albert Way

---

[18] John Hutchins, *The History and Antiquities of Dorset (interspersed with some remarkable particulars of natural history; and adorned with a correct map of the country, and view of antiquities, seats of the nobility and gentry)* 3rd edn, corrected by William Shipp and James Whitworth Hodson, 4 vols. (Westminster: John Bowyer Nichols & Sons, 1861), I, vii.

[19] Anon., 'The Organic World now in Progress', *Quarterly Review* 47 (March 1832), 132. The antiquarian William John Thoms asked proudly in 1859, 'Who that remembers the plates of Petrifactions to be found in old works on Natural History, or the heterogeneous fragments which used to be labelled Fossils in our museums, could, from an inspection of them, have ever believed it possible that their study should have resulted in that most important Science which we all now admire for its ingenuity and profundity – Geology?' See *Choice Notes from 'Notes and Queries'. Folk Lore* (London: Bell & Daldy, 1859), v.

[20] Lord George Gordon Byron, *Don Juan*, ed. E. Steffan and T.G. Steffan (Harmondsworth, Middlesex: Penguin, 1996), p. 403.

[21] Anon., 'Tylor on *Primitive Culture*', *Edinburgh Review* 135 (January 1872), 89-90. The reviewer acclaims that 'keen and persistent inquisition into the buried hearths and

proclaimed in his 'Introduction' to the first volume of the *Archaeological Journal* (March 1844):

> At the present time, the love and the study of ancient and historical monuments...no longer confined to a limited number of curio enquirers, have become a national and a prevalent taste. The progressive advance of such a taste may be marked from year to year, not less in the formation of numerous local societies, and private collections, or in costly undertakings for the support or restoration of ancient public monuments, than in publications, by means of which the obscurities of the science of Antiquity have been rendered comprehensible and acceptable to the public.[22]

This zeal spread to the scrutiny of provincial lore, which represented for one commentator 'a chapter in our history too long neglected, since by means of such information the greater part of all that is peculiar in our laws and manners might probably at one time have been traced to its origin, accounted for, and explained'.[23] Contemporary peasant customs, hitherto derided as the worthless wreckage cast aside by progressive culture, now became 'an object of keen scientific curiosity'.[24] E. B. Tylor's concept of the untutored rural masses as a limitless archive of cultural antiquities, introduced in his articles of the mid-1860s and scrupulously extended in his masterwork *Primitive Culture*, may have had a profound effect on Hardy's imaginative reconstruction of Wessex village life. With energetic eloquence Tylor urged a new generation of antiquarians to compile the folklore of European peasant life and to plot its likenesses with tribal behaviour:

> Look at the modern European peasant using his hatchet and his hoe, see his food boiling or roasting over the log-fire...hear his tale of the ghost in the nearest haunted house, and of the farmer's niece who was bewitched with knots inside till she fell into fits and died. If we choose out in this way things which have altered little in the long course of centuries, we may draw a picture where there shall be

---

homesteads, the sepulchral mounds and bergs, the cinerary urns and mortuary chambers of early ages.'

[22] Albert Way, 'Introduction', *Archaeological Journal* 1 (1844), 1.

[23] Anon., 'On the History and Prospects of Antiquarianism in England', *Edinburgh Review* 86 (October 1847), 318.

[24] Edward Caird, *The Evolution of Religion. The Gifford Lectures delivered before the University of St. Andrews in Sessions 1890-91 and 1891-2*, 2 vols. (Glasgow: James Maclehose & Sons, 1893), I, 13.

scarce a hand's breadth of difference between an English ploughman and a negro in Central Africa.[25]

Tylor contested that probing the irrationality and superstition of the village community, a 'now unfamiliar social institution', was no 'profitless task', and he gave folk-practices a documentary significance already ascribed to the broken urns and petrified organic remains uncovered by excavators.[26] General publications such as the *The Gentleman's Magazine*, *Athenaeum*, *Cornhill*, *Blackwood's Magazine* and *The Quarterly Review* reflected this intensified interest by offering more antiquarian, geological and archaeological discussion. Tylor placed some of his most succinct and persuasive early articles in *The Fortnightly Review*, which became in the latter third of the century, 'the acknowledged mouthpiece of advanced, free-thinking radicalism'.[27] He hoped that endeavours to locate the key to primeval periods would create an invaluable area of humanistic inquiry, as well as minister to the well-being of modern society, because the ideas and traditions of Victorian Britain – 'the heir of all the ages in the foremost files of time' as Tennyson described it in 'Locksley Hall'[28] – were the end-products of history. Tylor believed that the findings of anthropology would enable the 'great modern nations to understand themselves, to weigh in a just balance their own merits and defects, and even in some measure to forecast...the possibilities of the future'.[29]

Given the Victorians' passion for possessing the lost things of the past and making them part of their own experience, it is hardly surprising that their remarkable adventures in time would oscillate between exultation and despair. Though William H. Smith declared in 1863 that 'we shall be happy to receive whatever knowledge of the now forgotten past [the geologist] can bring to light',[30] his era was defined as much by crippling doubt as it was by serene confidence in scientific progress. Far from seeing the earth as a volume immeasurably rich in meaning, Sir Francis Palgrave argued, 'We must give it up, that speechless past; whether in Europe, Asia, Africa

---

[25] E. B. Tylor, *Primitive Culture: Researches into the Development of Mythology, Philosophy, Religion, Art and Custom*, 4th edn., 2 vols. (London: John Murray, 1903), I, 6. Hereafter referred to as *Primitive Culture*.

[26] E. B. Tylor, 'Maine's Village Communities', *Quarterly Review* 131 (1871), 176.

[27] John Gross, *The Rise and Fall of the Man of Letters: Aspects of English Literary Life Since 1800* (New York: Macmillan, 1969), p. 66.

[28] Alfred Lord Tennyson, *The Poems of Tennyson*, ed. Christopher Ricks, 3 vols. (Harlow, Essex: Longmans, 1987), II, 129. Hereafter referred to as *The Poems of Tennyson*.

[29] Quoted in Henrika Kuklick, *The Savage Within: The Social History of British Anthropology, 1885-1945* (Cambridge: Cambridge University Press, 1991), p. 7.

[30] [William H. Smith], 'Wilson's *Prehistoric Man*', *Blackwood's Magazine* 93 (1863), 544.

or America...on Lycian shore or Salisbury Plain; lost is lost; gone is gone for ever.'[31] Many suspected that once we go back beyond writing, our achievements would seem almost subhuman. Perhaps this was an alarmed response to the recurring nineteenth-century struggle between a scriptural account of origins with its emphasis on the designing hand of a providential creator, and that implied by the geological record, whose stony pages the pedantically studious Henry Knight must decipher while precariously suspended from the face of an escarpment in *A Pair of Blue Eyes* (1873). Tylor observed in 1866 how 'The old and simple theory which explains the world at large as directly animated by a life like our own, or directly resulting from such life, has been for ages at war with an ever-accumulating and ever-encroaching scientific knowledge'.[32] Apprehension also stemmed from finding, especially through Darwinism, an unacceptably primitive and bestial dimension of man. Although the English *Monthly Review* of 1832 saw evolution as 'the most stupid and ridiculous' idea to be hatched by 'the heated fancy of man',[33] this scientific theory would soon become, in the words of a more moderate journalist, 'part of the furniture of the human mind'.[34] Hardy's poem 'Drinking Song' ruminates on the status of humankind and its vexed relationship to other species: 'Next this strange message Darwin brings' that 'We all are one with creeping things;/And apes and men/Blood brethren,/And likewise reptile forms with stings'.[35] The Neanderthal skeleton was unearthed in 1857 by Fuhlrott and, as C.F. Keary recorded, 'when the skull and other parts of the skeleton were exhibited at a scientific meeting at Bonn, in the same year, doubts were expressed as to the human character of the remains'.[36]

Nevertheless, the unflagging drive to 'exhume' neglected epochs even spread to the discipline in which Hardy himself trained as a young man, architecture. A contributor to the 1857 *Edinburgh Review* announced that the accurate study of architectural ruins could produce findings to rival the momentous 'excavations' of earth sciences:

---

[31] Quoted in Sir John Lubbock, *Prehistoric Times, as illustrated by Ancient Remains and the Manners and Customs of Modern Savages*, 4th edn. (London: Frederic Norgate, 1878), p. 1.

[32] E. B. Tylor, 'The Religion of Savages', *Fortnightly Review* 6 (1866), 72.

[33] Quoted in Deborah Cadbury, *The Dinosaur Hunters. A Story of Scientific Rivalry And the Discovery of the Pre-historic World* (London, Fourth Estate, 2001), p. 184.

[34] T. W. Fowle, 'The Place of Conscience in Evolution', *Nineteenth Century* 4 (1878), 1. By 1880, the term 'origin of species' had apparently 'become a household name in science'. See Alfred R. Wallace, 'The Origin of Species and Genera', *Nineteenth Century* 7 (1880), 93.

[35] Thomas Hardy, *The Complete Poems of Thomas Hardy*, New Wessex Edition. ed. James Gibson (London: Macmillan, 1976), pp. 906-7. Hereafter referred to as *Complete Poems*.

[36] C. F. Keary (ed.), *The Dawn of History: An Introduction to Pre-historic Study* (London: Mozley & Smith, 1878), p. 13.

The architectural remains of past generations, sometimes scattered over wastes in which the primeval solitude has regained its empire over civilisation, sometimes buried under the strata of more recent periods of history, are the most conspicuous and enduring monuments of nations, of religions, and of empires which have left no other trace upon this earth [and] may be compared by their results to the knowledge extracted by the geologist and the naturalist from the physical condition or the organic remains of the globe.[37]

Hardy was fascinated by the branch of architecture devoted to Gothic restoration.[38] 'Of all the inventions of our age', Sidney Colvin remarked in October 1877, 'none have been adopted more rapidly or more unreservedly, from one end of Europe to the other, than this of architectural restoration'.[39] As a trainee architect, Hardy spent a great deal of time sketching Gothic features and restoring old churches. He had been working with Gothic ever since he began his pupillage with John Hicks at Dorchester in 1856. Gothic was the accepted style for church building, and the vogue was for 'renewal' of as many medieval qualities as possible in crumbling parish churches. Hardy assessed the grammar and archaeology of the neo-medieval style, in which Hicks himself specialized, and was employed in surveying and preparing preliminary studies of churches marked for renovation. When he relocated to London in 1862, it was specifically as 'a young Gothic draughtsman who could restore and design churches and rectory-houses'.[40] He is credited with the design of All Saints' Windsor, a Gothic church consecrated in 1864, with medieval tracery and a large rose window.

Although Hardy shared to an extent the antiquarian leanings of the neo-Gothic architects, it was tempered by the disabused wisdom that efforts at resuscitating a distant, prestigious past could only be at best mere forgeries.[41] Perhaps pangs of remorse for what he believed to be his own

---

[37] Anon., 'Fergusson's *Handbook of Architecture*', *Edinburgh Review* 105 (January 1857), 112-13.

[38] See Kenneth Clark, *The Gothic Revival: An Essay in the History of Taste* (London: Murray, 1928); George L. Hersey, *High Victorian Gothic: A Study in Associationism* (Baltimore: Johns Hopkin University Press, 1972); Basil F. L. Clarke, *Church Builders of the Nineteenth Century: A Study of the Gothic Revival in England* (Newton Abbot: David & Charles, 1969); James F. White, *The Cambridge Movement: The Ecclesiologists and the Gothic Revival* (Cambridge: Cambridge University Press, 1962).

[39] Sidney Colvin, 'Restoration and Anti-Restoration', *Nineteenth Century* 2 (1877), 446, 448.

[40] Thomas Hardy, *The Life and Work of Thomas Hardy by Thomas Hardy*, ed. Michael Millgate (London: Macmillan, 1984), p. 41. Hereafter referred to as *Life*.

[41] In his *Handbook of Architecture* (1855), James Fergusson wrote 'though Gothic art was a thing of our country and of our own race, it belongs to a state of society so different from anything that now exists, that any attempt to reproduce it now must at best be a masquerade,

extreme and disastrous renovations as an architect's assistant impelled him
to join the Society for the Protection of Ancient Buildings (1877). In his
essay 'Memories of Church Restoration' (1906), Hardy looked back 'in a
contrite spirit' at his own 'brief experience as a church-restorer and the
drastic treatment' he 'dealt out'.[42] He opposed this architectural craze
because it obscured or denied the intricate investment of different moments
of time in the one building or site. In A *Pair of Blue Eyes*, for example,
Henry Knight regrets the damage done by renovators in the substitution of
a mock medievalism for the true antiquity of architectural palimpsest in
Endelstow Church, whilst the narrow-minded and facile Parson Swancourt
feels no guilt at all.[43]

The backward-looking curiosity of Hardy's era ranged from the vogue
for Gothic revival and its veneration of the feudal era, to reconstructing the
prehistoric realm of which Stonehenge is such a challenging part.
Prehistory as a separate facet of research into humankind's past emerged in
the second half of the nineteenth century with the publication of Daniel
Wilson's *The Archaeology and Prehistoric Annals of Scotland* (1851).
Twelve years later, in the preface to the second edition of this book, Wilson
referred to 'the application of the term prehistoric introduced – if I mistake
not – for the first time in this work'.[44] C. F. Keary could claim that 'the
science of pre-historic archaeology' might 'stand in rivalry with geology as
the favourite child of this century'.[45] T. G. Bonney's 1866 article 'Stone
Circles and Megalithic Remains' for the *Gentleman's Magazine* recognized
how:

> The antiquity of the human race and the condition of man in the ages
> before written history are among the most interesting problems of the
> present time. Facts disclosed by the careful scrutiny to which the
> earth's crust has been subjected have gone far to overturn opinions
> formerly regarded as beyond question, and a spirit of eager and
> earnest inquiry has taken the place of almost contemptuous neglect.
> Caves and gravel-beds, peat-mosses and lakes, barrows and burial-
> places, are undergoing careful examination...Primaeval archaeology

---

and never can be a real or an earnest form of art'. Quoted in Anon., 'Fergusson's *Handbook of Architecture*', 140.
[42] Thomas Hardy, *Personal Writings*, p. 203.
[43] As a disgruntled anonymous contributor to the 1872 *Quarterly Review* observed of Gothic 'folly' in general: 'A large number of our recent churches...are made mere specimens of the transient ecclesiastical fashion, instead of permanent monuments of art.' See Anon., 'The State of English Architecture', *Quarterly Review* 132 (January 1872), 299.
[44] Quoted in Glyn Daniel and Colin Renfrew, *The Idea of Prehistory* (Edinburgh: Edinburgh University Press, 1988), p. 2.
[45] C. F. Keary, *The Dawn of History*, iii.

now not only occupies a large space in the transactions of scientific societies, but also has been made the subject of entire works by...[Daniel] Wilson[46]

In 1871 Heinrich Schliemann began to excavate at Ithaca and found Troy, proving the historic foundations of the Homeric poems and making the epic verse come alive again. The activities of Schliemann and his acolytes became a source of immense popular interest; readers enjoyed the florid reports of how 'the spade brought to light tomb after tomb, and how each tomb yielded its golden hoard'.[47] The modern world's discovery of ancient civilization through excavation was chronicled extensively in the pages of periodicals such as the middlebrow general interest weekly *The Illustrated London News*.[48] Schliemann epitomized the new spirit of more systematic, disciplined digging to replace the old-style random activity that often destroyed the very relics it was supposed to salvage. The 'father of scientific archaeology'[49] was General Augustus Lane Pitt-Rivers (1827-1900), the owner of the Cerne Giant[50] and Cranborne, 'The Chase' in *Tess of the d'Urbervilles*. It was here, in this region of 'Druidical oaks' (*Tess* 75), that Pitt-Rivers embarked on a series of excavations of prehistoric, Roman and Saxon sites.[51] His precise stratigraphic field methodology

---

[46] T. G. Bonney, 'Stone Circles and Megalithic Remains' in *The Gentleman's Magazine Library: A Classified Collection of the Chief Contents of 'The Gentleman's Magazine' from 1731-1868. Archaeology: Part II*, ed. George Laurence Gomme (London: Elliot Stock, 1886), p. 3.

[47] Anon., 'Schliemann's *Mycenae*', *Quarterly Review* 145 (January 1878), 68.

[48] The *Illustrated London News* is an apt example. Founded in May 1842, it began publication when Queen Victoria had reigned only five years and it was one of the few general periodicals to consistently report archaeological discoveries as a general practice. It was selling 20 000 copies within six weeks of initial publication and reached a circulation of 250 000 by 1852. See Peter W. Sinnema, *The Dynamics of the Pictured Page: Representing the Nation in the 'Illustrated London News', 1842-1892* (Aldershot, UK: Ashgate, 1998).

[49] Mark Bowden, *Pitt Rivers* (Cambridge: Cambridge University Press, 1991), p. 154.

[50] This aggressively masculine 180-foot figure, carved with crude naturalism in the chalky cliffs above Cerne Abbas village, is now regarded as a purely British artform, although William Stukeley, addressing the Society of Antiquaries on the subject of the Giant in 1764, believed it represented Hercules. Hardy was no doubt amused by the glaring incongruity of this pagan giant once overshadowing the Benedictine Abbey at Cerne Abbas. The 'Giant's Hill by Abbot's Cernel' is mentioned in *Tess of the d'Urbervilles* (Ch. 48) and in *Life's Little Ironies*: 'A Few Crusted Characters,' and 'Old Audrey's Experiences as a Musician'.

[51] The General took the name Pitt-Rivers in 1880, when he inherited the Rivers estates, more than 29 000 acres of land on the borders of Dorset, Wiltshire and Hampshire. This was among the richest archaeological real estate in Britain and indeed Europe. In 1895 Hardy and his first wife paid a week's visit to Rushmore, Pitt-Rivers's house fifteen miles southwest of Salisbury. Hardy composed a poem about the General's third daughter, 'Concerning Agnes' contained in the posthumously published *Winter Words* volume. For

established the science of archaeological excavation, as opposed to ransacking 'the sepulchres of former races'[52] for a primary burial with an urn or a bronze dagger that would grace a private collection. The fruits of this venture were contained in the lavishly illustrated, five-volume *Excavations in Cranborne Chase, Near Rushmore on the Borders of Dorset and Wilts* (1887-1905).[53]

For the Hardy whose imagination was inquisitive about time the rapid growth of archaeology and the concept of systematic archaeology were peculiarly problematic. He knew of course that his own county boasted an enormous wealth of material for the expanding army of prehistoric archaeologists; southern England had been occupied from the earliest times, and possessed an unusual number of field monuments.[54] As the author Mary Butts testified, residing in Hardy country was like living in a region 'with all its bones showing, whose fabric and whole essence is stone, which is dominated and crowned by stones; standing stones on the moors, cairn and castle...each field fixed by a phallos'.[55] Charles Warne, whose antiquarian account *Ancient Dorset* was published the same year as Hardy's *Under the Greenwood Tree* in 1872, paid fulsome tribute to 'The County of Dorset' which 'from an archaeological point of view, stands pre-eminent for the number, variety, and importance of its ancient remains, many of them existing in a perfect state of preservation. Its earthworks claim a place amongst the finest of the kind in Britain'.[56] As with his objections to church restoration, Hardy was susceptible to the emotional associations that gather round a building or site over countless generations. An apparently unglamorous object or area could store within its fabric the fading airs of bygone times. What if the discoveries made by spade and pickaxe obliterated these precious 'associations'? Although Pitt-Rivers

---

further information see Desmond Hawkins, *Concerning Agnes: Thomas Hardy's 'Good Little Pupil'* (Gloucester: Alan Sutton, 1982).

[52] Anon., 'Lyell's *Principles of Geology*', *Quarterly Review* 53 (April 1835), 408.

[53] A useful example of his earlier published work is 'An Examination into the Character and Probable Origins of the Hill Forts of Sussex', *Archaeologia* 42 (1868), 27-52; 53-76.

[54] Barry M. Marsden's *Pioneers of Prehistory: Leaders and Landmarks in English Archaeology (1500-1900)* (Ormskirk, Lancashire: Hesketh, 1983) notes the high level of antiquarian attention devoted to Wessex, particularly in the eighteenth and nineteenth centuries. See also John Michell, *Megalithomania: Artists, Antiquarians and Archaeologists at the Old Stone Monuments* (London: Thames & Hudson, 1982).

[55] Mary Butts, *The Crystal Cabinet: my childhood at Salterns* (Boston: Beacon Press, 1988), p. 12.

[56] Charles Warne, *Ancient Dorset: The Celtic, Roman, Saxon, and Danish Antiquities of the County, including the Early Coinage. Also an Introduction to the Ethnology of Dorset, and other Archaeological Notices of the County, by William Wake Smart* (Bournemouth: D. Sydenham, 1872), i.

believed he was a type of cultural embalmer, assiduously preserving the long forgotten dead, the digs by which he achieved this involved severe damage to the landscape.[57] The galling irony was that archaeological remains could be transferred into a permanent record only by dismantling the site. Hardy's resistance was not in the end to *discovery*, of course, but to the possibility of final destruction through a plundering and heedless quest for treasure.

And then there was the Hardy whose temperamental inclination and artistic tactic of 'imaginative archaeology' was eclectic and promiscuous, rather than rigorously systematic. Hardy wished to incorporate into his artistic vision both the tenacious resolve of a Tylor or Pitt-Rivers, and the jovial dilettantism of the amateur antiquarian. As his portrayal of Stonehenge reveals, Hardy was not going to be restricted only to prehistoric strata. He wished to display all the fan of time and each elaborate link in the chain between the earliest ages and late-Victorian society. The roving historical consciousness at work in *Tess* would have found some comfort in E. B. Tylor's definition of modern anthropology's purpose: 'Civilization, being a process of long and complex growth, can only be thoroughly understood when studied through its entire range; that the past is continually needed to explain the present, and the whole to explain the part'.[58] Yet Tylor's sense of the need for structure was strong too: he argued vehemently that the new science of man depended upon the painstakingly rational processes of minute observation, inference, and generalization. His books and articles exhorted students of the past to shun the desultory 'speculations of the old-fashioned antiquaries'[59] by setting themselves 'to walk on the solid ground of inductive reasoning'.[60] He would have endorsed the high-minded statement in the November 1829 issue of the *Gentleman's Magazine*:

> It is not the business of an Antiquary merely to...pile document upon document, extract upon extract...The judicious Antiquary has higher views than these: it is...to draw strong conclusions out of minute facts which have escaped the general eye...Without the exertion of a conjectural spirit, guided by sober caution, the Antiquary would

---

[57] For a concise account of Pitt-Rivers's theories on preserving and arranging archaeological artefacts see *Address by Lt.-General A. H. L. F. Pitt-Rivers at the opening of The Dorset County Museum, 1884* (Dorchester: The Friary Press, 1984).
[58] E. B. Tylor, *Researches into the Early History of Mankind and the Development of Civilization* (London: John Murray, 1865), p. 2.
[59] E. B. Tylor, 'Review of *The Lake Dwellings of Switzerland and other parts of Europe* by Ferdinand Keller', *Fortnightly Review* 6 (1866), 768.
[60] E. B. Tylor, 'William von Humboldt', *Quarterly Review* 124 (1868), 524.

indeed be little better than a heaper up of old bills, inventories, ballads, a dealer in verdigris and iron rust, or a collector of...bricks, stones, tiles and pipkins.[61]

In practice, however, few archaeologists embodied the ideal of 'the true antiquary' described by John Milner in his 1790 contribution to the *Gentleman's Magazine* entitled 'Barrows in Dorsetshire':

> In searching...into these rude memorials of our forefathers, the true antiquary will ever respect their remains; and whilst he enters into their views by endeavouring to revive their memory, he will also as far as possible consult their wishes, in leaving to their bones their ancient place of sepulture.[62]

In 'A Tryst at an Ancient Earthwork', first published in the March 1885 edition of the *Detroit Post*,[63] Hardy portrays an aged and unethical excavator obsessed with the 'barbarous grandeurs of past time'. This character was supposedly based on Edward Cunnington, the 'local Schliemann' of Dorchester, as Hardy ironically dubbed him in a paper prepared for a meeting of the Dorset Natural History and Antiquarian Field Club and read by Hardy himself on 13 May 1884.[64] The 'well-known antiquary with capital letters at the tail of his name' illegally exhumes from the ancient earthwork Maiden Castle a striking mosaic proving Roman occupation, a skeleton almost intact and a gold statuette of Mercury. Although he is prevailed upon to replace these finds, the beautiful statuette is found in the deceased man's effects. Hardy acknowledges that many amateurs pursued the study of antiquity not so much to wrest historical data from the material remains of the past as to gather curios. Charles Warne prefaced his *Celtic Tumuli of Dorset* (1866) with a stinging rebuke to the ham-fisted amateur diggers of his home county who desecrated 'time-

---

[61] Anon., 'The Society of Antiquaries Defended', *Gentleman's Magazine* (November 1829), 419.

[62] John Milner, 'Barrows in Dorsetshire' in *The Gentleman's Magazine Library: A Classified Collection of the Chief Contents of 'The Gentleman's Magazine' from 1731-1868. Archaeology: Part I*, ed. George Laurence Gomme (London: Elliot Stock, 1886), p. 99.

[63] This arresting anecdote was published in the *Detroit Post* as 'Ancient Earthworks and What Two Enthusiastic Scientists Found Therein'; in 1893 it appeared in the *English Illustrated Magazine* as 'Ancient Earthworks at Casterbridge'.

[64] Michael Millgate describes Hardy's portrait as 'almost' libellous, and notes that a paper read by Hardy to the Field Club in 1884 (relating to Max Gate excavations) was 'mysteriously omitted from the Club's published *Proceedings* for a full six years – possibly because of animosity on the part of Cunnington or one of his friends'. See *Thomas Hardy: A Biography* (Oxford: Oxford University Press, 1982), pp. 244-5.

hallowed monuments for no better purpose than the indulgence of a craving acquisitiveness and the adornment of glass cases with ill-understood relics'.[65] No doubt this is the kind of collector from whom Pitt-Rivers tried to distance himself. But for all his emphasis on the dig not as ill-conducted pillage but as thorough scientific pursuit, executed with military precision, Pitt-Rivers was himself an eager and miscellaneous ethnographical collector, amassing artefacts and displaying them in museums.[66]

The amateur spirit was rooted in a seventeenth- and eighteenth-century tradition that promoted the formation of fine discriminating tastes. The age of collectors produced the word dilettanti: those who revelled in the arts. It is impossible to ignore the aesthetic element in the growth of an antiquarian desire to uncover the partially concealed roots of the past. Tennyson captures well the levity of the dilettanti in *The Princess* (1847), when he enumerates a mixture of exotic items on display at Vivian Hall:

> And on the tables every clime and age
> Jumbled together; celts and calumets,
> Claymore and snowshoe, toys in lava, fans
> Of sandal, amber, ancient rosaries...
> The cursed Malayan kris, and battle-clubs
> From the isles of palm: and higher on the walls,
> Betwixt the monstrous horns of elk and deer,
> His own forefathers' arms and armour hung.
> (ll. 16-19, 21-4)[67]

The extent to which Hardy was motivated by dilettantism is an interesting question; the more so since several of his novels afford important, thought-provoking and incisive studies of the dilettante figure.[68] Hardy's experiences as a member of the Dorset Natural History and Antiquarian Field Club, which he joined during 1881, clearly influenced his droll portrayal of 'the South-Wessex Field and Antiquarian Club' in *A Group of Noble Dames* (1891), and in *The Hand of Ethelberta* (Chapter 31) he remarks on the dilettante frivolities which characterized antiquarian fieldwork as a popular pastime for the country parson or gentleman of

---

[65] Charles Warne, *Celtic Tumuli of Dorset: An Account of Personal and other Researches in the Sepulchral Mounds of the Durotriges* (London: T. Tegg & Sons, 1866), ii.

[66] See David K. Van Keuren, 'Museums and Ideology: Augustus Pitt-Rivers, Anthropological Museums, and Social Change in Later Victorian Britain', *Victorian Studies* 28 (1984), 171-89.

[67] Alfred Lord Tennyson, *The Poems of Tennyson*, II, 280.

[68] For a striking early portrait of the Victorian dilettante see Henry Knight in Hardy's third published novel, *A Pair of Blue Eyes*. Knight's London office is decorated with *objets d'art* from his Continental wanderings (Chapter 13).

leisure.[69] A contributor to the October 1847 *Edinburgh Review* deplored that 'large class of men – we might now add, women and children – led into the belief, that sufficient claim to the title of an antiquary may be obtained by measuring church windows, and rubbing brasses'.[70] And yet Hardy's broad but superficial knowledge of relics in his own region, along with that imaginative tactic of casually amassing fragments from various periods which is such a distinctive and deep-rooted feature of his art, takes its authority from the spirit of indiscriminate collection epitomized by John Brand (1744-1806), and continuing through Tylor's *Primitive Culture* to the monumental *Golden Bough* (1890), whose author Sir James George Frazer was, in Margaret Hodgen's opinion, 'a collector of popular and primitive antiquities in the tradition of Brand'.[71] Brand's *Popular Antiquities* became for informed, non-academic Victorians 'an automatic reference and authority on antique custom and odd superstition'.[72] It was mainly owing to his unflagging industry that the nineteenth century acknowledged with increasing formality that folk-practices and the myths to which they related told at least as much of the distant past as did tangible vestiges such as Stonehenge. To that extent his work acted as a crucial link between archaeology, amateur antiquarianism and the independent, comprehensive 'science' of anthropology embodied by Frazer. The sheer bulk of Brand's materials and the bewildering array of his sources encouraged erudite readers to uncover secrets 'hid in old parchments difficult to decipher, in the confusion of neglected libraries, in the dust of record-houses...or buried beneath the soil'.[73]

Hardy's friend and neighbour William Barnes (1800-89) seems to have 'placed' himself between the two extremes with effortless ease. A polyglot and polymath, he was in Hardy's words, 'probably the most interesting link between present and past forms of rural life that England possessed...a complete repertory of forgotten manners, words, and sentiments, a store

---

[69] See the 'Introduction' to the first volume of *Archaeologia Cantiana*: 'One of the charms of archaeology at least, like that of natural history, consists in its eminently social nature; in the employment it offers to all'. *Transactions of Kent Archaeological Society* 1 (1858), 19. On the nineteenth-century vogue for local archaeology see Charles Dellheim, *The Face of the Past. The Preservation of the Medieval Inheritance in Victorian England* (Cambridge: Cambridge University Press, 1982), pp. 45-58.

[70] Anon., 'On the History and Prospects of Antiquarianism in England', *Edinburgh Review* 86 (October 1847), 325.

[71] Margaret T. Hodgen, *The Doctrine of Survivals: A Chapter in the History of Scientific Method in the Study of Man* (London: Allenson, 1936), p. 116.

[72] Richard M. Dorson, *The British Folklorists: A History* (London: Routledge & Kegan Paul, 1968), p. 17.

[73] Anon., 'On the History and Prospects of Antiquarianism in England', *Edinburgh Review* 86 (October 1847), 307-8.

which he afterwards turned to such good use in his writings on ancient British and Anglo-Saxon speech, customs, and folklore'.[74] Barnes's poetry offers a vibrant picture of his childhood days in the Blackmore Vale, a lush, sheltered tract of Wessex countryside; however, his treatment of rustic life and its virtues is obviously selective. Hardy asserted that the Dorset poet 'held himself artistically aloof from the ugly side of things...we escape in his pictures the sordid miseries that are laid bare in Crabbe'.[75] Barnes's wood engravings comprise a gentle vision of southwestern England that was irreparably disturbed by modern agricultural technology and aggressive urban expansion. Yet he was not merely the historian and laureate of a passing rural tradition. Though he never displayed it with Hardy's searing intensity, Barnes too was keenly aware of parochial prejudice and cruelty.[76] Moreover, his poetry showed that he was an expert speaker upon the dialects of the western counties. In 1863, the Philological Society published Barnes's first edition of *A Grammar and Glossary of the Dorset Dialect*, with, as the subtitle declared, *The History and Outspreadings and Bearings of the South-Western English*. Through the *Glossary*, Barnes could indulge both his scholarly exactitude and his less scientific pleasure in casually collecting words and phrases contributed by readers of the *Dorset County Chronicle*.

For Hardy, it was a much greater dilemma to reconcile in his fiction the unwavering purposeful dedication of a Pitt-Rivers with the haphazard time-voyaging that disrupts established patterns and embraces frivolous fun. However, commentators persistently reduce to a quite mistakenly-assumed Barnesian straightforwardness Hardy's equivocal attitude to the past; even accusing him of a sentimental evasion of pressing contemporary issues. They cite the General Preface to the 1912 Wessex Edition in which he speaks of his endeavours to preserve 'a fairly true record of a vanishing life' with its 'country customs and vocations, obsolete and obsolescent'.[77] Also the Prefatory Note to *The Early Life of Thomas Hardy* justifies the inclusion of '[s]ome incidents of his country experiences' which 'may be considered as trivial', on the grounds that 'they embody customs and manners of old West-of-England life that have now entirely passed away'.[78] Critical orthodoxy, though, rarely acknowledges the inveterate ironist

---

[74] Thomas Hardy, 'The Rev. William Barnes, B.D.', *Athenaeum* (October 16, 1886), 501-2. Reprinted in *Personal Writings*, p. 101. See also Rev. O. P. Cambridge, 'In Memoriam Rev. William Barnes, B.D.', *Proceedings of the Dorset Natural History and Antiquarian Field Club* 8 (1887), xviii.

[75] Thomas Hardy, *Personal Writings*, p. 84.

[76] See for instance Barnes's poem 'The Love-Child'.

[77] Thomas Hardy, *A Pair of Blue Eyes*, p. 453.

[78] F. E. Hardy, *The Life of Thomas Hardy 1840-1928* (London: Macmillan, 1962), viii.

behind these words. In Louis MacNeice's poem 'Wessex Guidebook', Hardy is perceived as a quaint museum exhibit along with the period he supposedly tried to salvage. Hardy's 'fading hand' is of a piece with the other harmless specimens in the Dorset County Museum that MacNeice evokes in his portrayal of a region loaded with the detritus of its Celtic and Roman forebears:

> Flake tool; core tool; in the small museum
> Rare butterflies, green coins of Caracalla,
> Keep easy company with the fading hand
> Of one who chronicled a fading world;
> Outside, the long roads, that the Roman ruler
> Ruled himself out with, point across the land
> To lasting barrows and long-vanished barracks.[79]

Hardy's stance is much more demanding than either MacNeice's poem or Barnes's practice would suggest. Indeed, a complicating irony besets his free-ranging backward excursions in time, and this probably stems from his own ambiguous status as a *provincial* writer with *supraprovincial* aspirations. Hardy stood at a cultural crossroads, subtly responsive to the dislocating complexities of modernity yet driven by a historical responsibility to remember, record and reanimate dying traditions. We have the Hardy who shared Barnes's passion for local antiquarian matters, who built Max Gate close to a notable tumulus, Conquer Barrow near Dorchester, and in 1890 gave a paper on the urns and skeletons discovered in digging the foundations.[80] Yet there is also the Hardy who received an architectural training in the capital, 'the diffident...West Country lad' plunged 'into the very deep end of sophistication'. Indeed, 'the artistic and scientific side of a great metropolis drew him like a magnet'.[81] The author who documents the irrational beliefs and occult pastimes which enshrine fragments of a vanishing culture, is the same figure who, in his autobiography, tries to carve out a niche among the London glitterati, a social set whom he nevertheless satirized ruthlessly in *The Hand of*

---

[79] Louis MacNeice, *The Collected Poems of Louis MacNeice*, ed. E. R. Dodds (London: Faber & Faber, 1966), p. 452.

[80] See 'Some Romano-British Relics Found at Max Gate, Dorchester'; a speech read at the Dorchester Meeting of the Dorset Natural History and Antiquarian Field Club in 1884. Reprinted in *Personal Writings*, pp. 191-5 and in *Thomas Hardy's Public Voice: The Essays, Speeches, and Miscellaneous Prose*, ed. Michael Millgate (Oxford: Clarendon Press, 2001), pp. 61-4.

[81] See Robert Gittings, *Young Thomas Hardy* (Harmondsworth, Middlesex: Penguin, 1986), pp. 89, 90, 93.

Ethelberta (1875) and in the town episodes of *The Well-Beloved* (1892/1897).

Within this dualism, it is the theme of local attachment to which Hardy obsessively returns – a question dominating the fiction and sociology of the nineteenth century and after. Is it best for individuals to live within modest, simply organized communities, inheriting their ancestral lore and the land to which they tend? Is it that which holds the key to the community's continuing vitality? Hardy feared the moral and psychological consequences of discontinuity in man's environment and beliefs, which tended to shatter local bonds and traditional authorities. Yet, whereas William Barnes habitually saw the newest views of life intruding with predatory pervasiveness on the ordered calm of his poetic landscape, Hardy could react as an enlightened cosmopolite: paradoxically perhaps, the latest ideas were to him often the soundest.

So what was Hardy's true intention when, in MacNeice's words, he 'chronicled a fading world'? To claim that the goal of his imaginative excavations and discoveries was the same as Barnes's – to immortalize the mental as well as physical heirlooms of a remote antiquity – is fraught with difficulties. It could scarcely be maintained, for example, that his portrayal of the garish skimmity ride in *The Mayor of Casterbridge* records a cherished relic of peasant folk culture or makes a heartfelt plea for the perpetuation of that culture. Hardy is cannily oblique when he explores the legitimacy of widely accepted traditions, and reveals many vestigial remnants of ancient lore to be misguided, morbid or even destructive, such as the occult practices in 'The Withered Arm' and Susan Nunsuch's black witchcraft in *The Return of the Native* (1878). These habits and ideas, discarded by the front marchers of civilization and lingering on in back corners, attest, according to E. B. Tylor, 'how large a share stupidity and unpractical conservatism and dogged superstition have had in preserving for us traces of the history of our race'.[82] In the complex experience that is Hardy's promiscuous discovery of time and its circumstance in his fictions, he is quick to expose the impoverished remnants of a community's former strength as a highly integrated social structure.

This clear-sighted attitude clashes with the critical commonplace that the Wessex novels represent almost a Barnesian attempt 'to preserve an imaginative Eden',[83] contrasting the stable perfection of a pre-industrial agrarian order with a blighted and brutalizing consumerist epoch. Hardy's revisiting the crumbling abodes of history was not shaped by vacuous and

---

[82] E. B. Tylor, *Primitive Culture*, I, 150.
[83] R. A. Forsyth, 'The Conserving Myth of William Barnes', *Victorian Studies* 6 (1963), 328.

cloying sentimentality for 'traditional values' in an age of escalating technological advance. He knew how reverence for a lost rural paradise could become a form of lotus-eating that narcotized the population, making them forget the present and blot out the most urgent needs for reform. He did not believe that the customs and beliefs of Barnes's secluded pre-enclosure hamlets were uniformly attractive and life-affirming.[84] Hardy realized to what extent his people were both the lucky beneficiaries and helpless victims of the cultural traditions in which they were steeped. He repudiated Pitt-Rivers's naive, easy optimism that the uncovered remains of outmoded cultures might enrich and irradiate the modern moment. Indeed, his depiction of Stonehenge in *Tess* intimates that the origins of our cultural legacy are based on vicious deeds and are best left behind. Hardy was in his own fashion obsessed by the past. Though he recognized early the destabilizing outcome of his discoveries in the imaginative patterns of his work, nevertheless, his fictions both shadowed and foreshadowed the nascent sciences of man so as to fashion that provocative, unillusioned historical consciousness in *Tess*.

Hardy's imaginative assimilation of scientific and humanistic pursuits dedicated to reconstructing the course of man's collective past can be seen in an important way in *The Return of the Native* (1878), whose mumming episode is imbued by E. B. Tylor's crucial formulation of 'survivals'.[85] In his two-volume *Primitive Culture* (1871), Tylor had designated as 'survivals' those primitive or ancient forms of thought and practice, which obdurately resisted the impulse of change and lingered into later culture, thus revealing continuity between early and more developed forms of

---

[84] According to an 1837 survey, a traveller was likely to see 'the worst of houses and the poorest of labourers' in 'the wretched villages of Dorsetshire'. See Alexander Somerville, *The Whistler at the Plough; containing travels, statistics, and descriptions of scenery and agricultural customs in most parts of England; with letters from Ireland: also 'Free Trade and the League', a biographical history*, 3 vols. (Manchester: J. Marshall, 1852), I, 380. William Cobbett's comprehensive overview of bucolic England in *Rural Rides* (1830) identified some of the most shocking cases of destitution in the southern counties.

[85] On the concept of 'survivals' as 'the foundation stone for a school of anthropological folklorists' see Richard M. Dorson (ed.), *Peasant Customs and Savage Myths. Selections from the British Folklorists*, 2 vols. (Chicago: University of Chicago Press, 1968), I, 181. See also Joan Leopold, *Culture in Comparative and Evolutionary Perspective: E. B. Tylor and the Making of 'Primitive Culture'* (Berlin: Dietrich Reimer Verlag, 1980), pp. 49-54. On Tylor and the development of nineteenth-century anthropology see George W. Stocking, *Race, Culture and Evolution* (New York: The Free Press, 1968); *Functionalism Historicized: Essays in British Social Anthropology* (Wisconsin: University of Wisconsin Press, 1984); *Victorian Anthropology* (New York: Free Press, 1987).

civilization.[86] Although in his second edition of *Primitive Culture* Tylor felt it necessary to add a prefatory note explaining his apparent neglect of Charles Darwin, remarking that his system was structured from a different perspective, he was clearly indebted to Darwin's philosophy. Tylor did little to discourage the belief that his new term was borrowed from or associated with the concepts of fossilized or vestigial forms in geology or biology.[87] Indeed, commentators have viewed Tylor's doctrine as an anthropological version of the 'Tree of Life' described in Darwin's *The Origin of Species* (1859). The 'Tree of Life' illustrates Darwin's notion of the genealogy of species: one species ramifies into many, some of which become extinct; some branches die out altogether; and some species do not ramify at all, but instead continue to exist unmodified, while other originally contemporary species change and multiply greatly. Thus, according to Darwin and, later, to Tylor, many periods of evolution – both human and animal – exist simultaneously in the present. Charles Darwin saw that adaptation, no matter how slow, to a continuously changing environment by continuously changing species was the dynamics of evolution. Culture, as Tylor viewed it, was the mental adaptation of man to environment.[88] In *Primitive Culture* he likened his analysis of cultures to Darwin's groundbreaking research: 'What this task is like, may be almost perfectly illustrated by comparing these details of culture with the species of plants and animals studied by the naturalist.'[89]

Primitive Culture, regarded by Robert Ackerman as 'the founding document in modern British anthropology',[90] extended the Darwinian biological revolution to prehistoric man, making him precious in a way that he was not for geology, whose gigantic new temporal order reduced his significance as a creature of only recent emergence. Like many Victorian theorists of ancient religion, Tylor was agnostic, and may have had his own writings in mind when he wryly referred to those iconoclastic

---

[86] Hardy's references to Tylor are found in *The Literary Notebooks of Thomas Hardy*, ed. Lennart A. Björk, 2 vols. (London: Macmillan, 1985), I, entry 1336. Hereafter referred to as *Literary Notebooks*.

[87] From the 1870s, Tylor increasingly compared the anthropological study of the distribution of survivals with the geological study of the distribution of fossils within different strata: 'the institutions of man are as distinctly stratified as the earth on which he lives'. See 'On a Method of Investigating the Development of Institutions; Applied to Laws of Marriage and Descent', *Journal of the Anthropological Institute* 18 (November 1888), 269.

[88] In the antepenultimate paragraph of his *Origin of Species*, Darwin had called for the application of evolutionary principles to the study of mankind ('Much light will be thrown on the origin of man and his history').

[89] E. B. Tylor, *Primitive Culture*, I, 8.

[90] Robert Ackerman, *J. G. Frazer: His Life and Work* (Cambridge: Cambridge University Press, 1987), p. 77.

'investigations' which 'gained a special attention from being looked upon as hostile to Christianity by a large public'.[91] Tylor allied himself with cultural forces that had already been responsible for the attenuation of 'God' into a verbal convenience, and the erosion of theology as an explanatory system. He secretly enjoyed reminding his readers of the radical similarity between Judaeo-Christian traditions and those of pagan cults. Behind Christian legend, dogma and ritual was a substantial body of primitive and even barbarous 'survivals'. Tylor defined it thus:

> Among evidence aiding us to trace the course which the civilization of the world has actually followed, is that great class of facts to denote which I have found it convenient to introduce the term 'survivals'. These are processes, customs, opinions, and so forth, which have been carried on by force of habit into a new state of society different from that in which they had their original home, and they thus remain as proofs and examples of an older condition of culture out of which a newer has evolved.[92]

Hardy incorporated Tylor's concept into his reflections on the mummers' play that forms the centrepiece of Mrs Yeobright's Christmas festivities in *The Return of the Native*:

> of mummers and mumming Eustacia had the greatest contempt. The mummers themselves were not afflicted with any such feeling for their art, though at the same time they were not enthusiastic. A traditional pastime is to be distinguished from a mere revival in no more striking feature than in this, that while in the revival all is excitement and fervour, the *survival* is carried on with a stolidity and absence of stir which sets one wondering why a thing that is done so perfunctorily should be kept up at all. (*Native* 122. My italics)

That the mummers perform their parts without any genuine verve says much about the larger social occasion of which it is a part: the 'good supper' organized by Mrs Yeobright to commemorate the return from Paris of her only son Clym. The Wessex novels are replete with similar 'feast' episodes that throw into sharp relief the degree to which the nuclear 'family' is a locus of harmonious integration or the highest achievement of evolution. On the surface, Mrs Yeobright's Christmas festivities provide an opportunity for the Egdonites to rejoice in their own well-being, unfazed by a sense of unworthiness or class-anxiety. Closer inspection however

---

[91] E. B. Tylor, 'Lake Dwellings', *Quarterly Review* 125 (1868), 438.
[92] E. B. Tylor, *Primitive Culture*, I, 16.

reveals, instead of a whole community stirred by a common emotion, only glaring social gaps:

> [Mrs Yeobright] asked the plain neighbours and workpeople without drawing any lines, just to give 'em a good supper and such like. Her son and she wait upon the folks. (*Native* 133)

Normally, the act of feasting would symbolize the reanimating potentials of togetherness, a ritualized interaction organizing and renewing social bonds. *Primitive Culture* and James George Frazer's *Golden Bough* (1890) both proclaimed the untold value of the communal meal in examining the intricate mechanisms of primitive society.[93] Feasting went to the very heart of culture, in which food was an arcane 'language', a means of communicating with one's fellows and one's gods. Sigmund Freud, whose *Totem and Taboo* (1914) owes an immense debt to Frazer's discussion of sacrifice as a totemic communion sacrament, stressed how a feast was rooted in 'very ancient ideas' of the importance of eating and drinking as a group.[94] He believed that to translate the complex codes underlying food-sharing would enable anthropologists to attain detailed knowledge about the unconscious attitudes of society. From the outset of his literary career Hardy knew the major role feasting played in both the secular and religious life of human assemblies: bringing people together and helping produce the changes which take place within them. His early thinking was perhaps shaped by the zealous antiquarian John Brand's discussion of ancient beliefs enshrined in the annual round of calendar customs. Brand's discipline lacked Tylor and Frazer's scholarly rules of research or breadth of vision. Nevertheless, he argued with clarity and conviction about how many feasts of the calendar year derived from 'the times of Paganism' whose 'annual festivals were celebrated in honour and memory of their gods, goddesses and heroes, when the people resorted together at their temples and tombs'.[95] His immense work showed how major transitional crises of the life-cycle were marked in almost all communities by a

---

[93] Frazer was quick to acknowledge the impact of Tylor on his own conception of the feast as central antique ritual. Indeed, he went so far as to proclaim that Tylor's writings 'had first interested him in anthropology' and thereby 'marked an epoch' in his life. Frazer quoted in George W. Stocking, *After Tylor* (London: Athlone Press, 1998), p. 132.

[94] Sigmund Freud, *Totem and Taboo. Some Points of Agreement between the Mental Lives of Savages and Neurotics*, trans. James Strachey (London: Routledge & Kegan Paul, 1950), p. 134.

[95] John Brand, *Observations on the Popular Antiquities of Great Britain: chiefly illustrating the Origin of our Vulgar and Provincial Customs, Ceremonies, and Superstitions*, rev. with introd. Sir Henry Ellis, 3 vols. (1848-49; repub. New York: AMS Press, 1970), II, 1-2.

ceremonial distribution and consumption of food. Moreover, the ritualized sharing of food and drink as oblation and celebration was sanctified by Biblical example.[96]

In *The Return of the Native*, however, the Yeobrights distance themselves from their guests and so have little appreciation for the sacrament of solidarity which feasting represents. The withered parish of Egdon Heath is becoming atomized, and the fact that Mrs Yeobright and her son 'wait upon' their 'plain neighbours' is a gesture more of condescension than of warm social intimacy or ungrudging hospitality. If it were not for the need to give her son a memorable homecoming, there would be little chance of her consorting with the genial but lowly furze-cutters and other 'workpeople' who prefer to gather at Damon Wildeve's Quiet Woman Inn. The Egdonites are separated from one another not just by caste, but geographically as well. Mrs Yeobright's Blooms-End cottage, situated on the edge of the heath, is described as an 'obscure, removed spot' (*Native* 109). Though there is little change in community membership on Egdon, families do not live in close physical proximity to one another, so there are few stable social groupings whilst there are acute tensions within all the families. When Eustacia exploits for her own private ends the traditional fertility rituals of the heath, the bonfire-lighting and the mumming, she trivializes them by divesting them of what little communal resonance they have left. She has no conception of feasting as a sacrament of dynamic association, a sincere articulation of the search for belongingness to a clan. Clym himself does not favour the Egdonites' primitive mores, of which mumming is an integral part. He hopes to bring 'social evolution' and education to his unlettered neighbours, a 'programme for reform' that would destroy their ceremonials and ability to eat, work and play together without thinking about it.

Despite the failure of Mrs Yeobright's Blooms-End festivities to fuse a fragmenting community, Hardy will continue to explore 'survivals' as a means of inspecting the notion that in the continuance of folklore long after the disappearance of the circumstances in which it emerged, there might be glimpsed potent undercurrents of psychic activity. If, in the multifaceted experience which is Hardy's discovery of time and its circumstance, he is

---

[96] Many Scriptural incidents impart grandeur and spiritual significance to eating and drinking together: the marriage at Cana; the picnic supper by the sea of Tiberias for Jesus and his disciples after the Resurrection. The Blessing and the Grace affirm a direct link between God and the provision of good food, encouraging an attitude of veneration while eating. Acts 27:35: 'And when he had spoken thus he took bread and gave thanks to God in presence of them all, and when he had broken it he began to eat.' See Bridget Ann Henisch, *Fast and Feast: Food in Medieval Society* (University Park and London: Pennsylvania University Press, 1990).

quick to uncover the tattered remains of a community's former vigour as an integrated social order, he will nonetheless ask whether it is possible, in the Victorian setting, to revive in an energizing way mysterious beliefs such as those which form the ancient core of mumming. The word mummer, derived from the Danish 'Momme', signifying 'one wearing a mask', takes us back to the constables in *Tess* who in the dawn light of Stonehenge seem to be wearing ritual masks. Whereas in the Stonehenge scene Hardy shows several different strata of time – prehistoric (heliolatry), historic (ancient Greek tragedy) and modern (the sly Wagnerian flourish, the more homely dramas) – actively cross-fertilizing one another to produce a startling imaginative experience, the mummers' play fails to approach this nexus of past and present, savage and civilized. The pagan ceremony in which the play is rooted and the subsequent accretions of other material do not merge to the same exhilarating degree. Yet Hardy reverts to the anthropological occasion of feasting in the hope of exploring previously untrodden mental terrain. The value of his imaginative 'excavations' – speculating, for instance, whether folk materials might reveal the unconscious basis of individuality in automatic responsiveness – cannot be overstated in a pre-Freudian era. When Hardy read Frazer's *The Golden Bough* in the 1890s, the most extended attempt at the time to interpret and relate folk customs to the great myths and legends of the past, he saw that 'survivals' afforded irreplaceable insight into the earliest habits of thought. Andrew Lang spoke for the majority of late-Victorian anthropologists when he announced that 'we explain many peculiarities of myths as survivals from an earlier social and mental condition of humanity'.[97] Freud, an archaeologist of the mind, developed this research to show how the prehistoric impulses of the race were replicated in the unconscious layers of the individual psyche, tracing basic neurotic traits back to a common prehistory.

That Mrs Yeobright's party at least tantalizes the reader with intimations of fecundating energies is typical of Hardy's later creative adventures: trying to understand his culture's relationship to what has anticipated it; asking what are man's enduring, unchanging instincts; uncovering a residue of human response that the prevailing practices of an age cannot smother. This struggle to find a vital presence in 'survivals' – whether they are the tumuli and earthforts dotting the distant uplands around Casterbridge, traditional folklore, petrified organic remains or medieval churches threatened by Gothic revivalists – is at the core of Hardy's restless time-voyaging.[98]

---

[97] Andrew Lang, 'Myths and Mythologists', *Nineteenth Century* 19 (1886), 59.
[98] William Cowper Powys wrote admiringly of Hardy's acute sensitivity to anthropological curiosities: 'Tribe by tribe, race by race, as they come and go, leaving their monuments and

It is surprising that, although the questions raised by Hardy's reinflection of E. B. Tylor's anthropological doctrine are many and various, they are rarely canvassed by recent critical studies. For instance, divisions proposed in cultural study between self and other, and between 'here' and 'there', or between separate and incommensurate cultures inform the new social sciences and Hardy's own writing project. In early works such as *A Pair of Blue Eyes* through to what is technically Hardy's final published novel, *The Well-Beloved*, the division adumbrated between metropolitan 'centre' and agricultural 'periphery', and the notion of recuperating a lost collective identity are highly significant. Certainly the anthropological motif of the infiltration of communities from the outside is persistent in Hardy.[99] By developing the jaundiced perspective of a predatory interloper from the towns such as Edred Fitzpiers in *The Woodlanders*, Hardy could explore the outlandish pre-Christian practices secretly cherished and maintained by the rural peasantry among whom he grew up. Hardy entertains the possibility of overhauling stale Victorian conventions and refreshing them with new potencies drawn from a primordial and dateless past. But even when this earnest attempt meets with failure and disenchantment, he is, in *The Return of the Native* for instance, inspired by the artistic stimulus afforded by 'survivals', the irrational beliefs and practices so at variance with the 'enlightened' views of the educated classes.

In phenomena that had little apparent meaning and utility to the practical modern world, Hardy saw 'history defaced, or remnants that have escaped the shipwreck of time'.[100] His poem 'In a Museum', describes the oldest fossil bird, the *archaeopteryx macrura*, separated from Upper Jurassic Lithographic Stone in Solenhafen, Bavaria, and displayed as a skeleton cast at the Albert Memorial Museum of Queen Street, Exeter. Hardy, who saw the specimen in 1915,[101] wrote of it with reverent fascination (the skeleton of a body and tail is large, extending fifteen

---

their names behind, Hardy broods over them, noting their survivals, their lingering footprints, their long decline.' Quoted in Peter Casagrande, *Hardy's Influence on the Modern Novel* (London: Macmillan, 1988), pp. 69-70.

[99] See, for instance, Aeneas Manston in *Desperate Remedies*, Henry Knight in *A Pair of Blue Eyes*, Sergeant Troy in *Far from the Madding Crowd* and Angel Clare in *Tess of the d'Urbervilles*.

[100] Thus Francis Bacon described the remains of classical antiquity in *Advancement of Learning*. Quoted in Margaret T. Hodgen, *The Doctrine of Survivals: A Chapter in the History of Scientific Method in the Study of Man* (London: Allenson, 1936), p. 47

[101] The *Life* records that on June 10, 1915 Hardy 'motored with F[lorence]to Bridport, Lyme, Exeter and Torquay...Then back to Teignmouth, Dawlish, and Exeter, putting up at the "Clarence" opposite the Cathedral.' (p. 401)

inches; there are traces of long radiating feathers which may have added notably to its size):

> Here's the mould of a musical bird long passed from light,
> Which over the earth before man came was winging;

Hardy adds a characteristic comment:

> Such a dream is Time that the coo of this ancient bird
> Has perished not, but is blent, or will be blending
> Mid visionless wilds of space with the voice that I heard,
> In the full-fugued song of the universe unending.[102]

Nothing, in Hardy's view as articulated here, is truly obliterated. The bird's immortality, like that of any human being, is safe so long as memory works.[103] Hardy romanticizes the 'coo' of the ancient creature (although its song was probably closer to a primitive kind of croak), comparing it to a contralto voice that he has heard the previous evening, one that he still remembers for its 'sweet singing'. The poem is energized not only by the findings of prehistoric archaeology but also by physics: Hardy elaborates the notion that both sound and light continue to exist as waves, so that in theory birdsong and human utterance could chime together in the 'full-fugued song' formed by sound waves in the universe.

It is the essence of Hardy's art from the very outset to conjure up the relics of time – the objects and occasions which are the 'survivals' of history – to make them play tantalizingly round the immediate object of his concern, and to invite the reader to tease out the implications of the elaborate perspectives which result. And to address the way in which this requires Hardy to employ his full repertoire of tone from the insouciant and playful to the bitterly sardonic is one of the chief excitements of the study of his fictions.

---

[102] Thomas Hardy, 'In a Museum', *Complete Poems*, p. 430.
[103] For an early brief account of the Archaeopteryx, see W. H. Davenport Adams, *Life in the Primeval World (founded on Meunier's 'Les Animaux D'Autrefois')* (London: T. Nelson & Sons, 1872), pp. 194-5.

Chapter 2

Opening the Fan of Time

Desperate Remedies (1871)

> [Manston] reached a pit, midway between the waterfall and the engine-house...Into this pit had drifted uncounted generations of withered leaves, half filling it...Oak, beech, and chestnut, rotten and brown alike, mingled themselves in one fibrous mass. Manston descended into the midst of them, placed his sack on the ground, and raking the leaves aside into a large heap, began digging...A large hole – some four or five feet deep – had been excavated by Manston in about twenty minutes. Into this he immediately placed the sack, and then began filling in the earth, and treading it down...For a hiding-place the spot was unequalled. The thick accumulation of leaves, which had not been disturbed for centuries, might not be disturbed again for centuries to come, whilst their lower layers still decayed and added to the mould beneath. (302-3)[1]

The sense of stagnation within the historical process that links *Desperate Remedies* and *A Pair of Blue Eyes* is nowhere better highlighted than by the leaf-pit into whose depths Aeneas Manston descends to conceal the corpse of his dissolute first wife, Eunice. The pit, whose 'accumulation' of rotting leaves has 'not been disturbed for centuries', is a thought-provoking symbol in a novel concerned with absences of vitalizing force, a symbol which asks how seemingly dead levels of the past might interact with the modern moment and condition the future. Whilst Manston hopes to exploit the undisturbed compression of the years, Hardy meticulously uncovers the successive 'layers' of history surrounding his central characters: the excavated data revealing patterns of stultifying stagnation and spoiled fecundity. These layers represent the diverse periods entertained in the novel, from the timeless instinctual energies embodied by Manston, through the realm of Virgilian epic (conjured up by his Christian name), to the more recent historical strata that have moulded the identity of Carriford village. The Three Tranters Inn is a 'survival' of medievalism, old

---

[1] Thomas Hardy, *Desperate Remedies*, The New Wessex Edition, ed. with introd. C. J. P. Beatty (London: Macmillan, 1986). Hereafter referred to as *Remedies*.

Knapwater house bears traces of baronial activity, and the new Knapwater estate is a product of eighteenth-century taste. Hardy's overlapping strata of time have as their bedrock the figure of Manston, who in addition to hiding the body of his wife in the pit, is trying symbolically to 'bury' the primitive component of his own personality which impelled him to lash out and accidentally kill her. He is attempting to conceal the dead, while Hardy uncovers not vitality but the spirit of desiccation in his methodical excavation of history. Manston is the first character in the Wessex novels to struggle with, and be ultimately conquered by, his own mental inheritance. Like William Dare in *A Laodicean* (1881), Manston is the last illegitimate scion of a doomed aristocratic clan returning to the seat of his forefathers. He is not so much a character in any conventional sense as a moribund composite of conflicting forces. D. H. Lawrence proposes that Manston, like the leaf-pit into whose 'fibrous mass' (*Remedies* 302) he sinks, has a 'rottenness at the core' which inevitably spreads and ruins his best intentions.[2] As the result of illicit passion, 'farmed out' as an orphan, Manston has no legal existence; polite society has withdrawn its approval from him. Lacking a stable identity or vocation, he has little doubt that death is man's normal state. He writes in his suicide note: 'when we survey the long race of men, it is strange and still more strange to find that they are mainly dead men, who have scarcely ever been otherwise' (*Remedies* 319). Yet *Desperate Remedies* indicates that 'dead men' and blighted matter from one generation, however well submerged, can, paradoxically, actively defile the hopes and aspirations of the next. Manston at the novel's close yearns to retreat into quietism: 'having found man's life to be a wretchedly conceived scheme, I renounce it'. To return to a 'Time...Before the birth of consciousness'[3] – indeed to obliterate all memory of his having ever existed – he believes more natural than life itself.

Manston's plight as a victim not only of social misfortune but also of the buried self of subconscious motives, directed by desires he cannot fully comprehend,[4] makes him a more complex figure than the implacably evil stage villain and 'loose-principled adventurer' in Richard Carpenter's analysis of *Desperate Remedies*.[5] Hardy captures Manston's dread of being overtaken by imperceptible, but irresistible, forces which threaten, not from an external source, but more worryingly, from inside the self. The sexual

---

[2] D. H. Lawrence, *Study of Thomas Hardy and Other Essays*, ed. Bruce Steele (Cambridge: Cambridge University Press, 1986), p. 48.

[3] Thomas Hardy, 'Before Life and After', *Complete Poems*, p. 277.

[4] This conception of the bastard child in Victorian fiction receives detailed treatment in Nicola Shutt's unpublished DPhil thesis 'Nobody's Child: The Theme of Illegitimacy in the Novels of Charles Dickens, George Eliot and Wilkie Collins' (University of York, 1991).

[5] Richard Carpenter, *Thomas Hardy* (New York: Twayne, 1964), p. 40.

imperatives with which he grapples are, Hardy implies, of immemorial and obscure descent, and cannot be altogether expunged by the moral, social and psychological conditioning of civilized man. *Desperate Remedies* was published in the same year as E. B. Tylor's *Primitive Culture* (1871), a substantial portion of which is devoted to the examination of 'survivals' within the self and in the wider community. His 'Conclusion' asserts that there is 'no human thought so primitive as to have lost its bearing on our own thought, nor so ancient as to have broken its connection with our own life'.[6] Perhaps this ancient flow of instinctual being is bound up with what Henry Knight glimpses in the stony gaze of the trilobite in *A Pair of Blue Eyes* (Chapter 22), which threatens to undermine the almost anchorite seclusion of his arid bourgeois life.

Manston is a figure of atavistic potency, and he can be viewed as a tentative prototype for those 'satyrs' of the mature fiction, Edred Fitzpiers and Alec d'Urberville, who respect few decrees outside their own need for instant self-gratification. Satyrs were lecherous creatures allied with the natural forces of the woodland in Greek mythology. D. H. Lawrence argues that the primal drives which make Manston kill his wife and then attempt to marry Cytherea Graye could have been a wellspring of vital creativity in an earlier epoch: he is an 'aristocratic' male who 'fell before the weight of the average, the lawful crowd, but who, in more primitive times' might have formed a 'romantic' rather than a 'tragic' figure.[7] However, to be reinstated within the orthodox parameters of the dominant culture one must learn to smother or contain wayward instinctual energies. Manston lacks the necessary nervous equipment for this show of rational restraint and compliant conformity, which explains why he has been, of his own choice, beyond the pale for so long, an outcast.

Desperate Remedies not only reflects Hardy's abiding fascination with the cultural fossils of earlier epochs that are a salient part of our present-day terrain, but also with psychological 'survivals': ineradicable irrational elements in human conduct. Sir John Lubbock, whose *Origin of Civilisation* was published in 1870, suggested how 'some ideas' are 'rooted in our minds, as fossils are imbedded in the soil'.[8] This implies, however, that ancient ideas, although lodged in the human mind, cannot actively shape modern behaviour. But Hardy conceives of Manston in a way that bears out R. R. Marett's 1917 observation that 'savage impulses' always

---

[6] E. B. Tylor, *Primitive Culture*, II, 452.

[7] D. H. Lawrence, *Study of Thomas Hardy*, p. 48.

[8] Sir John Lubbock, *The Origin of Civilisation and the Primitive Condition of Man. The Mental and Social Condition of Savages*, 2nd edn., with additions (London: Longmans, Green, and Co., 1870), p. 1.

remain 'dormant in the heart of civilised man', ready to 'spring to life again'.[9] Herbert Spencer's *Principles of Psychology* (1855) would have given Hardy much to ponder in its assertion that the human mind inherits through the nervous system the legacy of its ancestors' adaptations. Manston's functional disorder may be a manifestation not simply of a nervous susceptibility, but of a morbid tendency which has its origins much further back in ancestral aberration. Throughout his first published novel, Hardy addresses what Wilkie Collins, in *Basil* (1852) calls, 'the workings of the hidden life within us which we may experience but cannot explain',[10] and sexual abnormality as a powerful determining influence over human behaviour. Manston cannot quell what may have been a basic component of the mental traits of his forebears:

> He was palpably making the strongest efforts to subdue, or at least to hide, the weakness...rather from his own conscience than from surrounding eyes...He made no advances whatever: without avoiding her, he never sought her...Something held him back, bound his impulse down...She was interested in him and his marvellous beauty, as she might have been in some fascinating panther or leopard – for some undefinable reason she shrank from him, even whilst she admired. (*Remedies* 117)

In Manston's feline beauty there is perhaps a Dionysian element. James Frazer later remarked how 'a feature in the mythical character of Dionysus' is that he was often 'represented in animal shape'.[11] With Hardy's mythological allusions we can create a scale of possibility in which the barely glimpsed Dionysian perspective acts as a suggestive starting point, working up to the unquestionably deliberate and elaborated handling of Giles Winterborne as a failed fertility figure in *The Woodlanders* (1887), and Tess Durbeyfield as a late-Victorian version of Persephone. Indeed, it is difficult, given the hypnotic power Manston exercises over Cytherea during the storm, not to think of the Dionysian in Nietzsche's thought: the principle of diabolic darkness, rapture, music and dance. Even at this early stage in his writing career, Hardy's fiction is susceptible to an analysis employing the mythological (and mythologized) past as an interpretive tool.

---

[9] R. R. Marett, 'The Psychology of Culture Contact, Presidential Address to the Folklore Society', *Folklore* 28 (1917), 14.
[10] Wilkie Collins, *Basil*, ed. Dorothy Goldman (Oxford: Oxford University Press, 1990), p. 29.
[11] Sir James George Frazer, *The Golden Bough: A Study in Magic and Religion*, ed. with introd. Robert Fraser (Oxford: The World's Classics, 1994), p. 399.

The stratum of ancient Greek mythology that is quarried to identify Manston as a prototype for the 'satyrs' of later novels is deliberately complicated by Hardy's use of Virgilian epic. What effect does he achieve by having Manston's Christian name invoke the greatest hero of Latin poetry, Aeneas? The 'Dutch clock...fixed out of level', ticking 'wildly in longs and shorts...its entrails hanging down...like the faeces of a Harpy' (*Remedies* 255) is more than an arresting image, with its grotesque animism, but indicates a challenging interaction of Roman myth and a modern era out of joint.[12] The Dutch clock signals not only Hardy's obsession with myriad time-schemes, but reveals how 'past and present wind easily onto the same pole in Hardy's art'.[13] Robert Gittings, however, is in no doubt that mere pedantry explains Hardy's classical borrowings, whose significance rarely extends beyond the immediate scene: 'this type of learned allusion...runs through all his work to the last, loading his novels with untoward digressive references to literature, painting, and architecture.'[14] Gittings misjudges not only the level of astuteness with which Hardy employs myth, but also the importance which many Victorian scholars attached to the task of unlocking 'all the secret drawers of ancient mythology'.[15] As early as 1839 one reviewer observed that 'within our memory this branch of knowledge [mythography] was the study of a chosen few, but now so widely has it spread as to form a subject of interest in general society'.[16] Hardy's prefatory note to 'William Barnes' implies that he studied Virgil with keen sensitivity, and there is a far deeper mythological purpose at work in *Desperate Remedies* than Gittings gives him credit for.[17] Moreover, Hardy's imaginative excavation of the *Aeneid* would continue long after his debut novel was published.[18]

---

[12] Harpies were monsters with a woman's face and body and a bird's wings and claws. These predatory creatures are taken from Book III of Virgil's *Aeneid*.

[13] Bert Hornback, *The Metaphor of Chance: Vision and Technique in the Works of Thomas Hardy* (Athens, Georgia: Ohio University Press, 1971), p. 43.

[14] Robert Gittings, *Young Thomas Hardy* (Harmondsworth, Middlesex: Penguin, 1976), p. 202.

[15] Max Müller, 'Postscript' to 'Solar Myths', *Nineteenth Century* 18 (1885), 920.

[16] B. E. Pote, 'Ancient Figurative Language: Creuzer and Knight', *Foreign Quarterly Review* 23 (1839), 36. For useful accounts of the popularity of mythographic writings during this period see Albert C. Yoder, 'Concepts of Mythology in Victorian England', unpublished Ph.D dissertation (Florida State University, 1971); and J. W. Burrow, 'The Uses of Philology in Victorian England', in *Ideas and Institutions of Victorian Britain*, ed. Robert Robson (London: Barnes & Noble, 1967).

[17] 'The speech of his [Barnes's] ploughmen and milkmaids in his *Eclogues*...is as sound in its syntax as that of the Tityrus and Meliboeus of Virgil whom he had in mind'. See Thomas Hardy, *Personal Writings*, p. 84.

[18] Hardy quarried the *Aeneid* for an epigraph ('Veteris vestigia flammae' IV, l. 23) to one of his most important volumes of verse, *Poems of 1912-1913*.

The ten-year-old Hardy was given a copy of Dryden's *Virgil* by his mother, a book 'of which he never wearied',[19] and it is quoted seven times in *Desperate Remedies*, either in the original Latin or in Dryden's translation. In the relationship between Cytherea Aldclyffe and her illegitimate son, Hardy offers a deeply ironic 'retelling' of Virgil's epic poem, for Manston is manipulated by his mother in a manner reminiscent of the way Venus steers Aeneas. Cythera, an island off southern Greece and the reputed birthplace of Aeneas's mother and protector Venus (hence called Cytherea), was consecrated for the worship of this love-goddess. Miss Aldclyffe is described as having 'a Roman nose in its purest form', and 'the round prominent chin with which the Caesars are represented in ancient marbles'. As Beatty remarks in his introduction to the New Wessex Edition of the novel, she 'behaves like a classical goddess in the Victorian world'.[20] Miss Aldclyffe presides over the parish from a classical building (*Remedies* 50), and her estate contains a Grecian temple in which she discusses love with her young namesake while two swans (birds often linked with Venus) cross 'the water towards them' (*Remedies* 176).

But what did Hardy see in the plight of the 'goddess-born' Trojan prince, who leads a group of exiles from the burning towers of Troy to found a new city in the West, which might shed light on the illegitimate Manston? Both characters are rootless wanderers who struggle to locate meaning and coherence in a world that has failed to give them any firm sense of identity. Both Virgil's Aeneas and Manston long for death, since neither feels he belongs to the cosmic order.[21] But whereas the destiny of Virgil's hero is to discover a site that will eventually become Rome and place the whole world under its laws, Manston's goal is to marry a girl in whom Miss Aldclyffe sees a younger, unsullied version of herself.[22] The foundation of Rome required a human sacrifice or the inhumation of a body or head as a guarantee of prosperity, which is ironically related to Manston's burial of his wife in the leaf-pit. However – and this for Hardy is the crucial point – Manston, given the extent to which he is betrayed by imperious impulses of anger towards his wife, could never aspire to the unflinching courage and severe self-discipline of his classical namesake, who is prepared to subordinate his own individual needs and desires to the grave responsibilities of his divine mission. Such stalwart devotion to duty,

---

[19] Thomas Hardy, *Life*, p. 21.
[20] C. J. P. Beatty, 'Introduction', *Desperate Remedies*, p. xxix.
[21] See Virgil, *The Aeneid*, trans. C. Day Lewis (The World's Classics: Oxford, 1986), p. 6; and *Desperate Remedies*, Ch. 21.
[22] See Richard Sylvia, 'Thomas Hardy's *Desperate Remedies*: "All My Sin Has Been Because I Love You So" ', *Colby Quarterly* 35:2 (June 1999), 102-16.

or *pietas*, is in sharp contrast to the savage instinctual energy in man, or *furor*, which engulfs Manston and hasten his downfall. He has insufficient 'ballast of brain' (*Remedies* 109) – the cool rational control Virgil recommended – to neutralize his unregulated feelings.

Desperate Remedies contains a stratum of Greek myth overlaid by allusions to an epic Roman poem which itself dynamically reinterprets mythological material. Hardy's continuing fascination with vestigial remnants and the interaction of diverse historical periods does not end with the satyrean Manston's psychological 'survivals'. The steward is himself a product of Miss Aldclyffe's tarnished and tangled history, which transports the reader from an ancient mythologized past to more parochial and immediate events. This restless time-voyage attests a more compelling imaginative quarrying than Hardy will manage in either *Under the Greenwood Tree* (1872) or *The Trumpet-Major* (1880), two Wessex novels cited by critics to show Hardy guilty of a simplistic and sentimentalizing retrospection. Cytherea Aldclyffe is 'a woman whose early seduction means that she has taken elaborate steps to conceal her past'.[23] Her efforts to deal with the 'shameful' consequences of this early liaison underline the theme of tainted fertility that Hardy also develops during Manston's descent into the 'underworld' of instinctual behaviour. Implicit in the penitential suffering of this aristocratic lady and her misbegotten son is a radical disconnection from the natural world's ongoing organic life, which Hardy broadens in his probing delineation of a devitalized country parish later presided over by Miss Aldclyffe. Through her figure Hardy's interest in ancestry is revealed as genuinely integral to his rich and complex sense of times past and present. As in *A Laodicean* (1881) and *Tess of the d'Urbervilles* (1891), Hardy's first and third published novels portray the irreparable collapse of a once revered patrician dynasty. But it is not just the Aldclyffe line that has, in the words of Parson Swancourt speaking of his own noble clan in *A Pair of Blue Eyes*, 'been coming to nothing for centuries' (132). Hardy's evocative description of the leaf-pit reveals decay accumulating, deepening; and so we observe the Aldclyffe decline infecting the surrounding district of Carriford – a hitherto healthy, thriving community where most of the novel's action is set.

Three architectural 'survivals', each telling its own story of Carriford in 'bygone times' (*Remedies* 100), are singled out by Hardy for especially minute attention: Knapwater House; the Old House or what remains of the original Elizabethan manor; and the Three Tranters Inn. The austerity of Knapwater's architecture and its remoteness from the village (more than a

---

[23] John Bayley, *An Essay on Hardy* (Cambridge: Cambridge University Press, 1978), p. 133.

quarter of a mile away), reflect a distinctive level of taste in the evolution of English country-houses, being 'regularly and substantially built of clean grey free-stone throughout, in that plainer fashion of classicism which prevailed at the latter end of the eighteenth century' (*Remedies* 50). The prosperity of its owners is mirrored in the fact that they could abandon the old Elizabethan house, which is now used in part as labourers' cottages, having become a 'carcase full of cracks':

> Against the wall could be seen ragged lines indicating the form of other destroyed gables which had once joined it there. The mullioned and transomed windows...were mostly bricked up...and the remaining portion fitted with cottage window-frames carelessly inserted, to suit the purpose to which the old place was now applied... (*Remedies* 83)

The alterations wrought to the place by time plus fashion, and the fact that two-thirds of this 'picturesque spot' have been either ruthlessly dismantled or ruined, reveal how modern requirements are steadily effacing the traces of a differently constructed past. The mullion – a vertical post dividing a window into two or more lights – has in time been replaced by the sash, the gables by cornices. When Manston moves in, further modifications are made to the Old House, such as pulling down the existing partitions to the labourers' cottages, to make it habitable for the steward, so that more 'layers' are added to what remains of the original structure. The Old House has become a 'palimpsest', on which its previous occupants have etched their experiences for posterity. A contributor to *Archaeologia Cantiana* observed that antique buildings such as manor-houses or farms 'bear upon their faces the legible records of the past',[24] since they have been defaced, readapted and refitted in the taste of successive ages between the medieval and our own. Lord Luxellian's estate in *A Pair of Blue Eyes* is a similarly incomplete 'script'. In 'an age of retrospect' and 'historical science',[25] the study of architecture was inextricably intertwined with antiquarian pursuits, and Hardy delights in playing the tireless local antiquarian with regard to the ancestral pile, noting how many accretions have gathered round it over the centuries. But again, the clues enabling us to unearth and appreciate how the Luxellian home came into being have been expunged by 'Time's unflinching rigour'. Like so many other types of

---

[24] Anon., 'Introduction', *Archaeologia Cantiana: Transactions of the Kent Archaeological Society* 1 (1858), 6.
[25] Thus Sidney Colvin described the Victorian age in 'Restoration and Anti-Restoration', *Nineteenth Century* 2 (1877), 448.

retrospective curiosity portrayed in *A Pair of Blue Eyes*, we must accept
that crucial details about origins are irrecoverable:

> The substantial portions of the existing building dated from the reign
> of Henry VIII; but the picturesque...spot had been the site of an
> erection of a much earlier date...A licence to crenellate...was granted
> by Edward II to 'Hugo Luxellian chivaler'; but though the faint
> outline of the ditch and mound was visible at points, no sign of the
> original building remained. (*Eyes* 86)

Though Hardy believes that the faded grandeur of the Old House
makes it a more appealing structure than the modern substitute, he has no
illusions as to the inevitability of change. Miss Aldclyffe's concern is that it
should be fit for 'adaptation to modern requirements' (*Remedies* 82). How
do we reconcile the critical stance affirming that Hardy tries throughout his
writing career to immortalize the broken remnants of a stately past with
Cytherea's coachman describing the dilapidated building as awkward,
unhandy, dismal and damp; situated 'too low down in the hollow to be
healthy' (*Remedies* 48)? The 'Elizabethan fragment' may be architecturally
unique, but the 'most ancient portion of this structure' attests the
unsalvageable state into which the local aristocracy has plunged, for
creepers clamber 'over the eaves of the sinking roof, and up the gable to the
crest of the Aldclyffe family perched on the apex' (*Remedies* 82). A grim
indication of the extent to which the Old House has plummeted from its
earlier majesty is in the outhouse, formerly used as a kitchen and scullery
but now functioning as brew-house and workshop (again more cryptic
'signatures' added to a time-crusted architectural manuscript). This is
where Manston stores his first wife's corpse – a once notable and imposing
edifice has become a charnel house. The family has not really moved on,
leaving this irrelevant, unwanted and decayed carapace behind. Although
vital progress can leave such a shell behind without it being an especially
negative rather than a positive indicator, the Aldclyffes have not replaced it
with an equivalent or greater energy with their new home.

The third building in Carriford that affords a gateway into a forgotten
age is the medieval posting-inn, the Three Tranters; it too is wasting away,
having long passed its bustling heyday. Hardy describes the place and
purpose of this tavern with a delicate sureness of touch:

> The...Inn, a many-gabled, mediaeval building, constructed almost
> entirely of timber, plaster, and thatch, stood close to the line of the
> roadside, almost opposite the churchyard, and was connected with a
> row of cottages on the left by thatched outbuildings. It was an

uncommonly characteristic and handsome specimen of the genuine roadside inn of bygone times; and standing on one of the great highways in this part of England, had in its time been the scene of as much of what is now looked upon as the romantic and genial experience of stage-coach travelling as any halting-place in the country. (*Remedies* 100)

For those with little practical experience of rural life Hardy implies, the Three Tranters seems a sample and museum piece (a 'specimen') from an idealized countryside. But travelling by stagecoach, far from being 'romantic and genial', was in fact very uncomfortable, and given the atrocious state of many English highways with their ruts and mires, hazardous as well, not to mention the likelihood of being ambushed in a secluded spot. Hardy draws attention to the paradox of a small community next to a once busy highway, but one which has been left to moulder, as ill-suited to the circumstances of contemporary living. For those late-Victorian readers hoping to find a Wessex Arcadia based on a life of the simplest virtues, Hardy offers no glib consolation. Carriford is merely a depressed enclave bypassed by history:

The railway had absorbed the whole stream of traffic which formerly flowed through the village and along by the ancient door of the inn, reducing the empty-handed landlord, who used only to farm a few fields at the back of the house, to the necessity of eking out his attenuated income by increasing the extent of his agricultural business if he would still maintain his social standing. (*Remedies* 100)

As Cytherea Graye realizes when she talks to the ironically named landlord Farmer Springrove, the roadside inn is a tattered relic of the medieval past. Although it has served for generations as a cherished community gathering-place, it is now a discarded husk, from which all positive energy has retreated. The old man admits that ' "the Inn and I seem almost a pair of fossils" ' (*Remedies* 106). In *A Pair of Blue Eyes*, Henry Knight will confront a genuine fossil through which Hardy 'exhumes' not just the Middle Ages but the whole desolate store of evolutionary history.

It is interesting to compare Hardy's description of the Three Tranters Inn with Dickens's earlier account of a similar country tavern, the Maypole, in *Barnaby Rudge* (1841), a historical novel about the events culminating in the Gordon riots. Although Dickens's work is set in England around 1775 – and Hardy's just under a century later – the similarities are telling. The Maypole has seen famous figures pass through its timeworn doors:

> The Maypole...was an old building with more gable ends than a lazy
> man would care to count on a sunny day; huge zig-zag
> chimneys...and vast stables, gloomy, ruinous, and empty. The place
> was said to have been built in the days of King Henry the Eighth;
> and there was a legend...that Queen Elizabeth had slept there one
> night while upon a hunting excursion, to wit, in a certain oak-
> panelled room with a deep bay window (43)[26]

Although numerous quaint stories and legends have been seamlessly woven
into the fabric of the Inn's history, this building is starting to look as
redundant and fossilized as Farmer Springrove's tavern in *Desperate
Remedies*. Emptiness and devitalization are as much a part of the
Maypole's identity as the layers of must and dust that settle over its
antiquated furniture. Dickens's assertion that this Tudor structure, wrapped
in its garment of ivy, is yet of 'a hale and hearty age' sits uneasily with the
pointed images of neglect and dissolution linked to the inn's exterior:

> With its overhanging stories [and] drowsy little panes of glass...the
> old house looked as if it were nodding in its sleep...the bricks of
> which it was built had originally been a deep dark red, but had grown
> yellow and discoloured like an old man's skin; the sturdy timbers
> had decayed like teeth. (44)

The discoloured bricks like 'an old man's skin' and timbers 'decayed
like teeth' anticipate, and perhaps even suggested to Hardy, features of the
Three Tranters, with its 'line of roofs...over the decayed stalls...sunk into
vast hollows till they seemed like the teeth of toothless age' (*Remedies*
100). Dickens's stark word-painting jars with the scholarly opinion that the
Maypole is a product of the author's appalled flight from a new society of
hectic capitalist enterprise into a nostalgically remembered past. The notion
that Dickens views the 'experience of stagecoach travelling' as 'romantic
and genial' (*Remedies* 100), is given the lie by his unglamorous portrayal of
English roads and the many risks confronting those who dare traverse
them.[27] Dickens knew as well as Hardy that the provincialism which had
sealed remote regions inside their own cultures was disappearing; and to
succeed in modern England often meant ready, clear-sighted acceptance of
city life with its unnerving technological innovations and squalid self-
interest.

---

[26] Charles Dickens, *Barnaby Rudge*, ed. with introd. Gordon Spence (Harmondsworth,
Middlesex: Penguin, 1986).
[27] See *Barnaby Rudge*, Chapter 3 'Rough Riders'.

The Three Tranters, like the Maypole Inn, creaks under the burden of the local past, and is a site bound up with intimations of mortality and disuse. Significantly, Farmer Springrove's desolate inn stands 'almost opposite the churchyard', and the white of his labourers' smock-frocks is repeated in the whiteness of its headstones (*Remedies* 100). Old Springrove's 'passed-away fortunes' (*Remedies* 100) are no more vividly suggested than in the tavern sign, whose boards are 'visible through the thin paint depicting [the forms of the Three Tranters], which were still further disfigured by red stains running downwards from the rusty nails above' (*Remedies* 100-101). The lifeblood of the inn, and of the entire parish, has been reduced to a trickle: fertile continuities have been irretrievably lost. The history of the village is not in busy and active symbiotic relationship with the present and future; it has been blankly overtaken by dizzying modernity and the past itself is laying a dead hand on improvement. Old Springrove's inn and the rustic culture it epitomizes contain the seeds of its own disintegration. Carriford is the victim of internal decay, and its moribund condition is further evidenced by its feeble attempts to combat the spread of the fire that constitutes the most dramatic event in the novel; the galvanizing force which once made the village and its tavern a self-sufficient organic unit has departed.

The Three Tranters does not yield an income sufficient to maintain old Springrove's social standing, so he is compelled to take on extra labours, such as a modest cider-making business. This produces a seemingly exuberant scene under the elms that impressed some early reviewers of *Desperate Remedies*, who felt Hardy was tapping into the overflowing ripeness of the region.[28] Mrs Oliphant might have used the portrayal of cider-making to prove that Hardy's true gift lay in celebrating man's harmony with the rhythms regulating seasonal change, and the prodigal fecundity of 'the rustic landscape, the balmy breathing of the cows, looming out of the haze in the mystery of the dawn – the rapture of the morning in the silent fields'.[29] The passage itself, however, tells a more sobering story:

---

[28] See R. G. Cox (ed.), *Thomas Hardy: The Critical Heritage* (London: Routledge & Kegan Paul, 1970), pp. 1-7.

[29] Ibid., p. 258. In an August 1871 letter to Macmillan accompanying the manuscript of *Under the Greenwood Tree*, Hardy wrote that he turned to rural life because in his previous novel *Desperate Remedies* 'the rustic characters and scenes...had been made very much of by the reviews.' See *The Collected Letters of Thomas Hardy*, ed. Richard L. Purdy and Michael Millgate, 7 vols. (Oxford: Clarendon Press, 1978-88), I, 1. Hereafter referred to as *Collected Letters*.

> Mr Springrove had been too young a man when the pristine days of
> the Three Tranters had departed for ever to have much of the host
> left in him now. He was a poet with a rough skin...Too kindly
> constituted to be very provident, he was yet not imprudent. He had a
> quiet humorousness of disposition, not out of keeping with a frequent
> melancholy, the general expression of his countenance being one of
> abstraction...On the present occasion he wore gaiters and a leathern
> apron, and worked with his shirt-sleeves rolled up beyond his
> elbows, disclosing solid and fleshy rather than muscular arms. They
> were stained by the cider, and two or three brown apple-pips from
> the pomace he was handling were to be seen sticking on them here
> and there. (*Remedies* 101)

The contradictions and self-cancelling elements of the account – 'Too
kindly constituted to be very provident...yet not imprudent...a quiet
humorousness...not out of keeping with...melancholy' – reveals Hardy
giving not an exact depiction of old Springrove's traits but a negation of
them into 'abstraction'. This tactic underpins the general atmosphere of
weary exhaustion pervading the novel. The farmer's rolled-up shirt sleeves
revealing arms stained with cider and starred with apple pips, his strange
languor and reserve – these aspects foreshadow the more intricate
presentation of Giles Winterborne's appearance and disposition in *The
Woodlanders* (1887).[30] That the tavern and its landlord are on the brink of
ruin is highlighted by the detail of his arms, which, if he were still spirited
and strong, would be 'muscular' rather than 'solid and fleshy'.

Inattention and diffidence severely curtail Farmer Springrove's
capacity for decisive action, traits linked to his mediocre management of
business affairs. Not only has this living embodiment of former days failed
to insure the Three Tranters and the adjacent cottages – which his lease
obliges him to rebuild after the fire – but he does not check that the burning
debris which causes disaster is far enough away from his thatched inn.[31]
Similarly, Giles Winterborne lacks the foresight to discharge his duties as
a husbandman in *The Woodlanders*. It is partly through sterile self-
abnegation that he loses his cottage, his livelihood and his fiancée; unable
to mate and procreate he dies along with other superseded forms of life.

---

[30] See in particular the 'Autumn's very brother' passage in Chapter 28 of *The Woodlanders*,
where Giles seems to rise out of the earth like a new Adam, his bare arms coated with pips
and flecks of apple flesh.

[31] Under the lifehold system, a tenant entered into agreement with the lord of the manor to
occupy a dwelling for a term of lives. Farmer Springrove is the sole lessee for the inn and
the adjoining cottages. Giles Winterborne's cottage is a lifehold (see *The Woodlanders*
Chapter 13).

Fire engulfs the Three Tranters Inn, and Hardy implies this cremation is a fitting end for fossilized buildings that no longer serve any life-sustaining purpose – an idea bolstered by the spirit with which Hardy has the fire devour Stancy Castle in *A Laodicean*. A tavern that has witnessed 400 years of history is reduced to a 'mere heap of red-hot charcoal' in a matter of minutes. A host of anthropomorphic images evoke the wicked sport which actively hostile forces make out of man's antique constructions:

> The autumn wind, tameless, and swift, and proud, still blew upon the dying old house, which was constructed so entirely of combustible materials that it burnt almost as fiercely as a corn-rick. The heat in the road increased, and now for an instant at the height of the conflagration all stood still, and gazed silently, awestruck and helpless, in the presence of so irresistible an enemy. (*Remedies* 144)

Two historical references from the early sections of *Desperate Remedies* are deployed in the account of the Three Tranters disaster, and seem deliberately placed as part of Hardy's conscious design: the Great Fire of 1666, which completely transformed the face of London (*Remedies* 36), and the burning down of Parliament House on the evening of 16 October 1834 (*Remedies* 26). Desmond Hawkins complains that Hardy 'loves to drag in an antiquarian titbit without much concern for its relevance';[32] but this misrepresents Hardy's intention, which is to suggest a larger dimension and meaning for his characters and their actions. If not assiduously deployed proleptic gestures or artful flashforwards, the two references provide a type for earlier anti-types. Hardy's depiction of the Three Tranters fire discloses the unsuspected crossing of paths. Perhaps the implication is that such paths have always been traversed and always will be.

The wells of vital creativity missing from so many aspects of Carriford life are embodied in young Edward Springrove. Possessing the energetic application, insistence and self-belief to work his way up from lowly origins to architect status (as Stephen Smith does in *A Pair of Blue Eyes*), he plays on the side of purposeful change, and tries to prevent a blighted Aldclyffe past from ruining his father's already enfeebled parish. Although the newly-arrived railway is depicted as having contributed to the slow decline of the Three Tranters, this dynamic mode of travel, along with other technological achievements like the telegram, is essential to young Springrove's solving the puzzle that surrounds the Knapwater estate and its dubious occupants. It is a force for good in the young man's exacting

---

[32] Desmond Hawkins, *Thomas Hardy* (London: Macmillan, 1950), p. 87.

detective work. Unlike the simple folk of Carriford, whose church services impart a code of living that ignores the impact modern inventions will make on traditional rustic ritual, Springrove appreciates the manifold pressures of the new order, but without losing touch with his birthplace. The only occasion on which we see him really drained and emasculated like his nervously thoughtful father is during the marriage of Cytherea Graye and Manston. The time is early January, as it was when Miss Aldclyffe refused to marry Cytherea's father – an example of a poisoned past seeping into present and future lives. Specifically, the time is the 5th of January, which is called 'Old Christmas Eve' – in the myth of history signifying a changing of ages, and annually the moment at New Year when one year shifts into another. At this decisive point of overlapping historical strata, the unclean medieval atmosphere of the Aldclyffe chantry acts as a kind of incubus draining Edward Springrove's strength.

> light from the candles streamed...across the chancel to a black chestnut screen on the south side...erected for the soul's peace of some Aldclyffe of the past. Through the openwork of this screen could now be seen illuminated, inside the chantry, the reclining figures of cross-legged knights, damp and green with age, and above them a huge classic monument, also inscribed to the Aldclyffe family, heavily sculptured in cadaverous marble.
> Leaning here – almost hanging to the monument – was Edward Springrove, or his spirit. (*Remedies* 200-201)

Charles Alfred Stothard, in *Monumental Effigies of Great Britain* (1833), believed that, by examining the memorials of the illustrious dead, we could 'arrest the fleeting steps of Time, and again review those things his arm has passed over, subdued, but not destroyed'. Effigies were important because 'to history they give a body and a substance, by placing before us those things which language is deficient in describing'.[33] His fiery enthusiasm for the endeavour of resuscitating the past was shared by Pugin. In *Contrasts* (1836), a key document of the central phase of the Gothic Revival, Pugin stressed that 'it is only by communing with the spirit of past ages, as it is developed in the lives of the holy men of old, and in their wonderful monuments and works, that we can arrive at a just appreciation

---

[33] Charles Alfred Stothard, *The Monumental Effigies of Great Britain, selected from our cathedrals and churches, for the purpose of bringing together, and preserving correct representations of the best historical illustrations extant, from the Norman Conquest to the reign of Henry the Eighth*, ed. Alfred John Kempe, London, 1833. New edn. with additions by John Hewitt (London: Chatto & Windus, 1876), p. 2.

of the glories we have lost'.[34] However, Hardy conveys the macabre side of the favourite Victorian pastime of studying tombs and vaults; he divests the patrician past of the romantic historical associations celebrated by Pugin and the overwhelming majority of nineteenth-century antiquarians. Edward Springrove, destined to join the new Victorian nobility of talent and enterprise, finds his strength sapped by the ghosts of a once sturdy family now on the brink of extinction. That Edward seems to be 'hanging' from a 'huge classic monument' implies the brute force upon which the feudal spirit depended. Hardy's brooding account of youth exposed to diseased aristocratic air is elaborated in *A Pair of Blue Eyes* when Elfride Swancourt feels uneasy looking at the solemn portraits of Lord Luxellian's forefathers.[35] She becomes 'somewhat depressed by the society of Luxellian shades of cadaverous complexion fixed by Holbein, Kneller, and Lely, and seeming to gaze at and through her in a moralizing mood' (*Eyes* 87). Again the focus falls on oppressive 'cadaverous' figures, which is heightened in a later scene when Elfride accompanies Henry Knight to survey the Luxellian crypt. Standing in the gloom surrounded by coffins, a ray of daylight lends her face a corpse-like 'blue pallor' (*Eyes* 325).

In *Desperate Remedies* Hardy illustrates not only recent historical layers, but through his portrayal of Manston reaches out to the vestiges of primitive experience, a chthonic potency which has survived the imposition of a stifling rationality bred by historical 'progress'. That Hardy couples the chronicle of a crumbling rural community (using its buildings as architectural 'survivals'), with the unearthing of an ancient satyrean propensity in the conception of Manston, shows a virtuosity few critics proclaim. Perhaps Hardy's cogent account of the netherworld currents within the aristocratic male, and their disastrous revolt against a profoundly constricting kind of respectability, remains the most crucial 'find' in this debut volume.[36]

---

[34] Augustus Welby Northmore Pugin, *Contrasts: or A Parallel between the Noble Edifices of the Middle Ages, and Corresponding Buildings of the Present Day; shewing the Present Decay of Taste*, introd. H. R. Hitchcock (New York: Humanities Press, 1969), p. 16.

[35] This scene anticipates the de Stancy portraits that exert a potent influence over another youthful figure who, like Edward Springrove, belongs to the new era of constructive advance, Paula Power in *A Laodicean*.

[36] For a salutary reappraisal of the novel see A. A. M. Bulaila, '*Desperate Remedies*: Not Just a Minor Novel', *Thomas Hardy Journal* 14:1 (February 1998), 65-74.

A Pair of Blue Eyes (1873)

> One stream only of sunlight came into the room from a window quite
> in the corner, overlooking a court. An aquarium stood in the
> window...an errant, kindly ray lighted up and warmed the little world
> therein, when the many-coloured zoophytes opened and put forth
> their arms, the weeds acquired a rich transparency, the shells
> gleamed of a more golden yellow, and the timid community
> expressed gladness more plainly than in words...Knight then went to
> the middle of the room and flung open his portmanteau, and Stephen
> drew near the window. The streak of sunlight had crept upward,
> edged away, and vanished; the zoophytes slept: a dusky gloom
> pervaded the room. And now another volume of light shone over the
> panes.
>   'There!' said Knight, 'where is there in England a spectacle to
> equal that? I sit there and watch them every night before I go home.
> Softly open the sash.'
>   Beneath them was an alley running up to the wall, and thence
> turning sideways and passing under an arch, so that Knight's back
> window was immediately over the angle, and commanded a view of
> the alley lengthwise. Crowds – mostly of women – were surging,
> bustling, and pacing up and down. Gaslights glared from butchers'
> stalls, illuminating the lumps of flesh to splotches of orange and
> vermilion, like the wild colouring of Turner's later pictures, whilst
> the purl and babble of tongues of every pitch and mood was to this
> human wild-wood what the ripple of a brook is to the natural forest.
> (*Eyes* 182, 186-7)

Henry Knight is introduced to us from the viewpoint of his earnest protégé
Stephen Smith. Knight's London residence at Bede's Inn boasts a marine
aquarium, through whose glass we look in uncomprehending security at a
multi-coloured aggregation of atoms that comprises for Knight the
zoological past, an exotic and entrancing world-within-a-world. Zoophytes
are creatures classified midway between plants and animals, such as sea-
anemones, corals and sponges. The aquarium is a symbol of Knight's
unhealthy detachment, which will be eroded by his subjective love for
Elfride and by the untrammelled nature that assails him on the Cliff without
a Name ten chapters later. Knight dabbles in literary and scientific research;
his sense of ruling power derives from diligently maintaining the pose of
aloof spectator, scrutinizing life through the safety of a glass partition. At
Bede's Inn – even the name suggests a monastic retreat from the hazardous
undercurrents of metropolitan life – he is a figure who does not immerse
himself in that life but merely *watches* from a position of unobserved
seclusion. Seething below his office window is the 'Humanity Show' (*Eyes*

186), the sinister movements of cramped, wasted lives in the atavistic enclave of lower London: the 'postern abuts on as crowded and poverty-stricken a network of alleys as are to be found anywhere in the metropolis' (*Eyes* 180).[37] This shabby 'spectacle' evokes the conclusion to Sir John Lubbock's *The Origin of Civilization and the Primitive Condition of Man* (1870) in which he describes 'countrymen of our own living, in our very midst, a life worse than that of a savage; neither enjoying the rough advantages and real, though rude, pleasure of savage life, nor yet availing themselves of the far higher and more noble opportunities which lie within the reach of civilized Man'.[38] For that most 'civilized' of men Henry Knight, the 'Humanity Show' implies the theatrical unreality of his controlled environment. Ensconced in well-appointed chambers that exude the scent of scholarship, Knight's personal world is abstracted from the distasteful facts of time in an artificial way. He has found a safe haven from the reproductive, familial and economic demands which harass the typical Victorian male. Hardy implies that Knight voyeuristically enjoys looking down from his 'box' on a low (in every sense) entertainment; examining the savage within, that swarming mass of human specimens brought into existence by the industrial revolution who, most of the English ruling establishment was convinced, would destroy English civilization if permitted any kind of political prominence.

Henry Knight is Hardy's first major study in a series of Victorian dilettantes, which culminates in the scathing portraits of Edred Fitzpiers in *The Woodlanders* (1887) and Angel Clare in *Tess of the d'Urbervilles* (1891).[39] In some respects Knight is a blueprint for Clare: overbearingly self-righteous, coldly idealistic, with 'an invincible objection to be any but the first comer in a woman's heart' (*Eyes* 246). Knight's rooms are adorned with casts, statuettes and medallions 'picked up' on antiquarian wanderings through 'France and Italy' (*Eyes* 182). During the course of the novel, he

---

[37] Hardy's memorable description is reminiscent of George Sims in *How the Poor Live* (1883), reporting the existence of 'a dark continent that is within easy walking distance of the General Post Office'. Quoted in Peter Keating, 'Introduction' to Keating (ed.), *Into Unknown England 1866-1913: Selections from the Social Explorers* (Manchester: Manchester University Press, 1981), p. 14.

[38] Quoted in Morse Peckham, *Victorian Revolutionaries. Speculations on Some Heroes of a Culture Crisis* (New York: George Braziller, 1970), p. 182.

[39] Knight suffers, as Angel Clare will, from the lack of 'a grosser nature' (*Eyes* 363). *The Spectator* (28 June 1873) was surprisingly perceptive about Hardy's portrait of the neurotic, selfishly intolerant scholar: 'For Knight is no carpet-knight, but quite the reverse – a lonely, unloving man, an acute, uncompromising critic, of severe rectitude, unable to conceive of purity and faithfulness in combination with timidity and vacillation, and therefore harsh and unjust.' Quoted in Marlene Springer, *Hardy's Use of Allusion* (London: Macmillan, 1983), p. 47.

embarks on similar expeditions to Dublin (*Eyes* 244) and in the neighbourhood of Endelstow in Cornwall (*Eyes* 257).[40] Described as a 'man of many ideas' (*Eyes* 400) and a 'fair geologist' (*Eyes* 271), Knight is one of the most relentlessly cerebral of Hardy's dilettantes, a figure who would consider himself in the vanguard of E. B. Tylor's 'army' of backward-looking rationalists devoted to collecting and preserving the trophies of distant epochs:

> Was there ever a time when lost history was being reconstructed, and existing history rectified, more zealously than they are now by a whole army of travellers, excavators, searchers of old churches, and explorers of forgotten dialects?[41]

Thus Tylor in *Primitive Culture* (1871). Two years later, Hardy published *A Pair of Blue Eyes*, a novel whose portrayal of the reflective pedant Henry Knight furnishes a scalding critique of the 'travellers', 'explorers' and 'searchers of old churches' eulogized by Tylor and his anthropological peers. Tylor's rhetorical question articulates a commitment to antiquarian investigation partly shared by Hardy himself, and one which invests his creation of Knight, a barrister by profession who has a sweeping variety of interests in bygone records from literature to excavated artefacts. Writing in 1880 Edward Walford, editor of *The Antiquary* magazine, paid tribute to the contemporary 'reverence for antiquity...which shows itself in the popular devotion to ancient art, whether in architecture, in painting, in design...and in the eager reception accorded to fresh discoveries of relics or works of antiquarian interest'.[42] But Hardy reveals a pensive attitude towards that crusading desire to make the Victorian age one of the most 'eventful periods of intellectual and moral history, when the oft-closed gates of discovery...[stood] open at their widest'.[43] Many of Knight's encounters with various strata of (pre)history take place through his relationship and experiences with Elfride Swancourt. Although her presence is 'weak' (*Eyes* 52), her eyes are 'her last and best treasure' (*Eyes* 33), whose depths might conceal a vibrant inner life. Knight's overriding need to probe Elfride's romantic past – as Angel Clare will Tess Durbeyfield's in the later novel – to guarantee that she is as chaste and spotless as his mental picture of her, highlights the edgy fascination of exploring people or things with a secret history, and the accompanying

---

[40] Knight later travels on the Continent to study medievalism and early French art (*Eyes* 414).
[41] E. B. Tylor, *Primitive Culture*, I, 281.
[42] Edward Walford, 'Preface', *Antiquary* 1 (1880), iii.
[43] E. B. Tylor, 'Conclusion', *Primitive Culture*, II, 452.

dread of what might be divulged. *A Pair of Blue Eyes* contains many dramas in which characters attempt to expose 'what went on in the country hundreds of years ago' (*Eyes* 204); ranging from the sham medievalism of Stephen Smith's neo-Gothic church restoration, the 'fossilized Tory' (*Eyes* 96) Parson Swancourt's frivolous forays into 'the mists of antiquity' (*Eyes* 66) using his much-thumbed genealogical dictionary, his daughter Elfride's compensating fantasies of romance-writing about 'the Early Ages' (*Eyes* 178) in her story *The Court of King Arthur's Castle*, to Knight's crisis on the Cliff without a Name, where he confronts a genuine imbedded fossil.[44]

The cliffhanger in Chapter 22 offers the most demanding time-perspective in a novel obsessed by visual angles and lenses (the various types of 'glass' through which Knight scrutinizes other life-forms in and around Bede's Inn).[45] When he is 'spitted' on a rock, the rarefied serenity of his London chambers will seem like a distant dream. Knight's marine aquarium, in which nature is trapped and prettified for the wandering eye, sharply contrasts with the untamed sea that lashes the foot of the cliff, waiting to consume him if he should slip and fall.[46] However, the imprisoned zoophytes prefigure the fossilized trilobite that – in an effective 'turning-of-tables' – so coldly stares Knight in the eyes as he hangs in front of it, reduced to its primitive level.[47] His ordeal begins with him sitting on the cliff displaying his scientific erudition to Elfride. He attempts to demonstrate the contrariwise circulation of air-currents up the face of the

---

[44] The Parson owns a *Genealogical and Heraldic Dictionary of the Landed Gentry of Great Britain and Ireland*. His hobby would have found favour with a writer for the inaugural edition of *Archaeologia Cantiana* who endorsed 'this reverence for ancient families' and urged new members to contribute 'letters and genealogies of families living or extinct in their neighbourhood'. See Anon., 'Introduction', *Archaeologia Cantiana* 1 (1858), 19. Delighting in 'patrician reminiscences' (*Eyes* 131), Parson Swancourt expatiates on 'Knight's fine old family name, and theories as to lineage and intermarriage connected therewith' (*Eyes* 216). Hardy was himself interested in genealogy, but he could also distance himself from, and lampoon, individuals who pored over family trees.

[45] For a thought-provoking reassessment of the eye imagery in the novel see Meoghan Byrne Cronin, '"As a Diamond Kills an Opal": Charm and Countercharm in *Thomas Hardy's A Pair of Blue Eyes*', *Victorians Institute Journal* 26 (1998), 121-47; Judith Bryant Wittenberg, 'Early Hardy Novels and the Fictional Eye', *Novel* 16:2 (Winter 1983), 151-64.

[46] Stephen Smith approaches Knight's chambers through a courtyard containing a sycamore tree: 'the thick coat of soot upon the branches, hanging underneath them in flakes, as in a chimney...Within the railings is a flower garden of respectable dahlias and chrysanthemums, where a man is sweeping the leaves from the grass' (*Eyes* 180-81). As in the marine aquarium, Nature is here attenuated, imprisoned and overseen by man: a stark contrast to Knight's cliff adventure in which the full weight of savage natural force is unleashed upon him.

[47] James Gibson writes that this episode 'may be the first cliff-hanger in our literature'. See *Thomas Hardy: A Literary Life* (London: Macmillan, 1996), p. 60

cliff: ' "Over that edge," said Knight, "where nothing but vacancy appears, is a moving compact mass. The wind strikes the face of the rock, runs up it, rises like a fountain over our heads...rising instead of falling, and air instead of water" ' (*Eyes* 264). Instead of applying his confident grasp of physical laws to his own behaviour and avoiding the verge, Knight freely indulges his curiosity. 'The labour of extricating laws from masses of facts', according to one reviewer, 'is a labour of love to the man of science.'[48] Unfortunately Knight's labour of love as a 'pioneer of the thoughts of men' (*Eyes* 271) makes him stray too close to the verge and a sudden gust of wind sucks his hat off; in a rash attempt to retrieve it he slips down the incline and ends up clinging to the edge of the cliff:

> Haggard cliffs, of every ugly altitude, are as common as sea-fowl along the line of coast between Exmoor and Land's End; but this outflanked and encompassed specimen was the ugliest of them all. Their summits are not safe places for scientific experiment on the principles of air-currents, as Knight had now found, to his dismay. (*Eyes* 270)

Ironically, Knight now finds himself clutching the dark shale, in the unforgiving grip of the very laws about which he had been holding forth. With a 'knot of starved herbage' (*Eyes* 268) the only thing keeping him from plunging into the sea, the tough-minded agnostic senses his own fragility, forced into a 'confrontation of man with the immense geological perspectives of earth's history'.[49] Knight has slipped over the border separating the living from the nonliving, and inanimate nature becomes for him a pitiless adversary.

> He reclined hand in hand with the world in its infancy. Not a blade, not an insect, which spoke of the present, was between him and the past. The inveterate antagonism of these black precipices to all strugglers for life is in no way more forcibly suggested than by the paucity of tufts of grass...on their outermost ledges. (*Eyes* 270)

This engrossing incident with its multiple ironies offers the most wide-ranging and comprehensive vision of former worlds in Hardy's fiction, and the sixth instalment of the serial version breaks off at the end of the novel's Chapter 21 showing Knight, exposed and unprotected, 'in the presence of a

---

[48] Anon., 'Sir John Herschel's *Astronomical Observations at the Cape of Good Hope*', *Quarterly Review* 85 (June 1849), 5.
[49] Desmond Hawkins, *Thomas Hardy: Novelist & Poet* (Newton Abbot, Devon: David & Charles, 1976), p. 137.

personalized loneliness' (*Eyes* 269).[50] Left for several minutes by Elfride, suspended over the abyss, he determines 'to make the most of his every jot of endurance' (*Eyes* 270), yet he is faced blankly with the prospect of his own mortality. For Knight the marked increase in the time-span of the imagined past accentuates his sense of existential isolation on the cliff, and he faces the cheerless prospect of humanity ending up like the extinct creatures entombed in 'the enormous masses of black strata' (*Eyes* 268). His plight offers a trenchant comment on what happens when, according to William Gladstone, we 'substitute a blind mechanism for the hand of God in the affairs of life'.[51] Yet Knight's inflated self-opinion makes him see his particular prospect at this moment as humanity's prospect: his journalistic art lies in representing the individual as the general experience with a robust certitude of tone. And he never quite overcomes this colossal egotism, though the cliff ordeal might have taught him to.

The cliff scene reveals Knight's difficulty of dealing with the grim testimony of the convoluted rock folds and the fossils shaped millions of years ago. It highlights an era 'long, beyond chronology'[52] against which his many credentials are set and qualified. By revealing Knight's response to the suffocating silences of geological time-spans, Hardy captures the loss and reduction of man's significance in his own sight. On the escarpment Knight's ordeal is one of learning about an implacable Nature red in tooth and claw: 'He could only look sternly at Nature's treacherous attempt to put an end to him, and strive to thwart her' (*Eyes* 271). Hardy's evocation of Knight's predicament is reminiscent of Leslie Stephen's article 'A Bad Five Minutes in the Alps', in which he imagines himself clutching a precipice after a mountaineering mishap, waiting for death.[53] Stephen's sketch was first published in *Fraser's Magazine* in November 1872 (volume 86); *A Pair of Blue Eyes* came out in serial form 1872-73. Stephen and Hardy capture the bleak practical reality of a confrontation with the physical external world. 'Pilloried on a bare rock', Stephen, like his

---

[50] For a geological discussion of the uncompromising stretch of Cornish coastline upon which Hardy's portrayal of the cliff is based see Richard Fortey, *Trilobite! Eyewitness to Evolution* (London: Flamingo, 2001), pp. 1-16. See also Lawrence Jones, 'Thomas Hardy and the Cliff without a Name', in *Geography and Literature: A Meeting of the Disciplines*, ed. William E. Mallory and Paul Simpson-Housley (Syracuse, New York: Syracuse University Press, 1987), pp. 168-84.

[51] W. E. Gladstone, 'Dawn of Creation and of Worship', *Nineteenth Century* 18 (1885), 706.

[52] Thomas Hardy, 'The Clasped Skeletons', *Complete Poems*, p. 873.

[53] Leslie Stephen, 'A Bad Five Minutes In The Alps' in *Essays on Freethinking and Plainspeaking* (London: Longmans, Green & Co., 1873), pp. 155-97.

fictional counterpart, struggles to maintain an objective rational stance, and succumbs to 'wild and tyrannous imaginings' about a hostile universe.[54]

Through a 'strange conjunction of phenomena' (*Eyes* 119), Knight notices that he is looking into the dead eyes of a fossilized trilobite, a distant cousin of crustaceans which Charles Darwin highlighted as an example of sudden extinction through failure to adapt. The armour-plating of didactic aphorism, which Knight wears with such aplomb in polite society is useless to him now as he dangles by his fingertips in the concavity of the cliff, reduced to the same level as a rudimentary life-form:

> The creature represented but a low type of animal existence, for never in their vernal years had the plains indicated by those numberless slaty layers been traversed by an intelligence worthy of the name. Zoophytes, mollusca, shell-fish, were the highest developments of those ancient dates. The immense lapses of time each formation represented had known nothing of the dignity of man. They were grand times, but they were mean times too, and mean were their relics. He was to be with the small in his death...at this dreadful juncture his mind found time to take in, by a momentary sweep, the varied scenes that had had their day between this creature's [trilobite's] epoch and his own. (*Eyes* 271-2)

It is appropriate that Knight, a feted member of the London smart set and an amateur geologist, should have to contemplate being 'with the small in his death'. Yet if there were a nuclear disaster, the zoophytes like those in Knight's marine aquarium would survive, not man. Knight is one of those 'nineteenth-century investigators' for whom 'the trilobite was an alien creature, whose connection to the world of living animals was remote, almost imponderable'.[55] After trying to impress Elfride by experimenting on air-currents, Knight realizes to his consternation that nature is practising experiments on him. He finds himself on the receiving end of a new conception of time that is a consequence of geological and physical data he had previously treated with blithe unconcern. The sense that instead of being 'Creation's crown and perfection',[56] he might be merely a drab facet of matter amid the sordid struggles of nature, threatens Knight's 'preternatural quiet' (*Eyes* 267). For a sophisticated cosmopolite always at

---

[54] In both episodes the weather is treacherous, and heavy rain makes the cliffs especially unsafe. Knight clings to his knot of vegetation, Stephen to a rhododendron root. This comparison was first made by John Halperin, 'Leslie Stephen, Thomas Hardy, and *A Pair of Blue Eyes*', *Modern Language Review* 75 (1980), 738-45.

[55] Richard Fortey, *Trilobite! Eyewitness to Evolution*, p. 86.

[56] Anon., 'Darwin's *Origin of Species*', *Quarterly Review* 108 (1860), 259.

one remove from physical experience, who prefers arcane sedentary pursuits to a direct apprehension of time, the trilobite's unblinking eyes reveal a cosmos in which man is an isolated intelligent mutation. However, the tone of the passage mingles this profound revelation with Hardy's puckish wit and legerdemain. Knight, whose capacity for detached, passionless contemplation is in no way stymied by being precariously suspended from the face of an escarpment, mentally composes an article for his highbrow journal *The Present*, converting the hectic disorder of lived experience into cool explanatory prose: 'The creature represented but a low type of animal existence'. The prospect of death galvanizes this sage as nothing in professional life does, giving him the will to live and providing copy for his next weightily authoritative piece! Knight feels his death would be a 'loss to earth of good material' (*Eyes* 275) – an impish Hardyan pun on the prose 'material' Knight could publish in *The Present*.

Uncontrolled nature in her 'experiment' shatters the imposed equilibrium of Knight's existence: 'The world was to some extent turned upside down for him' (*Eyes* 272). He is punished for aspiring to an impermissible objective detachment. However, Hardy is not trivializing Knight's enforced calm rationality here; that he manages a stoical self-possession is remarkable, and it plays no small part in keeping him alive. Still, even he is unable to sustain the rigid composure of composing his next erudite article when left alone on the black cliff, which he imagines as a remorseless foe: 'Grimness was in every feature, and to its very bowels the inimical shape was desolation' (*Eyes* 271). Hardy elaborates a pattern of antinomial dualism here, as Knight's conscious wishes and values are set against a hostile Darwinian universe. But the dilettante's skewed perception of a personified Nature that is callously unresponsive to the appeals of human suffering, is no truer than the trite ideological flights indulged by disciples of sublime scenery such as Angel Clare in *Tess*.

Through his eyeball-to-eyeball confrontation with the imbedded trilobite, Knight sees not so much his own life flashing before him as that of the whole melancholy procession of deep prehistory, a fan-like compression of an immensity of time. Knight's mind races back to the aeons before man as he shares in the vision of these crustacean-like creatures that patrolled the shallows of vanished oceans for three hundred million years. A moment of suppressed panic in the present offers Knight re-entry into a remote past of incomprehensible strangeness, a 'time' before 'the disease of feeling germed'.[57] After standing on the cliff-top using Elfride's telescope to watch the steamer that, unknown to him, carries his

---

[57] Thomas Hardy, 'Before Life and After', *Complete Poems*, p. 277.

romantic rival Stephen Smith home, Knight now observes the telescoping of different stages of evolving life:

> Time closed up like a fan before him. He saw himself at one extremity of the years, face to face with the beginning and all the intermediate centuries simultaneously. (*Eyes* 272)

The 'fan' image shows that in Knight's time-journey there are two starting points, original chaos at one end and himself at the other, a Victorian polymath. Then, the two ends of the evolutionary chain meet face to face, underlining his physical kinship with and derivation from unconscious primitive forms of life. In a series of tableaux of the past, he visualizes neolithic man, then animal forms 'of monstrous size', then further back to 'huge-billed birds' and 'swinish creatures as large as horses', and so backwards through uncountable ages to 'fishy beings of lower development' until reaching the trilobite, whose own evolution calibrated geological time itself. This perspective, achieved through a sense of the compression of discrete time-periods, is an arresting example of the scientific mind engaged in what T.H. Huxley called 'retrospective prophecy': 'the reconstruction in human imagination of events which have vanished and ceased to be'.[58]

In April 1858 Hardy's close friend and mentor, Horace Moule (upon whom many critics believe Knight to be based) gave him a copy of Gideon Algernon Mantell's *The Wonders of Geology* (1838).[59] Moule might have been thankful to offload this two-volume work (there would be eight British editions in all, making it the best-selling popular geology in Victorian England) because its findings sailed too close to the theological wind for it to be palatable to Moule's father, the rector of Fordington near Dorchester. Mantell (1790-1852) was an indefatigable dinosaur hunter and geologist who lived among the fossil-rich Mesozoic cliffs of England's south coast.[60] In 1824 he discovered *Iguanodon*, the second dinosaur known

---

[58] T. H. Huxley, 'On the Method of Zadig', in *Science and Hebrew Tradition* (London: Macmillan, 1901), p. 6.

[59] Gideon Mantell was among the most popular geological lecturers in Victorian England and as a writer unusually concerned to disseminate accurate scientific information throughout the public at large. His major books on earth science include *The Fossils of the South Downs* (1822), *Illustrations of the Geology of Sussex* (1827), *The Geology of the South-East of England* (1833), *The Wonders of Geology* (1838), *Medals of Creation* (1844), and *Petrifactions and Their Teachings* (1851).

[60] See Dennis Dean, *Gideon Mantell and the Discovery of Dinosaurs* (Cambridge: Cambridge University Press, 1999).

to science and the first herbivorous one.[61] Knight, himself an avid gentleman geologist and student of natural history, derives his reflections while spitted on the Cliff without a Name from Mantell's *Wonder of Geology*. Mantell treated the phenomenon of the trilobite with rapt attention: these humble, grey creatures had survived ice ages and volcanic eruptions to witness continents move, mountain chains elevated and eroded. Especially noteworthy is Mantell's focus on the trilobite's multifaceted eyes.[62] Knight's dazzling vision of geological strata folding up like a fan (*Eyes* 272), bears an uncanny resemblance to the 'Retrospect' at the end of Mantell's first volume, in which he imagines himself travelling back in time to 'a beautiful country of vast extent, diversified by hill and dale, with its rivulets, streams, and mighty rivers, flowing through fertile plains'.[63] Here Mantell gazes upon 'monsters of the reptile tribe, so huge that nothing among the existing races can compare with them, basking on the banks of its rivers, and roaming through its forests', just as Knight imagines the sight of 'Huge elephantine forms'. Travelling farther back in time, Mantell's voyager perceives 'winged reptiles of strange forms' sharing with the birds 'the dominion of the air'. Knight sees 'dragon forms and clouds of flying reptiles'.[64] Mantell continues, 'And after the lapse of many ages I again visited the earth; and the country, with its innumerable dragon-forms, and its tropical forests, all had disappeared, and ocean had usurped their place'.

---

[61] Gideon Mantell met Mary Anning in 1832, the 'fossil woman' (1799-1847) and a local celebrity in Dorset who, it is popularly supposed, uncovered in 1811 the first Ichthyosaur to be seen by human eyes. The earliest reports of Mary Anning's work were published by the Lyme historian George Roberts, 'The Fossil Finder of Lyme Regis', *Chambers Journal of Popular Literature*, vol. 7 (1857), 382-84. On Mantell and Anning's dedicated fossil-hunting see Adrian J. Desmond, *The Hot-Blooded Dinosaurs: A Revolution in Palaeontology* (London: Blond & Briggs, 1975); William D. Lang, 'Mary Anning and the Pioneer Geologists of Lyme', *Proceedings of the Dorset Natural History and Archaeological Society* 60 (1939), 142-64; Deborah Cadbury, *The Dinosaur Hunters* (London: Fourth Estate, 2001).

[62] Gideon Mantell, *The Wonders of Geology; or, A Familiar Exposition of Geological Phenomena*, 2 vols. (London: Henry G. Bohn, 1848), II, 793. Mantell devotes Section Twenty-two of his 'Lecture 8' to 'The Visual Organs of The Trilobites'. Section Six of his 'Lecture 6' discusses zoophytes, the exotic animal-plants on display in Knight's London rooms at Bede's Inn.

[63] Gideon Mantell, *The Wonders of Geology*, I, 447-9. The debt of this scene to Mantell was traced by Patricia Ingham, 'Hardy and *The Wonders of Geology*', *Review of English Studies* 31 (1980), 59-64 and elaborated in Roger Ebbatson's Penguin Classics edition (1985) of *A Pair of Blue Eyes*.

[64] As time 'closed up like a fan' before him, Knight views the ancestors from whom his formidable intellect evolved: 'Fierce men, clothed in the hides of beasts, and carrying, for defence and attack, huge clubs and pointed spears'. Mantell sees 'human beings, clad in the skins of animals, and armed with clubs and spears.'

When dry land reappears Mantell imagines 'herds of deer of enormous size, and groups of elephants, mastodons, and other herbivorous animals of colossal magnitude. And I saw in its rivers and marshes the hippopotamus, tapir, and rhinoceros.' Similarly, Knight dreams of 'the mastodon, the hippopotamus, the tapir, antelopes of monstrous size'. Hardy offers a fictional remoulding of this section from *The Wonders*, employing Mantell's imaginative structure and details to underscore that blend of high seriousness and comic upside-downness which from the reader's point of view is such a crucial part of this Knightly ordeal.

Gideon Mantell's vibrant artistic journey into 'periods of unfathomable antiquity'[65] is mirrored in Knight's gradual descent from the pinnacle of rational lucidity to the primeval darkness on the face of the escarpment. His profound loneliness and sense of reduced significance while dangling desperately at the edge of the cliff-face springs from the recondite messages decoded by such figures as Sir Charles Lyell, Robert Chambers and Charles Darwin in their scrutiny of those 'numberless slaty layers' (*Eyes* 271) of the geological record.[66] For these scholars the 'layers' of rock that enveloped the globe formed the pages of a history of the earth. As Knight learns, 'the spoils of the strata'[67] must have been shaped, not in a few thousand years of cataclysmic events, but over countless millions of years. A reviewer for *Blackwood's Magazine* acknowledged in 1860 that, 'a gulf of unknown span, not even dimly seen across, divides [historic or human time]...from the geologic ages which went before'.[68] The agnostic Knight would no doubt have encouraged making available the revelation of the rocks, undermining the entrenched power of theological conservatism.

'Time', to many early Victorians, was approximately six thousand years old, and Man removed by only a few generations of oral tradition from Adam.[69] Within the space of a few decades the predominant view of

---

[65] Gideon Mantell, *The Wonders of Geology*, I, 447.

[66] Chambers's most popular work was *The Vestiges of Creation* (1844); Lyell is best remembered for his immense *Principles of Geology* (1830-33), which played a major role in the development of Darwin's *The Origin of Species* (1859). Given that Hardy believed he was among the first 'acclaimers' of *The Origin* (*Life* 153), it is surprising that his published *Literary Notebooks* do not contain any direct quotations from Darwin and there is only one reference to the great geologist Lyell.

[67] [J. D. Forbes], 'Lyell on the Antiquity of Man', *Edinburgh Review* 118 (1863), 259.

[68] Henry Darwin Rogers, 'The Reputed Traces of Primeval Man', *Blackwood's Magazine* 88 (1860), 431.

[69] In 1650 the Archbishop of Armagh, James Ussher, had concluded that God created the earth the night preceding Sunday 23 October, 4004 years before the birth of Christ. His dating of the earth, far from being derided, was considered an astute piece of historical scholarship by some devout Victorian intellectuals, who followed his lead in the study of chronology using sacred texts. Samuel Lysons, in *Our British Ancestors: Who And What*

geological time shifted from that which could be comprehended imaginatively, to that which could only be grasped mathematically. This was, according to one contemporary observer, part of a 'great and sudden revolution'[70] in conceiving history. Although Davenport Adams enthused in 1872 that, 'Science…is at this moment casting its magic light upon a Past which everlasting shadows would seem to have concealed from our wistful ken',[71] science could only articulate a sense of the earth's true age by using strict, increasingly circumscribed methods of presenting data. J. Phillips conceded that the periods of time opened out by geological discovery 'can only be a matter for conjecture without limit'.[72] Yet Hardy evokes the *idea* of sixty million years – it means very little to us as a dry scientific fact – by having Knight confront the trilobite: an imaginative appreciation of a wide sweep of geological time and scale within which human hopes and anguish claim a pre-eminent value. 'Such being the vast importance of modern Science to the community', contended one reviewer, 'it is proportionately of consequence that its principles and its definite discoveries should be made generally known, and should be explained in such manner as to attract the popular imagination, and to enter fully into the popular mind'.[73]

Hardy registered and responded to – in his typically complex amalgams of historical and prehistorical strata – the demand from an informed, enthusiastic reading public that seminal scientific innovations be possessed by and portrayed in literature. When Sir John Lubbock's *Prehistoric Times* (1869) begins, 'The first appearance of man in Europe dates from a period so remote, that neither history, nor even tradition, can throw any light on his origin, or mode of life', it is Hardy's art, rather than the abstract purity of mathematical theorems, which helps 'to realize our conceptions of the enormous lapse of past time'.[74] William Wordsworth anticipated the day when the 'remotest discoveries of the chemist, the botanist, or mineralogist will be as proper objects of the poet's art as any upon which it can be

---

Were They? An Inquiry (Oxford and London: John Henry & James Parker, 1865), provides an Adamic chronology and angrily rejects 'recent geological theories' which can only 'astonish sober-minded people' (92).

[70] Charles Murchison, 'Editor's Note', in *Paleontological Memoirs and Notes of Hugh Falconer*, 2 vols. (London: Hardwicke, 1868), I, 486.

[71] W. H. Davenport Adams, *Life in the Primeval World, (founded on Meunier's 'Les Animaux d'Autrefois')* (London: T. Nelson & Sons, 1872), p. 22.

[72] [J. Phillips], 'Review of *Geological Evidences of the Antiquity of Man* by Charles Lyell', *Quarterly Review* 114 (1863), 370.

[73] Anon., 'Scientific Lectures – their Use and Abuse', *Quarterly Review* 145 (January 1878), 36.

[74] Anon., 'Lyell – on *Life and its Successive Development*', *Quarterly Review* 89 (September 1851), 412-51.

employed'.[75] Hardy makes the bottom dropping out of history seem like a massive shock to which the human psyche could barely adjust. Professional expounders of modern secular knowledge who wished to capture the immensity of unchronicled ages found themselves encroaching, like Gideon Mantell in his bravura 'Retrospect' from *The Wonders of Geology*, on a novelist's stock-in-trade. This would not be viewed as a problematic trend, for as Mantell himself remarked, 'our readers might well exclaim that the realities of Geology far exceed the fictions of romance!'[76]

After rising to prominence as a refined reviewer of contemporary fiction, Knight now has to read a tortuous narrative of the geological record, the 'pages' of whose 'stony register'[77] convey sobering messages about the process of evolutionary development. Yet intellectually he feels very superior, for the empty carapace of the trilobite intimates all that is degraded and base in the shadowy primordial past. The mute carcase of this arthropod lacks man's 'dignity', and later Hardy tells us that 'Knight, without showing it much, knew that his intellect was above the average' (*Eyes* 271). That there may be a shared genetic legacy between this irrelevant particle of life and himself would be a source of disgusted disbelief to Knight. Turned to stone, the trilobite is ultimately akin to the merciless inanimate forces Knight thinks are persecuting him; a conception of Nature described in Tennyson's *In Memoriam* 56 which 'from scarped cliff and quarried stone' cries 'A Thousand types are gone;/I care for nothing, all shall go'.[78]

Knight's 'inner eye' still works frantically as his grip begins to loosen, and continues to draft the learned article that he will finish if the churning sea does not take him first. The ordeal does not exorcise his pompous self-regard:

> The mental picture of Elfride in the world, without himself to cherish her, smote his heart like a whip. He had hoped for deliverance, but what could a girl do?...Was Death really stretching out his hand? (*Eyes* 272)

---

[75] Quoted in 'Introduction' to U. C. Knoepflmacher and G. B. Tennyson (eds.), *Nature and the Victorian Imagination* (Berkeley, Los Angeles: University of California Press, 1977), xviii.

[76] Gideon Mantell quoted in Deborah Cadbury, *The Dinosaur Hunters*, p. 155.

[77] Henry Darwin Read, 'The Reputed Traces of Primeval Man', *Blackwood's Magazine* 88 (1860), 424.

[78] The epigraph to Chapter 21 is from Tennyson, but from 'Break, Break, Break', while the epigraphs to Chapters 16, 20 and 28 are from *In Memoriam*, and there is further quotation from it in Chapter 35.

The Hardyan tactic of being simultaneously solemn and sly is apparent when the 'idiosyncratic mode of regard' shifts from addressing the entire evolutionary process, an awesome panorama, to 'those musing weather-beaten West-country folk who pass the greater part of their days and nights out of doors' (*Eyes* 272). These people from remote provinces should have a more pragmatic insight into natural process than the self-preening city-dweller. 'Nature seems', in the eyes of West-country folk, 'to have moods in other than a poetical sense: predilections for certain deeds at certain times, without any apparent law to govern or season to account for them'. Man's primitive subjective impressions are measured against Knight's scientifically rational mind.

> She is read as a person with a curious temper; as one who does not scatter kindnesses and cruelties alternately, impartially, and in order, but heartless severities or overwhelming generosities in lawless caprice...In her unfriendly moments there seems a feline fun in her tricks, begotten by a foretaste of her pleasure in swallowing the victim. (*Eyes* 272-3)

'Caprice', from the Latin *capra*, or goat (suggesting a fantastical goat leap), is an unaccountable change of mind or conduct. Nature's freakish fancy on the cliff recalls Elfride's 'freak' on the decrepit West Endelstow tower, when Knight saves the heroine from a fall (*Eyes* 219); only this time Knight is the creature in distress and Elfride, far from being the epitome of naïve playfulness and dreamy rashness, now becomes a brave, resourceful rescuer. The Italian *Capriccio*, a sudden movement, literally means 'horror', or 'head with the hair standing on end', and captures the essence of Knight's traumatic plight.

Under intense pressure, Knight's unemotional intelligence gives way to primitive superstition and the anthropomorphic delusion. That he personifies the pinnacle of rock and the natural forces assailing him reveals the projections of a terrified mind. A perception normally offensive to Knight's 'dignity', he adopts it now as upward gusts of rain stick 'into his flesh like cold needles' (*Eyes* 273). To his frayed nerves the wind 'was a cosmic agency, active, lashing, eager for conquest' (*Eyes* 273); the sun, 'a splotch of vermilion red upon a leaden ground – a red face looking on with a drunken leer' (*Eyes* 275). Knight, who prides himself on never deviating from the straight path of science, supremely self-assured in his own bourgeois values and his own civilizing mission, now betrays a closer affinity to those 'weather-beaten West-country folk' than he would ever admit to:

> Pitiless Nature had then two voices, and two only. The nearer was
> the voice of the wind in his ears rising and falling as it mauled and
> thrust him hard or softly. The second and distant one was the moan
> of that unplummeted ocean below and afar – rubbing its restless
> flank against the Cliff without a Name. (*Eyes* 274)

What Knight previously repudiated as puerile, he is now compelled to
embrace: a reading of the cosmos as subject to 'lawless caprice', the very
opposite of the scientific worldview he endorses under normal conditions, a
'universal regular sequence, without partiality and *without caprice*' (my
italics) discussed by George Eliot.[79] The next paragraph, however, reveals
that the intelligible physical laws governing the movement of air-currents
cause Knight's ordeal: the very same laws he expounded to Elfride on the
cliff-edge. It is his enforced subjective perception that engenders his
horrified lapse from rationalistic naturalism into superstitious dread, just as
daily exposure to seasonal rhythms shapes the outlook of West Country
folk, who know little of the scientific laws that condition Nature's malign
pranks.

   Hardy subtly exploits the imaginative possibilities of a primitive
worldview whilst foregrounding the underlying principles from which it
strays. The narrative tactic is supple enough to oscillate between a
naturalistic attitude of dispassionate scrutiny and humanistic identification
with Knight, whose thoughts and feelings have become confused in a
twilight world of undifferentiated dread. The potent impression of the
wilfully malevolent 'cosmic agency' evidencing Knight's tormented sense
of reality is balanced by objective data such as length of time, temperature
and colour: 'She will never come again; she has been gone ten minutes'
(*Eyes* 273). He then peers down at the sea: 'We colour according to our
moods the objects we survey' (*Eyes* 273). The animistic West-country
worldview is certainly appealing to Hardy and he takes a mischievous
pleasure in making a scientific rationalist accept it briefly as panic and
despair overwhelm his habitual sang-froid. Hardy remarks that the
animistic vision of nature is not 'poetical', for it has emerged from rough
contact with nature's tangible actualities, instead of fey romantic reveries.
If Knight, he implies, were not a cosmopolitan essayist able to pontificate
about air-currents, he would perhaps leave the cliff with more sympathy for

---

[79] George Eliot, 'The Influence of Rationalism: Lecky's History' in *Impressions of
Theophrastus Such: Essays and Leaves from a Note-book* (Edinburgh and London: William
Blackwood & Sons, 1901), p. 355. See also Edward Caird: 'The work of science is to find
law, order, and reason in what seems at first accidental, capricious and meaningless'. *The
Evolution of Religion. The Gifford Lectures delivered before the University of St. Andrews in
Session 1890-91 and 1891-2*, 2 vols. (Glasgow: James Maclehose & Sons, 1893), I, 1.

that 'primitive' instinctual outlook which is prone to allow sovereignty to subjective superstitions over objective knowledge. Yet for Knight, the conceit of nature red in tooth and claw is just a version of the more esoteric 'wild imaginings' that afflict Leslie Stephen during his 'Bad Five Minutes In the Alps'. Hardy does not always keep a clear line – and this is a deliberate ploy – between what is distorted subjective perception and the external fact. Indeed, the eerie personality of this site is acknowledged both by Elfride and the Hardyan narrator.

> It is with cliffs and mountains as with persons; they have what is called a presence, which is not necessarily proportionate to their actual bulk. A little cliff will impress you powerfully; a great one not at all...'I cannot bear to look at that cliff,' said Elfride. 'It has a horrid personality, and makes me shudder. We will go.' (*Eyes* 263)

Knight's ordeal ends when the tenacious will is weakening, and all seems lost. As his position becomes more precarious, Elfride shows unorthodox initiative by making a rope from her voluminous undergarments. What saves the Victorian dilettante is not just his survival instincts, but human intelligence, improvisational flair, and at the last minute when his muscles are seizing up with strain, the level-headed caution with which he tells Elfride to test every knot in the rope. Although Knight remains smugly scornful of the mental and practical capabilities of women, it is Elfride's ready adaptability that helps to outwit 'pitiless Nature', giving the lie to Samuel Chew's assertion that she is a figure of wavering impulsiveness, 'unable to face a situation determinedly'.[80] Hardy might even regard Knight's recovery of his rational faculties as irrefutable evidence of genuine superiority in respect to unreasoning creation, and not as mere vanity: his having Elfride test the knots not only ensures his survival but is an example of his fitness to survive. She pulls him to safety, and as they embrace she notices the disappearance of the steamboat that we know carries Knight's superseded rival and protégé.

'The literal cliff-hanger', remarks Ronald Blythe, shows Knight's intellectual pride 'questioned and humbled'.[81] The intensity of his atavistic adventures amid the comfortless grandeur of the north Cornish seaboard should have drastically undermined the sententiousness of his formulaic ideas. But even after his devastating trials he misreads, unchastened.

---

[80] Samuel Chew, *Thomas Hardy: Poet and Novelist* (New York: Russell & Russell, 1964), p. 30.
[81] Ronald Blythe, 'Introduction', *A Pair of Blue Eyes*, The New Wessex Edition (London: Macmillan, 1976), p. 26.

Although subjected to a severe physical test and plunged into philosophical obscurity, the essayist emerges with his hubris unshaken. There is in Knight no modest 'acceptance of his creatureliness'.[82] That his and Elfride's cooperation in rescue might be a symbol of reconciliation between austere naturalistic rationalism and instinctual energy is smothered by his failure to act decisively at this key point and the pair do not kiss. His crippling neurosis about unsullied innocence prevents him responding positively to her sexual declaration: 'Knight's peculiarity of nature was such that it would not allow him to take advantage of the unguarded and passionate avowal she had tacitly made' (*Eyes* 279).[83] Knight's surname whimsically suggests a rescuer on a white charger who has begun a medieval quest for fresh innocence and 'untried lips' (*Eyes* 355). D. H. Lawrence understood the destructive absurdity of Knight's 'quest' in his *Study of Thomas Hardy* (1914). He labelled the fastidious man of letters a 'Virgin Knight': 'a thing, finally, of ugly, undeveloped, non-distinguished or perverted physical instinct'.[84] Knight's stubborn insistence on a male definition of perfect purity indicates not only personal sexual frigidity but also the corrosive effects of a society regulated by the moral double-standard which Hardy attacks more forthrightly in *Tess of the d'Urbervilles* (1891). Seeing Elfride effectively naked – she is dressed only in a diaphanous outer garment which clings to her like a glove – Knight cannot force the moment to its crisis and he desexualizes her: she becomes to him 'as small as an infant' (*Eyes* 279). To quarry the otherness of the female is a crucial part of this Victorian dilettante's initiation into previously uncharted recesses of the secret self. But he is hopelessly constrained by genteel convention, and averts his eyes from the sight of Elfride's almost unclothed body.

Knight's reaction to the self-exposing Elfride concludes in darkly comic fashion an episode in which layers of tectonic history (and of clothing) are peeled away, to profoundly destabilizing effect. Hardy depicts a nature from which all garments of make-believe have been removed to reveal her grislier features.[85] Yet Knight succeeds in insulating himself from the trilobite's stare and from Elfride's body. Although the cliffhanger

---

[82] Douglas Brown, *Thomas Hardy* (London: Longmans, 1961), p. 134.

[83] Knight, who lives entirely verbally, using his immense scholarship as a substitute for sexual knowledge, finds it strange, having met Elfride, 'to look at his theories on the subject of love, and reading them now by the full light of a new experience, to see how much more his sentences meant' (*Eyes* 246). Even when Knight starts to love her, he uses the feeling as raw material for a planned paper on the 'Artless Arts' (*Eyes* 229).

[84] D. H. Lawrence, *Study of Thomas Hardy*, pp. 47, 49.

[85] Hardy's poem 'The Lacking Sense', *Complete Poems*, p. 116-17, offers a less complex picture of Nature as an unconscious and unwitting creature who has 'wounded where she loves', for 'sightless are those orbs of hers'.

forms the central dramatic event in *A Pair of Blue Eyes*, and is for Knight his most demanding test, he has to uncover yet more 'remnants of mortality' (*Eyes* 320). Six chapters later, he makes the most gruesome 'excavation' of his life when he stumbles across the still-warm body of Mrs Jethway, buried under the rubble of West Endelstow's toppled tower. But Knight is once again barred from any lasting self-discovery by his ineradicable need to transform a welter of felt experience into magisterial written text. It is telling that he locates the widow Jethway, a woman with her own acute interest in the past, although she has no pretensions to Knight's learned antiquarianism. She spends her life travelling between West Endelstow churchyard where her son Felix is laid and that of a village near Southampton where she visits the graves of her mother and father. This old woman, whose morbid fixation on dead things Hardy shows as turning to vindictiveness and evil, meets with a violent death during one of her nocturnal visits to her son's tomb. As Knight feels the widow's hair, he mentally drafts the article that he will no doubt send to *The Present* about uncovering a corpse during a late-night ramble through a remote country parish: 'It is a tressy species of moss or lichen...It is a mason's whitewash-brush...It must be a thready silk fringe' (*Eyes* 387).

Knight's subterranean adventures also include a visit to the 'underworld' of the Luxellian crypt accompanied by Elfride. As one of the 'searchers of old churches' celebrated by E. B. Tylor, Knight professes a respect for the emotional associations which accumulate round a building or site over innumerable generations. Elfride had earlier reflected that her 'existence' might have a 'grave side' (*Eyes* 146) and this is confirmed in the gloom of the vault. In the crypt stray shafts of daylight lend her face a 'blue pallor' (*Eyes* 325) – an ominous chiaroscuro effect showing that this figure's destiny is to join forever 'the black masses lining the walls' (*Eyes* 320). The final scene of the novel, when Smith and Knight watch Lord Luxellian grieving over Elfride's coffin (Chapter 40) can be measured against Knight's theatrical experiences at Bede's Inn, using the poverty-stricken lives of the alleyway as a source of voyeuristic fascination:

> In the new niche of the crypt lay [Elfride's coffin], bright and untarnished in the slightest degree.
> Beside [it] was the dark form of a man, kneeling on the damp floor, his body flung across the coffin, his hands clasped, and his whole frame seemingly given up in utter abandonment to grief...He murmured a prayer half aloud, and was quite unconscious that two others were standing within a few yards of him.
> Knight and Stephen had advanced to where they once stood beside Elfride on the day all three met there, before she had herself gone

down into silence like her ancestors, and shut her bright blue eyes for
ever. (*Eyes* 450)

Even here Knight maintains the dilettante's unwillingness to surrender
completely to the experience of the situation. As at Bede's Inn, he is largely
insulated from the truths of the fan of time. Hardy's description of the
impotent mourning over Elfride's coffin in the Luxellian family vault, with
reference to 'her bright blue eyes' which are now shut forever, reminds us
how she is consistently presented not as a character in the mainstream
Victorian sense – like anything found in Trollope for instance – but as an
occasion, a 'quarry' which invites excavation. However, the exterior of this
unworldly beauty is never truly pierced; the buried self remains an
inscrutable mystery because right to the end neither the socially deferential
Stephen Smith nor his cultured mentor Knight ever see the real Elfride:
'Stephen fell in love with Elfride by looking at her: Knight by ceasing to do
so' (*Eyes* 244). The 'unmapped country'[86] of Elfride's feelings remains
something beyond either man's capacity to chart. She dies an elliptical
compound of frivolity and initiative, conceit and humility, evasiveness and
rash candour.

Until twenty years ago, critical orthodoxy had consistently treated *A
Pair of Blue Eyes* reductively, dismissing it as an idyllic and slight
romantic comedy.[87] Norman Page remarks that despite moments of special
insight into the elaborate dynamics of selfhood, Hardy's third published
novel is written for the most part, 'with a self-consciously stylized
adherence to the conventions of tone, language and action of popular
fiction...Credible human response remains largely buried under the
machinery of romance and sensationalism.'[88] The reality however is quite
the opposite. *A Pair of Blue Eyes* should be propelled from a peripheral to
a more pivotal place in the Hardy canon; it is an angular work of ingenious
inventiveness. Indeed, the macabre absurdity of Knight's Poe-esque
unearthing of the Widow Jethway's corpse unsettles the reader's generic

---

[86] George Eliot, *Daniel Deronda*, ed. Terence Cave (Harmondsworth, Middlesex: Penguin,
1995). The 'great deal of unmapped country within us which would have to be taken into
account in an explanation of our gusts and storms'.
[87] A number of influential Hardy scholars have argued for a more sympathetic and balanced
reappraisal of *A Pair of Blue Eyes*. See Peter Widdowson, *Hardy in History: A Study in
Literary Sociology* (London: Routledge, 1989); Mary Rimmer, 'Club Laws: Chess and the
Construction of Gender in *A Pair of Blue Eyes*', in Margaret R. Higonnet (ed.), *The Sense of
Sex: Feminist Perspectives on Hardy* (Urbana and Chicago: University of Illinois Press,
1993), pp. 203-20; the Penguin Classics introductions to *A Pair of Blue Eyes* by Roger
Ebbatson (1986) and Pamela Dalziel (1998); and Jane Thomas, *Thomas Hardy, Femininity
and Dissent: Reassessing the 'Minor' Novels* (London: Macmillan, 1999).
[88] See *Thomas Hardy* (London: Routledge & Kegan Paul, 1976), p. 144.

and sentimental expectations more vigorously than anything in *Desperate Remedies*. Hardy also elaborates the irony of Knight, the metropolitan man of letters – and not the homely rustic figures supposedly 'in touch with nature' – as recipient of a stark vision in which 'immense lapses' of the past unfold before him on the twisted cliffs of Cornwall. Hardy strips away the mask of deep time to expose many disconcerting facts about the evolutionary mechanism and a grave lack of stability within it. Even then Knight does not learn from his atavistic experience: the fussy perfectionist cannot make effectual use of his 'excavations'; they may briefly destabilize his nourishing delusion of existence, but Hardy suggests there is a virtue in that. Perhaps this may all be the 'truth' that lies in Elfride's eyes: she is the figure through whom all these discoveries are made. And she ends as an empty shell of a body in a sarcophagus, a stage prop. But what incredible insights are made available, even if they cannot be entirely capitalized on by Knight and other characters inside the novel. At a very personal level, the outlandish findings of *A Pair of Blue Eyes* gratify Hardy's own sense of imaginative excitement by offering means of invoking the complex historical strata that form the groundwork of the modern moment.

Chapter 3

Paganism Revived?

Far from the Madding Crowd (1874)

> the shearing supper, the long smock-frocks and the harvest-home,
> have...nearly disappeared in the wake of the old houses...The change
> at the root of this has been the recent supplanting of the class of
> stationary cottagers, who carried on the local traditions and humours,
> by a population of more or less migratory labourers, which has led to
> a break of continuity in local history, more fatal than any other thing
> to the preservation of legend, folk-lore, close inter-social relations...
> For these the indispensable conditions of existence are attachment to
> the soil of one particular spot by generation after generation.[1]

Taken from the preface to Hardy's fourth published novel *Far from the
Madding Crowd,*[2] the passage above has been used to bolster the critical
commonplace that Hardy mourns the disintegration of popular village
culture, as if it were a more enabling and ennobling mode of life 'in pagan
harmony with the deeper rhythms of existence.'[3] In fact, *Far from the
Madding Crowd* and *The Return of the Native*[4] assess the need for
'continuity' with a cautious and watchful provisionality, reflecting Hardy's
radical ambivalence about the status and imaginative potency of links with
a local heritage. Both Weatherbury[5] in the earlier novel and Egdon Heath in
the later are populated by figures 'attached to the soil', dependent upon it
for their livelihood, and who tend it 'generation after generation'. Hardy
displays throughout these two novels a probing insight into the larger issues

---

[1] Thomas Hardy, *Far from the Madding Crowd*, ed. with introd. Suzanne B. Falck-Yi
(Oxford: The World's Classics, 1993), pp. 4-5. Hereafter referred to as *Crowd.*
[2] Carl Weber dates the action of *Far from the Madding Crowd* as 1869-73. It started to
appear as a serial in the *Cornhill Magazine* in January 1874, which makes the time of the
events of the tale almost contemporary. See *Hardy of Wessex: His Life and Literary Career*
(London: Routledge & Kegan Paul, 1965), p. 224.
[3] James W. Tuttleton, *Vital Signs: Essays on American Literature and Criticism* (Chicago:
Ivan R. Dee, 1996), p. 298.
[4] Thomas Hardy, *The Return of the Native*, ed. with introd. Simon Gatrell (Oxford: The
World's Classics, 1986). Hereafter referred to as *Native.*
[5] There is an ancient earthwork in Dorset called Wetherbury Castle.

of time, which is for the most part absent from the comfortably undisturbing narratives of *Under the Greenwood Tree* (1872) and *The Trumpet-Major* (1880). His thought-adventures are now more alert to the body of survivals called 'folklore' (*Crowd* Preface: 4). When Hardy was working on *Far from the Madding Crowd,* the term 'folk-lore' had only been in use to denote the traditional beliefs, legends and customs current among the rural peasantry for about twenty-five years.[6] William John Thoms, writing in the *Athenaeum* (22 August 1846) under the pseudonym Ambrose Merton, proposed the term 'folk-lore' as a 'good Saxon compound to refer to what we in England designate as Popular Antiquities.' In 1850 Charles Newton noted the inestimable value of this lore, lingering 'like an echo on the lips of the peasantry, surviving in their songs and traditions, renewed in their rude customs with the renewal of Nature's seasons'.[7] Among the 'rude customs' of the Wessex peasantry, Hardy singles out the anthropological occasion of feasting. By mentioning the 'shearing-supper' and the 'harvest-home' in his Preface, he draws attention to traditional communal feasts that already possessed a special meaning for early Victorian antiquarians as part of their sustained cultural inquiry into the continuity of primitive beliefs from the savage to the modern European peasant.[8] John Brand's *Popular Antiquities*[9] and William Hone's *Every-Day Book and Table Book*[10] both mention the sheep-shearing feast; but it is Joseph Strutt's *Sports and Pastimes of the People of England,* first published in 1801, that offers the most intriguing explanation:

> There are two feasts annually held among the farmers of this country, which are regularly made in the spring, and at the end of the summer...The first is the sheep-shearing, and the second the harvest-home; both were celebrated in ancient times with feasting and variety of rustic pastimes: at present, excepting a dinner, or more

---

[6] A President of the Folk-Lore Society Edward W. Brabrook, in a memorial on the death of Queen Victoria in 1901, wrote how 'the very existence' of 'the study of folklore...is bounded by Her Majesty's reign'. See *Folk-Lore* 12 (1901), 98.

[7] Charles Newton, 'On the Study of Archaeology', *Archaeological Journal* 8 (1850), 1.

[8] Andrew Lang, in the last quarter of the nineteenth century, would become a leading exponent of the view that 'the folk-lore of civilized is often identical with the superstitions of savage races'. See his 'Preface', *Folk-Lore Record* (London: Nichols & Sons, 1879), p. iii.

[9] John Brand, *Observations on the Popular Antiquities of Great Britain: chiefly illustrating the Origin of our Vulgar and Provincial Customs, Ceremonies, and Superstitions,* rev. with introd. Sir Henry Ellis (1848-49; repub. New York: AMS Press, 1970), II, 34-7.

[10] William Hone, *The Every-Day Book and Table Book or, Everlasting Calendar of Popular Amusements, Sports, Pastimes, Ceremonies, Manners, Customs, and Events,* 3 vols. (London: T. Tegg & Son, 1835), pp. 559-61.

frequently a supper, at the conclusion of the sheep-shearing and the harvest, we have little remains of the former customs.[11]

Bathsheba's 'shearing-supper' (*Crowd* 150) and Sergeant Troy's 'Harvest Home' (*Crowd* 252), comprise the first two of three significant feasts in *Far from the Madding Crowd,* and as Strutt contests, although 'the particular manner in which the sheep-shearing was celebrated in old time is not recorded', it might, like many country wakes, have 'derived in origin from some more ancient rites practised in the times of paganism'.[12]

> They sheared in the great barn, called for the nonce the Shearing Barn, which on ground plan resembled a church with transepts. It not only emulated the form of the neighbouring Church of the parish, but vied with it in antiquity. Whether the barn had ever formed one of a group of conventual buildings nobody seemed to be aware: no trace of such surroundings remained. (*Crowd* 150)

The continuity of work is formally celebrated but through Hardy ironically observing it from a standpoint of historical discontinuity, since the Victorian age experienced a vogue for church restoration that shattered the very medievalism it was supposed to resuscitate. Church worship, Hardy implies, suffered almost as much grievous disfigurement from the hand of time as did church exteriors.[13] Acknowledging the 'flimsiness' of his own religious convictions in 1851, Ruskin complained, 'If only the Geologists would let me alone, I could do very well, but those dreadful hammers. I hear the clink of them at the end of every cadence of the Bible verses.'[14] The freethinkers, who railed against a supine acquiescence in dogma, probably nurtured Hardy's sceptical ideas at this stage of his literary career, and Leslie Stephen (1832-1904) may be seen as a seminal figure. His *Essays on Free Thinking and Plain Speaking* (1873) and *Agnostic's Apology* (1876) are both from the period when Hardy was associated with him in his role as editor of the prestigious *Cornhill Magazine*.[15] 'The one

---

[11] Joseph Strutt, *The Sports and Pastimes of the People of England. Including the Rural and Domestic Recreations, May Games, Mummeries, Shows, Processions, Pageants, and Pompous Spectacles, from the Earliest Period to the Present Time.* New edn. with index William Hone (London: T. Tegg & Son, 1838), p. 363.

[12] Ibid., p. 365.

[13] As Laureate, Tennyson warned against the 'fierce and careless looseners of the faith'. See 'Love Thou Thy Land' (1834) and 'To the Queen' (1872).

[14] Quoted in *The Norton Anthology of English Literature*, vol. 2, gen. ed. M. C. Abrams (New York and London: W. W. Norton & Company, 1986), p. 924.

[15] See Tony Slade, 'Leslie Stephen and *Far from the Madding Crowd*', *Thomas Hardy Journal* I:2 (1985), 31-40. Hardy was invited (2 May 1902) by the historian Frederic

duty which at the present moment seems to be of paramount importance is the duty of perfect intellectual sincerity', Stephen announced in the first of his *Essays*, which interrogated the moral authority of a Christian world-view.[16] The 'duty' Stephen discusses relates to a newfound intellectual emancipation: 'Let us think freely and speak plainly, and we shall have the highest satisfaction that man can enjoy.'[17]

The shearing scene develops a correspondence between Weatherbury's church and its barn, thus emphasizing a natural religion that flouts the hidebound and humourless traditions of ecclesiastical Christianity. Unsurprisingly Leslie Stephen, overseeing the serialization of Hardy's story for his magazine, found the whole episode 'excellent'.[18] Anglicanism, as Hardy perceives it during this scene, cannot hold its place as an enlivening and pervasive feature of English life, for the 'days of creeds are as dead and done with as days of Pterodactyls.'[19] The shearing barn, however, with its 'dusky, filmed chestnut roof, braced and tied in by huge collars, curves and diagonals, was far nobler in design because more wealthy in material than nine-tenths of those in our modern churches' (*Crowd* 150). For ceremonial and communal purposes Bathsheba's barn has greater merit:

> One could say about this barn, what could hardly be said of either the church or the castle, akin to it in age and style, that the purpose which had dictated its original erection was the same with that to which it was still applied. Unlike and superior to either of those two typical remnants of medievalism, the old barn embodied practices which had suffered no mutilation at the hands of time...Standing before this abraded pile the eye regarded its present usage, the mind dwelt upon its past history, with a satisfied sense of functional continuity throughout, a feeling almost of gratitude, and quite of pride, at the permanence of the idea which had heaped it up. (*Crowd* 150)

This is a rare occasion in Hardy's fiction when 'medievalism and modernism' have 'a common standpoint' (*Crowd* 151), since the 'defence

---

William Maitland (1850-1906) to contribute to the latter's *The Life and Letters of Leslie Stephen* (London: Duckworth, 1906). Hardy responded with a lengthy and affectionate reminiscence, interspersed with quotations from Stephen's letters. Reprinted in Michael Millgate (ed.), *Thomas Hardy's Public Voice: The Essays, Speeches, and Miscellaneous Prose* (Oxford: Clarendon Press, 2001), pp. 258-65.

[16] Leslie Stephen, *Essays on Free Thinking and Plain Speaking*, p. 32.

[17] Ibid., p. 362.

[18] Letter to Hardy, 17 February 1874, Hardy Memorial Collection, Dorset County Museum.

[19] Thomas Hardy, *Life*, p. 358.

and salvation of the body by daily bread is still a study, a religion and a desire' (*Crowd* 151). By 'defence of the body' Hardy points to the barn's use not just for threshing and shearing but also for clothing the skin, protecting it against the elements. Past and present are coupled in a manner that elevates the barn above the other two 'survivals' of medievalism.

Through his considered portrayal of the shearing barn, Hardy implies that, in technologically primitive societies, religion was woven seamlessly into the rich fabric of daily routine; there was no crude division between the sacred and the secular; so that spirit and body became part of the same numinous experience. In one space of encounter were united the worship of divinity, the bringing together of harvest and the ensuing thanksgiving for a god-given fertility. A robust sense of solidarity distinguishes the collective work done at the farm by Bathsheba's employees, and Hardy reveals how agricultural skills are instrumental in producing new arrangements of feeling between individuals. He contests that the urgent needs of the body comprise an alternative, more profound religion predating the Church of England, which as a national institution is not what it once was, and may even be founded upon a grave error: salvation of the Christian soul. The castle is outmoded and redundant because the military threat it was designed to counteract is a thing of the remote past. Moreover, the communal act of feeding that follows the shearing has strong sacramental suggestiveness, discovering the spiritual in the body, for we have not yet reached that absolute destructive antagonism between body and mind which *Jude the Obscure* articulates with chilling ironic insistence. But Hardy shows how this unique experience has been displaced by religion with its misguided stress on keeping the place of veneration pristine and unpolluted, for the celebratory feast is removed from Bathsheba's barn, the emblem of reconciliation with nature and corporate identity. Perhaps Hardy acknowledges the irreversible effects of continuous cultural refinement.

In striking contrast to Mrs Yeobright's genteel communal meal, class distinctions at Bathsheba's table are almost bridged by an unaffected enjoyment of togetherness, in a way which recalls Strutt's definition of the 'mell-supper': 'Mell is plainly derived from the French word *mesler*, to mingle together, the master and servant promiscuously at the same table.'[20] The eighteenth-century antiquarian Henry Bourne explains that this class-levelling is the very essence of an authentic feast experience: 'Servant and his Master are alike, and every Thing is done with an equal Freedom. They sit at the same Table, converse freely together, and spend the remaining Part of the Night in dancing, singing, etc. without any Difference or

[20] Joseph Strutt, *Sports and Pastimes*, pp. 364-5.

Distinction.'[21] But the seating arrangements at the shearing-supper reveal that an unbridgeable social gulf exists between the gentlewoman farmer and her workforce. The shearers feast outside in the yard, and the end of the table is pushed through a window of the manor-house, so that Bathsheba may sit inside; separated from, and superior to, her employees.[22]

But in what tone does Hardy depict this particular feast, which transports us back, he says, to 'the early ages of the world' (*Crowd* 166)? The rejoicing is too contrived and decorous, pandering to a Victorian bourgeois readership that delighted in visions of an unblemished rural hinterland before it was buried invisibly beneath railways and roads. Hardy's illustration of the stability associated with the recurrent rhythms of agricultural life deliberately teases us, along with the novel's title, by evoking a sanitized version of pastoral in which the 'peasant' is innocent of modern corruption.[23] As in Milton's *Lycidas*, Shelley's *Adonais* and Matthew Arnold's *Thyrsis*, that which is of fathomless antiquity has degenerated into an ornate, highly stylized literary form designed to please a moneyed urban audience. The shearing-supper also evokes Arnold's 'Scholar-Gypsy': the Oxford-educated dilettante revelling in mannered artifice, viewing his physical surroundings through the eyes of Theocritus. Andrew Lang's review of Hardy's novel for the January 1875 *Academy* is helpful here, for it proposes that *Far from the Madding Crowd* is set retrospectively in a mistily timeless past, instead of the 'Bad Seventies',[24] a turbulent period in a region beset by acute social and economic problems: 'the country folk in the story have not heard of strikes...they have, to all appearances plenty to eat and warm clothes to wear and when the sheep are shorn in the ancient town of Weatherbury, the scene is one that Shakespeare or that Chaucer might have watched. This immobile rural existence is what the novelist has to paint.'[25] About the pitiless

---

[21] Henry Bourne, *Antiquitates Vulgares; or, the Antiquities of the Common People* (Newcastle, 1725), p. 229. Quoted in Robert W. Malcolmson, *Popular Recreations in English Society, 1700-1850* (Cambridge: Cambridge University Press, 1973), p. 81.

[22] See Rosemary Jann, 'Hardy's Rustics and the Construction of Class', *Victorian Literature and Culture* 28:2 (2000), 411-25.

[23] On Hardy's 'pastoralism' in this novel see Fred Reid, 'Art and Ideology in *Far from the Madding Crowd*', in *The Thomas Hardy Annual No. 4*, ed. Norman Page (London: Macmillan, 1985), pp. 91-126.

[24] For social context see Michael Millgate, *Thomas Hardy: His Career as a Novelist* (London: Bodley Head, 1971), p. 103; J. H. Bettey, *Rural Life in Wessex 1500-1900* (Guernsey: Alan Sutton, 1987); J. P. D. Dunbabin, *Rural Discontent in Nineteenth Century Britain* (London: Faber & Faber, 1974); G. E. Mingay, *Rural Life in Victorian England* (London: Heinemann, 1977).

[25] Quoted in Ian Gregor, *The Great Web: The Form of Hardy's Major Fiction* (London: Faber & Faber, 1974), p. 45.

dispossession of the Dorset smallholder, the pulling down of cottages and the pauperization of rural labourers, this section of the novel remains reticent. Instead, Hardy exploits the hint of Greek idyll, with Oak – who 'could pipe with Arcadian sweetness' (*Crowd* 45) – playing his flute while the shearers relax in the June sunset. The half-ironic vocabulary connects classical characters with their Wessex counterparts – they are also reveller-swains, and soon feel the ambiguous merriment of 'the gods in Homer's heaven' (*Crowd* 165).

The anthropological occasion of feasting is for Hardy murkier and more provocative than this serene supper implies, for it excludes the socio-economic changes that were corroding the seemingly solid structures of agricultural existence. Moreover, the potentially fatal contagion of erotic imperatives introduced through Troy, and Farmer Boldwood's nervous pathology must infringe upon the immutable bucolic scene. 'Life at high-pressure', according to the Victorian physician Thomas Stretch Dowse, 'is the prominent feature of the nineteenth century, and we cannot be surprised when we find that the so-called nervous diseases and exhaustions, dipsomania and insanity, are increasing beyond all proportion to the rapid increase of the population.'[26] The darker intimations of life 'at high-pressure' absent from the shearing-supper invest Francis Troy's 'Harvest Home', which also acts as his 'Wedding Feast' (*Crowd* 252). The sergeant disdains the 'continuity' exalted in the first communal meal by Bathsheba and her farmworkers. Since he 'has never made any basic decisions about the conduct of life',[27] and is too obtuse to meditate on origins or consequences, Troy stands apart from a creature of tortured consciousness like Boldwood. That the soldier notices nothing outside the moment and has little conception of past or future is indicated by his prodigal gesture of giving Bathsheba his father's watch – the only token of his aristocratic heredity he himself owns. Believing he can dominate the moment as he can dominate women, he is in a sense 'released' from time: fatuously unaware of the historical process, he persistently overlooks its effects on people and places. Hardy uses the soldier to inspect with sophisticated scepticism the notion of 'continuity' as a thing prized in itself. Yet he reminds us that Troy is a result of the very earliest continuity of all: the sex-impulse, formed from an instinct predating that need for 'close inter-social relations' (*Crowd* Preface: 5) upon which the shearing-supper is based. This martial figure, described by Fanny Robin as: 'a man of great respectability and

---

[26] Thomas Stretch Dowse, *On Brain and Nerve Exhaustion (Neurasthenia), and on the Nervous Sequelæ of Influenza* (London: Ballière, Tindall, Cox, 1894), p. 51.
[27] Geoffrey Thurley, *The Psychology of Hardy's Novels: The Nervous and the Statuesque* (St. Lucia, Queensland: University of Queensland Press, 1975), p. 80.

high honour – indeed, a nobleman by blood' (*Crowd* 115) is to Hardy 'the erratic child of impulse' (*Crowd* 187). This refers not simply to his passions, which are sudden and strong, or to his wandering nature, but to his being a *product* of impulse: 'A slight romance attaches to [Troy]. His mother was a French governess, and it seems that a secret attachment existed between her and the late Lord Severn' (*Crowd* 115).

As with the first 'satyr' in the Wessex novels, Aeneas Manston from *Desperate Remedies* (another 'natural' or illegitimate child whose name evokes romance that is mythical and distant from reality), and continuing into the more exacting types of Edred Fitzpiers and Alec d'Urberville, Troy is of patrician origin and acknowledges no laws outside his own need for sensual delight. That the sergeant's offspring by Fanny Robin is stillborn however implies Hardy might have treated him as a more demanding character than 'an unscrupulous sexual adventurer'[28] – perhaps even as a blueprint for the failed fertility figure of the mature fiction.

In the Great Barn that only a few months earlier had revealed harmony between the shearers and their place of work, Troy transforms a harvest-home feast and dance commemorating his marriage to Bathsheba into a 'debauch' (*Crowd* 256). Although Troy's revel is profoundly damaging – a bizarre nightmare version of the shearing-supper – it does have an appealing quality in that the participants find short-lived respite from the dragging predictability of their daily routine. Able to charm and ease his way into the good graces of others, Troy, in stark contrast to Farmer Boldwood, appreciates the socializing and romantically seductive use of music. However, Hardy shows Troy's event to be wrong through Gabriel Oak, whose honest forthrightness and vigilance make him the one true preserver of communal coherence. Unlike the sergeant, Oak lives in the daily presence of continuity; he upholds the steady routines of farm life with a tenacious devotion to duty. Moreover, by covering the hayricks he indicates that 'the defence and salvation of the body' (*Crowd* 151) is uppermost in his mind, as opposed to Troy, who imperils the whole district by his effrontery and luxurious idleness when he refuses to believe in the approaching late-August storm. Yet Troy's harvest revel is problematic in a way that the ersatz, exaggerated shearing ritual is not. Against the wholesome pastoralism of the first ceremonial meal, we have in the sergeant's recklessly flamboyant and raucous gathering (from which women and children are barred) a Bacchic moment dislocated from the deadening morality of the dominant culture, exploding the modest regard for precedent embodied by Oak.

---

[28] Martin Seymour-Smith, *Hardy* (London: Bloomsbury, 1995), p. 197.

The principles of sybaritic indulgence and self-abandonment imbuing Troy's harvest-home are in pointed contrast to Farmer Boldwood's 'Christmas-Eve party' (*Crowd* 370). He seems a more contemporary figure at his insipid and fervourless event, a creature whose thinking takes us away from origins.[29] Many of those at the shearing also attend Boldwood's house, but the party only testifies to the farmer's life of brooding unease and alienated solitude.

> It was not that the rarity of Christmas parties in the parish made this one a wonder, but that Boldwood should be the giver. The announcement had had an abnormal and incongruous sound, as if one should hear of croquet playing in a cathedral aisle...Such a thing had never been attempted before by its owner, and it was now done as by a wrench...a shadow seemed to rove about the rooms saying that the proceedings were unnatural to the place and the lone man who lived therein. (*Crowd* 370-71)

In his daily routine Boldwood is more responsive to a stringent code of bourgeois gentility that necessitates a joyless abstention from worldly pleasures. His desires are arguably stronger than Troy's, but stifled under a veneer of Puritanical austerity, with Hardy comparing his emotional make-up to 'a hotbed of tropic intensity' (*Crowd* 126). Although Hardy is quick to censure Troy's frantic sensation-seeking during the harvest-home, the soldier possesses, unlike his romantic rival, a vital passion for music as a sort of binding agent, as well as a primitive instinct to affirm corporate belonging.[30] Freed from stern army discipline, Troy gladly surrenders to the mechanism of a rite that combines dissipation with inspiration, and persuades Bathsheba's male workforce to do likewise. Boldwood though is paralysed by acute self-consciousness; he treats many of his guests with nervous condescension, and no amount of carousing can offset the dismal atmosphere of entombed emptiness that defines his home.

Farmer Boldwood's mental development, like Clym Yeobright's in *The Return of the Native*, has gone beyond the evolution of the animal. With these ascetic figures Hardy offers two different versions of crippling

---

[29] For more positive, favourable readings of Boldwood's characterization see Frank R. Giordano, Jr., *'I'd Have My Life Unbe': Thomas Hardy's Self-Destructive Characters* (Alabama: University Of Alabama Press, 1984), pp. 101-15.

[30] See John Hughes, *'Ecstatic Sound': Music and Individuality in the Work of Thomas Hardy* (Aldershot: Ashgate, 2001); Alisa Clapp-Intyre, *Angelic Airs, Subversive Songs: Music as Discourse in the Victorian Novel* (Athens, Ohio: Ohio University Press, 2002); C.M. Jackson-Houlston, *Ballads, Songs and Snatches: The Appropriation of Folk Song and Popular Culture in British Nineteenth-century Realist Prose* (Aldershot: Ashgate, 1999), pp. 140-72.

selfhood as a moribund force. Frazer's *Golden Bough*, and Freud after him in *Totem and Taboo*, are both centrally concerned with the onset of thought and how it occasions primitive man's 'fall' from a position of lofty confidence in his own ability to harmonize with and marshal natural forces. Hardy is not writing an allegory of a Frazerian moment when man first becomes keenly aware of his own faculty of consciousness, with mind emerging as the dominant entity in human experience. But throughout his literary career he shows a serious interest in an anthropological model, addressing with sympathetic sensitivity how an individual's evolution from primitive nomad to civilized cipher entails the loss of a preconceptual sense of vitality. With Boldwood, Hardy implies that cerebral activity is the source of grim introspection and radical self-estrangement. Consequently, the staid yeoman cannot begin to evoke the boozy camaraderie that infuses the other crucial Christmas feast in the early novels, Reuben Dewy's party in *Under the Greenwood Tree* (47). The elation of Dewy's dance even envelops Fancy Day, usually so mindful of the dowdy formalities and conventions tirelessly maintained by orthodox Christianity and the urban bourgeoisie. Dewy's guests show an euphoric alertness to music's 'insistent calls of joy';[31] they are rejuvenated through the contagious powers and intricate felicities of sound. Unlike Dewy's event, which attempts to buttress and perpetuate the peculiar shape of a close-knit community, Boldwood's flat celebration is merely an *ad hoc* aggregation of individuals. Moreover, social barriers are kept intact: 'At the lower end, which had been arranged for the workfolk, specially, a group conversed in whispers, and with clouded looks' (*Crowd* 388). Instead of a welcome respite from the dreary middle-class strictures that hinder spontaneity and personal growth, Boldwood creates only glum foreboding. He has no conception of the fact that festival works outside the customary limits and traits of conscious identity as a safe and socially productive outlet for repressed energy. This is why the notion of a ceremonial meal occurs so often in Victorian anthropological accounts of religious ritual. Tylor, Frazer and their acolytes translated the ancient language of this event with its stress on the spiritual significance of an encounter which generates new motifs of sensory awareness freed from the restraining inhibitions of genteel etiquette.

When Boldwood succumbs to jealous rage and shoots Troy at the Christmas-Eve party, he is revealed as a disturbing amalgam of primal sub-rational drives and modern psychosis. This episode, by far the most unsettling of the three feasts, enacts an elemental struggle between masculine forces: the celibate neurasthenic tormented by time pitted against

---

[31] Thomas Hardy, 'After the Burial', *Collected Poems*, p. 876.

a 'satyr' who is impervious to its manifold pressures. A sumptuous gathering intended to foster social adhesion ends in the irrational derangement of sexual passion and murder. Hardy focuses on the release of tensions that were previously unacknowledged, but which exert a powerful destructive influence upon the personality. Boldwood's behaviour bears out the omniscient narrator's observation that 'man, even to himself, is a palimpsest, having an ostensible writing, and another beneath the lines' (*Crowd* 254).[32] This recalls Thomas de Quincey's vivid image of layers of experience in the memory: the mind as a palimpsest on which successive writings have been imprinted and seemingly erased, but capable of recovery through a sudden shock to the system:

> countless are the mysterious handwritings of grief or joy which have inscribed themselves successively upon the palimpsest of your brain; and, like the annual leaves of aboriginal forests, or the undissolving snows on the Himalaya, or light falling upon light, the endless strata have covered up each other in forgetfulness. But by the hour of death, but by fever, but by the searchings of opium, all these can revive in strength. They are not dead, but sleeping...In some potent convulsion of the system, all wheels back into its earliest elementary stage.[33]

Through Boldwood's killing of Troy, Hardy illustrates how quickly the crisp contours of the civilized self dissolve when 'some potent convulsion of the system' causes an atavistic return of supposedly long-buried and forbidden impulses.

The three feasts in *Far from the Madding Crowd* indicate that Hardy's treatment of historical 'continuity' allows him to explore irresolutions deep within his own thinking. A communal experience that should underline the value of safeguarding links with remote antiquity – Bathsheba's shearing-supper – seems fake and unchallenging when compared to Troy's riotous harvest-home, whose almost Homeric excesses represent perhaps a more credible aspect of early society. Some of the most compelling results of imaginative 'excavation' in this novel are evident during Boldwood's Christmas party. He is employed by Hardy to suggest that a cultivated

---

[32] In 1901 Hardy was asked if he remembered the contents of love-letters he used to write for the village girls. He replied: 'Possibly, in a sub-conscious way. The human mind is a sort of palimpsest, I suppose; and it's hard to say what records may not lurk in it.' See William Archer, *Real Conversations* (London: Heinemann, 1904), p. 32.

[33] Thomas De Quincey, 'Suspiria de Profundis', in *Confessions of an English Opium-Eater and Other Writings*, ed. with introd. Grevel Lindop (Oxford: The World's Classics, 1996), p. 146.

individual, no matter how much he strives to control his own instinctual impulses with the exercise of moral self-management, remains an archaic man at the deepest level of his temperament. Boldwood's fate throws into sharply ironic relief Tennyson's admonition to 'move upwards, working out the beast,/And let the ape and tiger die'.[34] Since there are no meaningful channels of interpersonal communication in Boldwood's life, he can only exorcise the 'beast' – a savage visceral reality beneath the skin – through homicidal rage and then attempted suicide. The wealthiest and apparently most dignified man in the parish is also its most susceptible member due to his feelings of isolation from the sentiments that seem to bind the rest of rural society. His disastrous feast comments on a rational order whose central weakness is its failure to brook or embrace the passional energies of primitive life lurking within it. This finding is part of Hardy's gradual movement within the novel towards a difficult and in some ways discomfiting vision of the feast as essential social ritual in anthropological terms. Although *Far from the Madding Crowd*'s analysis of feasting shows that the model of a cohesive rustic community in touch with nature is an illusion, it is not as pervasively problematic as the superstitious but resilient world of Egdon Heath.

The Return of the Native (1878)[35]

In this novel Hardy considers the possibility of overturning the effects of a Frazerian 'fall', and achieving redemptive contact with the fecund life of the earth through 'close inter-social relations' (*Crowd* Preface: 5) and pagan ritual. Again Hardy draws on his own ambivalent attitude towards those conceptions and fancies of primitive thought that have been varnished over by Christianity but scarcely hidden by it. James A. Farrer's description of these phenomena recalls De Quincey's evocative analogy between certain ancient ideas and archaeological or geological formations. Farrer, like many late-Victorian antiquarians, tried to reconstruct the mental life of early man based on the model provided by earth sciences:[36]

> Like old Roman or British remains, buried under subsequent accumulations of earth and stones, or superficially concealed by an

---

[34] Alfred Lord Tennyson, *In Memoriam*, sec. 118, ll. 27-8.
[35] *The Return of the Native* is set in the years 1842-43.
[36] See for instance Henry Gay Hewlett: 'Between the physical history of the Earth and the intellectual history of its chief inhabitant there are some striking features of resemblance.' 'The Rationale of Mythology', *Cornhill Magazine* 35 (1877), 407.

overgrowth of herbage, uninjured during all the length of time, [folk-beliefs] have lain unobserved...just beneath the surface of nineteenth-century life, as indelible records of our mental history and origin.[37]

Did Hardy share Farrer's confidence that a mass of pagan ideas might lie totally *uninjured* 'beneath the surface of nineteenth-century life'? Or was he closer to Tylor's more considered position, that certain survivals 'have been rolled and battered like pebbles by the stream of time, till their original shapes can no longer be made out'?[38] *The Return of the Native* indicates Hardy's unresolved and fascinated musing over whether the domain of folk-culture might be salvaged; and was that reclamation desirable, if provincial lore could not be justified by proving its relevance to humankind's deepest emotional needs?

> The instincts of merry England lingered on here with exceptional vitality, and the symbolic customs which tradition has attached to each season of the year were yet a reality on Egdon. Indeed, the impulses of all such outlandish hamlets are pagan still: in these spots homage to nature, self-adoration, frantic gaieties, fragments of Teutonic rites to divinities whose names are forgotten, have in some way or other survived medieval doctrine. (*Native* 389-90)[39]

Egdon is a much richer repository of 'survivals' than Weatherbury in *Far from the Madding Crowd*: heavy with the detritus of history, the heath and its inhabitants uphold a life that has defied to some extent the wear and tear of time.[40] Hardy frames the action with rituals marking the onset and close of a pagan winter. No fatal 'break of continuity in local history' (*Crowd* Preface: 4) has occurred: to 'recline on a stump of thorn in the central valley of Egdon' is to know 'that everything around and underneath had been from prehistoric times as unaltered as the stars overhead' (*Native* 6). Hardy's comment that 'the instincts of merry England' linger on the Heath with 'exceptional vitality' is more troubling, as the first pagan practice in the novel reveals: the 5 November bonfire-lighting. Strutt remarks, '[i]t has been customary in this country, from time immemorial,

---

[37] James A. Farrer, *Primitive Manners and Customs* (London: Chatto & Windus, 1879), p. 276. Andrew Lang described the superstitions of the rural peasantry in a similar fashion as 'fossils of rite and creed', lying 'close to the surface of civilised life'. See *Custom and Myth* (London: Longmans & Co., 1884), pp. 11-13.

[38] E. B. Tylor, *Primitive Culture*, I, 271.

[39] Edition cited.

[40] C. F. Keary explained how 'the conservators of heathenism' are 'villagers, or the dwellers on uncultivated lands'. See 'Some Phases of Early Religious Development', *Nineteenth Century* 4 (1878), 360.

for the people, upon occasions of rejoicing...to make large bonfires upon the close of the day'.[41] Yet the Egdon bonfire-builders have no inkling of their antecedents in a barbaric past. It is only Hardy, with his delight in what was rapidly becoming antiquarian lore, who can chronicle the history of Guy Fawkes night:

> It was as if these men and boys had suddenly dived into past ages and fetched therefrom an hour and deed which had before been familiar with this spot. The ashes of the original British pyre which blazed from that summit lay fresh and undisturbed in the barrow beneath their tread...Festival fires to Thor and Woden had followed on the same ground, and duly had their day. Indeed, it is pretty well known that such blazes as this the heathmen were now enjoying are rather the lineal descendants from jumbled Druidical rites and Saxon ceremonies than the invention of popular feeling about the Gunpowder Plot. (*Native* 15)

On a cursory reading, the participants enjoy the dynamic spirit of mutuality stressed in Hardy's preface to *Far from the Madding Crowd* and during the shearing scene. The Great Barn, which allied bygone with contemporary life and seemed a fitting tribute to collective human effort throughout the ages, is here replaced by the barrow. But the ancient burial mounds which litter the forbidding Egdon landscape, 'untouched and perfect as at the time of their erection' (*Native* 387), have little use in the present, except as natural 'museums of early culture'[42] for fervent archaeologists. Their purpose is not for labour like the barn, but to mock human effort while reminding observers how man might in death resist the obliterating forces of time. Do we find here though the same unpretentious zest as that displayed by the rustics who frequent Warren's Malthouse in the earlier novel: a portrait of unaffected social belonging and delight in conversation which preaches the 'gospel of the body' (*Crowd* 151)? Although bonfire-lighting is intended as a gesture of impious defiance, stressing 'Promethean rebelliousness' against 'foul times, cold darkness, misery and death' (*Native* 15), the actual event presided over by the decrepit and illiterate crew of Egdonites seems to portend their extinction rather than to prevent it. Apparently divorced from any historical continuity with their heritage, the ashes created by their fire are connected with the undisturbed ashes of an original British pyre.

---

[41] Joseph Strutt, *Sports and Pastimes*, p. 372.
[42] E. B. Tylor, *Primitive Culture*, I, 61.

Bonfire-lighting reveals 'how slowly the relics of Paganism disappear among country people',[43] yet despite Grandfer Cantle's ebullience the custom remains a feeble, ossified relic. Appropriately, the conversation of the Egdonite 'celebrants' focuses on various forms of dissolution and failure: the ageing process; the unfortunate outcome of many marriages; how human ambitions are regularly thwarted; and the sexual impotence of Christian Cantle, a simpleton whose name suggests how the strictures of Anglican tradition have emasculated healthy paganism. They also comment on Clym Yeobright's reputation on the heath as 'an artist and scholar' (*Native* 170): gifts they both worship and instinctively distrust. These Egdonites hardly embody the preconceptual dash of a non-thinking society before the onset of mind as described in the first book of *The Golden Bough*. Even though their lives are regulated by rituals and memory rather than by ideas (' "You be bound to dance at Christmas because 'tis the time o' year; you must dance at weddings because 'tis the time o' life" ' (*Native* 20)), the Guy Fawkes crowd are a far cry from the Frazerian man-gods dominating the elements by sheer force of will. However, Hardy's tone during this episode is not one of jaded resignation or sour disillusionment at failing to find in all its vivacity the reincarnated spirit of pagan idolatry. He enjoys the incongruity of these aged heathdwellers desperately trying to inject carnivalesque splendour into the custom. And the anthropological resonances of bonfire-lighting are undeniably potent for him. James A. Farrer writes:

> The three great festivals of the Druids took place on Mayday Eve, Midsummer Eve, and on All Hallow-e'en. On those days went up from cairns, foothills and Belenian heights fires and sacrifices to the sun-god Beal...These fires have descended to us as the famous Beltane fires, lit still, or till lately, in Ireland, Scotland, Northern England, and Cornwall...usually on hill tops, with rejoicing and merriment and leaping through the flames on the part of all ages and sexes of the population. It is possible that this leaping through the flames is a relic of the time when men fell victims to them, a modification of the more barbarous custom.[44]

---

[43] *Pall Mall Gazette* (29 June 1867) quoted in Charles Hardwick, *Traditions, Superstitions and Folk-Lore (chiefly Lancashire and the North of England): Their affinity to others in widely-distributed localities: Their Eastern Origin and Mythical Significance* (London: Simpkin, Marshall & Co., 1872; repr. Manchester, England: E. J. Morten, 1973), p. 38.

[44] James A. Farrer, *Primitive Manners and Customs* (London: Chatto & Windus, 1879), pp. 296-7.

The elderly Grandfer Cantle is one of the unlikely figures who furnishes the 'rejoicing and merriment', although there are no flames to leap through on Blackbarrow, only 'a circle of ashes flecked with red embers and sparks, the furze having burnt completely away' (*Native* 28). But Hardy implies that the Egdonites, despite 'whirling' (*Native* 28) about their bonfire in a mad measure, are really performing a dance of death. John Goode, in arguing how the peasant community 'has become farcical and shabby'[45] does not acknowledge that these are the very qualities that appeal to Hardy's sprightly wit and idiosyncratic visual angles. Of particular note is the bizarre, even Grand Guignolesque way in which the timeworn faces of the group are illuminated by the bonfire's infernal glow against the foreboding blackness of the Heath. Hardy effortlessly transfigures the 'shabby' Egdonites by focusing on the 'brilliant lights and sooty shades which struggled' upon their 'skin and clothes' (*Native* 15), making everything seem fluid and inchoate. Near the flickering flames the labourers tend to lose all characteristic moral identity:

> the permanent moral expression of each face it was impossible to discover, for as the nimble flames towered, nodded, and swooped through the surrounding air the blots of shade and flakes of light upon the countenances of the group changed shape and position endlessly. All was unstable; quivering as leaves, evanescent as lightning. Shadowy eye-sockets deep as those of a death's head suddenly turned into pits of lustre: a lantern-jaw was cavernous, then it was shining: wrinkles were emphasized to ravines, or obliterated entirely by a changed ray. (*Native* 15)

The bonfire, along with many other cultural 'survivals' in *The Return of the Native*, reveal that Hardy's natural pleasure in chiaroscuro and incongruity will vitalize the art where the confidence might so easily be shaken. The 'dance of death' performed by Grandfer Cantle and his eccentric cronies, whose spectral, mummylike faces create a memorable vision, exemplifies Hardy's personal sense of imaginative exhilaration, and prevents the scene from appearing merely farcical or forlorn.[46]

The mummers' play, unlike the bonfire-lighting, is enacted by young people, and on a cursory analysis promises a more animated encounter with primitive fecundating energies. The mumming, bearing 'the marks of many

---

[45] John Goode, *Thomas Hardy: The Offensive Truth* (Oxford: Basil Blackwell, 1988), p. 46.

[46] The dramatic contrast of light and dark which Hardy exploits when portraying the Egdonites around the bonfire was replete with possibilities for illustrators of the novel. See Pamela Dalziel, 'Anxieties of Representation: The Serial Illustrations to Hardy's *The Return of the Native*', *Nineteenth Century Literature* 51(1996), 84-110.

different epochs and influences',[47] is part of Mrs Yeobright's party for her returned son Clym. However, whereas Hardy reveals warmth of human companionship during Bathsheba's shearing-supper, the distribution of food and drink at Mrs Yeobright's home reveals that Egdon, unlike Weatherbury, is atomizing. The Heath-folk no longer represent the self-sufficient agricultural communities that fashioned traditional drama, dance and poetry, imbuing it with the pulse of spontaneous joy and the subliminal sensations of correspondence. The festivities, which in the earlier novel indicated Bathsheba's ungrudging hospitality, here only show a dwindling sense of fellowship. Any chance of 'close inter-social relations' (*Crowd* Preface: 4) has been attenuated by the geographical distance between each cottage on the Heath, and more seriously by class distinctions. Mrs Yeobright is the daughter of a clergyman who married beneath him, and represents 'a species of stuffy local gentility'.[48]

The mummers' play which forms the centrepiece of Mrs Yeobright's evening entertainment is a stubborn 'survival' of ancient ritual and has been enacted in Egdon homes 'generation after generation' (*Crowd* Preface: 5). One of the earliest Dorset authorities to make any reference to this custom of the festive season was William Barnes, who in his *Grammar and Glossary of the Dorset Dialect* alludes to mummers as 'a set of youths who go about at Christmas, decked with painted paper and tinsel, and act in the houses of those who like to receive them a little drama, mostly, though not always, representing a fight between St. George and a Mohammedan leader, and commemorative, therefore, of the Holy Wars'.[49] But Hardy's 'youths' perform the play without élan, in marked contrast to D. H. Lawrence's rustics in *The Rainbow* who greet the mumming with 'loud applause, and shouting and excitement as the old mystery play of St. George, in which every man present had acted as a boy, proceeded, with banging and thumping of club and dripping pan.'[50] Despite the fact that the Egdon mummers do not enjoy playing their roles – half-heartedness is the most obvious characteristic of a true 'survival' – Hardy uses the occasion

---

[47] Charlotte Burne, 'The Collection of English Folk-Lore', *Folklore* 1 (1890), 320.

[48] John Paterson, 'An Attempt at Grand Tragedy', in R. P. Draper (ed.), *Hardy: The Tragic Novels* (London: Macmillan, 1975), p. 209.

[49] Quoted in John Symonds Udal, *Dorsetshire Folk-Lore (with a Fore-Say by William Barnes)*, 2nd edn., reprinted from original 1922 edn. (St. Peter Port, Guernsey: Toucan Press, 1970), p. 83.

[50] D. H. Lawrence, *The Rainbow*, ed. Mark Kinkead-Weekes (Cambridge: Cambridge University Press, 1989), p. 131.

as a means of testing the notion that a counterforce to social sterility could be located in the origins of mumming itself.[51]

But how much could Hardy have known of the pagan provenance of this traditional entertainment? Ruth A. Firor contends that he possessed a exhaustive knowledge of mumming – 'he meticulously preserved details of costume, gesture and mode of declamations' – and that he exploited the pagan roots of the play: 'on the whole, the mummers' play in *The Return of the Native* is considerably closer to the primitive source of folk-drama, we may safely believe, than the majority of extant folk-plays'.[52] John Paterson confidently proclaims that its 'Christian veneer scarcely conceals its pre-Christian character as fertility rite celebrating the death of the year and its resurrection in the spring'.[53] These readings assume that Hardy's methods of using folk materials are bracingly modernist. He included only those details which were a proper part of the folk tradition, and declared in a letter that the 'legendary matter & folk-lore in my books is traditionary, & not invented...this being a point on which I was careful not to falsify local beliefs & customs'.[54] Robert Squillace, though, is sceptical about whether Hardy could have registered the primitive core of this ritual, ignoring subsequent cultural and oral accretions. He maintains that critics

> have often misinterpreted the meaning of the mummers' play Hardy depicts in *The Return of the Native* by crediting him with knowledge about the pagan origins of mumming that he almost certainly did not possess. At the root of this error is a tendency to attribute a modern sensibility to a premodern writer...The evidence that Hardy knew

---

[51] For a fuller account of the history and significance of the mummers' play see Alan Brody, *The English Mummers and their Plays* (Philadelphia: University of Pennsylvania Press, 1970); E. K. Chambers, *The Medieval Stage*, 2 vols. (Oxford: Oxford University Press, 1903) and *The English Folk Play* (Oxford: Clarendon Press, 1917); R. J. E. Tiddy, *The Mummers' Play* (Oxford: Clarendon Press, 1923). T. F. Ordish's 'English Folk Drama', *Folk-Lore* 4 (1893) is an interesting late-nineteenth century attempt to answer some of the questions raised by the play.

[52] Ruth Firor, *Folkways in Thomas Hardy* (Philadelphia: University of Pennsylvania Press, 1931), pp. 202-3.

[53] John Paterson, '*The Return of the Native* as an Antichristian Document', *Nineteenth Century Fiction* 14 (1959), 121-2.

[54] Thomas Hardy, *Collected Letters* III, 93-4. Hardy wrote to his close friend, the anthropologist Edward Clodd in 1894: 'I may say, once for all, that every superstition, custom, &c., described in my novels may be depended on as true records of the same (whatever merit in folklorists' eyes they may have as such) – and not inventions of mine' (*Collected Letters*, II, 54).

nothing about the connection between mumming and fertility rites is in fact overwhelming.[55]

It is true that until the 1850s very little extensive analysis of the mummers' play existed and the only printed sources for the texts of the performances were obscure local histories, rare antiquarian collections and commercial chapbooks. Mumming is mentioned in William Hone's *Every Day-Book* of 1826,[56] and Robert Chambers furnished 'a specimen of the mumming-drama' for the *Book of Days* (1869).[57] In the latter half of the nineteenth-century folklore, and the mummers' play as part of it, began to emerge as a key area of scholarly inquiry. William John Thoms reproduced numerous play texts in *Notes and Queries* between 1850 and 1880, while he was still editor. The two major authorities on English folk practices available to readers in the 1870s, Joseph Strutt's *The Sports and Pastimes of the People of England* and John Brand's *Observations on Popular Antiquities,* both link the beginnings of the play to the Saturnalia, the Roman festival of disguise and misrule, as does Thomas Dudley Fosbroke in his *Encyclopedia of Antiquities* (1843 edn.).[58] Hardy's friend, J. S. Udal, an officer of the *Folk-Lore Society,* whose article 'Christmas Mummers in Dorsetshire' was published in the *Folk-Lore Record* (1880), also fails to reach the proper conclusion about this 'survival'.[59] The first, albeit tentative, reading of mumming as a mutilated fragment of primitive rites in which a god-personification of either the year or the sun is symbolically slain and revivified to safeguard fecundity in springtime would not arrive until the publication of James Frazer's *Golden Bough* (1890), twelve years after *The Return of the Native* was serialized in *Belgravia.* In the early years of the twentieth century, E. K. Chambers would further emphasize

---

[55] Robert Squillace, 'Hardy's Mummers', *Nineteenth Century Literature* 41 (1986), 172, 174. Squillace's article offers a sophisticated analysis of mumming in *The Return of the Native.*

[56] William Hone, *The Every-Day Book and Table Book or Everlasting Calendar of Popular Amusements, Sports, Pastimes, Ceremonies, Manners, Customs, and Events incident to each of the Three Hundred and Sixty-Five Days, in Past and Present Times* 3 vols. (London: T. Tegg & Son, 1835), II, 1645.

[57] Robert Chambers (ed.), *The Book of Days. A Miscellany of Popular Antiquities in connection with the Calendar including Anecdote, Biography & History, Curiosities of Literature and Oddities of Human Life and Character,* 2 vols. (London and Edinburgh: W. & R. Chambers, 1869), II, 740.

[58] Fosbroke describes the mummers as 'amusements derived from the Saturnalia, and so called from the Danish *mumme,* or Dutch *momme,* disguise in a mask.' *Encyclopaedia of Antiquities; and elements of archaeology, classical and medieval,* 2 vols. (London: T. Tegg & Sons, 1843), II, 608.

[59] J. S. Udal, 'Christmas Mummers in Dorsetshire', *Folk-Lore Record* 3:1 (1880), 87-116.

how the pattern of slaughter and revival at the core of the play might represent 'the annual death of the year or the fertilization spirit and its annual resurrection in spring'.[60] For Chambers and students of the play who followed in his wake, the combat, death and resurrection were the most accessible features in tracing mumming back to its source in agricultural fertility rites.

Hardy not only benefited artistically from the Victorian scientific revolution, but also anticipated it in key respects. We cannot say categorically that he never suspected how the roots of this traditional entertainment involving Saint George's victory in single combat over the Turkish Knight extended deep into a ceremonial past. What is enacted is conflict at its most elemental level, stripped to a basic essential: opposing forces. Hardy's painstaking evocation of the mummers' play signals an anthropological fascination with those combat elements distorted by time which fortify the twentieth-century concept of this event as a tattered vestige of fertility ritual, whose actions once served a necessary, effective and magical purpose. But there is also an attractively mischievous tone to this scholarly precision. Hardy was well aware of antiquarian collectors whose pedantic pursuit of exactitude in discussing and reconstructing 'survivals' deadened rather than piqued a reader's curiosity about the nascent sciences of humankind. Ironically, these 'experts' could only encounter a 'survival' by using that rational scientific intelligence which prevented them from inward participation in it. Nevertheless, Hardy offers a slight hint that the play might be an instance of unconscious paganism flowing beneath the surface of conscious Christianity:

> Like Balaam and other unwilling prophets, the agents seem moved by an inner compulsion to say and do their allotted parts whether they will or no. This unweeting manner of performance is the true ring by which, in this refurbishing age, a fossilized survival may be known from a spurious reproduction. (*Native* 122)

'Inner compulsion' and 'unweeting' [unthinking] 'manner of performance' imply that some primitive raw material of which mumming is composed has taken hold of the young people. Hardy, in his reminiscences of local 'survivals' of ancient customs in William Archer's *Real Conversations,* describes the event and the chanting, inflectionless delivery of words with almost mystic reverence:

---

[60] E. K. Chambers, *The Medieval Stage*, I, 218.

> Rude as it was, the thing used to impress me very much – I can
> clearly recall the odd sort of thrill it would give. The performers used
> to carry a long staff in one hand and a wooden sword in the other and
> pace monotonously around, intoning their parts on one note, and
> punctuating them by nicking the sword against the staff.[61]

However, in *The Return of the Native* play, Hardy offsets any glimpse
of a substantially felt pagan presence, or instinctual force generated by the
content of the play, by saying that a genuine performance is 'fossilized': an
almost functionless culture element like bonfire-lighting. The fact of
'survival' does not necessarily entail some vital symbolic truth has
endured. An idea, Tylor remarked, 'the meaning of which has perished for
ages, may continue to exist simply because it has existed.'[62] But certain
rituals are supposed to withstand the myriad pressures of modern
civilization and communicate experiences beyond the confines of the social
language, feelings that go 'too deep in the blood and soul, for mental
explanation or description'.[63] Mumming has become merely a lacklustre
and stale set of automatic actions enforced by habit. It is no longer a
ceremony that offers spiritual sustenance to the Egdonites, and anticipates
R. J. E. Tiddy's assessment of the state of the play in the early twentieth
century as 'a perfunctory piece of fooling'.[64] The procession and
performance which was once believed to bring thriving abundance to the
land, and to the tribe dwelling on it, is now a trite, luck-bringing
perambulation.[65] Tylor recognized that the 'serious business of ancient
society' will eventually 'sink into the sport of later generations, and its
serious belief...linger on in nursery folk-lore'.[66]

The mummers' play, like the communal bonfire, does not quite deliver
an untarnished example of 'paganism revived' in the novel because of the
irreversible changes that time has inflicted on the external physical world.
The outlandish formal actions of the play are rooted in a reality alien to our
own. Applying a Darwinian model to the historical process, Tylor argued
that society's oldest customs must either adapt or become superfluous, just
as biological forms do in an evolving natural world:

---

[61] William Archer, *Real Conversations*, p. 35.

[62] E. B. Tylor, *Primitive Culture*, I, 71.

[63] D. H. Lawrence, *Phoenix: The Posthumous Papers of D. H. Lawrence*, ed. with introd. Edward D. McDonald (London: William Heinemann, 1961), p. 296.

[64] R. J. E. Tiddy, *The Mummers' Play* (Oxford University Press, 1923; Chicheley: Paul P. B. Minet, 1972), p. 70.

[65] T. F. Ordish, in 'Folk Drama', *Folk-Lore* 2 (1891), 314-35, and 'English Folk Drama', *Folk-Lore* 4 (1893), 149-75, argues that folk rituals in general lost much of their vigour with the emergence of specifically Christian drama.

[66] E. B. Tylor, *Primitive Culture*, I, 16.

The history of survival, in cases like those of the folk lore and occult arts...has for the most part been a history of dwindling and decay. As men's minds change in progressing culture, old customs and opinions fade gradually in a new and uncongenial atmosphere, or pass into states more congruous with the new life around them.[67]

From a strictly anthropological perspective the mumming may appear 'as lifeless now as the fossil shells on the shore of some ancient coral sea'.[68] Yet Hardy's art, responding to 'survivals' precisely because they are not 'congruous with the new life around them', is in this episode a bracing substitute for the primitive potency which once imbued the play.

The remainder of the play ended; the Saracen's head was cut off, and Saint George stood as victor. Nobody commented, any more than they would have commented on the fact of mushrooms coming in autumn or snowdrops in spring. They took the piece as phlegmatically as did the actors themselves. It was a phase of cheerfulness which was, as a matter of course, to be passed through every Christmas, and there was no more to be said. (*Native* 139)

The seasonal imagery tantalizes by affording another hint that Hardy saw his Egdonites as the unknowing continuators of an earlier pre-Christian faith rooted in and growing out of a cycle of birth and death in the agricultural year. Although the coolness with which the audience responds seems to confirm the reading that mummers are a bizarre irrelevancy in the Victorian era, Hardy's prose does not show a corresponding languor. The oddity of this traditional entertainment elicits some of his most delicately nuanced writing. Eustacia Vye, in order to meet the man who might take her to the hub of the romantic world, must first of all bargain using her sexuality,[69] then disguise it in a performance for a community whose ignorant insularity and petty jealousies she despises. She is also well aware that by appearing as the Turkish Knight she has broken the tradition of the ceremony as a strictly masculine ritual; this is for the reader a crucial source of dramatic tension. Alan Brody states how the 'custom of reserving the task of performing the play for men only is one that has endured to the twentieth century. Even in its most decadent form, this exclusiveness still

---

[67] Ibid., I, 136.

[68] James A. Farrer, *Primitive Manners and Customs* (London: Chatto & Windus, 1879), p. 77.

[69] Eustacia obtains the Turkish Knight role in exchange for holding Charley's hand.

obtains.'[70] Eustacia risks exposure and opprobrium so that she might enjoy Clym voyeuristically, casting furtive glances at him through the strands of her mummer's mask. Under normal circumstances, she would not be welcome in Mrs Yeobright's home because of her dubious reputation.

The want of zest that distinguishes both the performance and reception of the mummers' play at Mrs Yeobright's cottage offers a sharp contrast to Eustacia's highly charged dance with Damon Wildeve at the East Egdon picnic or 'gypsying'. Hardy's drifting and mesmeric prose-rhythms convey rapturous movement within a charmed scene of shared intensities:

> A whole village-full of emotion, scattered abroad all the year long, met here in a focus for an hour. The forty hearts of those waving couples were beating as they had not done since, twelve months before, they had come together in similar jollity. For the time Paganism was revived in their hearts, the pride of life was all in all, and they adored none other than themselves. (*Native* 261-2)

In the original terms of the manuscript the East Egdon gypsying was defined not simply by an apparent recrudescence of paganism but as a fevered disavowal of whatever sober authority Christianity might claim to possess: 'Christianity was eclipsed in their hearts, Paganism was revived, the pride of life was all in all, they adored themselves & [*sic*] their own natural instincts.'[71] Hardy conveys an enchanted sense of spiritual possibility or involuntary transport similar to that in Tennyson's early 'Armageddon':

> All sense of Time
> And Being and Place was swallowed up
> Within a victory of boundless thought.[72]

Hardy paints a more complicated portrait than Bathsheba's shearing-supper of people overwhelmed by the profoundly visionary nature of the moment. This episode evokes the urgent intoxications of Sergeant Troy's 'Harvest-Home' in the Great Barn: a revel sustained by the modulations of erotic delirium, inducing self-forgetfulness and euphoric trance, thus

---

[70] Alan Brody, *The English Mummers and their Plays* (Philadelphia: University of Pennsylvania Press, 1970), p. 20.

[71] Hardy's reference to the eclipse of Christianity appeared in the text of the serial edition of 1878 (*Belgravia, An Illustrated London Magazine*, XXXVI, 244), but was expunged from the text of the first edition (Vol. 2, p. 280) published in the same year. This omission gives some indication of the virulent censorship current in the late 1870s.

[72] Alfred, Lord Tennyson, *The Poems of Tennyson*, I, 82.

affording transient release from the inexorable forward motion of mechanical time and the lumpishness of daily labour. For Eustacia and Wildeve, the gypsying suspends their powers of dignified self-control: it 'had come like an irresistible attack on whatever sense of social order there was in their minds, to drive them back in the old paths' (*Native* 260).

But does Eustacia re-enter through spirited dance-steps into a primal condition of existence delineated during the first book of *The Golden Bough*: a position of natural conviction and security that results from regarding the environment as an extension of herself over which she has complete command, in which nourishment offers itself whenever hunger arises? What prevents Hardy's portrayal of the gypsying from being perceived as thwarting the negative effects of a Frazerian 'fall' is the illicit nature of Eustacia's dance. As with lighting the bonfires and the mummers' play, Eustacia exploits folk-practices to serve her own selfish ends; so even her presence at East Egdon pollutes the spirit of yearning for imaginative and interpersonal connection upon which the village festivity rests. Any multiplied consciousness of her surroundings or experience of erotic and expressive enthusiasm is therefore of a menacing, de-limited kind, for she has 'imbibed much of what was dark' in the heath's tone.[73] This ominous force seems in keeping with the threatening presence of the heath itself; the spot – whose animistic romanticism is reminiscent of *Wuthering Heights* (1847) – exhales darkness as 'rapidly as the heavens precipitated it. The obscurity in the air and the obscurity in the land closed together in a black fraternization towards which each advanced half way' (*Native* 3-4).

There is an unsettling incongruity about Eustacia's captivated participation both in the mummers' play and in the gypsying, because these anthropological occasions are founded upon fertility rites of dateless antiquity, yet never during the novel does she approximate to a fertility figure. Instead, she embodies during her ecstatic dance with Wildeve a destructive emasculating force, reminiscent of Frazer's later conception of Cybele, the Phrygian goddess whose novices participated in the 'ghastly rite' of castrating themselves so that their deity could discharge her benevolent functions.[74]

If there is an occasion in the novel when the shattered relationship with Frazerian nature is briefly restored, we must not refer to the 'symbolic customs' (*Native* 389), but ironically to the experiences of a single

---

[73] That there is a darker potency connected with dance is underlined by Hardy's short story, 'The Fiddler of the Reels.' On dance and the occult see Roderyk Lange, *The Nature of Dance: An Anthropological Perspective* (London: Macdonald & Evans, 1975).

[74] The third 12 volume edition of *The Golden Bough* (1906-15) contains Frazer's discussion of Cybele.

individual who does not even cherish folklore – Clym Yeobright, whose altruistic fantasy of educating the illiterate heathfolk constitutes a major threat to the 'nearly perished' links 'between obsolete forms of life and those which generally prevail' (*Native* 7-8). The vestigial rites of the Egdonites are extinct in the higher social strata – 'that rookery of pomp and vanity, Paris' (*Native* 101) – where Clym, a prosperous diamond merchant, has allegedly absorbed the central tenets of scientific humanism.

Although they are very different figures, Hardy employs Clym, as he does Troy in *Far from the Madding Crowd*, to investigate the idea of continuity as a thing treasured in itself. Through the returned native, Hardy suggests the dangers of a too exclusively civilized or analytical mode of mental life. Clym has suffered the alienating effects of transplantation from communal to modern society; his look shows 'a natural cheerfulness striving against depression from without' (*Native* 139). The disease of thought[75] is firmly taking hold: 'The beauty here visible would in no long time be ruthlessly overrun by its parasite thought...an inner strenuousness was preying upon an outer symmetry' (*Native* 138). His long-term goal – to effect the 'passing from the bucolic to the intellectual life' (*Native* 174) – would if successful divorce the Egdonites from the folk-practices such as 'club-walking' (*Native* 45) and maypole-dancing that give at least some semblance of shape and coherence to their world. Yet Clym's philanthropic dream of bringing theoretical intelligence and social evolution to the underprivileged Egdonites would also expunge the more unglamorous and baleful 'instincts of merry England' (*Native* 389), in particular the savage ignorance of Susan Nunsuch's black witchcraft. According to the anthropologist John Lubbock writing in 1870, 'a belief in witchcraft still flourishes among our agricultural labourers and the lowest classes in our great cities'.[76] Tylor treated occult tendencies as dysfunctional 'survivals' – 'fragments of a dead lower culture embedded in a living higher one'[77] – dragging back into darkness a society whose ultimate ambition must be to achieve rational clarity. That Clym might prompt a 'break of continuity in local history' (*Crowd* Preface 4), and clear away the cobwebs of superstition from this secluded corner of Wessex, would be no cause for mourning. And yet this deracinated figure, an earnest proponent of 'advanced' thinking in whose face 'could be dimly seen the typical

---

[75] See Matthew Arnold's 'Stanzas from the Grande Chartreuse': 'Before this strange disease of modern life,/With its sick hurry, its divided aims,/Its heads o'ertaxed, its palsied hearts' (ll. 203-5).
[76] Sir John Lubbock, *The Origin of Civilisation and the Primitive Condition of Man. Mental and Social Condition of Savages*, 2nd edn., with additions (London: Longmans, Green, & Co., 1870), p. 136.
[77] E. B. Tylor, *Primitive Culture*, I, 72.

countenance of the future' (*Native* 169), might be closer to the instinctual life of the heath than Susan Nunsuch. Egdon embodies a mental disposition radically different from that to which he has been accustomed in Paris. What seems at first merely the regressive pastoralism of an Arnoldian scholar-gypsy is an ability to visualize the 'forgotten Celtic tribes' who once occupied this terrain. Clym's tense modernity is combined with acute receptivity to the heath's primeval rhythms:

> He walked along towards home without attending to paths. If anyone knew the heath well it was Clym. He was permeated with its scenes, with its substance, and with its odours. He might be said to be its product...His toys had been the flint knives and arrow-heads which he found there...when he looked from the heights on his way, he could not help indulging in a barbarous satisfaction at observing that in some of the attempts at reclamation from the waste, tillage, after holding on for a year or two, had receded again in despair, the ferns and furze-tufts stubbornly reasserting themselves. (*Native* 175-6)

The antiquarian landmarks of this region – such as its 'Druidical stone' (*Native* 188) – exert a compelling hold over Clym's imagination; at a local barrow excavation (*Native* 191), he unearths a 'pot of bones' which he gives as a grotesque love-token to Eustacia instead of his mother. Clym, an 'exemplar of the modern spirit',[78] ironically prizes 'the rusty implements of a bygone barbarous epoch' (*Native* 196). His primitive rapport with the soil of a county which William Stukeley and later antiquarians believed to be one of the earliest colonized portions of Britain exceeds that possessed by any of his 'non-thinking' neighbours.

> He was in a nest of vivid green...The air was warm with a vaporous warmth, and the stillness was unbroken. Lizards, grass-hoppers, and ants were the only living things to be beheld. The scene seemed to belong to the ancient world of the carboniferous period, when the forms of plants were few, and of the fern kind. (*Native* 205-6)

Hardy's imaginative reconstruction of Clym's environment combines evocative 'romantic' terms with recent scientific lingo ('carboniferous' had only been current since 1799). The arcane mystery of Egdon is accentuated by revealing its even more mysterious evolution from 'prehistoric times' (*Native* 6). A transient modern moment conveyed by immediacy of

---

[78] Peter A. Dale, 'Thomas Hardy and the best consummation possible', in John Christie and Sally Shuttleworth (eds.), *Nature Transfigured: Science and Literature, 1700-1900* (Manchester and New York: Manchester University Press, 1989), p. 210.

sensation (the warmth of the air, the bold colours and clear shapes, the living insects) is surrounded by the measureless scale of the geological past. The heavy, sensuous atmosphere has a restorative effect on Clym, as he rediscovers a primordial, deeply buried mental state, making 'the incipient marks of time and thought' 'less perceptible' on his face (*Native* 207).[79] Renouncing his quixotic pursuits, the partially blind Clym, whose beliefs once affirmed the 'irrepressible New', now sinks into the soothing monotony of furze-cutting, the most basic and gruelling heath occupation. Merryn Williams writes that Clym 'cannot really go back to being a land worker when his whole life has made him, inescapably, an intellectual'.[80] Yet Clym, inwound with the flora and fauna, attains his desire for regression and almost seems the very emanation of his pagan setting. This might be the closest we get to a reversal of the Frazerian lapse into alienating self-consciousness, the effects of which are displayed through the morbidly introspective Boldwood:

> [Clym's] daily life was of a curious microscopic sort, his whole world being limited to a circuit of a few feet from his person. His familiars were creeping and winged things, and they seemed to enroll him in their band...The strange amber-coloured butterflies which Egdon produced...quivered in the breath of his lips, alighted upon his bowed back, and sported with the glittering point of his hook as he flourished it up and down. Tribes of emerald-green grasshoppers leaped over his feet, falling awkwardly on their backs, heads, or hips, like unskilful acrobats...Huge flies, ignorant of larders and wire-netting, and quite in a savage state, buzzed about him without knowing that he was a man. In and out of the fern-brakes snakes glided in their most brilliant blue and yellow guise...Litters of young rabbits came out from their forms to sun themselves upon hillocks, the hot beams blazing through the delicate tissue of each thin-fleshed ear, and firing it to a blood-red transparency in which the veins could be seen. (*Native* 253-4)

Clym stands at the centre of this vividly detailed description, swinging the 'glittering point of his hook' up and down through the crowd of fluttering, leaping and sunning creatures. Hardy lets us see Egdon's

---

[79] Clym's response to the ancient presence of Egdon prefigures the evocation of the Cornish moors in D. H. Lawrence's *Kangaroo* (1922). Like Hardy, Lawrence apprehended an almost palpable past in 'survivals': 'And then the Cornish night would gradually come down upon the dark, shaggy moors, that were like the fur of some beast, and upon the pale-grey granite masses, so ancient and Druidical...he felt he was over the border, in another world. Over the border, in that twilit, awesome world of the Celts.' (263)

[80] Merryn Williams, *A Preface to Hardy* (London and New York: Longman, 1976), p. 100.

swarming life from an angle or a distance so near as to make it startling. He contrasts the tangible hardness and sharpness of Clym's glittering hook with the diaphanous wings of butterflies, legs of grasshoppers, fern fronds and the blood running through painfully fragile and transparent baby rabbit ears. Clym's merger with the earth appears at first a major access of power: re-entry into a state of primordial warmth, attaining 'a mystical peace, positive and profound.'[81] The slightly comic anthropomorphism of Hardy's relaxed description is appealing; he evokes a sense of thronging profusion and sensual fullness as the tangible forms of bees, butterflies, grasshoppers and rabbits vie for space in Clym's clump of furze. This colourful menagerie of a few feet radius, fearlessly flocking around a human being, conveys little threat on a cursory reading. But in this world of sensory stimulation, we are alerted to an uneasy and potentially dangerous presence. The crowding and proximity is unnerving: bees circle close to Clym's body, butterflies quiver in his breath, the flies are 'huge' and 'savage', and snakes lurk in the underbrush. Sheila Berger observes how Clym 'seems to eliminate the margin between himself and the heath'.[82] He is such an inseparable part of the landscape he tends that even his own mother fails to recognize him: 'The silent being who thus occupied himself seemed to be of no more account in life than an insect. He appeared as a mere parasite of the heath...entirely engrossed with its products, having no knowledge of anything in the world but fern, furze, heath, lichens, and moss' (*Native* 278-9).

Commentators frequently treat the furze-cutting scene as Clym's exultant surrender to the instinctual self amid the austere contours of his birthplace. But is he allowed direct access to the original springs of humanity, reuniting himself 'with the strong, free flow of life' that rises 'out of Egdon as from a source'?[83] Clym's rapt immersion in the terrain and his response to Egdon as a numinous presence entails not so much a prelapsarian rapport with the creatures around him but a frightening loss of individuality. Brought into eerie communion with the meanest forms of life, he seems a mindless extension of the heath. Spending sixteen hours a day cutting furze and sleeping largely for the remainder, he becomes obsessed with a milieu whose barren, sandy soil and prehistoric tumuli evoke a gigantic graveyard. Instead of creating a vision of primitive man's

---

[81]   J. C. Dave, *The Human Predicament in Hardy's Novels* (London: Macmillan, 1985), p. 52.
[82]   Sheila Berger, *Thomas Hardy and Visual Structures: Framing, Disruption, Process* (New York and London: New York University Press, 1990), p. 60.
[83]   D. H. Lawrence, *Study of Thomas Hardy and Other Essays*, ed. Bruce Steele (Cambridge: Cambridge University Press, 1986), p. 85.

ability to subject natural phenomena to his will, Hardy presents a type of emasculation or even death, with Clym dissolving into the heath as part of the landscape's pigmentation. However, Hardy's prose captures Clym's sense of drugged absorption in the vast impersonality of the heath, and underlines the robust vitality with which he reacts to deadening types of disappointment. The familiar figures and forms of a natural cosmos achieve the most astonishing transmutations in the crucible of his art. Hardy brings the human eye abnormally close to natural objects and deploys the transfiguring effects of sunlight ('hot beams blazing through the delicate tissue of each thin-fleshed ear'). This self-celebrating exercise in visual accuracy remind us that similar imaginative resources prevent the bonfire and mumming episodes from seeming merely examples of frayed and fossilized ritual.

Hardy's endeavours in *Far from the Madding Crowd* and *The Return of the Native* to grapple with the intricate problems of layered organic continuity, and uncover a framework of inclusive relatedness that could act as a rite of reconciliation with nature, end in failure and dissatisfaction. Furthermore, as he demonstrates in the later novel, the origins of Egdon and the experiences of the Celtic tribes who subsisted on it cannot be fully recaptured, only explained: Hardy's amateur antiquarian voice lovingly details how this gaunt but majestically sombre heath upon which time makes but little impression is in the Domesday Book.[84] If Egdon's tumuli and 'the mouldered remains' they contain refuse to yield any secrets as to how contemporary life might be enhanced based on a past model, then Hardy will use these mute naturalized monuments to create surprising effects redolent of Gothic supernaturalism: '[Eustacia] sighed bitterly, and ceased to stand erect, gradually crouching down under the umbrella as if she were drawn into the barrow by a hand from beneath' (*Native* 358). When different historical moments are brought together in the exposition of an anthropological event, for example the November bonfires or the mummers' play, they tend to generate incongruities that point towards an unpalatable truth. But *The Return of the Native* reveals how the creative spirit which savours incongruity is undaunted by the fact that existing folk-rites may be no more than 'debris carried along the waves of time'.[85] When we move to *A Laodicean* (1881) and *Two on a Tower* (1882), the brilliant eccentricity of Hardy's art combats, and even arrests, the steady intensification of the moribund in his work.

---

[84] 'Its condition is recorded therein as that of heathy, furzy, briary wilderness, – "Bruaria". Then follows the length and breadth in leagues' (*Native* 5).
[85] Stanley Arthur Cook, *The Study of Religions* (London: Adam & Charles Black, 1914), pp. 149-50.

Chapter 4

Stories of Today

A Laodicean (1881)

> [T]he singing of the wire, which for the last few minutes he had quite
> forgotten, again struck upon his ear, and retreating to a convenient
> place he observed its final course: from the poles amid the trees it
> leaped across the moat, over the girdling wall, and thence by a
> tremendous stretch towards the keep where, to judge by sound, it
> vanished through an arrow-slit into the interior. This fossil of
> feudalism, then, was the journey's end of the wire, and not the
> village of Sleeping-Green. (22)[1]

Hardy's *A Laodicean* and *Two on a Tower* are perhaps more deeply
concerned than any of his previous novels with the subtle processes of his
own artful composition. *A Laodicean* functions as a refuge or 'fair retreat'[2]
for Hardy to experiment with tone and more sophisticated modes of visual
perspective. He allows himself unprecedented freedom to manoeuvre and
to refine the controlled historical promiscuity or 'eclecticism' (*Laodicean*
104), of which Stancy Castle is the central symbolic setting. These two
fictions, written one after the other, are a bracing expression of Hardy's
erratic time-voyaging, mischievously gathering in an often capricious
arrangement the scattered fragments of the past. In earlier chapters a key
question has been how Hardy reacts to discovering through roving thought-
adventure the absolute destructiveness of history, which bars energetic
contact with bygone periods. But he assuages any distress by viewing the
action from a radically shifting series of perspectives. George Somerset – a
Gothic architect and avid amateur antiquarian like his creator – is thrilled
by the sight of the 600-year-old Stancy Castle, a 'fossil of feudalism',
bizarrely equipped with up-to-date paraphernalia such as the buzzing

---

[1] Thomas Hardy, *A Laodicean*, ed. with introd. Jane Gatewood (Oxford: The World's
Classics, 1991). Hereafter referred to as *Laodicean*.
[2] Francis Bacon, 'Of Simulation and Dissimulation': 'The advantages of simulation and
dissimulation are three', of which 'the second is, to reserve to a man's self a fair retreat; for
if a man engage himself by a manifest declaration, he must go through, or take a fall'. See
Essays (London and New York: Oxford University Press, 1921), p. 15.

telegraph wire and neo-Greek gymnasium. Somerset's interest in this medieval 'survival' reflects Hardy's own retrospective curiosity: an imaginative possession of history by 'the class of *dilettanti*', the 'people that know all about styles and dates – travelled men, sketchers, ecclesiologists, and the like'.[3] Somerset's 'unlimited appreciativeness' (*Laodicean* 12), resisting a single-minded devotion to any one style, and temperamentally wary of the closed-off nature of philosophical systems, is portrayed as a force for good. That up-to-date contrivances and antique remnants might coexist is a concept Hardy can revel in:

> There was a certain unexpectedness in the fact that the hoary memorial of a stolid antagonism to the interchange of ideas, the monument of hard distinctions in blood and race, of deadly mistrust of one's neighbour in spite of the Church's teaching, and of a sublime unconsciousness of any other force than a brute one, should be the goal of a machine which beyond everything may be said to symbolise cosmopolitan views and the intellectual and moral kinship of all mankind. (*Laodicean* 22-3)

Where we might have expected a provocative clash Hardy impishly provides a romantic harmony. That *A Laodicean* displays a superabundance of this creative zest which both dazzles and amuses is apparent when Paula's telegraph message to Somerset 'sped through the loophole of Stancy Castle keep, over the trees, along the railway, under bridges, across three counties – from extreme antiquity of environment to sheer modernism – and finally landed itself on a table in Somerset's chambers in the midst of a cloud of fog' (*Laodicean* 210). 'When railways and telegraphs extend from London to the remotest cities and villages', observed a contributor to the 1842 *Quarterly Review*, 'the sensation of time may be transmitted along with the elements of language'.[4] Another writer remarked in 1877 that the 'telegraph has taken such a large place in the practical business of life, that the world in general is apt rather to look upon electricity only in light of an agent of rapid communication'.[5] This dynamic energy is conveyed by Hardy's descriptive prose: the wit resides not merely in Paula's using a telegraph machine inside the mouldering remains of feudal glory, then transmitting her note across a landscape dotted with dolmens and tumuli; we also see how the sense of breathless velocity evoked by modern communication contrasts with the rustic lethargy of 'Sleeping-Green',

[3] Anon., 'The State of English Architecture', *Quarterly Review* 132 (January 1872), 298.

[4] Anon., 'The *Encyclopaedia Britannica*', *Quarterly Review* 70 (June 1842), 57.

[5] Anon., 'The Science of Electricity as applied in Peace and War', *Quarterly Review* 144 (July 1877), 139.

whose inhabitants are far removed from the tide of progress. For Paula, time is precious; she belongs to that 'rising generation' who 'would think themselves ill-treated if they did not read in the *Times* each morning the report of any important event which had occurred in India the day before'.[6]

Whereas *Far from the Madding Crowd* and *The Return of the Native* hark back to the mid 1870s and early 1840s respectively, portraying communities relatively untouched by recent technology, *A Laodicean* and *Two on a Tower* are self-consciously 'stories of today', striking a note of deliberate contemporaneity. The plots of both exploit scientific gadgetry and the ways in which it modifies humankind's view of itself and its place in an accelerating and rapidly fluctuating world. Frederic Harrison asserted in the early 1880s: 'Take it all in all, the merely material, physical, mechanical change in human life in the hundred years, from the days of Watt and Arkwright to our own, is greater than occurred in the thousand years that preceded, perhaps even in the two thousand years or twenty thousand years.'[7]

Instead of offering a jaded, escapist complaint against the profligacy of the present, *A Laodicean* comprises a brisk, outgoing endorsement of modernity. Hardy reacts sensibly and humorously to the cultural anxieties about the alleged deleterious effects of late-Victorian life. He honours the apostles of scientific experimentation, and how they accommodate (as well as reanimate) the unlikeliest vestiges of the past. He does not depict Paula, the modern flower in her medieval flowerpot, as an 'upstart interloper'[8] or a shallow *parvenue* whose newfangled toys represent the polluted forces of a decadent bourgeoisie.[9] Pugin in *Contrasts* (1836), his manifesto for the Gothic Revival, angrily denounces 'the lukewarm feelings with which religion is regarded by the majority in this country'.[10] However, it is one of the novel's greatest triumphs that Paula, the 'lukewarm' woman, who aims to manufacture Hellenic pottery in her imposing Norman castle (*Laodicean* 36), becomes the embodiment of entrepreneurial flair. Paula has few

---

[6] Anon., 'The Science of Electricity as applied in Peace and War', 144.

[7] Frederic Harrisson, 'A Few Words about the Nineteenth Century', in *The Choice of Books* (London: Macmillan, 1907), p. 424. The essay first appeared in the *Fortnightly Review*, April 1882.

[8] Norman Page, *Thomas Hardy* (London: Routledge & Kegan Paul, 1976), p. 107.

[9] Robert Langbaum believes that Hardy is 'prefeminist' in his portrayal of Paula Power. See *Thomas Hardy in Our Time* (London: Macmillan, 1995), p. 83. See also Jane Thomas, *Thomas Hardy, Femininity and Dissent: Reassessing the 'Minor' Novels* (London: Macmillan, 1999).

[10] A. W. N. Pugin, *Contrasts*, introd. H. R. Hitchcock (New York: Humanities Press, 1969), p. 48.

qualms about taking 'contradictory views of life'.[11] Hardy also enjoys the image of her polished second-measuring castle clock – 'bearing the name of a recent maker' (*Laodicean* 25) – incongruously set amid Stancy Castle's decaying mortar.[12] William Dare's use of his 'patent photographic process' on the eerie de Stancy portraits (*Laodicean* 196), is another instance of Hardy presenting with beguiling verve the 'hymns ancient and modern' in the Victorian age.[13] An artistically minded photographer, writing in 1852, lamented that 'perhaps no science or art that has been revealed to mankind, has had to encounter a greater amount of opposition and prejudice than the science of photography'.[14] However, Hardy shows that photography can fit smoothly into the established hierarchy of pictorial media then in place in European culture. This jars with John Ruskin, who in 1872 declared of photographs that 'for geographical and geological purposes they are worth anything; for art purposes, worth – a good deal less than zero'.[15]

Though not unqualified in his embrace of the latest inventions, Hardy employs them with originality to demonstrate how a new medium – Dare's photography for instance – entertains an archaic medium (the mildewed ancestral portraits), and so opens up demanding new perspectives for his art. Hardy's imaginative dexterity and dash is the more notable given the stark series of disappointments in *The Return of the Native*. With regard to *A Laodicean* Desmond Hawkins writes, 'Hardy's friendliest critics have never found it easy to summon much enthusiasm for this, the third and last of his "novels of ingenuity" '.[16] But after *The Return of the Native*, Hardy comes out fighting, refreshed, energized. When George Somerset visits Sir William de Stancy, he finds the impecunious aristocrat settled snugly amid the 'mushroom modernism' of 'Myrtle Villa' whose '[g]enuine roadside respectability sat smiling on every brick of the eligible dwelling' (*Laodicean* 44). This mordant irony is elaborated when the baronet, a retired roué whose conversation Somerset expects to be 'the essence of

[11] Anon., 'Debased Hellenism and the New Renaissance', *Church Quarterly Review* 10 (April 1880), 107. Quoted in Thomas Hardy, *Literary Notebooks*, I, entry 1189.

[12] See David S. Landes, *Revolution in Time: Clocks and the Making of the Modern World* (Cambridge, Mass.: Harvard University Press, 1983).

[13] See Mark Durden, 'Ritual and Deception: Photography and Thomas Hardy', *Journal of European Studies*, 30:1 (March 2000), 57-69.

[14] H. Vines, *A Brief Sketch of the Rise and Progress of Photography, with Particular Reference to the Practice of Daguerreotype* (Bristol, 1852), p. 32.

[15] Quoted in Doug Nickel, 'The Camera and other Drawing Machines', in *British Photography in the Nineteenth Century*, ed. Mike Weaver (Cambridge: Cambridge University Press, 1982), p. 1.

[16] Desmond Hawkins, *Thomas Hardy. Novelist and Poet* (Newton Abbot, Devon: David & Charles, 1976), p. 82.

historical romance' (*Laodicean* 45), expatiates instead on contemporary money markets and the overriding need for frugality. This nimble wit is apparent when Somerset immerses himself in 'that volume of the county history which contained the record of Stancy Castle'. He becomes so preoccupied with the 'early times' of the noble edifice that he forgets how the minutes of the modern chronometer are rushing by:[17]

> he read that 'when this picturesque and ancient structure was founded, or by whom, is extremely uncertain. But that a castle stood on the site in very early times appears from many old books of charters'...He read on to the times when it first passed into the hands of 'De Stancy, Chivaler', and received the family name...
> Bang went eight strokes of the clock: it was the dinner hour...
> 'There, now I can't go, anyhow!' he said bitterly, jumping up, and picturing her receiving her company...Profoundly indifferent to the early history of the noble fabric, he felt a violent reaction towards modernism, eclecticism, new aristocracies, everything, in short, that Paula represented. (*Laodicean* 104)

Perhaps the most memorable escapade in this teasing wit occurs when the 'New Light' Paula briefly experiences the sights, sounds and smells of the 'Dark Ages':

> [Paula] was transported to the Middle Ages. It contained the shops of tinkers, braziers, bellows-menders, hollow-turners, and other quaintest trades...It was a street for a medievalist to revel in, toss up his hat and shout hurrah in, send for his luggage, come and live in, die and be buried in. She had never supposed such a street to exist outside the imaginations of antiquarians. Smells direct from the sixteenth century hung in the air in all their original integrity and without a modern taint. The faces of the people in the doorways seemed those of individuals who habitually gazed on the great Francis, and spoke of Henry the Eighth as the king across the sea. (*Laodicean* 399)

In his *Life of Carlyle*, published in the 1880s, J. A. Froude declared that Carlyle's unparalleled greatness as a historian resided in his ability 'to bring dead things and dead people actually back to life; to make the past

---

[17] For discussions on the significance of chronometric time in the Wessex Novels see William Frank Horwath, 'The Ache of Modernism: Thomas Hardy, Time and the Modern Novel', unpublished dissertation, University of Michigan, 1970; Nancy Ting-Man Wong, 'Human Time in the Wessex Novels', unpublished dissertation, University of Pittsburgh, 1973.

once more the present, and to show us men and women playing their parts on the mortal stage as real flesh-and-blood human creatures'.[18] Paula Power's medieval experience is an acerbic comment on Froude's assessment. Hardy relishes the artistic challenge of reviving the sights and sounds of former days, making 'the past once more the present'. Indeed, his time-voyage reveals an improvisatory finesse rarely found in his earlier fiction. He illustrates how an amateur antiquarian, always eager to separate the genuine 'survival' from a false copy, would rejoice at inhaling a sixteenth-century odour in all its original pungency. The passage is not throwaway or frivolous, but reveals in Hardy (who then confers it on Paula) a keen imagination empowered by incongruity so that we might perceive the complex workings of a brave new world from surprising angles. At an earlier point in the novel, he has George Somerset fall into the darkened well of a stairless tower in Stancy Castle like a Count of Monte Cristo and his watch is stopped by the fall (*Laodicean* 75). Hardy playfully evokes unexpected fairytale and chivalric images and notions: Somerset waves his white handkerchief through an arrow-slit like a medieval princess awaiting rescue by a fearless Arthurian knight. Hardy does not recoil in shock from an environment dominated by a Norman castle whose owner invites Somerset to construct a neo-Greek courtyard within its weather-stained walls, or a railway track weaving around prehistoric barrows.[19]

The dilettante's commonsense 'eclecticism' that Hardy indulges to such disarming effect extends to the assorted decorations and modish reading matter on display in Paula's living quarters. As well as 'books from a London circulating library, paper-covered light literature in French and choice Italian, and the latest monthly reviews', we see

> upon a small easy chair...a Bible, the *Baptist Magazine*, Wardlaw on Infant Baptism, Walford's County Families, and the *Court Journal*. On and over the mantelpiece were nicknacks of various descriptions, and photographic portraits of the artistic, scientific, and literary celebrities of the day. (*Laodicean* 38)

---

[18] James Anthony Froude, *Thomas Carlyle: A History of his Life in London, 1834-1881*, 2 vols. (London: Longmans, Green, & Co., 1884), II, 342.

[19] This could be a sly reference to the efforts of William Barnes and his fellow antiquarians to divert the Great Western Railway from Poundbury, the Romano-British hill-fort to the immediate northwest of Dorchester, and from Maumbury Ring in the town itself. See Alan Chedzoy, *William Barnes: A Life of the Dorset Poet* (Wimborne, Dorset: Dovecote Press, 1985); Charles Lock, 'Hardy and the Railway', *Essays in Criticism*, 50:1 (January 2000), 48-50.

'These things' Hardy writes, 'ensconced amid so much of the old and hoary, were as if a stray hour from the nineteenth century had wandered like a butterfly into the thirteenth, and lost itself there.' His tone implies an amused and slightly baffled fascination with this heterogeneous clutter; he is stirred and stimulated by the 'cosmopolitan, fashionable modernity'.[20] He himself moves promiscuously between those archaic and contemporary styles which best appeal to his own idiosyncratic temperament. 'To regard all things and principles of things as inconstant modes or fashions', Pater remarks in *The Renaissance*, 'has more and more become the tendency of modern thought.'[21] The book on county families and the *Court Journal* reflect Paula's concern for social standing; the Bible and *Baptism Magazine* indicate religious denomination and establish her as a dabbler in eclectic religious philosophy.[22] Hardy later described *A Laodicean* as a 'mechanical and ordinary production',[23] but its treatment of archaic features grafted onto a disconnected present is *extra*ordinary, continually courting oddness and whimsicality. Hardy refuses to be trapped by an overwhelming feeling of malaise; he conquers it, using arch humour as an expression of defiance and superiority.

A Laodicean possesses a new optimism about the way modernity takes account of 'survivals'. It is slavish respect for, or unthinking absorption in, the artefacts, styles and institutions of medieval times that is shown as sham, turning malignant. Captain de Stancy's 'close study of the castle history' and 'notes which referred to the pedigree of his own family' (*Laodicean* 183), is merely an attempt to wheedle his way into Paula's affections.[24] We might expect the architectural purist in Hardy, who calls for 'the protection of an ancient edifice against renewal in fresh materials' in his 1906 essay 'Memories of Church Restoration', to deride Paula's wish to build a Greek colonnade in the precincts of her Norman castle. She wants a fountain in the middle, and 'statues like those in the British Museum' – perhaps a plan to transport the Elgin Marbles into this isolated portion of Wessex! Ironically, Hardy's purist impulse is voiced by the unscrupulous architect Havill, whose letter to a newspaper disparages the neo-Hellenic spirit and Paula's criminal lack of veneration for the battered

---

[20] Joe Fisher, *Hidden Hardy* (London: Macmillan, 1992), p. 104

[21] Walter Pater, *The Renaissance: Studies in Art and Poetry*, ed. with introd. Adam Phillips (Oxford: The World's Classics, 1986), p. 186.

[22] On the religious questions posed by *A Laodicean* see Timothy Hands, *Thomas Hardy: Distracted Preacher? Hardy's Religious Biography and its Influence on his Novels* (London: Macmillan, 1989).

[23] See Thomas Hardy, *Life*, p. 154.

[24] Admittedly, de Stancy's campaign of impressing Paula is undertaken somewhat reluctantly and only at the urging of Dare.

magnificence of Stancy Castle, which has outlasted English Civil Wars only 'to be made a complete ruin by the freaks of an irresponsible owner' (*Laodicean* 109).

Havill's tirade is couched in terms reminiscent of 'The State of English Architecture', a waspish article published in the 1872 *Quarterly Review* condemning 'this Gothic reign of terror' which sacrifices 'simplicity of outline and rhythm of parts' for 'meretricious vanity' and 'agonizing superfluity of contrivance'.[25] With his relish for exploiting uncoordinated impressions and contradictory positions, Hardy uses in *A Laodicean* the outlandish fusion of obsolete and chic that is Gothic renovation, yet he disavows it in his essays and poems.[26] Hardy comes across as simultaneously a child of his era (reflecting its perverse mixture of bright confidences and enervating angst), and within that a writer giving a response to it that is uniquely his own. Externalizing his own individual impulse when confronting the paradoxes of the period, he seems fretful when the spirit of the age was marked by hubristic eloquence (for example, about the perfectibility of man). But, as Havill's letter reveals on a subject close to Hardy's heart, he could be dryly amused in the light of vitriolic resistance to 'dainty', 'soft-handed' gentleman architects whose 'amateur dilettante diversions' were supposedly desecrating an august English heritage.[27] An 1831 reviewer claimed that 'incongruity is, in our estimation, a strong, perhaps a conclusive argument, against the adaptation' of 'the Gothic style'.[28] On this matter of sharp controversy, Hardy offers not a jeremiad on the 'puerile' pseudo-Gothic[29] but a jubilee; he divorces himself from the censorious Havills of late-Victorian England, and acclaims Paula's crusading desire to quarry multifarious techniques of construction and design. He sees in it the intrepid, visionary eclecticism to which he was instinctively drawn: his natural imaginative habit of randomly collecting motifs from diverse past cultures and placing them in increasingly eccentric

---

[25] Anon., 'The State of English Architecture', *Quarterly Review* 132 (January 1872), 309, 310, 319.

[26] See Hardy's poems, 'The Levelled Churchyard', *Complete Poems*, p. 157; and 'The Obliterate Tomb', *Complete Poems*, p. 383.

[27] As the anonymous reviewer for the 1872 *Quarterly* complains: 'Never has there been such wanton destruction of the historic associations and genuine artistic character and expression of our ancient buildings as they have suffered in the last thirty years.' See 'The State of English Architecture', 305, 312, 333.

[28] Anon., 'Old English Domestic Architecture', *Quarterly Review* 45 (July 1831), 472. For different perspectives on this debate within the periodical frame see also Anon., 'Hamilton &c. on Architecture', *Quarterly Review* 58 (February 1837), 61-82; Anon., 'Principles of Gothic Architecture', *Quarterly Review* 69 (December 1841), 111-49.

[29] Anon., 'Hope's *History of Architecture*', *Quarterly Review* 53 (April 1835), 342.

arrangements.[30] Hardy's inquiries are not merely into continuity with the past; he shows a concern with prudent adaptation to the present, and astute awareness of the future.

Paula Power's fanciful improvements to her castle home are not associated with that which is undesirable or life-denying; rather Hardy warns against uncomprehending immersion in the patrician past. The de Stancys are a lost yet partially preservable thirteenth-century order; like Rings-Hill Speer, which dominates the landscape of *Two on a Tower*, defunct sites should be put to an entirely new use. No dirge for a dying past, *A Laodicean* reinforces Paula's nobility of talent and ambition, and scoffs at the enervated de Stancys, whose defective medievalism cannot meet the exigencies of the modern moment. If Hardy espoused the shrill rhetoric of Havill's letter, the novel would be a cautionary tale of orderly feudalism displaced by tasteless and turbulent democracy. But like Paula, Hardy enjoys casually raiding the storehouse of history, given the Victorians' deepening knowledge of unfamiliar epochs and cultures. She represents to Somerset, who quotes the hero of 'Locksley Hall', 'the march of mind – the steamship, and the railway, and the thoughts that shake mankind' (l.128).[31] Though conscious of the unreliable technology of the train – one nearly runs Somerset over – Hardy's upbeat attitude towards the railway and the tunnel built by Paula's pioneering father underpins his strategy of furnishing a dilapidated Norman castle with 'the leading inventions of the day'.[32] Hardy does not bemoan the sudden loss of a 'pre-railroad' existence like Thackeray: 'They have raised those railroad embankments up, and shut off the old world that was behind them. Climb up that bank on which the irons are laid, and look to the other side – it is gone.'[33] The geologist Gideon Mantell grumbled that the railway had 'completely metamorphosed the English character' by bringing '[e]ternal

---

[30] The architect Thomas Leverton Donaldson wrote in 1842: 'We are wandering in a labyrinth of experiments, and trying by an amalgamation of certain features in this or that style of each and every period...to form a homogenous whole with some distinct character of its own.' See *Preliminary discourses pronounced before the University College of London, upon the commencement of a series of lectures, on Architecture, 17 October, 1842* (London: J. Smith, 1842), p. 30. Donaldson presented Hardy with the silver medal of the Royal Institute of British Architects on 16 March 1863 for his essay on the application of coloured brick and terra-cotta to modern architecture.

[31] Tennyson was a passenger on the first train from Liverpool to Manchester in 1830. See Robert Bernard Martin, *Tennyson: The Unquiet Heart* (Oxford: Clarendon Press, 1980), p. 121.

[32] Anon., 'The *Encyclopaedia Britannica*', *Quarterly Review* 70 (June 1842), 55.

[33] William Makepeace Thackeray, 'The Roundabout Papers No. 8', *Cornhill Magazine* 2 (1860), 504.

hustle, movement with the greatest rapidity, constant change'.[34] Dickens's attitude to the ongoing expansion of the British rail network could be apocalyptic: 'beyond the Station, an ugly dark monster of a tunnel kept its jaws open, as if it had swallowed them and were ravenous for more destruction.'[35] Hardy repudiates rhetoric of severe trauma and the ideas of social collapse which were strenuously promulgated by the opponents of railway travel; he offers instead a more temperate, reassuring assessment:

> Somerset looked down on the mouth of the tunnel. The absurdity of the popular commonplace that science, steam, and travel must always be unromantic and hideous, was proved on the spot. On either slope of the deep cutting, green with long grass, grew drooping young trees of ash, beech, and other flexible varieties...The vertical front of the tunnel, faced with brick that had once been red, was now weather-stained, lichened, and mossed over in harmonious hues of rusty browns, pearly greys, and neutral greens. (*Laodicean* 95)

Rather than brutally 'cutting down antiquities...destroying and defacing on all sides',[36] the tunnel has been happily absorbed into its surroundings and naturalized by time. Hardy is not repelled by this glaring incongruity but evinces a feeling of quiet wonder at the tunnel's deceptively organic appearance, and clashes with the sombreness of *Desperate Remedies*, in which the emergence of rail travel has left Old Springrove's Three Tranters Inn a cheerless roadside relic. In 1862 James Fergusson paid fulsome tribute to the design of tunnels: 'Some of the entrances to the tunnels which are found on most railways in England are as grand as any city gates, and

---

[34] Quoted in Dennis Dean, *Gideon Mantell and the Discovery of Dinosaurs*, p. 261.

[35] Charles Dickens, 'Associations of Childhood', *All the Year Round* (30 June 1860), 274. See also Harland S. Nelson, 'Staggs's Gardens: The Railway Through Dickens's World', *Dickens Studies Annual* 3 (1980), 41-53.

[36] Anon., 'The Dorset County Museum and Library', *The Dorset County Chronicle*, 3 January, 1884. Reprinted in *Address by Lt.-General A. H. L. F. Pitt-Rivers at the opening of The Dorset County Museum, 1884* (Dorchester: The Friary Press, 1984), p. 16. Hardy must have savoured the delicious irony that the projection of the South Western Railway from London to Dorchester in 1845 played a crucial role in the founding of the Dorset County Museum (with William Barnes as one of its secretaries). At the resolutions of the preliminary meeting held on 15 October 1845, it was decided that 'in consideration of the importance of this district with respect to natural history and both British and Roman antiquities, and, more especially at this time, when the disturbance of the surface of the county in the formation of railroads is likely to bring to light specimens of interest in these several departments of science, it is advisable to take immediate steps for the establishment of an institution in this town containing a museum and library for the county of Dorset.'

grander than many triumphal arches that are to be found in Europe.'[37]
Hardy would have supported this sentiment rather than take a Ruskinian
view of the railway's utilitarian meanness,[38] although he does not quite
follow a rapt journalist in hailing the railway as 'the greatest blessing which
science has ever imparted to mankind'.[39] We are invited, however, to regard
the railway not simply in terms of mechanical function but as an object
worthy of aesthetic appreciation: the moss and the effects of weather,
bringing the massive stonework into the organic cycle of nature, thus
making technology seem picturesque and romantic. This is a far cry from
Dickens's *Dombey and Son*, which anxiously alerts us to the massive
lesions carved into the land by railway tracks.

Hardy's representation of the ancient Wessex countryside, overspread
with telegraph poles and John Power's railway, is not the searing vision of
a bleak dystopian fiction. Rather he hails 'those *new arts* which are on the
eve of altering the forms and habits of social life. The wonders of railway
intercourse, of locomotive engines, tunnels...steam-boats' and the almost
magical 'powers of the electro-magnetic telegraph'.[40] *A Laodicean* shuns
the didactic simplicity of Augustus Welby Pugin's juxtapositions of old and
new in *Contrasts* (1836).[41] The etched title-page in the first and second
editions refers to 'a parallel between the noble edifices of the fourteenth
and fifteenth centuries and similar buildings of the present day; shewing the
present decay of taste'. Pugin measures the 'structures that the puny hand
of modern times has raised',[42] such as railway stations and poorhouses,
against the churches and stately monuments from an age of unshakeable
faith. Hardy's tunnel episode, instead of illustrating the unrelieved sterility

---

[37] James Fergusson, *History of the Modern Styles of Architecture: being a sequel to the Handbook of Architecture* (London: John Murray, 1862), p. 477. William Wordsworth by contrast, in poems such as 'On the Projected Kendal and Windermere Railway' and 'Proud Were Ye, Mountains' (both 1844), speaks out against the railway's 'rash assault' on the 'beautiful romance of nature' and denigrates the 'mischief' of the 'long-linked Train'.

[38] See Ruskin's 'The Lamp of Beauty' chapter from *The Seven Lamps of Architecture*.

[39] Anon., 'The London and North-Western Railway', *Quarterly Review* 84 (December 1848), 2.

[40] Anon., 'The *Encyclopaedia Britannica*', *Quarterly Review* 70 (June 1842), 54-5. The reviewer quotes from *The Morning Chronicle*, 8 June 1842: 'Railroad travelling...is a delightful improvement of human life. Man is become a bird: he can fly longer and quicker that a Solon goose...Everything is near – everything is immediate: time, distance, and delay are abolished' (71). See also W. E. Gladstone, 'Free Trade, Railways, and Commerce', *Nineteenth Century* 7 (January-June 1880), 367-88. Gladstone admires 'the constant progress of mechanical invention' and 'the marriage of the steam-engine to the rail, and its enlistment in the business of locomotion by land' (371).

[41] Augustus Welby Northmore Pugin, *Contrasts*, introd. H. R. Hitchcock (New York: Humanities Press, 1969).

[42] Ibid., p. 35.

of Victorian life with its 'tide of innovations and paltry novelties',[43] upholds the manifold opportunities created by Paula's venturesome and reformist generation. In Pugin's medievalism, Hardy sees only an ossified, fixed feudal order.

But does Hardy really show the traditional aristocracy as impotent and feckless in a heady present that boasts 'the application of…steam to travelling, of electricity to telegraphs'?[44] Sir William de Stancy pragmatically suggests that 'nothing can retain the spirit, and why should we preserve the shadow of the form?' (*Laodicean* 46-7). Gothic romance, whose conventions Hardy vigorously updates in *A Laodicean* for the neo-pagan days of the 1870s, usually dictates that a sinister independent life should be given to the central archetype, a mansion or castle, whose 'historic past' touches its occupants 'with a yet living hand' (*Laodicean* 205-6). Horace Walpole, in *The Castle of Otranto* (1765), describes the portrait of Manfred's grandfather groaning and stepping out of its frame; so Hardy makes Paula, while observing the dingy de Stancy portraits, feel that they have stretched out a tentacle from their genealogical tree to absorb her into their mass.[45] Captain de Stancy is like the reanimation of an ancestral type, and the pressures of the castle start to tell on Paula, a dissenter set among chambers of antique lumber and the dust of old carvings. Her infatuation with the de Stancy lineage suggests a perennial capacity of human nature to invent ancient triumphs and sentimentalize traditional beliefs or institutions; even though, like the dreary, cracked de Stancy portraits, and indeed the originals themselves, they have fallen into desuetude. The aisle of the de Stancy church contains the family tomb of 'cross-legged knights' reminiscent of the chantry in Knapwater church which enervates Edward Springrove in *Desperate Remedies*.[46] In *A Laodicean*, Paula actually wishes she were a true aristocrat; she is attracted to the historical tombs of these highborn figures (*Laodicean* 112). Hardy's central polemic is to show that this old patrician spirit has a poisonous power that threatens to deprive Paula of her pioneering vitality.

Through the concept of Captain de Stancy himself and his bastard son William Dare, Hardy reveals how difficult it is to lay the medieval spirit to rest. Sir William's soldier son is an elaboration of the 'satyr' figure already seen in Aeneas Manston from *Desperate Remedies* (1871) and Sergeant

---

[43] A. W. N. Pugin, *Contrasts*, p. 55.

[44] Anon., 'Popular Science', *Quarterly Review* 84 (March 1849), 318.

[45] Another possible influence on *A Laodicean* is Nathaniel Hawthorne's *The House of the Seven Gables* (1851), an exploration of hereditary guilt, which also artfully juxtaposes Gothic stock-in-trade and modern inventions (Holgrave is a daguerreotypist).

[46] '[T]he reclining figures of cross-legged knights, damp and green with age'. See *Desperate Remedies*, pp. 200-201.

Troy in *Far from the Madding Crowd* (1874). The depiction of Sir Blount in *Two on a Tower* – who abandons his wife for the frisson of big-game hunting in Africa – continues in a droller vein Hardy's exploration of this invariably highborn type. In contrast with Troy though, de Stancy has vowed to be celibate and a teetotaller, as a means of correcting an earlier indiscretion that produced an illegitimate child. Far from being 'a pantomime pair of aristocratic schemers of whom the father is an ineffective voyeur',[47] de Stancy and his son reveal Hardy's increasing sensitivity to the resonances of mythic material in a modern setting. Unlike Dickens's depiction of Esther Summerson in *Bleak House* (1853), William Dare is not a developed investigation of the illegitimate psyche, but seems rather an 'agency' or a collection of skills, the warped product of untrammelled sexuality. He embodies the primitive instinctual force that is an inescapable part of aristocratic inheritance in the Wessex world:

> the moonlight streamed into the room, across the bed whereon Dare was sleeping. He lay on his back, his arms thrown out; and his well-curved youthful form looked like an unpedestaled Dionysus in the colourless lunar rays. (*Laodicean* 144)

Like the pagan divinity to whom he is compared, Dare is a drinker associated with satanic darkness and shape-changing (through his patented photographic process which corrupts and distorts images).[48] In 1857 Lady Elizabeth Eastlake maintained that photography is 'too profoundly interwoven with the deep things of Nature to be entirely unlocked by any given method'.[49] But Dare is initiated into the secrets of this 'new and mysterious art' so that he can alter negatives to make the temperate and sensible Somerset appear drunk (*Laodicean* 319).[50] This prefigures the ancestral portraits that seem to be laughing in the flickering flames at the climax of the novel. Through his conception of the 'Dionysian' Dare, Hardy hesitates on the brink of an imaginative commitment to exploring vestiges of a primeval past imbedded in mythic material, a commitment

---

[47] John Goode, *Thomas Hardy: The Offensive Truth* (Oxford: Basil Blackwell, 1988), p. 67.

[48] 'From its inception', Lindsay Smith writes, 'photography held a connection with magic. The "black", which associates that "black art from France" with magic, is apparent both in the literal chemical stains upon the body of the photographer and in the "negative" status of the photographic medium, which quickly became known for its inauthenticity in its sovereign ability to deceive.' See Lindsay Smith, *The Politics of Focus: Women, Children and Nineteenth-Century Photography* (Manchester: Manchester University Press, 1998), p. 2.

[49] [E. Eastlake], 'Photography', *Quarterly Review* 101 (April 1857), 456.

[50] Ibid., 442.

that reaches fruition in *The Woodlanders* and *Tess*. This is not to suggest that a heightened awareness of ancient tales in Victorian literature suddenly began with Hardy: the imaginative treatment of myth is almost as ancient as myth itself. In nineteenth-century England, Matthew Arnold was moving in Hardy's direction in poems such as 'Balder Dead' from *Poems, Second Series* (1855), using with new alertness the common nonrational heritage of mankind which myth enshrines. But Hardy was born at a more propitious time, for as Edward A. Freeman attested in 1866, 'The origin of mythical narratives in general, and the relation of the myths of one nation to those of others, is an important and fascinating subject, and one which has lately been zealously taken up by a special school of inquirers'.[51] In the vanguard of this 'special school' was E. B. Tylor, who affirmed that the 'turning of mythology to account as a means of tracing the history of laws of mind, is a branch of science scarcely discovered till the nineteenth century'.[52] His writings contained much to stimulate Hardy's imagination: 'The very myths that were discarded as lying fables, prove to be sources of history in ways that their makers and transmitters little dreamed of. Their meaning has been misunderstood, but they have a meaning.'[53] It is this meaning that Hardy's mature fiction, despite or perhaps *because of* an accelerating sense of historical crisis, strives to unravel.

The Dionysian Dare is, for his father, a constant and humiliating reminder of that sexual energy that might once have had a genuine place in an ancient clan, but which is now a moribund destructive passion which de Stancy feels he must stifle at every opportunity. Dare lures his father into voyeuristically watching the virginal Paula perform her gymnastics, and de Stancy's volatile instinctual impulses disastrously reassert themselves.

> [Captain de Stancy] went forward, and looked through the hole into the interior of the gymnasium. Dare withdrew to some little distance, and watched Captain De Stancy's face, which presently began to change...Paula, in a pink flannel costume, was bending, wheeling, and undulating in the air like a gold-fish in its globe...A bitter recollection of his vow, together with a sense that to gaze on the festival of this Bona Dea was, though so pretty a sight, hardly fair or gentlemanly, would have compelled him to withdraw his eyes, had not the sportive fascination of her appearance glued them there in spite of all. (*Laodicean* 172-3)

---

[51] Edward A. Freeman, 'The Mythical and Romantic Elements in Early English History', *Fortnightly Review* 4 (1866), 641. See also George Grote, 'Grecian Legends and Early History', *Westminster Review* 39 (1846), 173-4.

[52] E. B. Tylor, *Primitive Culture*, I, 275.

[53] Ibid., I, 281.

Bona Dea refers to Fauna, the wife or daughter of the fertility god Faunus in Roman mythology. Women celebrated her cult with a mysterious festival that was forbidden to men. Dare, knowing de Stancy is bored by questions of aristocratic pedigree, manages to awaken in his father by this tactic of grossly sensual appeal an unlikely interest in matters of lineage and even the role his ancestors played as Cavaliers in the English Civil War (*Laodicean* 183); restoring to him the sexual potency of which he himself is a product.

Though never making it explicit, Hardy evokes a scene redolent of the Actaeon and Diana narrative: the famous legendary hunter who inadvertently stumbled upon the goddess of chastity bathing naked and who was transformed into a stag, then torn to pieces by his own hungry hounds. By placing de Stancy's immolation in a mythological context, Hardy comments on the nature of voyeurism and the overwhelming shock of instinctual feeling. Through Dare's manipulation, we see rekindled in de Stancy a new awareness of aristocratic identity by removing the civilized veneer of late-Victorian polite society. A 'fermentation' begins in de Stancy, 'a purely chemical process' (*Laodicean* 173), causing the release of repressed energies. But this liberation of satyrean passion as the captain unearths his heritage is not a genuine 'survival' at all, but the comically grotesque recovery of aristocratic esteem.

Just as de Stancy crumbles under the weight of his own long-retarded instinctual energies, so his ancestral home is devastated by a conflagration that originates within its mildewed walls, for medievalism contains the seeds of its own abject collapse. The burning down of the mansion or castle may be a 'standard item in the repertoire of Gothic melodrama',[54] but Hardy's handling is original and of a piece with his habit of revitalizing the conventions elsewhere in the novel. When Dare sets the castle alight, his ancestors' approval is imaged in their faded portraits, which flicker into life. The arsonist unwittingly frees Paula and Somerset from the oppressive residue of the past: an appropriate close to a novel in which Hardy's imaginative vision has been *released* to exuberant effect:

> a light shone upon the lawn from the windows of the Long Gallery, which glowed with more brilliancy than it had known in the meridian of its Caroline splendours. Thereupon the framed gentleman in the lace collar seemed to open his eyes more widely; he with the flowing locks and turn-up mustachios to part his lips; he in the armour, who was so much like Captain De Stancy, to shake the plates of his mail with suppressed laughter; the lady with the three-

---

[54] Michael Millgate, *Thomas Hardy: His Career as a Novelist*, p.170.

> stringed pearl necklace...to nod with satisfaction and triumphantly
> signify to her adjoining husband that this was a meet and glorious
> end.
>   The light increased, and blown upon by the wind roared round the
> pictures, the tapestries, and the cradle, up to the plaster ceiling and
> through it into the forest of oak timbers above. (*Laodicean* 426)

The fire at Farmer Springrove's Three Tranters tavern in *Desperate Remedies* (1871) has tragic consequences. Here the conflagration is presented as an exultant outpouring of elemental energy, with enough strength to engulf 'the forest of oak timbers above', material from which the 'cradle' is made. This is a 'meet' way for a fossil of feudalism to vanish – a *tour de force* of release. Final extinction becomes consummation, for in the end the captain's family are in hopeless disarray: Sir William dead; de Stancy himself ruined, alone, defeated by the undying moments of a remorseless, retributively demanding history; and the inoffensive Charlotte retreating into an Anglican order of nuns. Rather than yield to humiliating modern compromise in the shape of neo-Greek modification, the medieval spirit of Stancy Castle defiantly turns its last aggressive impulse upon itself. Perhaps Dare, the final degenerate scion of a devastated family, is the only character in *A Laodicean* who has 'authority' to burn down the castle, a symbol of his own thwarted hereditary instincts. Despite the encouraging signs of new inventions at the outset (the buzzing telegraph wires), at the denouement Stancy castle and its antique contents are reduced to ashes by the arson of a man who can effortlessly control and pervert technological advance (the deforming photographic process). The dazzling paraphernalia of a progressive society hold no fear for Dare, an instrument of his clan's most antisocial impulses.

Hardy scholars of the last fifty years have rarely delivered so many discouraging negative comments as they have about *A Laodicean*, often labelling it the worst Wessex novel.[55] They have been less perspicacious than the often hysterical and tendentious reviewers of the late nineteenth century.[56] After *The Return of the Native*, whose imaginative excavations

---

[55] J. B. Bullen writes that *A Laodicean* 'provides little evidence of the imaginative fire which characterizes Hardy at his best'. See *The Expressive Eye: Fiction and Perception in the Work of Thomas Hardy* (Oxford: Oxford University Press, 1986), p. 118. Albert Guerard calls it 'the dreariest of Hardy's novels'. *Thomas Hardy. The Novels and Stories* (Cambridge, Mass.: Harvard University Press, 1949), p. 52; Richard Carpenter condemns it as 'a potboiler of the worst sort.' *Thomas Hardy* (New York: Twayne, 1964), p. 62.

[56] The *World* saw *A Laodicean* as a 'curious...mixture of sensationalism, philosophy, religion, spiritual affection, and carnal suggestiveness' (11 January 1882, p. 18), while the *Observer* found it 'original in its mixture of pedantry and simplicity, melodrama and philosophy' (2 April 1882, p. 1).

uncover such dissatisfying shards and splinters of earlier cultures, *A Laodicean* displays Hardy's insistent virtuosity. Stancy Castle, rich in romantic historical associations – as Ruskin said, an old building 'connects forgotten and following ages with each other'[57] – becomes a symbol not just of temporal conjunction but also of the ways in which Hardy can revivify the seemingly moribund relics of forgotten periods. He is excited by the artistic possibilities offered by 'survivals' because they cast their shadows across many different eras. He reacts with an exuberance that undercuts the ideologically limiting construction of Hardy as a monolithically pessimistic author. The image of a medieval castle, crusted with myriad bygone experiences, stimulates him to new insights when he might have been uneasy over an apparent collision of past and future. He repeatedly challenges our generic expectations, forcing us to re-evaluate habitual ways of seeing situations sharply out of joint. In *A Laodicean*, he persuasively contends that energy resides in modernity's accommodating our heritage (e.g. Paula's maverick plans for her castle home) rather than the past's unbecoming and graceless attempt to ingratiate itself with the modern spirit (Captain de Stancy). This even extends to the machinery of Gothic supernaturalism, situating the conventional orphan of the castle in the bewildering milieu of Victorian scientific, social and political ferment. Although commentators would have us believe that Hardy was magisterially dismissive of Gothic stock-in-trade, it appears in this novel to exert an irresistible hold over his imagination.

In the next section it is apparent how the incongruities revealed by 'survivals', which provide numerous occasions for Hardy to indulge an extravagant play of fancy in *A Laodicean,* signally fail to do so in *Two on a Tower.* Rings-Hill Speer is the key symbolic setting of the later novel as Stancy Castle is to its predecessor. Hardy's technique of surveying an antique object and all its subsequent accretions is evident once again:

> The column had been erected in the eighteenth century as a substantial memorial of [Viviette's] husband's great-grandfather, a respectable officer who had fallen in the American War...The fir-shrouded hill top was (according to some antiquaries) an old Roman camp – if it were not (as others insisted) an old British castle, or (as the rest swore) an old Saxon field of Witenagemote – with remains of an outer and an inner vallum. (6-7)[58]

---

[57] John Ruskin, *Seven Lamps of Architecture* in *The Works of John Ruskin*, ed. E. T. Cook and Alexander Wedderburn, 39 vols. (London: George Allen, 1903-12), VIII, 234.
[58] Thomas Hardy, *Two on a Tower*, ed. with introd. Suleiman M. Ahmad (Oxford: The World's Classics, 1993). Hereafter referred to as *Tower*.

Hardy seems amused by the typical antiquarian bickering over the question of the site's history, while at the same time acknowledging his own sustained absorption in the true beginnings of a structure, custom, superstition or rite; for a fascination with the aetiology of things, whether discovering the origin of species or the source of the Nile, was a dominant feature of Hardy's lifelong passion for Victorian science.

In *A Laodicean* Hardy judges the past represented by the highborn de Stancy as a fake desiccated potency, crude and clumsy in its endeavour to harness the modern spirit. Aristocratic heritage is equally unimportant to the present application of the Speer: Hardy indicates there can be no miraculous reinstatement of former patrician glories. The best we can expect is that the abandoned husks of a fossilized past can be cleverly modified to a contemporary purpose. But *Two on a Tower* does not repeat *A Laodicean*'s boisterous display of authorial ambition. Indeed, we can regard the two novels as the obverse and reverse sides of Hardy's comic brio. *Two on a Tower*'s cynical humour and darkly oracular tone replace the earlier work's brashness and linguistic invention.

Two on a Tower (1882)

> Under any other circumstances Lady Constantine might have felt a nameless fear in thus sitting aloft on a lonely column, with a forest groaning under her feet, and palaeolithic dead men feeding its roots; but the recent passionate decision stirred her pulses to an intensity beside which the ordinary tremors of feminine existence asserted themselves in vain. (*Tower* 108-9)

Hardy's intricate visual angles and deft use of incongruity – which keep the encroaching bleakness at bay in *A Laodicean* – now make things graver and more disconcerting in *Two on a Tower*. Whereas capricious wit is a bold exercise of power in the earlier novel, stealing laughter in the midst of danger, the humour of *Two on a Tower* is never permitted to be simply amusing and collapses amid the general ruin. Lady Viviette Constantine 'sitting aloft on a lonely column' evokes images of the Nelson monuments that were spontaneously created close upon the news of the famous Lord's naval victory (1805) in the Battle of Trafalgar. Monuments like that in Trafalgar Square (under construction between the 1820s and 1840s) commemorated the heroic virtues of men; rarely were they built to honour a woman. Viviette's position at the top of the Speer also suggests the Christian ascetics who demonstrated their devotion to God by living on similar towers, such as Saint Simeon Stylites (390-459), the first and most renowned of the Pillar-Hermits, who occupied a pillar for thirty years.[59] Hardy's pairing of images not ordinarily fused, which on a cursory reading make little sense together, – the male Christian ascetic and the married patrician lady – reveals a grim aptness after all: Viviette has been compelled to assume an enervating existence of severe self-repression as a gesture of devotion to her dissolute husband.[60] She has taken a 'solemn oath' (*Tower* 20) not to mingle in genteel society until his return from Africa, so her clandestine visits to the Speer have much more serious implications than they will for the young astronomer with whom she is in love.

In the unsettling image of 'palaeolithic dead men' Hardy ponders, as he did when portraying the relationship between Dare and de Stancy in *A Laodicean*, to what extent the psychological past is a dead event in modern society. Tylor's *Primitive Culture* convincingly demonstrated that 'through remoter periods, as we recede more nearly towards the primitive conditions of our race, the threads which connect new thought with old do not always vanish from our sight'.[61] To what extent then did the individual inherit from preceding generations not only his physiological but also his psychological structures? That the remains of 'palaeolithic dead men' actively fertilize the roots of the trees groaning beneath Viviette's feet is suggestive. Hardy implies that mental 'survivals' are still operant, governing human behaviour from below the threshold of rational consciousness. He skilfully exploits Rings-Hill Speer to introduce a vertical time-scheme: palaeolithic dead men buried beneath a Romano-British earthwork on which is built an eighteenth-century tower surmounted by Swithin's equatorial telescope. The archaeological term 'palaeolithic' was coined by Sir John Lubbock, author of the seminal *Prehistoric Times* (1865),[62] to designate a first Stone Age greatly antedating all written records:

> From the careful study of the remains which have come down to us, it would appear that Pre-historic Archaeology may be divided into four great epochs.
> I. That of the Drift; when man shared the possession of Europe with the Mammoth, the Cave Bear, the Woolly-haired rhinoceros,

---

[59] See Alfred Lord Tennyson, *The Poems of Tennyson*, I, 593.

[60] See Richard D. Sylvia, 'Hardy's Feminism: Apollonian Myth and *Two on a Tower*', *Thomas Hardy Journal* 12:2 (May 1996), 48-59.

[61] E. B. Tylor, *Primitive Culture*, I, 274.

[62] The book became a bestseller for half a century; the seventh edition was published in 1913.

and other extinct animals. This we may call the 'Palaeolithic' period.[63]

Hardy glimpses through the 'palaeolithic dead men' passional imperatives that do not submit to the rigid proprieties governing polite Victorian society. Does the social milieu of *A Laodicean* and *Two on a Tower* complicate these imperatives, or are the timeless energies simply malicious, inexorably cruel natural laws under whose sway we see in different degrees Captain de Stancy and Viviette? Although Hardy retains an honest ambivalence about this issue, he shifts towards the latter conclusion when Louis Granville discovers Viviette is carrying an illegitimate child by Swithin. As a result, he embarks on a journey to marry her off to the Bishop of Melchester. The incongruities which in *A Laodicean* supply so much material for Hardy's lively play of fancy here strike a more provocatively contentious and disturbing note:

> Louis entered the train at Warborne, and was speedily crossing a country of ragged woodland which, though intruded on by the plough at places, remained largely intact from prehistoric times; and still abounded with yews of gigantic growth and oaks tufted with mistletoe. It was the route to Melchester. (*Tower* 254)

Louis's route to a stronghold of Christianity on the modern train ironically takes him through some of the most ancient pagan landscape in Wessex. The 'oaks tufted with mistletoe' foreshadows Hardy's description of The Chase in *Tess* ('a truly venerable tract of forest land, one of the few remaining woodlands in England of undoubted primaeval date, wherein Druidical mistletoe was still found on aged oaks'), and is a potent image, given the antiquarian Charles Hardwick's comments in his *Traditions, Superstitions and Folklore* (1872):

> The mistletoe and the oak were both of sacred...origin amongst the Aryans...It is a parasite...everywhere believed to spring from seed deposited by birds on trees. When it was found on the oak, the Druids ascribed its growth directly to the gods.[64]

---

[63] Sir John Lubbock, *Pre-historic Times as illustrated by Ancient Remains and the Manners and Customs of Modern Savages*, 4th edn. (London: Frederic Norgate, 1878), p. 2. Lubbock also coined the term 'Neolithic' to refer to the later or polished Stone Age.

[64] Charles Hardwick, *Traditions, Superstitions and Folklore (chiefly Lancashire and the North of England): Their affinity to others in widely-distributed localities: Their Eastern Origin and Mythical Significance* (London: Simpkin, Marshall & Co, 1872; repr. Manchester, England: E. J. Morten, 1973), p. 67.

He comments later, 'The peculiar and regular equiangular form of the branches of the mistletoe, doubtless, had much influence in its selection as a mystical plant endowed with supernatural properties'.[65] It is possible that Hardy knew of ancient boundary and bridal oaks in Dorset, like the ones Hardwick mentions, 'around which newly-married couples danced three times and afterwards cut a cross...unquestionably one form of the many phallic symbols.'[66] The Greenwood Tree under whose branches the celebration of Dick and Fancy's wedding takes place is an oak. Eight years after the publication of *Two on a Tower* in 1890, James Frazer would thoroughly investigate the mythical significance of the mistletoe and the oak trees on which it was commonly found. The plant was 'from time immemorial', the 'object of superstitious veneration in Europe'.[67] Women believed that carrying mistletoe about with them would enable them to conceive.[68]

It seems highly probable then, considering the nature of Louis's mission to Melchester, that Hardy slyly exploits the link between 'oaks tufted with mistletoe' and pagan fertility rites, a link which first reviewers of the novel such as the *Saturday Review* no doubt found 'extremely repulsive' (18 November 1882, 675).[69] Convinced in *Two on a Tower* of the impossibility of dissociating oneself from enslavement to prescribed forms of social and sexual etiquette, Hardy incorporates more twisted and macabre effects into his comic repertoire. The prehistoric features of the Wessex countryside suggest the volatile passional imperatives (the begetting of a bastard) traditionally and naturally connected with the primitive world, as folklore attests and which Frazer and Freud confirmed. The scene shows Hardy obdurately refusing to honour the false pieties of his culture. Michael Millgate observes that Hardy 'was creating future trouble for himself by allowing the story to drift towards topics and situations of doubtful propriety'.[70] *A Laodicean*'s witty address never descends into the cruel, even venomous glee with which Hardy depicts the

---

[65] Ibid., p. 255.

[66] Ibid., p. 75.

[67] Sir James George Frazer, *The Golden Bough*, p. 750.

[68] Ibid., p. 751. See also pp. 796-800: 'The inference is almost inevitable that The Golden Bough was nothing but the mistletoe seen through the haze of poetry or of popular superstition.'

[69] The *Literary World* found the whole episode 'outrageous'; the *Daily News* 'intensely cynical'; the *Athenaeum* 'little short of revolting'. *The Spectator's* critic wrote, 'this is a story as unpleasant as it is practically impossible'. See *Thomas Hardy: The Critical Heritage,* ed. R. G. Cox (London: Routledge & Kegan Paul, 1970), pp. 98-101.

[70] Michael Millgate, *Thomas Hardy. A Biography* (Oxford: Oxford University Press, 1982), p. 229.

ruined Lady Constantine becoming the 'spiritual queen of Melchester' (*Tower* 184) after passing off Swithin's child as the middle-aged bishop's. Hardy's tone here shows that while he was able to confront and entertain disaster in a resourceful manner during *A Laodicean*, in his next published novel his personal penchant for irony, mischief and the incongruous is itself galling, making the general prospect seem worse, not better.

The same tension and bitterness behind an incongruous situation imbues the portrayal of Swithin's marriage preparations in the tower cabin. Hardy's roving archaeological imagination again charges the Speer with arresting associations, but the disenchanted tone of the writing remains the dominant quality. Hardy considers the issue that was a source of such ugly controversy in the final novels: the features of a genuine marriage and its relationship to the religious rite and the legal contract, which guarantees its social acceptance. In *A Laodicean,* Hardy might have countered the oppressive fact of an unbridgeable gulf between primitive and modern conceptions of marriage by adopting a fresh way of observing it; here the 'find' remains painfully stark, the narrative voice almost despairing.

> It was a strange place for a bridegroom to perform his toilet in, but considering the unconventional nature of the marriage a not inappropriate one. What events had been enacted in that earthen camp since it was first thrown up nobody could say; but the primitive simplicity of the young man's preparations accorded well with the prehistoric spot on which they were made. Embedded under his feet were possibly even now rude trinkets that had been worn at bridal ceremonies of the early inhabitants. Little signified those ceremonies to-day, or the happiness or otherwise of the contracting parties. (*Tower* 118)

This sharp representation of incongruity, striking a note of irrecoverable loss, is unalleviated by any nimble flourishes of alternative perspective. Hardy focuses on young rabbits watching Swithin's 'preparations through the open door from the grey dawn without, as he bustled half-dressed in and out under the boughs, and among the blackberries and brambles that grew around' (*Tower* 117-18). It is as if Hardy wants to believe Swithin has the 'primitive simplicity' to establish a rapport with his prehistoric surroundings, and be subsumed in the natural world like the partially blind, furze-cutting Clym Yeobright on Egdon Heath. But to establish this kind of primal link is unfeasible for a dispassionate agent of modernism.

In *A Laodicean* there was a spirited insouciance in the 'New Light' Paula taking possession of Stancy Castle, a medieval 'survival'. However, there can be no such harmony between the astronomer and his even older surroundings; for as Seymour-Smith observes, Swithin is a 'hard-faced Darwinian',[71] a rationalist agnostic scholar whose training renders him incapable of fully immersing himself in the eerie ambience of the site, beneath which many 'ancient Britons lie buried' (*Tower* 60). Swithin aspires to join that astronomical elite who 'spend the best years of their lives in recording for the benefit of a remote posterity the actual state of the heavens.'[72] Swithin cannot be assessed as a vigorous modern equivalent of the ancient seers and sun-worshippers who stood on more basic temple-towers and mediated between the heavenly and sublunary realm, blessed with the almost magical gift of decoding the riddles of the stellar universe. Although Rings-Hill Speer is 'the temple of that sublime mystery on whose threshold he stood as priest' (*Tower* 61), Swithin is a clear replacement of that ancient type utterly divorced from him in attitude, function and sympathy. Hardy concedes that his own handling of incongruity is making the general scene bleaker not better, and looks *beyond* the human for fecundating energies, but exposes only 'horror' at the intractable 'vacancy' of the night sky.

> There were gloomy deserts in those southern skies such as the north shows scarcely an example of...The inspection of these chasms brought [Swithin] a second pulsation of that old horror which he had used to describe to Viviette as produced in him by bottomlessness in the north heaven. The ghostly finger of limitless vacancy touched him now on the other side...Space here, being less the historic haunt of human thought than overhead at home, seemed to be pervaded with a more lonely loneliness. (*Tower* 268)

The 'lonely loneliness' reflects Hardy's anxious sense that language does not possess the expressive resources to capture in consolingly human or familiar terms the awesome vastness of astronomical distance. That the world revealed by Swithin's telescope is at once frightening and indifferent would have resonated with Tennyson, for whom astronomy was one of the 'terrible muses' (geology being the other) in his poem 'Parnassus' (1889).[73] These two sciences were often connected in that they both opened up

---

[71] Martin Seymour-Smith, *Hardy* (London: Bloomsbury, 1995), p. 292.

[72] Anon., 'Sir John Herschel's *Astronomical Observations at the Cape of Good Hope*', *Quarterly Review* 85 (June 1849), 8.

[73] Swithin's account of 'the voids and waste places of the sky' also looks backwards to the third lyric of Tennyson's *In Memoriam*: 'From our waste places comes a cry,/And murmurs from the dying sin.'

perspectives that seemed to dwarf humankind and its history. [74] Sir Charles Lyell throughout his *Principles of Geology* (1830-33), compares the 'immensity of past time' revealed by Victorian geology to the austere 'sublimity' of the astronomer's gaze: 'Worlds are seen beyond worlds immeasurably distant from each other, and beyond them all, innumerable other systems are faintly traced on the confines of the visible universe'.[75] In 1885 Hardy noted the following from a review on Henry Amiel: 'To look on our own time from the point (of view) of universal history, on history from the point of view of geological periods, on geology from the point of view of astronomy – that is to enfranchise thought.'[76] But Hardy cannot react buoyantly to the existential emptiness of this vision in *Two on a Tower*, for he is fast losing faith in his ability to offer sanguine ways of registering the 'unacceptable'. In this disquieting incident *Two on a Tower* foreshadows that crisis point when all the resources of Hardy's art conspire to produce a feeling of unmitigated desolation.

A Laodicean was effective 'sanctuary' for Hardy after the potentially oppressive discoveries made in *The Return of the Native*; a chance to fully exercise a dextrous wit that not only offset previous distress but made us see late-nineteenth century England, and the immense forces shaping it, from idiosyncratic angles. In his treatment of Stancy Castle there are few signs of a writer who 'could not forgive the progress that was destroying old legend, folklore, and rustic individuality'.[77] Hardy would not have wished, like Tennyson's elderly spokesman in 'Locksley Hall Sixty Years After', observing a civilization in ceaseless flux, to stifle the cry of progress 'till ten thousand years have gone'.[78] Although alert to the ways in which they could be corrupted, Hardy is generally thrilled by the new inventions set amid a crumbling edifice that could make the farthest reaches of the earth less isolated. But in the description of the galaxies overhead in *Tower* there is an overpowering feeling of blighted hope which typifies Hardyan incongruity in the novel as a whole, because the subtle varieties of tone which his humour can accommodate are not permitted anything like as free

---

[74] See Jim Barbon, 'Star-Crossed Love: The Gravity of Science in Thomas Hardy's *Two on a Tower*', *Victorian Newsletter* 94 (Fall 1998), 27-32.

[75] Sir Charles Lyell, *The Principles of Geology, Being an Attempt to Explain the Former Changes of the Earth's Surface, by Reference to Causes now in Operation*, 3 vols. (London: John Murray, 1830-33), I, 63.

[76] Thomas Hardy, *Literary Notebooks*, I, 1340.

[77] Jerome Hamilton Buckley, *The Triumph of Time. A Study of the Victorian Concepts of Time, History, Progress and Decadence* (Cambridge, Mass.: Harvard University Press, 1966), p. 63.

[78] Alfred Lord Tennyson, 'Locksley Hall Sixty Years After' (1.78), *The Poems of Tennyson*, III, 228.

an expression. This is the principal reason why *Two on a Tower* is a slighter story than *A Laodicean*. Often passed over in embarrassed silence by Hardy scholars, *A Laodicean* evinces a determination to sustain wonder against the imminence of historical upheaval. Around Stancy Castle he weaves disparate bygone moments and locates positive reminders of artistic strength and coherence. This technique attests his bravery in grappling with the unhappier implications of his own unique artistic vision. However *Two on a Tower*, written at a mid-point in Hardy's literary career (twelve years after *Desperate Remedies* and twelve years before *Jude*), is a more uneasy and fitful work, at times even tragic, in which the menacing threat of time is felt more than its soothing promise of social amelioration.[79] The puckish Hardy of *A Laodicean* who thrives on the anomalous position 'survivals' occupy in contemporary culture is increasingly troubled in *Two on a Tower* by his own witty address; sensing its inadequacy to allay the flagrant hypocrisy besetting his cultural moment. Consequently, he puts more emphasis on social issues themselves in the mature fiction, thus widening the breach between his natural imaginative habits and the pointed social critique.

At this stage in his literary career, Hardy's attitude to the English bourgeoisie becomes more impatient and abrasive, showing how 'instincts did not square well with the formalities' of 'existence' (*Tower* 48); and his richest vein of satirical vivacity turns in on itself. Yet the anthropological material contained in these two novels prepare for *Tess*'s elaborate use of mythic themes. *A Laodicean*'s incident involving Captain de Stancy secretly spying on Paula Power in her gymnasium has been frequently rejected as fatuous, but Hardy uses the ironical backcloth of myth to comment on irrational forces that are unleashed for destructive human ends. Hardy's reading of Tylor may have encouraged his tendency to see myth as linguistic amber preserving the most powerful mental processes of the earliest epochs. John Addington Symonds was in no doubt that 'the truth to be looked for in myths is psychological'.[80] Max Müller contested that myths are 'antiquities...showing us, far better than any stone weapons or stone idols, the growth of the human mind during a period which, as yet, is full of the most perplexing problems to the psychologist, the historian, and the theologian'.[81] During an age of widespread disruption, the quest for

---

[79] Irving Howe suggests however, in *Thomas Hardy* (New York: Macmillan, 1967), Ch. 4, that *Two on a Tower* is romantic comedy.

[80] John Addington Symonds, *Studies of the Greek Poets*, 2 vols. (London: Smith, Elder & Co., 1873), II, 15. Hardy's friend Edward Clodd was also confident that mythography would illuminate 'the genesis and development of mind'. See *Myths and Dreams* (London: Chatto & Windus, 1885), p. 5.

[81] Quoted in E. B. Tylor, 'South-Sea Island Mythology', *Quarterly Review* 142 (1876), 235.

mythical roots that gains momentum in the mature fiction might convey a sense of temporal continuity for the self. In 1822 Hartley Coleridge asserted that 'Man is not so utterly changed as to discern no truth or fitness in that...pile of representative fiction, which Greece built up in the years of her pride and energy'.[82] Hardy's unique version of the Actaeon and Diana tale, and his portrayal of Dare as a Dionysus figure, suggests that he believed we could recognize ourselves in mythical images of the bygone victories, struggles and defeats of humanity. 'The myths of the Greeks and Aryans', wrote Andrew Lang, 'are charged with the wildest, most incredible, most absurd, and morally most abominable narratives.'[83] Yet Hardy implies that ancient myth, and the often nonrational, violent and disorienting elements it includes, may help readers to reconcile themselves to the unavoidable constraints inflicted, by nature and by civilized society, upon the human condition through all history. It is this sense of a possible mental connection with his remotest forebears that Hardy becomes increasingly preoccupied with in the final novels. The role he plays in the rediscovery of mythic themes, probing 'the times of the Classical Dictionary' (*Tower* 9) in modernist literature, should therefore not be underestimated.

---

[82] Hartley Coleridge, 'On the Poetical Use of the Heathen Mythology', *London Magazine* 5 (1822), 119. More than fifty years later, W. A. Gill would argue that myth articulated many 'truths' relevant to poetry, religion, history and natural science. See 'The Origin and Interpretation of Myths', *Macmillan's Magazine* 56 (1887), 121.

[83] Andrew Lang, 'Myths and Mythologists', *Nineteenth Century* 19 (1886), 58.

Chapter 5

The Unmanned Fertility Figure

The Mayor of Casterbridge (1886)

> A spacious bow-window projected into the street over the main portico, and from the open sashes came the babble of voices, the jingle of glasses, and the drawing of corks. The blinds moreover being left unclosed the whole interior of this room could be surveyed from the top of a flight of stone steps...for which reason a knot of idlers had gathered there...
>
> The interior of the hotel dining-room was spread out before her, with its tables, and glass, and plate, and inmates. Facing the window, in the chair of dignity, sat a man about forty years of age...
>
> Susan Henchard's husband, in law at least, sat before them...He was dressed in an old-fashioned evening suit, an expanse of frilled shirt showing on his broad breast; jewelled studs, and a heavy gold chain. (33-4)[1]

When Susan and her daughter arrive in Casterbridge, Michael Henchard is seemingly at the apex of his mercantile prosperity and political prominence in the county town, celebrating his mayoral authority at a grand formal dinner.[2] Hardy offers a carefully detailed yet deliberately superficial view of the First Citizen, whose ostentatiously impressive appearance is signalled by 'jewelled studs' and a 'heavy gold chain'. The bow window separating this scene of civic ritual at the best hotel almost places a stage-frame around the great feast and implies that Henchard's status as the most

---

[1] Thomas Hardy, *The Mayor of Casterbridge*, ed. with introd. Dale Kramer (Oxford: The World's Classics, 1987). Hereafter referred to as *Mayor*. The main part of action falls between 1846 and 1849, and in timescale it follows immediately after *The Return of the Native* whose action belongs to 1842-43.

[2] In Robert Barnes's illustrations accompanying *The Mayor*'s serialization in *The Graphic*, Henchard seems not just a fine, upstanding Victorian gentleman but almost a monumental figure while presiding over Casterbridge as its First Citizen. See Philip V. Allingham, 'Robert Barnes' Illustrations for Thomas Hardy's *The Mayor of Casterbridge* as Serialised in *The Graphic*', *Victorian Periodicals* 28:1 (Spring 1995), 27-39. Also Arlene M. Jackson, *Illustration and the Novels of Thomas Hardy* (Totowa, New Jersey: Rowman & Littlefield, 1981), pp. 96-105.

illustrious member of the town-council (*Mayor* 37) is specular rather than authentic. Indeed, he appears suspiciously like the Henchard effigy of the later skimmity-ride: a 'stuffed figure, with a false face' (*Mayor* 277). The King's Arms episode derives its dramatic impact from the incongruous images of a scornfully sober and impeccably dressed Henchard presiding over a sumptuous meal in his honour, and the impoverished young hay-trusser who nineteen years earlier auctions his wife and child in a fit of drunken frustration at Weydon-Priors Fair. Even the watching Susan is stunned by the nature of her husband's transformation: 'When last she had seen him he was sitting in a corduroy jacket, fustian waistcoat and breeches, and tanned leather leggings, with a basin of hot furmity before him. Time the magician had wrought much here' (*Mayor* 35). Hardy telescopes the timespan between the present and the earlier picture so that the revelation to Susan of her labourer husband as a local luminary contrasts all the more sharply with her painful recollections of his surly aggressiveness. That this wayward, captious and inarticulate rustic now acts both as a churchwarden and chief magistrate, indicates the darker tone of a novel in which Hardyan incongruity, while it has never been merely whimsical or ebullient, has become a tool of subversion rather than diversion. The way Henchard is perceived here as the epitome of bourgeois probity is constantly at variance with what he really is.

Besides his mayoral duties, Henchard holds the social function of leading corn-factor, but by supplying bad flour which makes bread that runs all over the ovens, he has not met his basic obligation to the community standing outside the King's Arms. He has overreached himself; and we learn that there has never been such 'unprincipled' bread in the town before (*Mayor* 32). Hardy uses the adjective not just to convey dialectal vigour but to place in a derisive light Henchard's meteoric ascent to the position of judicial and economic head of Casterbridge. Ironically, this 'corn-king', who appears elevated well beyond the harm of petty criticism, is actually on the brink of financial collapse, and must bear responsibility for polluting the staff of life. He deserves immediate dethronement instead of being lionized. Although he nonchalantly converted his wife and child into cash at Weydon-Priors Fair, he cannot reverse the deleterious organic processes that have already taken place in Casterbridge, and make 'wholesome' the 'growed' wheat (starting to sprout in the ear before being gathered). Hardy, through his withering depiction of the feast and the furore surrounding the bad grain, indicates a fundamental failure of confidence in Henchard's position as prime corn-factor. In this bustling farming town which is the 'pole, focus, or nerve-knot of the surrounding countryside', fertility is the people's most highly prized value:

'the subjects of discussion were corn...sowing and reaping, fencing and planting' (*Mayor* 62); shops are replete with agricultural equipment; and even the rain floats 'like meal'. But Henchard is preoccupied with accumulating capital instead of fulfilling his role as spokesman for and servant of the populace. His grip on the corn-trade is slipping, and for this the poorer folk must suffer. The banquet is a mock representation of worldly and material supremacy: a puppet show of empty poses hiding a disreputable past.

Hardy mingles the black farce of an almost bankrupt Henchard and his half-drunken merchant cronies toasting what is in truth his fragile official authority with the more sombre vision of Casterbridge's 'plainer fellows' (*Mayor* 33) standing outside in the street gaping at the dissipation. These 'plainer fellows', although scholars have frequently debated their choric function, act more precisely as a 'congregation', observing a ceremonial at whose centre is the mayor – not in affectionate awe but with deep disenchantment now. The arrogant insensitivity of Henchard and his colleagues as they listen to the strains of a song called 'The Roast Beef of England' (*Mayor* 32), reveals how out of touch he has become with the mood of the hungry townspeople. Hardy implies, as he does in many other occasions of secular binding together in the novels, that there may be a pagan undercurrent to the King's Arms spectacle. A cursory glance reveals no obvious link between the august formality of Henchard's banquet and paganism. However, it is said of the mayor's wealthier guests: 'Three drinks seemed to be sacred to the company – port, sherry and rum; outside which old-established trinity few or no palates ranged' (*Mayor* 35). Hardy slyly undercuts the Christian associations of the language, reminding us of the rum-laced furmity concocted in a witch's cauldron at Weydon-Priors Fair,[3] whose echoes of ancient practice and suspension of moral standards commemorate a more heretical, 'underworld' fertility.[4] The primitive-wife auction in the seamy, claustrophobic Furmity Tent demolishes the

---

[3] 'A haggish creature of about fifty...slowly stirred the contents of the pot' (*Mayor* 8).

[4] George Laurence Gomme observes: 'In Dorsetshire and Wiltshire fairs are held upon sites which are often marked by the remains of ancient works, or distinguished by some dim tradition of vanished importance'. See *Folklore as an Historical Science* (London: Methuen & Co., 1908), p. 45. Greenhill sheep-fair in *Far from the Madding Crowd* is held on the 'remains of an ancient earthwork' (348). See also Robert W. Malcolmson, 'The liberating powers of drink at fairs and festivities were commonly celebrated in popular stories and songs: moderation, at these times, could be abandoned, restraint thrown aside, and immoderation flaunted to the full.' *Popular Recreations in English Society, 1700-1850* (Cambridge: Cambridge University Press, 1973), pp. 76-7.

sacramental union of Christian marriage.[5] In this atavistic episode, Henchard ritualistically casts off his wife as if she were the malign influence that has shattered his prospects.

Hardy would have appreciated the pagan resonance of communal feasting described in antiquarian collections such as John Brand's *Popular Antiquities*. This afforded a huge unsifted mass of data on which he may have drawn more than once in depicting festivities like mumming and the maypole-dance. Brand explained that feast occasions similar to Henchard's ceremonial dinner were often associated with holidays, and, although the pre-Christian origins of certain holidays were forgotten over time, these gatherings were still essential for the unity of the family or other social groups because they gave participants an opportunity to rejoice in their own well-being. Tranter Dewy's Christmas revel in *Under the Greenwood Tree* performs this salutary function, creating an enabling atmosphere of protective fellowship, and is arguably the most successful communal meal in the Wessex novels. As Hardy's perception of the struggle between natural impulse and bourgeois protocol grows more despondent, so his treatment of feasting darkens, and the occasions – Bathsheba's shearing-supper, Mrs Yeobright's tea-party for her returned son Clym, Giles Winterborne's 'roaring supper' for the Melburys – become increasingly tarnished by paltry concerns for caste. The King's Arms banquet is a more complex experience than these other moments because there would be nothing improper in Henchard placing an extreme stress on class distinctions if he and the other 'initiates' held the unconditional trust and esteem of those watching. The notion of Henchard asserting his 'apartness' from the assembled throng on the pavement is sound; the circumstances rather make it wrong: tactless at best, inflammatory at worst. The shutters of the King's Arms bow window are purposely left open so that the uninvited townsfolk can witness the magnificence of an elaborate banquet. But Hardy's grim facetious humour strips the social veneer from the First Citizen's elder guests, who are 'sniffing and grunting over their plates like sows nuzzling for acorns' (*Mayor* 35).

Henchard, although our initial glimpse of him as a public dignitary is defined by pomp and lavish fare, ends up starving to death on Egdon Heath in a mud hovel that anticipates the primitive shelter under which Winterborne deteriorates in *The Woodlanders*. Both men die in the midst of a nature with whose rhythms they are supposed to have an instinctive rapport (the mayor also acts as hay-merchant; Winterborne is a tree-planter

---

[5] See Leonora Epstein, 'Sale and Sacrament: The Wife Auction in *The Mayor of Casterbridge*', *English Language Notes* 24:4 (June 1987), 50-56; Thomas J. Tobin, 'Women as Others in *The Mayor of Casterbridge*', *McNeese Review* 36 (1998), 19-36.

and cider-maker). Hardy portrays these two men as fertility figures whose powers of promoting social cohesion, wealth and plenty are no longer operant. Hardy's chronicle of their downfall invites comparison with James Frazer's conception of the priest guarding the shrine of the fertility goddess Diana at Nemi,[6] whose strangeness and barbarity are evoked in the opening pages of *The Golden Bough* (1890). Although scholars have treated the feud between Henchard and the man who ousts him, the young Scot Farfrae, as a direct confrontation of two fundamentally antithetical types, the Frazerian perspective has not been employed. The custom of killing the priest-king of Nemi occurred either when his physical and sexual potency appeared to be vanishing or at the close of a reign of preordained length.[7] Defeating the priest in single combat was meant to dispel any disease or affliction so that the vitality of life might continue unhampered. A candidate for the priesthood only succeeded to office 'by slaying the priest, and having slain him, he retained office till he was himself slain by a stronger or a craftier'.[8] Hardy could not have known the ritual of unceasing assassination at Nemi, but he was familiar with country festivities of a sort that afforded the more homely staple – mumming, the sword dance, children's ceremonial games – which survived longest in local life precisely because they enacted a form of elemental combat. The quarrel between Farmer Boldwood and his tormentor Sergeant Troy for Bathsheba's hand in *Far from the Madding Crowd* (1874) is an early anticipation of this conflict between opposing forces (illustrated by 'John Barleycorn' and countless other folksongs).

Frazer's account of the fertility priest at Nemi and the violent ritual to which he must submit offers itself as a means of addressing the dominant course of events in *The Mayor* and *The Woodlanders*. Both novels focus on a native countryman's quarrel with, and gradual displacement by, an educated figure from afar, 'seemingly possessed of mysterious powers'.[9] The middle-aged Henchard feels a duty to defend his territory against the threat of a youthful pretender, and he repeatedly provokes Farfrae to contests of manliness and commercial acumen, without grasping that the two are not the same. Henchard's prolonged and fruitless battle with Farfrae, whose newfangled methods of economy the mayor can neither comprehend nor surpass, is what drives the earlier story along. Henchard

---

[6] Hardy mentions 'Diana Multimammia' towards the end of *The Mayor* (330), which refers particularly to her temple at Ephesus where she was depicted with many breasts.

[7] The Mayor of Casterbridge is elected annually to control the town's affairs.

[8] James Frazer, *The Golden Bough*, p. 11.

[9] Michael Millgate, *Thomas Hardy: His Career as a Novelist* (London: Bodley Head, 1971), p. 249.

cannot win because he is a corn-king displaced into corn-dealing, where the Scot will of course reign supreme because his skills of enlightened industry are much better attuned to the evolving agricultural order. The older man's potency should be directed towards the growing of grain, not the dealing in it. Hardy uses martial rhetoric to dramatize the escalation of the vendetta:

> A time came when, avoid collision with his former friend as he might, Farfrae was compelled, in sheer self-defence, to close with Henchard in mortal commercial combat...As soon as their war of prices began everybody was interested, and some few guessed the end. It was, in some degree, Northern insight matched against Southron doggedness – the dirk against the cudgel – and Henchard's weapon was one which, if it did not deal ruin at the first or second stroke, left him afterwards well-nigh at his antagonist's mercy. (*Mayor* 116)

Although Henchard is determined to conquer his adversary, his 'weapon' does not 'deal ruin at the first or second stroke' because the 'amazing energy' (*Mayor* 114) for which he was once widely venerated is now moribund. His social and economic eclipse by Farfrae is effectively conveyed through the competing festive entertainments each man organizes for the townspeople of Casterbridge. In contrast to his King's Arms banquet, the figurehead mayor tries to dissolve the proprieties of social distance and establish kinship with those less fortunate than himself when he holds his abortive event upon 'an ancient square earthwork' (*Mayor* 104). Henchard, hoping to humiliate Farfrae by projecting himself as virile leader of the agricultural community, provides 'a mammoth tea, of which everybody who lived in the borough was invited to partake without payment'. But this flamboyantly generous act, supposedly designed to foster social cohesiveness and avow common interests, is an even bigger failure than the Christmas party Winterborne arranges for Grace Melbury in *The Woodlanders*. Henchard's proposed merrymaking is washed out by rain, and its dismal conclusion in a solemn distribution of food to the poor and needy clashes with the unforced gaiety, music and dancing of his opponent's party, which shows the logistical proficiency of a resourceful business mind. Farfrae wins popularity by keeping his rival entertainment dry with the aid of an ingeniously constructed tent.

Henchard's increasingly acrimonious contest with Farfrae for control of the market town and the corn upon which it depends, is given added richness by Hardy's sophisticated historical vision. He illuminates the main dramatic action of 'Northern insight matched against Southron doggedness' (*Mayor* 116) by placing it against a scrupulously detailed backdrop of discord and strife down the centuries. The locale is 'dotted with barrows, and trenched with the remains of prehistoric forts' (*Mayor* 18), such as 'Mai Dun, of huge dimensions and many ramparts' (*Mayor* 310). Casterbridge appears 'haunted by history',[10] but specifically a history of conflict (Celtic versus Roman, Saxon versus Norman), whose latest enactment is the rancorous trade-war between Henchard and his Scottish opponent. In this region cluttered with the rubble of bygone battles, Hardy elaborates two topographical features that 'comment' on the central event: the Roman amphitheatre[11] and High-Place Hall. That Hardy gives such prominence to these 'survivals' in the novel may reflect the extent of his involvement with antiquarian ventures between 1880 and 1886. This included his joining the Society for the Protection of Ancient Buildings and The Dorset Natural History and Antiquarian Field Club, as well as his designing and constructing Max Gate. The amphitheatre has witnessed such gruesome spectacles as gladiatorial combats during the Roman occupation and later executions on the town gibbet, as well as more recent 'pugilistic encounters almost to the death' (*Mayor* 73). The ancient arena has lost little of its aura of disharmony, even though the days of crude physical encounter may be over. In the forbidding solitude of this site, Henchard arranges to meet the wife he humiliated and sold nearly twenty years ago:

> Casterbridge announced old Rome in every street, alley, and precinct. It looked Roman, bespoke the art of Rome, concealed dead men of Rome. It was impossible to dig more than a foot or two deep about the town fields and gardens without coming upon some tall soldier or other of the Empire, who had lain there in his silent unobtrusive rest for the space of fifteen hundred years...
>
> The amphitheatre was a huge circular enclosure, with a notch at opposite extremities of its diameter north and south...It was to Casterbridge what the ruined Coliseum is to modern Rome, and was nearly of the same magnitude... Melancholy, impressive, lonely, yet accessible from every part of the town, the historic circle was the frequent spot for appointments of a furtive kind...But one kind of

---

[10] Craig Raine, 'Conscious Artistry in *The Mayor of Casterbridge*', in Charles P. C. Pettit (ed.), *New Perspectives on Thomas Hardy* (London: Macmillan, 1994), p. 169.

[11] The Roman amphitheatre of Maumbury Ring in Dorchester was partially excavated in the early autumn of 1908, with follow-up excavations over the next few years, and shown to have been of Neolithic origin. Hardy was a fascinated observer at some of the 1908 digs and found himself mentioned in a few of the reports of the activity that appeared in *The Times* (e.g. 24 September 1908). On 30 September Charles Moberly Bell, of *The Times*, wrote and invited Hardy to contribute some reflections of his own. The resulting article is reprinted in Michael Millgate (ed.), *Thomas Hardy's Public Voice*, pp. 284-90.

appointment – in itself the most common of any – seldom had place
in the amphitheatre; that of happy lovers. (*Mayor* 70-71)

In his 'Presidential Address' to the first 'Proceeding' of The Dorset
Natural History and Antiquarian Field Club, J. C. Mansel-Pleydell called
this Roman amphitheatre 'one of the most perfect of the kind in Great
Britain'.[12] And yet so unpleasant are the memories that inhabit the Ring in
Hardy's rendering that no romantic liaisons occur there. He exploits with
malicious glee the incongruity of Henchard choosing this baleful spot to
resurrect his marriage with Susan, a secluded earthwork that has held
notorious public executions like that of Mary Channing in 1705, 'who had
murdered her husband' and 'was half strangled' then 'burnt there in the
presence of ten thousand spectators' (*Mayor* 71).[13]

Casterbridge contains not only a site of primitive struggle in the Roman
Ring – an arena 'still smooth and circular, as if used for its original purpose
not so very long ago' (*Mayor* 72) – but also the nearby corn-market which
has become the modern 'centre and arena of the town' (*Mayor* 181), where
the 'spectacular drama' of Henchard and Farfrae's 'trade-antagonism'
(*Mayor* 115) is enacted. Overlooking the corn-market is High-Place Hall,
the residence of Henchard's former mistress Lucetta. The extraordinary
position of her mansion in the county town – a point at which the genteel
upper world and the cheerless underworld collide – throws into unexpected
relief the theme of dissension and rivalry which more obviously touches the
amphitheatre. The market-face of the Hall with its Palladian symmetry and
reasonableness,[14] is macabrely counterpointed by the rear of the house
whose contorted mask stares at 'one of the little-used alleys of the town'.[15]

[12]   John Clavel Mansel-Pleydell, 'Presidential Address', *Proceedings of the Dorset Natural
History and Antiquarian Field Club* 1 (1876), 8.
[13]   In John Cowper Powys's semi-autobiographical novel *Maiden Castle* (1936), Dud No-
Man, a novelist, writes his own version of Hardy's *Mayor of Casterbridge* in the form of the
story of Mary Channing. Dud's hasty purchase (for eighteen pounds) of the young
equestrienne Wizzie Ravelston from a circus near Dorchester recalls Henchard's sale of
Susan and Elizabeth-Jane for five guineas in *The Mayor*.
[14]   The Palladian style, a dominant architectural style in England from 1715 to 1760, is often
characterized by academic adherence to classical forms. Squire Dornell's Falls-Park
residence in 'The First Countess of Wessex' from *A Group of Noble Dames* (1891), boasts a
'Palladian front' from whose 'regular features' it derived 'a dignity which the great, many-
gabled, heterogenous mansion of his wife could not eclipse.' The new house that Barnet
builds in 'Fellow-Townsmen' is another example of Palladian architecture. See *Wessex
Tales*, ed. with introd. Kathryn R. King (Oxford: The World's Classics, 1991), p. 117.
[15]   Hardy's bizarre placing of High-Place Hall is reminiscent of Henry Knight's Bede's Inn
residence from *A Pair of Blue Eyes* (1873), strangely situated in the midst of opposing
currents of metropolitan movement: the postern 'abuts on as crowded and poverty-stricken a
network of alleys as are to be found anywhere in the capital' (*Eyes* 180).

Around this building Hardy weaves associations of a chill menace, and the spirit of incongruity informing his portrait offers a telling contrast to *A Laodicean*'s prankish activity:

> Looking round at the door which had given her egress...[Elizabeth-Jane] saw that it was arched and old – older even than the house itself. The door was studded, and the keystone of the arch was a mask. Originally the mask had exhibited a comic leer, as could still be discerned; but generations of Casterbridge boys had thrown stones at the mask, aiming at its open mouth; and the blows thereon had chipped off the lips and jaws as if they had been eaten away by disease...
>
> The position of the queer old door and the odd presence of the leering mask suggested one thing above all others as appertaining to the mansion's past history – intrigue. By the alley it had been possible to come unseen from all sorts of quarters in the town – the old play-house, the old bull-stake, the old cock-pit, the pool, wherein nameless infants had been used to disappear. (*Mayor* 141-2)

The Hall, to which Henchard pays surreptitious visits to reach some agreement with Lucetta on their future relationship, reflects the mayor's status as a failing fertility figure, already intimated at the King's Arms. The placing and physical attributes of this residence express something of the discrepancy between slick surface and raw reality informing the grand dinner. The Hall's facade implies an image of senatorial splendour and grace that Henchard strives to project as First Citizen. But behind the trappings of affluence are unmistakable signs of spoiled fecundity: the Hall's heraldic emblem, formerly depicting a 'comic leer', now has chipped lips and jaws hinting at syphilitic dissolution, and reminds us of the damaged seed which undermines Henchard's credibility in the eyes of the hungry townspeople. Lucetta's mansion sits awkwardly not just in a street that backs onto a dingy alleyway from which a wanderer could reach a 'pool' where illegitimate children were drowned (another sign of spoilt fertility), but is a disturbingly surreal presence in a historical novel defined by fastidious realistic detail, evoking with antiquarian gusto an era before 'time and progress' obliterated 'many or most of the old-fashioned features' (*Mayor* 61 n.) of the town near which Hardy had been born in 1840, and in which he had been educated and employed until 1862. His Casterbridge is not a purely imaginative construction like Anthony Trollope's Barchester, and it is more meticulously observed than R. D. Blackmore's Exmoor setting in the popular historical novel *Lorna Doone* (1869). But the sordid back portion of Lucetta's mansion recalls the Gothic gloom and nightmarish intensity of Dickens's London in *Bleak House*

(1853), where the pristine veneer of aristocratic homes blinds an observer to the presence of nearby disease-ridden tenements.[16] This is far from being the 'dear, delightful Wessex'[17] implied by the tasteful facade of Lucetta's mansion, and emphasizes perhaps the most unsettling incongruity of all: that a picturesque and seemingly flourishing market town closely integrated with the surrounding cornfields should contain Mixen Lane.[18] The ever-worsening condition of the Lane, with its damp urban atmosphere, white-apron-wearing prostitutes and glaring symbols of crime (the gallows, gaol and hangman's cottage) is an index of Henchard's breakdown in his quasi-religious role as First Citizen. The damaged crop he supplies will have calamitous repercussions for the Lane, whose squalor is such that an 'altar of disease' might 'have been erected' there. That High-Place Hall shares with a Mixen Lane tavern called 'Peter's Finger' – arguably the most deprived and depraved portion of Casterbridge – the structural feature of two doors (and the back one associated with unlawful activity) is an irony whose impact is of a piece with the many ominous effects Hardy's witty repertoire has adopted since *A Laodicean*.

The Casterbridge slums, Roman ruins and High-Place Hall (from which wayfarers could reach 'the old bull-stake' and 'cock-pit') all afford lurid reminders of vicious 'blood sports': the savagery of a merciless competitive fight for survival at myriad moments in time. That Hardy's anthropological consciousness enables us to fix the gradual displacement and demise of Henchard in this context of turbulent encounter does not diminish the fact that the mayor's collapse is a uniquely tragic moment in parochial history. Henchard's fall as First Citizen is so compelling because he is the last genuine fertility figure, ejected by an individual markedly inferior to him in several respects. Although Farfrae makes the corn and hay traffic thrive as never before, and almost completely restores the blighted grain – indeed 'whatever he touched he prospered in' (*Mayor* 115) – we are never encouraged to see him, according to the seasonal rite of Frazer's defeated corn-king, as the replacement 'priest' who possesses foreknowledge of the land's fertility and a capacity to share in nature's secrets. His gift of curing the corrupted seed owes nothing to priestly magic but to strictly scientific endeavour. Through his exact use of modern methods such as 'ciphering and mensuration' (*Mayor* 107), the Scot wrests

---

[16] Hardy's evocation of High-Place Hall gainsays Lance St John Butler's contention that Casterbridge is 'almost as far removed from Dickens' London as the smallest villages in Wessex.' See *Thomas Hardy* (Cambridge: Cambridge University Press, 1978), p. 56.

[17] Thomas Hardy, *A Group of Noble Dames* (Dover: Alan Sutton, 1993), p. 42.

[18] Mixen Lane is to Hardy's Casterbridge what Tom-all-Alone's is to Dickens's London in *Bleak House* (1853).

control of Henchard's source of wealth, his substantial Georgian house in Corn Street and his women, first a would-be wife, then a would-be daughter. The unqualified success of his feast in town as opposed to Henchard's washed-out gathering resides in the precautionary measures of a cunning and wary rationalist. Hardy knows that Farfrae must prevail; but, as Geoffrey Thurley observes, 'Farfrae is not the stuff tragedy is made of'.[19]

Farfrae cannot fully assume his predecessor's mantle of fertility figure because he has no firm sense of the profoundly sacred; he goes through the motions of religious observance without accompanying them with the sincere intentions that give lasting human value.[20] The young Scot's relaxed easy-going temperament and lack of long-term goals, the very traits that enable him to ingratiate himself with sundry levels of Casterbridge society, indicate a personality whose blandness lends Henchard's fatally passionate nature an awesome magnitude. Unencumbered by the destructive changeability of his predecessor's emotions, the wily opportunist Farfrae modifies his actions to fit the circumstances. This is why his wooing of Lucetta seems perfunctory at best. Henchard's ruinous acts of rage carry more weight than Farfrae's manoeuvrings because he is capable of mythical stature.[21] The Scot's lukewarm, measured affections and tearful ditties for the country 'he loved so well as never to have revisited' are irrelevant next to Henchard's violent pride and ultimate desire to obliterate all vestiges of himself from Wessex.

Henchard embodies raw experience before the sophisticated evolution of concepts or metaphysical abstractions; he is himself a 'survival', the likes of which will never be seen again. Hardy conceives him not so much as a compilation of attributes to be dissected, as an anthropological phenomenon: an intensely literal individual, who understands his surroundings only when he has tangible contact with them. The animal and elemental imagery associated with him ('leonine', 'tigerish', 'a bull breaking fence', 'a great tree in the wind', his 'volcanic' temper) indicates the primitive past of brute strength still operant in his instinctual impulses, whose effects are devastating in a progressive modern civilization. Indeed, 'something fetichistic' (*Mayor* 19) resides in Henchard's beliefs: he lives by an ancient persuasion that meaning occupies the universe, but it is a

---

[19] Geoffrey Thurley, *The Psychology of Hardy's Novels: The Nervous and the Statuesque* (St. Lucia, Queensland: University of Queensland Press, 1975), p. 145.

[20] Contrast Henchard's penitential oath to abstain from alcohol that comes from the deepest core of his being, with Farfrae's superficial, bourgeois attitude to church-going.

[21] As C. M. Jackson-Houlston argues, Henchard possesses 'the tragic stature of a man of ancient times left stranded by the tides of the present'. See *Ballads, Songs and Snatches: The Appropriation of Folk Song and Popular Culture in British Nineteenth-century Realist Prose* (Aldershot: Ashgate, 1999), p. 154.

meaning that maliciously eludes him. The antiquarian James A. Farrer writes in *Primitive Manners and Customs* (1879):

> the fetichistic mode of thought is undoubtedly a low, and to us an absurd one. Burnings in effigy may probably be traced to it, and the stories so common in the annals of witchcraft of waxen images stuck with pins or burned, in order to injure a person they represented, undoubtedly belong to it.[22]

Henchard wonders towards the end of the novel whether 'somebody has been roasting a waxen effigy of me, or stirring an unholy brew to confound me! I don't believe in such power; and yet – what if they should ha' been doing it!' (*Mayor* 190). The Frazerian priest-kings of Nemi were regarded as possessing supernatural powers, but here Henchard thinks he is a hapless victim of magic, not a deft practitioner of it: 'he could not help thinking that the concatenation of events' was 'the scheme of some sinister intelligence bent on punishing him' (*Mayor* 127). On 18 December 1890, shortly after he finished writing *Tess*, Hardy made the following entry in his notebook:

> Mr. E. Clodd[23] this morning gives an excellently neat answer to my question why the superstitions of a remote Asiatic and a Dorset labourer are the same;– 'The attitude of man,' he says, 'at corresponding levels of culture, before like phenomena, is pretty much the same, your Dorset peasants representing the persistence of the barbaric idea which confuses persons and things, and founds wide generalizations on the slenderest analogies.'
> (This 'barbaric idea which confuses persons and things' is, by the way, also common to the highest imaginative genius – that of the poet.)[24]

Beneath the opulent props of selfhood displayed at his King's Arms feast, Henchard is similar to the 'Dorset labourer' of Clodd's description: unable to free himself from the 'barbaric idea which confuses persons and things'. This notion would become a cornerstone of Frazer's examination

---

[22] James A. Farrer, *Primitive Manners and Customs* (London: Chatto & Windus, 1879), p. 281.
[23] Edward Clodd was Hardy's friend and a popular mythographer of the 1880s. Clodd's contention was in fact the necessary foundation for comparative anthropology.
[24] Thomas Hardy, *Life*, p. 241. Hardy's wry parenthetic observation had precedent: E. B. Tylor, at the end of Chapter 8 of *Primitive Culture* (1871), writes: 'A poet of our own day has still much in common with the minds of uncultured tribes in the mythological stage of thought.'

of magic in the third edition (1911) of his *Golden Bough,* a phenomenon he subdivided into two related classes, homeopathic and contagious. Henchard fears the former kind in which a magician imitates the effect he wants to produce, often using an image of the person to be affected.[25] Moreover the mayor, who belongs to an earlier stage of mental evolution than Farfrae, perceives magic as a means not only of coercing the direction of his personal destiny but also the movements of the impersonal market. Why else would this First Citizen, surrounded by 'gentlepeople and such like leading volk' (*Mayor* 33) at the King's Arms, risk his reputation as a well-bred gentleman by secretly consulting a weather-prophet, Mr Fall, who lives on the seedy outskirts of town (*Mayor* 185)? Fall's nickname 'Wide-O', identifies Henchard's original sin (he widowed himself) as well as the zero he is fast becoming to his fellow councillors, creditors and subjects in Casterbridge. There is a strong element of bleak humour afforded by the 'clean-living' Henchard, an image of almost puritanical rigour at his sumptuous King's Arms dinner, adopting increasingly 'shady' (*Mayor* 73) tactics to win the 'commercial combat' with Farfrae. Martin Seymour-Smith's critical position – '*The Mayor of Casterbridge* is high tragedy, with little of Hardy's usual humour in it'[26] – does not quite reflect the blackly comic undercurrent in Hardy's depiction of Henchard's furtive consultation of the weather-prophet and his groping endeavours to shape events favourably. His meeting with the 'conjurer' encourages him to buy and store immense quantities of grain in the hope of foul weather and a sharp rise in prices, and when the first burst of sunshine causes him hastily to sell it off at a loss, nature turns violently against him as it did during his festive entertainment.

Henchard's final desperate bid to arrest Farfrae's rapid rise to the privileges he himself once enjoyed at the King's Arms, reveals Hardy's interest in a bygone moment greatly predating the construction of Mixen Lane, High-Place Hall or even the ancient Rome 'announced in every street, alley, and precinct' (*Mayor* 71). References to gladiatorial contests that once took place inside the 'deserted earthwork' (*Mayor* 72) prepare for the climactic primitive hand-to-hand duel enacted in the claustrophobic 'arena' of Farfrae's hayloft, the wrestling bout between the disgraced

---

[25] The antiquarian Charles Hardwick offers a less scientifically rigorous analysis of what Frazer eventually termed homeopathic or 'imitative' magic: 'Witches were supposed to compass the death of any obnoxious individual by making an image of the victim in wax. As this slowly melted before a fire, or under other applied heat, it was believed the original would in like manner sicken and decay. This superstition yet obtains to a great extent in the East.' *Traditions, Superstitions and Folk-Lore* (London: Simpkin, Marshall & Co., 1872; Manchester, England: E. J. Morten, 1973), p. 98.

[26] Martin Seymour-Smith, *Hardy* (London: Bloomsbury, 1995), p. 367.

former mayor and his Scottish successor. The transition from the grotesque comedy of a penniless, grubby Henchard playing a patriotic parody-mayor, offering to shake hands with the Royal Personage, to the fiery intensity of the wrestling in which the older man has the self-imposed handicap of one arm tied behind his back, is adroitly managed. After losing the 'commercial combat' (*Mayor* 116), Henchard feels the only means left of reasserting his superiority is by a trial of 'manliness' or physical strength. That he does not seize his opportunity and press home his murderous advantage over the prone Farfrae is due to his recalling the spontaneous affection he once felt for the Scot (*Mayor* 273). Henchard, a creature of strikingly primitive outlook, who 'could not catch his thoughts without pronouncing them' (*Mayor* 17), is destroyed when confronted by honest feeling, for he cannot carry out his ruthless design. Again, it is the apparently weaker antagonist who prevails. That the once overbearing Henchard, a male chauvinist whose 'haughty indifference' to females is 'well-known' in Casterbridge (*Mayor* 83),[27] now appears 'womanly' in his bearing is deeply disorientating. He is 'mastered' by the 'weaker' sex. His massive, vital frame seems to shatter:

> So thoroughly subdued was he that he remained on the sacks in a crouching attitude, unusual for a man, and for such a man. Its womanliness sat tragically on the figure of so stern a piece of virility. (*Mayor* 274)

Henchard is 'unmanned': a word first used in the Roman amphitheatre when he renounces his desire for revenge over Lucetta, agreeing to return her letters.

The unmanning of Hardy's fertility figure traditionally linked with thriving abundance in the agricultural world is not simply a case of a loss of confidence in Henchard's ability to 'read' nature's signs. Hardy makes an explicit connection between Henchard's loss of official position and dormant sexual energy. In previous novels, Hardy demonstrates the central overwhelming place of passion in human life through its predatory agents, Aeneas Manston, Francis Troy, Captain de Stancy, and Edred Fitzpiers in *The Woodlanders*, whose sexual behaviour has no regard for the artificial barriers of class. A principal concern that emerges from *A Laodicean* and *Two on a Tower* discussed in the previous chapter – showing how the injurious effects of passion are exacerbated by a repressive bourgeois morality – is extended in *The Mayor* and *The Woodlanders*. But in the earlier story Henchard's 'virility' (*Mayor* 274) is oddly lacking a sexual

---

[27] Henchard, as the Hardyan narrator says elsewhere, is a 'woman-hater' (*Mayor* 78).

component. Henchard has the bellicose temper that would lead us to expect a vigorous sexuality, not a solemn disavowal of it.[28] With subtlety Hardy raises the question of the relationship between agricultural and human fertility. Henchard never truly loves his first spouse Susan, and during the wife-auction at Weydon-Priors Fair he rails against the severe economic drain of marriage, ranting about the 'ruin of good men by bad wives' and the disintegration 'of many a promising youth's high aims and hopes...the extinction of his energies' (*Mayor* 10). After Susan dies Henchard accidentally discovers Elizabeth-Jane is not his daughter after all, but Newson's; his own child died a short time after the wife-sale. In Henchard, Hardy's typical pattern of a fatherless woman[29] is replaced by a wifeless and daughterless man – 'getting on towards the dead level of middle age' (*Mayor* 149) – lacking the human fertility to perpetuate his line. His business and fortune – and indeed his survival in the latter stages of the novel when, no longer able to supervise the autumnal harvest, he is relegated to petty retailer status in a humble seedman's shop 'overlooking the churchyard' (*Mayor* 240), relies on distributing other people's seed for the spring planting, yet he has surrendered control of his own. Human seed also fails to burgeon for his successor Farfrae, whose wife Lucetta dies while carrying his child, and their merger of commercial enterprise and inherited wealth ends without issue.

Frazer's scholarly quest to decipher the atavistic and inscrutable rites of kingly succession at Nemi involving the priest of 'Diana Multimammia' (*Mayor* 330), offers a challenging perspective on the dominant course of events in *The Mayor of Casterbridge*. The next section indicates that *The Woodlanders* invites a more informed Frazerian interpretation. Giles Winterborne is an enigmatic figure identified with the Hintock orchards as Michael Henchard is with the Casterbridge corn whose quality and profusion he cannot guarantee. Neither individual manages to safeguard his particular realm of nature from an insidious outside threat: Winterborne barely has sufficient resources to muster even a semblance of solid resistance. Hardy refines the situation of Frazerian conflict between the ailing 'priest' of the Hintock grove and a challenger who belongs to a higher (though not necessarily better) stage of cultural evolution. Roy Morrell's contention that Henchard's 'impulses' are 'to separate himself'

---

[28] Rosemary Sumner, taking the opposite position, argues that Henchard is capable of violent and extreme sexual feelings. See *Thomas Hardy: Psychological Novelist* (London: Macmillan, 1981), pp. 57-81.

[29] For example, Bathsheba Everdene in *Far from the Madding Crowd*, Thomasin Yeobright and Eustacia Vye in *The Return of the Native*, Anne Garland in *The Trumpet-Major*, and Paula Power in *A Laodicean*.

and 'to survive alone'[30] apply equally to the defeatist Winterborne at the
end of *The Woodlanders*, whose vocation Hardy briefly describes in *The
Mayor*:

> It happened that to-day there rose in the midst of them all two or
> three tall apple trees standing as if they grew on the spot; till it was
> perceived that they were held by men from the cider districts who
> came here to sell them, bringing the clay of their county on their
> boots. (*Mayor* 154)

The Woodlanders (1887)

> [Grace Melbury] flew round the fatal bush where the undergrowth
> narrowed to a gorge. Marty arrived at her heels just in time to see the
> result. Fitzpiers had quickly stepped forward in front of Winterborne,
> who, disdaining to shift his position had turned on his heel; and then
> the surgeon did what he would not have thought of doing but for Mrs
> Melbury's encouragement and the sentiment of an eve which effaced
> conventionality. Stretching out his arms as the white figure burst
> upon him he captured her in a moment, as if she had been a bird.
> (112)[31]

On Midsummer Eve the young women of Little Hintock participate in the
pagan survival of sowing hemp-seed under moonlight to cast a spell that
will bring forth a reaper (lover) into material form. Grace Melbury's
venture into this 'low' culture of nature-worship ironically results in
capture by a rakish member of 'high' society, the physician Edred
Fitzpiers. Hardy's use of the word 'captured' in this context may have had
a special resonance for readers in 1887 who had studied the pioneering
work of the social evolutionary tradition of anthropological research, such
as John McLennan's *Primitive Marriage: An Inquiry into the Origin of the
Form of Capture in Marriage Ceremonies* (1865).[32] For McLennan, 'the

---

[30] Roy Morrell, *Thomas Hardy: The Will and the Way* (Kuala Lumpur, Singapore:
University of Malaya Press, 1965), p. 24.

[31] All references are to Thomas Hardy, *The Woodlanders*, ed. with introd. Dale Kramer
(Oxford: The World's Classics, 1986). Hereafter referred to as *Woodlanders*.

[32] See also E. B. Tylor, 'On a Method of Investigating the Development of Institutions;
Applied to Laws of Marriage and Descent', *Journal of the Anthropological Institute* 18
(November 1888), 245-72. As well as being an effectively condensed summary of twenty-
five years of social evolutionary argument, this paper reflects to what extent marriage by
capture had been an issue of sharp controversy among Tylor's peers since the publication of
McLennan's *Primitive Marriage* in 1865. Hardy, in an 1895 letter to his friend Edward

central idea in the symbol' of marriage by capture 'was the carrying off of the woman, in defiance of her kindred and of their efforts to protect her'.[33] Giles Winterborne's[34] failure to shield Grace from the advances of his more cosmopolitan romantic rival indicates to what extent the ethos of the urban sophisticate has diminished the vigour of Little Hintock and its traditional forms and agents. Critical orthodoxy, while it has registered this crisis, does not explore fully how these two male figures embody contrasting perceptions of power at play in the dense, all-enclosing forest setting. The native Winterborne paradoxically appears both literally and metaphorically out of touch during this vivid scene because he is enfeebled (and ultimately killed) by the *chivalrous* mentality that, in a stable social structure, should belong to Fitzpiers, whose Arthurian-Norman name implies cultivation and urbanity in its modish antiquity. The chivalry infecting and working through Winterborne – leaving him a sterile asexual force – is projected against the libertine excesses that drag Fitzpiers back from lofty intellectual pursuits into a crude existence of seduction and abandonment. The latter is a character whose sexual appetite is at odds with his dilettantism; whose infidelities are not just casual but, in the entire pattern of the novel, symptomatic of a grave imbalance in the natural world which relates to Winterborne himself. What at first appears a coarse yet vital fertility unexpectedly lodged in Fitzpiers is really an overwhelming impulse to play the 'satyr' figure, and watch himself playing it. Midsummer Eve, for centuries arguably the most important and widespread of the annual festivals of Europe, affords a suitable 'stage' on which this predatory interloper might perform. Within minutes of catching Grace in his arms and declaring that he will keep her there forever, he transfers his attention to the hoydenish Suke Damson, whom he chases across the fields.[35] He re-enacts with her the 'superstitious sowing' in a hay mead under the full moon. D. H. Lawrence, by labelling Fitzpiers 'a weak, pitiable person',[36] fails to acknowledge his impudent daring in a region to which he is utterly foreign.

Clodd, wrote, 'the modern views of marriage are a survival from the custom of capture & purchase, propped up by a theological superstition.' See Hardy, *Collected Letters*, II, 92.
[33] John F. McLennan, *Studies in Ancient History* (London: Bernard Quaritch, 1876), p. 313.
[34] 'Winterborne' is a common Dorset place-name derived from the phenomenon of streams which dry up in summer, but whose fountains periodically break, as it is termed in the winter. The bursting of these springs is always delayed until the occurrence of a gale of wind, however wet the season. The Victorian antiquary J. J. Foster noted in seventeen villages in Dorset whose names are compounds of Winterbourne. See J. J. Foster, 'Dorset Folk-lore', *Folk-Lore Journal* 6 (1888), 115-19.
[35] Satyrs were frequently painted pursuing nymphs, the lesser female fertility deities usually linked with water and vegetation.
[36] D. H. Lawrence, *Study of Thomas Hardy*, p. 47.

This fickle visitant from the *beau-monde* betrays an indolent disregard for the consequences of his own desires, which he can realize through swift, decisive action, unlike the resigned stoic Winterborne, who is supposedly 'perfectly at home in the woods'.[37] Although Fitzpiers lacks the charisma to fit his own self-image as a flamboyant bohemian, he is in touch with his sexuality and aggressively fulfils it. His volatile energies are always the stronger and give him victory on a night when the rural community should be celebrating its own well-being and affinity with the fecund life of the soil.

That Winterborne, the man most closely involved with the Hintock trade in trees and their by-products (apples, barks, spars), is stymied by civilized constraint and finds his place usurped on Midsummer Eve by a 'town' man, reflects Hardy's perception that few things in this secluded region can be 'natural' any more. When Winterborne is sent to Sherton Abbas Market to collect the newly educated Grace, whose arrival he awaits with tremulous hope, he carries with him 'a specimen appletree' (*Woodlanders* 26), which serves as his heraldic emblem and implies Hardy is invoking the 'Wild Man' figure of the medieval mummers' play (traditionally shown holding a tree). But Winterborne could not be further removed from the untrammelled ferocity and perverse lasciviousness of his medieval counterpart.[38] Ironically, Hardy conceives Fitzpiers as the genuinely wild force: he is neither integrated with nor constrained by the woodland world, and he effortlessly violates its pagan survivals and its women. The Hintocks are there for him merely to act out his need for immediate self-gratification and sexual mastery. Through Fitzpiers's intrusive urban influence the Midsummer Eve festival has lost whatever religious authority it might once have possessed. Instead of affording access to suprahuman potencies, the Midsummer sowing has degenerated into an 'ungodly performance' (*Woodlanders* 110) – decadent, injurious and ill-adapted to the exigencies of contemporary life, 'a knick-knack' or 'a ridiculous proceeding with no apparent meaning'.[39] The ritual of scattering hemp-seed was originally related to a primitive conception of marriage designed to render the vegetation fertile by a process of 'imitative' magic; that is to say, actual sexual union was intended to induce fertility in humans, crops, and animals. James George Frazer explained in *The Golden Bough*, first published in 1890, 'If rude man identifies himself, in a manner,

---

[37] J. B. Bullen, *The Expressive Eye*, p. 170.
[38] Winterborne is 'a bachelor of rather retiring habits' whose 'trusty man and familiar Robert Creedle' is 'a survival from the days when Giles's father held the homestead and Giles was a playing boy' (*Woodlanders* 54).
[39] John F. McLennan, 'Bride-Catching', *Argosy* 2 (1886), 41.

with nature; if he fails to distinguish the impulses and processes in himself from the methods which nature adopts to ensure the reproduction of plants and animals...he may infer that by yielding to his appetites he will thereby assist in the multiplication of plants and animals.'[40] Fitzpiers yields to his 'appetites', but partly out of a malicious boredom that degrades the colourful history of this curious survival. Winterborne, as this episode throws into relief, is the very image of static and vulnerable disconnection; he can counteract neither the interference of Fitzpiers, nor the pernicious values of the culture that has instructed him. Winterborne's need to conform to Grace's newly acquired standards of propriety leads on Midsummer Eve to erotic frustration and futility rather than to cathartic release. Ian Gregor's assertion that moribundity in *The Woodlanders* is felt to be 'at once personal, communal, and located within nature itself',[41] ignores the deathliness of rapidly encroaching metropolitan manners which is Hardy's paramount preoccupation. Winterborne's endeavours to improve the quality of his own life and that of others in Little Hintock crumble under the weight of keenly felt social pressures.[42]

The Woodlanders comprises a more harrowing recognition than do Hardy's previous fictions of a defeated rural environment in the degree to which its traditional agent Winterborne, the apparent custodian of the forest and its antique culture, is 'unmanned' by a socially constructed consciousness. The idea of Winterborne as a nurturing, potent fertility figure is further stripped of credibility when Grace Melbury transforms him through misperception into an anthropological image of himself. In Chapter 28 she accompanies her husband Fitzpiers to see him off on what he claims is a strictly professional call, but which she suspects to be an illicit tryst with Mrs Charmond. Grace watches Fitzpiers moving through the fertile landscape as though it is quite separate from him. At 'the supreme moment' of 'bounty' in White-Hart Vale, when 'the hedges were bowed with haws and blackberries', Fitzpiers is directed by a selfish, destructive passion which can only further blight the traditional life of the woodland. Grace sees him as engrossed with something in his own imagination, having no rapport whatsoever with his organically abundant environment:

---

[40] James Frazer, *The Golden Bough*, p.104.

[41] Ian Gregor, *The Great Web: The Form of Hardy's Major Fiction* (London: Faber & Faber, 1974), p. 145.

[42] Shirley A. Stave writes that 'Hardy's portrayal of Little Hintock is that of a fragile vestige of the past continually buffeted by the values of contemporary society; with each blow, the community is weakened and the ideals that have served to bestow identity upon the folk are called into question'. See Shirley A. Stave, *The Decline of the Goddess: Nature, Culture and Women in Thomas Hardy's Fiction* (Westport, Conn.: Greenwood Press, 1995), p. 74.

> And so the infatuated surgeon went along through the gorgeous autumn landscape of White-Hart Vale, surrounded by orchards lustrous with the reds of apple-crops, berries, and foliage, the whole intensified by the gilding of the declining sun. The earth this year had been prodigally bountiful, and now was the supreme moment of her bounty. In the poorest spots the hedges were bowed with haws and blackberries; acorns cracked underfoot, and the burst husks of chestnuts lay exposing their auburn contents as if arranged by anxious sellers in the fruit-market. In all this proud show some kernels were unsound as her own situation, and she wondered if there were one world in this universe where the fruit had no worm, and marriage no sorrow. (*Woodlanders* 155)

Although the betrayed wife's point of view is foregrounded and made clear by 'she wondered', Hardy alerts us to her perceiving consciousness earlier by such clues as 'burst husks of chestnuts...as if arranged by anxious sellers in the fruit-market': features of an unspoilt natural location remind her of an urban market place. While her husband, lacking true instinctual sympathy with the earth, rides obliviously through a landscape of astonishing beauty, Grace notices an unflattering likeness between the unrelieved misery of her marriage and the general decay concealed beneath the autumn splendour.

The 'infatuated surgeon' passage deliberately parallels in structure the 'Autumn's very brother' description a page later. As Grace dwells on the irony of her husband going off to meet his mistress on the gentle mare given to her by Giles Winterborne, the man himself appears out of the valley. Rays of the declining sun, which reflected on the white coat of Fitzpiers's horse as he vanished into the distance, now shine off the blades of Winterborne's cider-making apparatus. Whereas Grace's image of Fitzpiers suggests a disruptive and incongruous figure amid the 'gorgeous' autumn landscape, the vision of Winterborne mediated through her consciousness exemplifies the ongoing organic life of the Hintocks. With a violent resurgence of affection for what she thinks are his unblemished country virtues, Grace sees him as *belonging* to the tangible natural world in all its aspects, and achieving his apotheosis as autumnal fertility figure. But this passage is not an example of 'uneducated vision'.[43] Grace desperately wants to believe that her childhood companion has been transfigured by the season; she celebrates his affinity with and, by implication, magical possession of the vibrant physical world. But this captivating light-enhanced illusion is unsustainable. Winterborne himself is

---

[43]   James Krasner, *The Entangled Eye: Visual Perception and the Representation of Nature in Post-Darwinian Narrative* (Oxford: Oxford University Press, 1992), p. 97.

never conscious of reaching a unique harmony with the rhythms governing
seasonal change, or that he personifies the earth's thriving abundance.

> He looked and smelt like Autumn's very brother, his face being
> sunburnt to wheat-colour, his eyes blue as corn-flowers, his sleeves
> and leggings dyed with fruit stains, his hands clammy with the sweet
> juice of apples, his hat sprinkled with pips, and everywhere about
> him that atmosphere of cider which at its first return each season has
> such an indescribable fascination for those who have been born and
> bred among the orchards. Her heart rose from its late sadness like a
> released bough; her senses revelled in the sudden lapse back to
> Nature unadorned. The consciousness of having to be genteel
> because of her husband's profession, the veneer of artificiality which
> she had acquired at the fashionable schools, were thrown off, and she
> became the crude country girl of her latent, early instincts.
>   Nature was bountiful, she thought. No sooner had she been cast
> aside by Edred Fitzpiers, than another being, impersonating
> chivalrous and undiluted manliness, had arisen out of the earth, ready
> to her hand. This, however, was an excursion of the imagination
> which she did not wish to encourage, and she said suddenly, to
> disguise the confused regard which had followed her thoughts, 'Did
> you meet my husband?' (*Woodlanders* 156)

Even before the perspective is explicitly made that of Grace at 'Her
heart rose from its late sadness', the tone of the passage, whose intoxicating
sensuousness is suspiciously Keatsian, implies that Grace is indulging 'an
excursion of the imagination'.[44] 'Imagination' here is not a positive or
healthy sign of social integration or spiritual aspiration but an index of the
perceptual aberrations to which Grace's immature mind is prone. Instead of
being filled with a sense of personal distress, brooding over how 'some
kernels' in White-Hart Vale are 'as unsound as her own situation'
(*Woodlanders* 155), Grace thinks 'Nature is bountiful' after Winterborne's
emergence, whom she reinvents in his ritual aspect coated with pips and
flecks of apple flesh; a figure who not only seems to blend with, but
assumes the overflowing ripeness of the region. She pictures autumn's
texture, produce, colour and smell in loving detail, accentuating the
countryman's apparent affiliation with natural processes. Fitzpiers can
boast, to Grace's mind, of no such intimate kinship with this landscape; he
is regarded as moving through the lush environment as though it is quite
separate from him. Hardy exploits the irony that if Grace's fanciful

---

[44] See George Wotton, *Thomas Hardy: Towards a Materialist Criticism* (Dublin: Gill &
Macmillan, 1985), pp. 55-7; and J. Hillis Miller, *Thomas Hardy: Distance and Desire*
(Cambridge, Mass.: Harvard University Press, 1970), p. 83.

identification of Winterborne with the cider-making process is carried to its logical conclusion, then this figure of natural fruition must surely be at risk of John Barleycorn's fate, or of being pressed like his own apples. In the autumn rites harvesting is associated with death. Hardy implies that we must accept the necessary decline and disappearance of the old year-spirit, and its replacement, achieved by brutal means, by a formidable new force. Winterborne *should* be dislodged – only, of course, Fitzpiers is grotesquely unfit to be considered Little Hintock's new nature-spirit.

Grace's naive pastoral thought-adventure conjures up an Emersonian 'Nature' where 'all mean egotism vanishes' and the 'greatest delight which the fields and woods minister is the suggestion of an occult relation between man and the vegetable'.[45] Yet her rapt vision completely smothers the fact that the diffident Winterborne possesses an intelligently natural knowledge and culture to which her expensive finishing school and Fitzpiers's sinister dabbling into esoteric lore could never lay claim. The hallucinatory intensity of her 'Autumn's very brother' gloss reveals more about her status as an irremediably *split* person, than it does about Winterborne, whose genuine qualities are ignored while she indulges her fantasies of a Hintock tutelary spirit. She is consistently presented as an imperfectly manufactured product of polite culture, 'as it were in mid-air between two storeys of society' (*Woodlanders* 164), this 'impressionable creature who combined modern nerves with primitive feelings' (*Woodlanders* 223). Although she feels as if she has returned to a momentous, dynamic relationship with her surroundings, the newly bourgeois Grace can never revert to being a 'crude country girl' like Marty South, who occupies the lowest social and economic level of woodland life. Grace half-heartedly rebels against the 'artificiality' paid for by wealth generated from her indulgent father's business of exploiting the forest (cutting down trees for timber). Her nostalgic dream of being restored through Winterborne, whose sunburnt face and cornflower-coloured eyes she associates with a vegetative deity, to the untutored native she once was is a delusion only equalled by her father's fancy that a recent divorce law will make a 'grown' Grace 'wholesome' again, erasing the 'stain' of her humiliating entanglement with Fitzpiers. 'The encounter', according to David Lodge, 'is a kind of epiphany for Grace, a moment of truth'.[46] These comments however afford little insight into her motives for weaving around Winterborne vaguely literary generalizations. Geoffrey Thurley remarks

---

[45] Ralph Waldo Emerson, *The Complete Works of Ralph Waldo Emerson*, 4 vols. (Cambridge, Mass.: Harvard University Press, 1971-87), I, 140.
[46] David Lodge, 'Introduction', *The Woodlanders*, The New Wessex Edition (London: Macmillan, 1975), p. 20.

that 'Giles is a Dionysiac worshipper of the earth and the seasons...a pagan'.[47] It is difficult to imagine Winterborne as a 'Dionysiac worshipper', given his lonely self-absorption, while his 'pagan' status is undercut by Grace's view of him rising like a new Adam out of the earth, 'impersonating chivalrous and undiluted manliness' (*Woodlanders* 156). His 'manliness'[48] in her eyes is an ever-withering sexless force, in stark contrast to the exploitative sensualism of Fitzpiers. Grace, caught between a frivolous nostalgia for treading the old tracks, and a keen desire for rapid cultural advancement, endows the countryman with a prelapsarian innocence, striving to sublimate her attraction; for she does enjoy Winterborne sexually, but only as a voyeur would enjoy the inaccessible observed object, a psychological enigma always outside her rarefied social sphere. This trait is shared by her husband Fitzpiers, who is not only a voyeur of others but also of his own emotions. Lucille Herbert believes that Hardy 'could very plausibly be represented as standing beside Henry James as "a watcher at the window...a figure with a pair of eyes, or at least with a field glass."'[49] But it is Fitzpiers who is seen 'quizzing [Grace] through an eyeglass' (*Woodlanders* 51), always on the lookout from his house on the hillside for the next fleeting frisson.

If Grace's extravagant evocation of 'Autumn's very brother' reveals how much she may wish to see Winterborne as the epitome of an organic relationship between man and the potency of nature, his inhibiting self-restraint is still painfully apparent because of the gentility she has imposed on him and with which she secretly feels most comfortable. Winterborne senses that his own 'homeliness' offends Grace's 'acquired tastes' (*Woodlanders* 166), so he apes a 'chivalrous...manliness': the very trait she exploits in One-Chimney Hut at the climax of the novel, effectively killing him by her own superfine moral scruples. The unnatural role Winterborne must play when Grace is present ends, as on Midsummer Eve, in dourness and detachment. That he shows his devotion to her during the 'Autumn's very brother' scene only by stroking a flower worn 'in her bosom' is a pathetic gesture, implying 'the abstraction of a somnambulist':

> Her abandonment to the seductive hour and scene after her sense of
> ill-usage, her revolt...against social law, her passionate desire for

---

[47] Geoffrey Thurley, *The Psychology of Hardy's Novels: The Nervous and the Statuesque*, p. 119.

[48] Grace refers again later to the 'manliness' she believes to inhabit 'unvarnished' men such as Winterborne (*Woodlanders* 166).

[49] Lucille Herbert, 'Hardy's Views in *Tess of the d'Urbervilles*', *Journal of English Literary History*, 37 (1970), 78. Herbert's quotation is taken from James's Preface to *The Portrait of a Lady*, in the New York Edition (1907-17), vol. 3.

primitive life, may have showed in her face. Winterborne was
looking at her, his eyes lingering on a flower that she wore in her
bosom. Almost with the abstraction of a somnambulist he stretched
out his hand and gently caressed the flower. (*Woodlanders* 157)

Winterborne explains why he caressed the flower: 'It would not have
occurred to me if I had not seen something like it done elsewhere'
(*Woodlanders* 157) – ironically by the 'debonair' Fitzpiers to Mrs
Charmond. The cider-maker's somnambulism foreshadows *Tess* in which
Angel Clare, during a moment of sleepwalking, carries the un-intact
protagonist and lays her in an empty coffin (Chapter 37). Both men feel
they must 'bury' the sexual instinct so as to obey a spurious 'social law'
and its rigorous standards of respectability. The consequence for
Winterborne is 'an abeyant mood' and 'a taciturn hesitancy' (*Woodlanders*
205) that destroys any chance of happiness he might have, or indeed might
confer, in the Hintocks. Winterborne's true home should be the Norse
'Niflheim' (*Woodlanders* 73), a gloomy fogland where the forlorn spirits of
those who have perished of old age or sickness, the unfulfilled, are destined
to remain.[50]

Later in the novel, when Grace is recuperating from her first illness,
Winterborne 'rose upon her memory as the fruit-god and the wood-god in
alternation...sometimes leafy, and smeared with green lichen...sometimes
cider-stained and starred with apple-pips' (*Woodlanders* 209). However,
Winterborne is a far cry from the regenerative figure of Grace's making
because he, like his workmate Marty South, epitomizes a ruined and
exploited human nature which cannot develop *naturally* if it is forced to
serve the demands of a new bourgeois culture and its false consciousness of
decorum, chivalry, and sexual 'correctness'. In the bitter recognition that
Grace stylizes Winterborne, and that his status as 'wood-god' can only be
at best a poetic guise, Hardy charts the death of a potent and beneficent
nature spirit whose reality can no longer be profoundly entertained in the
imagination. To Grace, Winterborne is simply a 'screen' on which she
might project her fey mythical fantasies, no doubt fuelled by reading
sentimental and idealistic forms of Romantic poetry at her fashionable
finishing school. Crucially, he has his own naturally informed culture
which is betrayed by Grace and Old Melbury, who thinks Winterborne is
not of sufficiently high caste for his daughter. Grace cannot appreciate the
tree-planter's 'sort of sympathy between himself and the fir, oak, or beech
that he was operating on; so that the roots took hold of the soil in a few

---

[50] Hardy may have had in mind Arnold's 'Balder Dead' (1855) in which 'The plains of
Niflheim, where dwell the dead' (1.172) is the region to which Balder is banished.

days' (*Woodlanders* 49). He and Marty South have an affinity with the forest expressed in terms of their shared intuitive understanding of a secret 'script' peculiar to Little Hintock. But their inherited culture is almost extinct, ousted by the refined arts of which both Grace and Fitzpiers are the dubious beneficiaries:

> The casual glimpses which the ordinary population bestowed upon that wondrous world of sap and leaves called the Hintock woods had been with these two, Giles and Marty, a clear gaze. They had been possessed of its finer mysteries as of commonplace knowledge; had been able to read its hieroglyphs as ordinary writing; to them the sights and sounds of night...amid those dense boughs...were simple occurrences whose origin, continuance, and laws they foreknew... they had, with the run of the years, mentally collected those remoter signs and symbols which seen in few were of runic obscurity, but all together made an alphabet...The artifices of the seasons were seen by them from the conjuror's own point of view. (*Woodlanders* 248-9)

Winterborne, unlike Michael Henchard who visits a 'conjuror' (Wide-Oh Fall) in Hardy's previous published novel *The Mayor of Casterbridge* (1885), is himself endowed with 'a gentle conjuror's touch in spreading the roots of each little tree, resulting in a sort of caress, under which the delicate fibres all laid themselves out in their proper directions for growth' (*Woodlanders* 50). His caress, quite spontaneous and unconscious, is intended to nurture the young trees. Yet when he strokes the flower worn by Grace in the 'Autumn's very brother' episode (*Woodlanders* 157), Winterborne's 'caress' intimates only stammering inadequacy and sexual repression. The fertile bond supposed to exist between Winterborne and his trees is what the novel creates an almost religious yearning for, even as it repeatedly punishes him for this affinity. When Winterborne descends from the great elm on which John South is fixated in his last illness, it is like a tree-spirit detaching itself: 'the tree seemed to shiver, then to heave a sigh: a movement was audible, and Winterborne dropped almost noiselessly to the ground' (*Woodlanders* 73). Although his 'gentle conjuror's touch' with the Hintock orchards implies he may be best qualified to cure Old South's solitary and fearful obsessiveness, Winterborne is once again superseded by Fitzpiers, whose modern medical training is tested during this memorable episode. Henry Joseph Moule, a respected antiquarian who became curator of the Dorset County Museum, refers to the source of Old South's obsession in a letter to Hardy as the 'elm-tree totem'.[51] The term 'totem' is

---

[51] Thomas Hardy, *Personal Writings*, p. 71.

North American, and was first used in an English text in 1791 by the traveller and interpreter James Long, who requisitioned it from the language of the Ojibway Indians. John F. McLennan examined the worldwide reverence for the mystical power of trees in an 1869 essay for *The Fortnightly Review* entitled 'The Worship of Animals and Plants'.[52] The terms 'totem' and 'totemism' passed into general circulation in English when James George Frazer published his seminal survey *Totemism* in 1887, the same year as Hardy's *Woodlanders*. Frazer defined it thus: 'A totem is a class of material objects which a savage regards with superstitious respect, believing that there exists between him and every member of the class an intimate and altogether special relation.'[53] Marty South explains how her ailing father perceives the elm outside their cottage as 'an evil spirit', 'exactly his own age' sprouting up 'when he was born on purpose to rule him, and keep him as its slave' (*Woodlanders* 78).[54] In the section of *Primitive Culture* devoted to animistic 'survivals', Tylor details how tree-worship stubbornly persists in remote rural settlements:

> The peasant folklore of Europe still knows of willows that bleed and weep and speak when hewn, of the fairy maiden that sits within the fir-tree, of that old tree in Rugaard forest that must not be felled, for an elf dwells within, of that old tree on the Heinzenberg near Zell, which uttered its complaint when the woodman cut it down, for in it was Our Lady, whose chapel now stands upon the spot.[55]

Old South keeps time to the movements of his elm – 'As the tree waved South waved his head, making it his fugleman with abject obedience', and believes it will fall on him: 'There he stands, threatening my life every minute that the wind do blow' (*Woodlanders* 70).[56]

---

[52] John F. McLennan, 'The Worship of Animals and Plants. Part 1', *Fortnightly Review* 6 (1869), 407-27.

[53] Sir James George Frazer, *Totemism and Exogamy*, I, 3.

[54] Jean Brooks describes John South's tree as 'a kind of Hintock Igdrasil' See *Thomas Hardy: The Poetic Structure* (London: Elek, 1971), p. 222.

[55] E. B. Tylor, *Primitive Culture*, II, 201.

[56] This complex scene raises many questions as to whether Hardy deliberately exploited anthropological investigations into the worship of definite external objects. In the mid-1860s E. B. Tylor was developing his theory of animism, observing that a 'childlike mind which can so attribute to any lifeless object a personal existence, a share in human life and thought...is indeed in the condition to which the religion and philosophy of the lower races for the most part evidently belong.' See E. B. Tylor, 'The Religion of Savages', *Fortnightly Review* 6 (1866), 72. C. F. Keary also focused on 'relics...of an earlier stratum of thought' such as 'river, tree or mountain worship' found in 'out-of-the-way spots'. See C. F. Keary, 'Some Phases of Early Religious Development', *Nineteenth Century* 4 (1878), 361.

The connection between Old South and the tall elm swaying outside his window is a macabre parody of Winterborne's 'sympathy between himself and the fir, oak, or beech': a quasi-mystical correspondence between woodlander and trees has collapsed into debilitating neurosis and harmful superstition. Winterborne, acting on Fitzpiers's advice, fells the elm, but when the old man sees the vacant patch of sky left behind he has a fit and dies of shock.[57] The consequences of felling South's tree, whose seriousness Winterborne cannot as yet fully comprehend, clash with the blackly comic effect of Fitzpiers's callous exclamation, 'Damned if my remedy hasn't killed him!' (*Woodlanders* 79). The remedial effects of his 'advanced' modern science, whose principles fail adequately to account for the ways and agencies of primitive irrationality, hasten the patient's death. In the novel felling the elm becomes a criminal act (technically a theft), since it is performed without the authorization of their affluent neighbour Mrs Charmond. The civilized and rational law that safeguards her rights as estate-owner would have the effect of protecting this vestige of tree-worship, which was historically a persistent subversion of Christianity.[58] Winterborne's destructive operation on the elm, whose lower boughs are lopped off before it is cut down ('shrouding' as it is called in Little Hintock), is inextricably intertwined with the falling-in of lives which limits his tenure of the cottages where the Souths also live, because old South is the last life in the life-holding.[59] Half his income, and Marty's home, are taken away at a stroke.

Winterborne's 'gentle conjuror's touch', if permitted free rein, might have saved John South (and the cottages) whereas Fitzpiers's medical science only precipitated his death. Yet it is difficult to reconcile Winterborne's 'marvellous power of making trees grow' (*Woodlanders* 49), with the horrific accounts of the detrimental operation of natural forces within the forest. Winterborne, the whimsical 'wood-god' of Grace's fantasies, can do little to resuscitate the creative potential of his birthplace. His inability to defend his locale from ugly decay shows in the numerous

---

[57] E. B. Tylor was among the first English anthropological scholars seriously to explore that primitive stage of thought 'where the individual tree is regarded as a conscious personal being, and as such receives adoration'. See *Primitive Culture*, II, 215.

[58] In his 1883 *Westminster Review* essay on Hardy's work, Havelock Ellis took special notice of Hardy's portrayal of trees and the almost religious power they had for him: 'Mr. Hardy is never more reverent, more exact, than when he is speaking of forest trees'. Ellis related this to 'lingering echoes of the old tree-worship', and to 'Nature-worship' in general. See Cox, *Thomas Hardy: The Critical Heritage*, pp. 103-32.

[59] Under the life-hold system, a tenant entered into agreement with the lord of the manor to occupy a dwelling for a period of lives. Farmer Springrove's Three Tranters Inn and the adjoining cottages in *Desperate Remedies* is also a life-hold.

descriptions of stunted and mutilated tree-life. It is dangerous, Hardy implies, to set much store by Grace's perceptions of the Hintock plantations and copses for they signal more her nagging anxieties rather than the actual condition of the physical world, for instance the 'trees close together' she notices when alone at Winterborne's One-Chimney Hut, 'wrestling for existence, their branches disfigured with wounds resulting from their mutual rubbings'; and the 'dead boughs...scattered about like ichthyosauri in a museum' (*Woodlanders* 234). Only Grace could compare features of a natural setting to a familiar urban location, especially one considered a hallmark of advanced civilization and synonymous with intellectual and moral edification. Also the seasonal cycle and effects of shadow, sunbeams, mist and storm all conspire to evoke a fictional environment unceasingly and ominously changing. However, the presentation of trees in terms of the 'Unfulfilled Intention' is a portrayal whose sheer starkness cannot be attributed to chiaroscuro or to Grace's unreliable observation. We are deliberately enticed into the pastoral prettiness of the opening image, before being exposed to the myriad disturbing features awaiting those who tread further into the forest depths:

> They went noiselessly over mats of starry moss, rustled through interspersed tracts of leaves, skirted trunks with spreading roots whose mossed rinds made them like hands wearing green gloves, elbowed old elms and ashes with great forks in which stood pools of water that overflowed on rainy days and ran down their stems in green cascades. On older trees...huge lobes of fungi grew like lungs. Here, as everywhere, the Unfulfilled Intention, which makes life what it is, was as obvious as it could be among the depraved crowds of a city-slum. The leaf was deformed, the curve was crippled, the taper was interrupted; the lichen ate the vigour of the stalk, and the ivy slowly strangled to death the promising sapling. (*Woodlanders* 40-41)

The increasingly grotesque somatic imagery – which Hardy repeats for trees in the 'wilder recesses' of Mrs Charmond's park with its ugly fungoid and parasitic growths[60] – is a far cry from *Under the Greenwood Tree* (1872), whose narrator evinces a rapt veneration for the woods. Hardy draws an analogy, and attributes the state of both Little Hintock and urban

---

[60] '[S]limy streams of fresh moisture, exuding from decayed holes caused by old amputations, ran down the bark of the oaks and elms' (*Woodlanders* 149); see also the half-dead oak 'hollow, and disfigured with white tumours, its roots spreading out like claws grasping the ground' (*Woodlanders* 161).

civilization to a common cause, the 'Unfulfilled Intention'.[61] This abstract formulation implies the extreme and unrelenting cruelty that nature imposes upon itself when engaged in a Darwinian struggle for survival. The violence of the disfigurement that Hintock trees inflict on one another is the most unsettling feature of Hardy's rural wasteland. One species seems to devour another; ivy slowly strangles 'the promising sapling', indicating the relationship between malformation and ruthless exploitation. Little Hintock is no better than the vast modern metropolis, whose bleak associations of crime, infant mortality and 'roofs of slated hideousness' are famously described by Tennyson's disenchanted elderly speaker in 'Locksley Hall Sixty Years After'.[62] The 'Unfulfilled Intention' also applies to Winterborne, who cannot halt the spread of disease in this area. Hardy reveals that individual beings and their plans are as vulnerable to social and psychological forces as saplings are to ivy.

It is fitting that Winterborne should be allied with Autumn because the season owes its distinctive colour and profusion to dying vegetation. The cider-maker and tree-planter, who in Grace's eyes rises out of the earth like a new Adam in Chapter 28, is eerily consumed by unhusbanded nature in Chapters 41 and 42. This time however, instead of bringing sunshine, Autumn 'was coming in with rains' (*Woodlanders* 229). Once allied with the prodigal fecundity of the Hintocks, the delirious Winterborne dissolves into the sylvan surroundings by imperceptible degrees. His enfeeblement and absorption back into the forest is not the true source of tragedy here, for in the full cycle of nature, growth and decay, sowing and reaping, are equally necessary. Hardy's acute sense of disaster stems from the fact that the tree-planter and cider-maker has not been *fertile* in his time: the galling irony is that Winterborne completes the cycle of life without fulfilling his priestly function. His role has been swiftly usurped by Fitzpiers who cannot fulfil it either, as the grim farce involving Old South's elm-tree attests. Winterborne's ritual death is marked by successive steps down the evolutionary ladder:

> [There] were low mutterings; at first like persons in conversation, but gradually resolving themselves into varieties of one voice. It was an endless monologue, like that we sometimes hear from inanimate nature in deep secret places where water flows, or where ivy leaves

---

[61] That Hardy suggests here 'a universal crippling in creation, a condition apparently inescapable for both the old world of Little Hintock and the new world of Sherton and beyond' see Linda K. Hughes and Michael Lund, 'Linear Stories and Circular Visions: The Decline of the Victorian Serial', in *Chaos and Order: Complex Dynamics in Literature and Science*, ed. N. Katherine Hayles (Chicago: University of Chicago Press, 1991), p. 174.

[62] Alfred, Lord Tennyson, *The Poems of Tennyson*, III, 230.

flap against stones; but by degrees [Grace] was convinced that the
voice was Winterborne's. (*Woodlanders* 235)

Winterborne's cough sounds like 'a squirrel or a bird' (*Woodlanders*
230), then his voice floats upon the weather 'as though a part of it'
(*Woodlanders* 233), and finally becomes indistinguishable, 'an endless
monologue, like that we sometimes hear from inanimate nature in deep
secret places'. He becomes first part of the animal world, then of the
inanimate world of water, wind and stone. But the process of dying
continues: Winterborne's final murmurs are 'like a comet; erratic,
inapprehensible, untraceable' (*Woodlanders* 236). Hardy draws on (with
heartfelt sincerity or stinging irony?) the traditions of pastoral elegy in
having all nature perform rites of mourning for the death of a god: 'The
whole wood seemed to be a house of death, pervaded by loss to its
uttermost length and breadth. Winterborne was gone and the copses seemed
to show the want of him; those young trees, so many of which he had
planted...were...sending out their roots in the direction that he had given
them with his subtle hand' (*Woodlanders* 245). The novel closes with a
shorn Marty South delivering a threnody to the unmanned warden of the
Hintock orchards. Her words are the only recognition we get from within
Winterborne's locale of his singular capabilities. In its simple unadorned
lyricism, Marty's tribute is natural elegy, neither self-conscious nor stilted:

> 'Whenever I plant the young larches I'll think that none can plant as
> you planted; and whenever I split a gad, and whenever I turn the
> cider wring, I'll say none could do it like you. If ever I forget your
> name let me forget home and heaven!...But no, no, my love, I never
> can forget 'ee; for you was a good man, and did good things!'
> (*Woodlanders* 276-7)

This tutelary nymph of Little Hintock, whose feminine contours are 'so
undeveloped as to be scarcely perceptible in her' (*Woodlanders* 276), is a
representative like the man she loves, of 'Unfulfilled Intentions' and the
barren asexual current running through society in the forest.[63]

Although Fitzpiers may be ultimately the true destroyer of Winterborne
and his farcical substitute as 'King of the Wood',[64] the countryman is also
the victim of Grace Melbury, who relies on his 'freedom from grosser

---

[63] For a reading of Marty as an essentially sterile figure see Penny Boumelha, *Thomas Hardy and Women: Sexual Ideology and Narrative Form* (Brighton: Harvester, 1982), pp. 107-8.

[64] 'The King of the Wood' is the title James George Frazer gives to the first book of his *Golden Bough*.

passions' and enervating impersonations of 'scrupulous delicacy' (*Woodlanders* 236). Although Marjorie Garson's standpoint is perhaps too strident, observing that Grace reflects Hardy's 'instinctive terror of the woman who castrates and kills',[65] the latter's adherence to legal and social etiquette causes Winterborne's demise in the gloomy Hintock glade. Grace's stay at One-Chimney Hut in the deepest part of the forest occurs when fleeing her adulterous husband and the unceasing gossip of her neighbours. In the first of a series of bizarrely comic touches showing the two lovers hampered by the Christian marriage contract and the stringent moral code it prescribes, whose might neither Winterborne's 'strong arms' nor Grace's refined boarding-school education can conquer, she is confronted by exactly the traits from which she has fled: the dreary inhibitions of social protocol. As on Midsummer Eve, Grace's impetuous foray into the forest paradoxically results in a meeting with forms or instruments of civilized culture. Winterborne's homely morality is unyielding as he wishes to make amends for his treachery in kissing her while knowing her to be Fitzpiers's wife – more than six months earlier! In refusing her invitation to an impropriety that might ruin her reputation, Winterborne moves from house to hovel to shelter; specifically a woodcutter's fuel shelter.

The Woodlanders introduces for the first time in Hardy's fiction 'the legal formalities for dissolving [a] union' (*Woodlanders* 206), and his desire to amend an imprisoning covenant. The One-Chimney Hut episode's peculiar tonal shifts are rooted in his biting manipulation of inherited literary forms, showing each one to be ludicrously inappropriate as a means of expressing or relieving the social malaise infecting Little Hintock. Hardy scornfully invokes the Snow White story during Grace's flight through an enchanted forest, for it is depicted with unearthly 'fairy tale' touches:

> the plantations were always weird at this hour of eve – more spectral by far than in the leafless season...there were strange faces and figures from expiring lights that had somehow wandered into the canopied obscurity...She had walked three or four miles westward... that prescriptive comfort and relief to wanderers in woods – a distant light – broke at last upon her searching eyes. (*Woodlanders* 224, 225)

However, Winterborne's mysterious dwelling unmagically boasts only one cramped shabby room. Hardy satirizes 'the mechanical plot of

---

[65] Marjorie Garson, *Hardy's Fables of Integrity: Woman, Body, Text* (Oxford: Clarendon Press, 1991), p. 121.

marriages and intrigues',[66] by making Grace sound an oddly comic note of the embarrassed lover: 'This is awkward'(!). The convoluted measures taken to stop the couple sleeping together (locking the door, securely bolting the shutters, leaving food on a windowsill) are redolent of broad farce or Chaucerian fabliau. In such genres the lovers' passions and ingenuity are gauged by the sturdiness and complexity of the barriers put in their path. But Winterborne hardly qualifies as a fabliau hero ready to employ any ruse so that he may gain access to the object of his desires. Hardy disconcertingly adopts a tone of mock-Romantic sentimentality and pathos when the scene moves to Winterborne's 'wretched little shelter' (*Woodlanders* 228). The countryman's noble martyrdom is embellished by poetic locutions: 'damp obscurity', 'the frailty that besieged him' and 'purity of the affection' (*Woodlanders* 228). Hardy settles on melodrama when Grace finally drags Winterborne's drenched body indoors: 'How Grace performed that labour she never could have exactly explained' (*Woodlanders* 235). Her 'labour' forcibly reminds us that her leisured lady inaction throughout the novel results not from inherent weakness but from the advantages of intellectual and moral refinement purchased by her snobbish father.

Hardy's unnerving oscillations between knockabout farce and tragic pathos to convey Winterborne's unmanning is also highlighted by the wild-goose chase initiated by Old Melbury and his geriatric 'search-party' (*Woodlanders* 273) whose anti-climactic upshot is the discovery that Grace has returned to her remorseful husband, Fitzpiers.[67] The rustic ruminations on marriage and Old Melbury's comic mortification over Grace – 'I thought you went out to get parsley!' – clash with Marty South's requiem over Winterborne's grave. The cider-maker, whom Grace compares to a resplendent primitive fruit-god in Chapter 28, ends his days weak and exhausted, tapping at his own window for scraps of food. The cheerless autumnal wood in which he collapses, with its 'brown leaves', 'dead boughs' and 'perishing woodbine stems' (*Woodlanders* 234), anticipates Frazer's highly charged description of Diana's fertility priest warily circling his tree in the sacred grove at Nemi, at the outset of *The Golden Bough* (1891):

---

[66] Joe Fisher, *Hidden Hardy* (London: Macmillan, 1992), p. 147.

[67] Hardy was concerned to strengthen the impression that Grace's return to her unfaithful husband was a tragedy for her. Hardy's 1889 revisions to the dramatized version of the novel make her future discontent explicit; see Michael Millgate, *Thomas Hardy: A Biography* (Oxford: Clarendon Press, 1982), p. 299.

we picture to ourselves the scene as it may have been witnessed by a belated wayfarer on one of those wild autumn nights when the dead leaves are falling thick, and the wind seems to sing the dirge of the dying year. It is a sombre picture, set to melancholy music...the sighing of the wind in the branches, the rustle of withered leaves underfoot...and in the foreground...a dark figure with a glitter of steel at his shoulder[68]

Frazer's 'belated wayfarer' – conjuring up distinctively literary travellers such as Wordsworth's 'lonely wanderer,' or the Byronic 'Highland rover' – is similar to Hardy's hypothetical 'rambler' at the beginning of *The Woodlanders*. Yet Hardy, with amused savagery, debunks the scholar-gypsy genre by revealing this 'rambler' of back-lanes and by-ways to be the foppish and hopelessly lost Barber Percomb, who eventually arrives at Little Hintock to purchase Marty South's 'chestnut' hair (*Woodlanders* 9). This selfish defoliation of 'nature's adornment' – she is 'shorn' as if in a sacrificial rite – embodies the destiny of a countryside, an underclass and a gender; as well as anticipating Frazer's account of the belief (a 'real article of primitive faith') that human hair was inextricably bound up with physical and sexual potency.[69]

While Winterborne 'pursues doggedly a downward path to a miserable grave',[70] forced by Grace Melbury to espouse the chivalric maxim that counsels repression of sexual appetites, Fitzpiers deliberately indulges his 'grosser passions'. This extrovert virility demonstrates his fitness to survive the vicissitudes that his own disruptive energies had stirred into action on Midsummer Eve. He was very much the centre of the story Hardy first offered to Macmillan with the possible alternative title *Fitzpiers at Hintock*. This implies that he was originally conceived as a more inscrutable figure than the 'third-rate Shelley' David Lodge calls him.[71] Hardy says apparently straightforwardly:

His face was rather soft than stern, charming than grand, pale than flushed; his nose – if a sketch of his features be *de rigueur* for a person of his pretensions – was artistically beautiful enough to have been worth modelling by any sculptor not over busy, and was hence devoid of those knotty irregularities which often mean power; while the classical curve of his mouth was not without a looseness in its

[68] James Frazer, *The Golden Bough*, p. 12.

[69] Ibid., p. 768.

[70] Geoffrey Thurley, *The Psychology of Hardy's Novels: The Nervous and the Statuesque*, p. 106.

[71] David Lodge, 'Introduction', *The Woodlanders,* The New Wessex Edition (London: Macmillan, 1975), p. 16.

> close. Either from his readily appreciative mien, or his reflective
> manner, his presence bespoke the philosopher rather than the dandy
> (*Woodlanders* 78)

The 'soft...charming...pale' face hints at the superior birth and schooling on which Fitzpiers so obviously prides himself. Hardy slyly remarks that the nose of this minor aristocrat without land or fortune would be 'worth modelling by any sculptor' if he was 'not over busy'. But 'the classical curve of his mouth' is 'not without a looseness in its close': the fatally magnetic glamour conceals a dilettante humbug. That the narrator has to assure us Fitzpiers's presence indicates 'the philosopher rather than the dandy' is strange, because it insists on the reality of his Platonic aspiration while at the same time implying its profound insecurity.

Fitzpiers aims to be a conscientious follower of Plato's belief in a world of abstract ideas, of which material manifestations on earth are only imperfect copies. He is also intrigued by 'the shadowy parts of science which lie beyond the boundary of well-defined discoveries'.[72] But this 'philosopher', in spite of his best intentions, dedicates more time to the 'rank literatures of emotion and passion' than to 'the books' of 'science' (*Woodlanders* 94). The contradiction in him of the roles of Platonic idealist and the incurable sensual materialist, who is not only imaginatively unfaithful but physically so, makes him a distinct, less moral variation on the type that includes Angel Clare and *The Well-Beloved*'s Jocelyn Pierston (there is a kinship in name). Fitzpiers struggles to release himself from the material grip of the natural world yet is dragged back by sexual imperatives into a satyrean existence. The primitive urge for licence, of which he is both a reluctant victim and triumphant hierophant, overwhelms his pseudo-scientific ambition to discover by dissection the point at which the ideal touches the real. Hardy perceives the sexual force inhabiting Fitzpiers to be the dominant natural energy at play in human affairs. In a bitterly grotesque finale, Fitzpiers's perseverance is rewarded because he flouts bourgeois norms and still claims Grace, in whom he experiences a renewed interest. Her proclaimed infidelity with Winterborne is ironically the stimulus for his inconstant idealizing desire. Fitzpiers's corrupt attitude intimates the final and irreversible erosion of faith in the capacity of elemental potencies to inform and inspire the human world by a destructive dilettantism that dishonours their traditional mythological representation. In Hardy's next published novel, *Tess of the d'Urbervilles*, Fitzpiers's dual personality splits into antipodal characters. His satyrean qualities appear at their crudest in Alec d'Urberville, while the intellectual pretensions and Platonic

---

[72] Anon., 'Popular Science', *Quarterly Review* 84 (March 1849), 327.

idealism are passed onto the asexual Christian, Angel Clare. However, in the conflict of natural potencies, Angel triumphs; Alec and Tess – both sexually charged figures – are sacrificed.

Chapter 6

Killing the God

Tess of the d'Urbervilles (1891)

> [T]ill comparatively recent times, the country was densely wooded. Even now traces of its earlier condition are to be found in the old oak copses and irregular belts of timber that yet survive upon its slopes, and the hollow-trunked trees that shade so many of its pastures.
>
> The forests have departed, but some old customs of their shades remain. Many however linger only in a metamorphosed or disguised form. The May-Day dance...was to be discerned...in the guise of the club-revel, or 'club-walking', as it was there called. Its singularity lay less in the retention of a custom of walking in procession and dancing on each anniversary than in the members being solely women...The club of Marlott alone lived to uphold the local Cerealia. It had walked for hundreds of years, if not as benefit-club, as votive sisterhood of some sort; and it walked still.
>
> The banded ones were all dressed in white gowns – a gay survival from Old-Style days, when cheerfulness and Maytime were synonyms...Ideal and real clashed slightly as the sun lit up their figures against the green hedges and creeper-laced house-fronts; for, though the whole troop wore white garments, no two whites were alike among them. Some approached pure blanching; some had a bluish pallor; some worn by the older characters...inclined to a cadaverous tint. (18-19)[1]

Marlott club-walking,[2] like Midsummer Eve in *The Woodlanders*, shows Hardy reacting with mature complexity to the bizarre incongruity of an archaic folk-practice which has, through social or religious conservatism, 'survived' into a new historical age. A late nineteenth-century parish society with its yearly feast and procession appears 'crusted' with myriad old associations. The 'local Cerealia' alerts us to the way in which the event was derived from medieval Mayday festivities. The glaring absence

---

[1] Thomas Hardy, *Tess of the d'Urbervilles*, ed. with introd. Juliet Grindle and Simon Gatrell (Oxford: The World's Classics, 1988). Hereafter referred to as *Tess*.
[2] See William Barnes's poem, 'Whitsuntide an' Club Walken' in *Poems of Rural Life in the Dorset Dialect* (London: Kegan Paul, Trench & Co., 1888), p. 37.

of men from this yearly event reveals that Christianity has suppressed and neutered the *Old-Style* May-Days and the Maypole, the 'stinkyng ydol' of Puritan invective, around which 'yung men and maides' used to dance.[3] May rejoicings evolved out of pagan springtime rituals to stimulate the rapid revival and growth of vegetatio n upon which tribes were dependent for life.[4] Sexual intercourse between male and female celebrants was believed to fulfill the sacred function of rendering the organic world fertile. Later Puritan writers saw this endeavour to promote natural abundance by a process of imitative magic as merely an excuse for unchecked wildness that had to be guarded against at all costs.[5] The 'singularity' of the woman-only club signals how pagan fertility worship based on sex and magic has been deposed by an arid Christian creed whose central tenets, as *Jude* makes clear, encourage a profound mistrust of biological imperatives.

In addition to illustrating how the women's club-walk has lost contact with the original sexual and mythic implications of the 'Cerealia', Hardy also excavates more recent historical territory. In the same chapter we are made aware of Tess's embarrassment as she and other white-gowned members of the 'votive sisterhood' (*Tess* 19) witness the mock grandeur of her father, the shiftless tranter Jack Durbeyfield, riding home from 'The Pure Drop' tavern in his 'triumphal chariot' (*Tess* 21). The amateur antiquarian Parson Tringham has informed him that he is really 'Sir John d'Urberville', a lineal descendant of a once illustrious family who 'came from Normandy with William the Conqueror' (*Tess* 14). That a drunken Sir John, riding back to his basic cottage in a 'chariot', has discovered his red blood is really blue, shows Hardyan humour grounded in anxiety and dread, for the consequences of Tringham's 'revelation' are catastrophic for Tess. Using the anthropological curiosity of 'club-walking', Hardy conducts a bravura thought-adventure through prerecorded history (the remains of a primeval oak forest), Romano-British (Cerealia fertility rites) and medieval periods.

Representing the 'highest' stage of cultural evolution (or so he thinks) is Angel Clare, accompanied by his two Anglican elder brothers Felix and

---

[3] Phillip Stubbes, *Anatomie of Abuses* (1583), qtd. in James Frazer, *The Golden Bough*, p. 90.

[4] Nathaniel Hawthorne exploits the pagan provenance of May-Day in his short story, 'The Maypole of Merry Mount'.

[5] As Andrew Lang observed, 'the Puritans were conscious that much Pagan custom had been tolerated by the Church, and had survived, not only in ecclesiastical usage, but in popular festivals'. See Lang's 'Presidential Address' in *The International Folk-Lore Congress 1891. Papers and Transactions*, eds. Joseph Jacobs and Alfred Nutt (London: David Nutt, 1892), p. 4.

Cuthbert, who pause in their study of *A Counterblast to Agnosticism*[6] to watch a gathering whose provenance in pagan idolatries is unknown to them, since they inquire 'as to the meaning of the dance and the white-frocked maidens'. Hardy savours the irony of the puritanical Clare brothers being spectators at this 'ungodly' event in which Marlott's maidens hold peeled willow wands (possibly shortened and portable versions of the Maypole, an emblem of phallic potency).[7] However, any amusement is tempered by underlying gravity, given the disastrous effects Angel's misperceptions of Tess will have when they meet again at Talbothays.

At the outset of his literary career, Hardy speculated whether the esoteric meaning folk-practices had for the communities who originally shaped them was recoverable in the late-Victorian world. He sought in cultural 'survivals' a wisdom that might yield badly needed correctives and solutions to contemporary problems. But through the Marlott club-walking *Tess* finally lays these hopes to rest after the grievous disappointments of *The Return of the Native*'s mummers' play and the sowing of hemp-seed in *The Woodlanders*: both fertility rituals ill-adapted, even in a 'disguised form' (*Tess* 19), to the exigencies of contemporary society. Like Blackmore Vale's 'hollow-trunked trees' (*Tess* 19), these ceremonies have been rendered empty shells by time, witnesses of the earliest ages whose testimony is meagre at best, revealing habits of mind radically different from our own. Not even Hardy's capricious visual angles can animate the traditional parade, in which genuine 'maidens' oddly mingle with some of Marlott's most venerable female inhabitants, whose 'wrinkled faces' had 'almost a grotesque, certainly a pathetic, appearance in such a jaunty situation' (*Tess* 19). The incongruity of these aged women undercuts the notion that the annual May-time procession and dance might be, as Angel and his brothers assume, 'part of a rural idyll'.[8] Sunlight imparts to the white garments of the 'older characters' a 'cadaverous tint', and the whole episode indicates that Hardy's time-voyaging no longer comprises a defiant expression of artistic vigour. Desperate, embattled and searching, the Hardy of *Tess* creates deep disquiet instead of *A Laodicean*'s sprightly verbal

---

[6] In the manuscript of *Tess*, Hardy uses the title *Answers to Essays and Reviews* for the book that the Clare family read, almost the same title as the actual *Replies* (1862) to the controversial manifesto of liberal theology *Essays and Reviews*.

[7] William Stukeley, in his *Itinerarium Curiosum* (1724), p. 24, describes a May-Pole in Lincolnshire 'where...the boys annually keep up the festival of the *Floralia* on May Day, making a procession to this hill with May gads (as they call them) in their hands. This is a white willow wand, the bark peel'd off, ty'd round with cowslips, a thyrsus of the Bacchinals.' Quoted in John Brand, *Popular Antiquities*, I, 241n. See Langdon Elsbree, 'Tess and the Local Cerealia', *Philological Quarterly* 45 (October 1961), 606-8.

[8] Joe Fisher, *Hidden Hardy* (London: Macmillan, 1992), p. 162.

performances that permit the reader to assess a potentially threatening situation from a piquant perspective. Tess participates willingly in a rural event whose mythic aspect Christianity has made inaccessible to all except the omniscient narrator. The cheerfulness of the celebrants harks back to the 'days before the habit of taking long views had reduced emotions to a monotonous average' (*Tess* 19). Yet these dancers cannot freely immerse themselves in the event as their remote ancestors did. A once sacred ritual commemorating the return of fecundity to the earth after the winter months has lapsed into a 'crude exposure to public scrutiny' (*Tess* 20). The emergence of an unproductive introspection alien to the 'fancies and prefigurative superstitions' (*Tess* 47) in which the heroine is steeped becomes apparent in the club-walkers' 'inability...to dissociate self-consciousness from their features' (*Tess* 20). The 'ache of modernism' – those 'feelings which might almost have been called those of the age' (*Tess* 129) – infects Tess as much as Angel Clare.

In earlier novels, most notably in *A Laodicean* with its nimble depiction of the 'fossil of feudalism' Stancy Castle, Hardy was able to reach beyond a sense of stagnation and energize the seemingly frayed relics of previous generations through his idiosyncratic mode of regard. But the status of these impish effects in Hardy's artistic repertoire begins to alter drastically in *Two on a Tower*, whose experiments in spectatorship produce more menacing results, a trend which intensifies in *The Mayor of Casterbridge* and *The Woodlanders*. Hardy is no longer certain that by manipulating tone or perspective he can present the moralities and social verities of his cultural heritage so as to temper their corrosive impact. His inability to modify painful features of late-Victorian England, only the 'light' in which they are seen, becomes a source of increasing frustration to him. Yet in *Tess* even sunbeams reveal a deathly 'bluish pallor' or a 'cadaverous tint' (*Tess* 19). That 'Ideal and real clashed slightly as the sun lit up' the club-walkers is ominous because *Tess* contains arguably more competing perspectives and chiaroscuro than any other Hardy novel. Relentlessly innovative though they are, Hardy's 'ways of seeing' intimate melancholy embitterment – already implicit in Fitzpiers's sub-Shelleyan follies and Grace's whimsical fantasy of Winterborne as a woodland god – with his own alternative views as fostering only harmful misconception or unwholesome, objectifying voyeurism.

The Marlott club-walk hints at the continual presentation of Tess in terms of the way she is 'seen' by others, until the inner meaning of her character seems composed wholly of other people's crude and reductive readings of her. Hardy, in his controversial subtitle, ironically misapplying the terminology of conventional Christian morality, declares that his 'Pure

Woman' is 'faithfully presented'.[9] But he knows how easily an 'image' of Tess supplants the thing itself, so the claim that she is 'faithfully presented' becomes ridiculous in a novel that continually fetishizes her visual presence. She is an assortment of all the object images the novel defines her as, primarily deriving from egoistic male spectators such as the pious Clare brothers at the Marlott parade. From the moment Tess is identified by her white muslin dress at the club-walking until she is 'unfurled' as a black flag over Wintoncester gaol, Hardy intentionally does the opposite of uncovering the innermost secrets of her being. This acute failure of representation is central to the novel's polemic. Tess's struggles to become a subject in her own right, mistress of her words and body, end in defeat.[10] The obsessive erotic imaging of Tess as a visual object, fetishistically focusing on body parts (her hair, mouth, eyes, arms) buries the 'real' woman under a mass of misleading or contradictory 'impressions' or 'seemings'.[11] As the opening quotation implies, an unacknowledged protagonist of *Tess* is the illuminative medium through which people and places are viewed. A perception of potency carries with it a formidable set of complications which lead us to question seriously what we are looking at or through: sunbeams (Marlott club-walk and harvest), flickering shadows or the glow of candlelight (Sorrow's baptism), pollen dust (the Chaseborough revel) and dense luminous fog (the night of rape/seduction under the 'Druidical oaks' of The Chase). These distorting media accentuate the tragic consequences of not seeing clearly and problematize the mythological representation, hinted at by the 'local Cerealia', which Hardy persistently employs in relation to his heroine who, according to Shirley A. Stave, 'becomes emblematic of the Great Goddess, the informing spirit of a Pagan consciousness'.[12]

   Tess of the d'Urbervilles continues where *The Mayor of Casterbridge* and *The Woodlanders* finish, in that it chronicles the death of a figure traditionally associated with the blossoming organic fecundity of an

---

[9] See Susan Bernstein, 'Confessing and Editing: The Politics of Purity in Hardy's *Tess*', in *Virginal Sexuality and Textuality in Victorian Literature*, ed. Lloyd S. Davis (Albany, New York: State University of New York Press, 1993), pp. 159-78.

[10] See Jules David Law, 'Sleeping Figures: Hardy, History and the Gendered Body', *English Literary History* 65:1 (Spring 1998), 223-57; David Garlock, 'Entangled Genders: Plasticity, Indeterminacy, and Constructs of Sexuality in Darwin and Hardy', *Dickens Studies Annual* 27 (1998), 287-305.

[11] Only on two crucial occasions does Tess vanish from the voyeuristic view: when Alec commits 'the act of darkness' with her under the Druidical oaks of The Chase, and when she is executed by hanging. The fundamental realities of her existence, which the Persephone myth articulates (sex and death), are unknowable.

[12] Shirley A. Stave, *The Decline of the Goddess: Nature, Culture, and Women in Thomas Hardy's Fiction* (London: Blackwood, 1995), p. 101.

agricultural milieu. Like Michael Henchard and Giles Winterborne before her, Tess Durbeyfield is the 'survival' of a moribund mythology whose actuality we no longer accept, because Hardy has fallen out with some of his own favourite techniques. This stems from his awareness of a profound and genuine loss, or perversion, of what is natural.

Whereas the principal centre of interest in *The Mayor* and *The Woodlanders* invites comparison with the violent primitive combat at Nemi that opens Frazer's *The Golden Bough* (1890), Tess Durbeyfield's story is a demanding revision of the archetypal pattern of losing, grieving and searching in the Persephone myth – one of the most emotionally charged and resonant Greek divine tales. The 'mother', Demeter/Ceres, was founder of the Eleusinian mysteries, protectress of the flourishing corn, and goddess of agriculture in general; her daughter Kore, the 'maiden', was otherwise known as Persephone or Proserpine.[13] Hardy was fully aware of the scalding ironies and incongruities he could exploit by an extended parallel between the traditional ballad narrative of the violation of female innocence and the abduction and rape of Persephone by Pluto, the Underworld Lord. Hardy would have endorsed John Addington Symonds's assertion in 1890 that 'Our artists, whether poets, painters, or musicians, are...right to employ the legends of past ages for the expression of thoughts and emotions belonging to the present...Myths, by reason of their symbolic pregnancy and spontaneity of origin, are everlastingly elastic'.[14] A myth was such a vague, amorphous configuration that it could, in Symonds's opinion, be easily adapted to the conceptions of succeeding generations.[15] According to A. H. Sayce, myth 'takes its colouring from each generation that repeats it, and clothes it with the passions and the interests and the knowledge of the men in whose mouths it lives and grows'.[16] This is a crucial point, because Hardy felt no inconsistency in absorbing mythic materials into a novel that aimed to be topical, showing female vulnerability to male exploitation and to the implacable rigours of class convention. He uses the rich complexities of the Persephone tale as an imaginative 'lens' through which to gauge late-Victorian England and its discontents. His classical allusions buttress the social critique that becomes increasingly shrill in the mature novels, which

---

[13] 'Kore' becomes 'Persephone' after she is abducted and claimed by Pluto.

[14] John Addington Symonds, 'Nature Myths and Allegories', in *Essays Speculative and Suggestive*, 2 vols. (London: Chapman & Hall, 1890), II, 196-7.

[15] For a searching analysis of Hardy's *Tess* in relation to Symonds's ideas on myth see Glen Wickens, 'Hardy and the Aesthetic Mythographers: The Myth of Demeter and Persephone in *Tess of the d'Urbervilles*', *University of Toronto Quarterly* 53:1 (Fall 1983), 85-106.

[16] A. H. Sayce, *The Principles of Comparative Philology* (London: Trubner & Co., 1875), p. 320n.

are all obsessively preoccupied with the legal and physical relations between the sexes.[17]

An obstructive critical prejudice dismisses Hardy's mythological framework in *Tess* as little more than the faltering display of classical scholarship by a self-educated vulgarian. However, from the moment Hardy altered the description of the Marlott club-walking from 'Vestal rite' in the manuscript to 'local Cerealia' for the *Graphic* serialization, he was determined that the Persephone myth, far from being an incidental detail, would be seamlessly woven into the imaginative fabric of his narrative. With the replacement of the Roman goddess of fire, Vesta,[18] by Ceres/Demeter, goddess of the corn-bearing earth, as the tutelary deity of the festivities, Hardy brings a more worrying note into the May Day event, whose resonances are felt throughout the novel. His final substitution of 'local Cerealia' for the earlier amendment may have been connected to the artistic stimulus provided by reading *The Golden Bough*, Frazer's immense compilation of sexual-religious mythology across many cultures, during the early months of 1891.[19] A darkly prophetic undercurrent distinguishes the revised club-walk episode, foreshadowing the polemical purpose of later chapters in which Hardy examines the relationship between virginity, fecundity and purity; and life, death and rebirth. His placing of the mythological motif near the beginning of the novel creates an expectation that Tess, like Ceres the Italo-Roman goddess of agriculture identified with the Greek Demeter, is destined to experience traumatic loss and grief; and, like Persephone, in her overall aspect of unsullied maidenhood, to endure physical violation at the hands of a sexually predatory stranger, and make a symbolic visit to the Underworld. From an early period of composition then, Hardy was brooding over how allusions to the Demeter and Persephone story might be subtly extended into a pattern of symbolic

---

[17] Critics inevitably speculate on an autobiographical motivation: '[Hardy] would have realised as he wrote *The Mayor, The Woodlanders, Tess* and *Jude* that his emotional concern over his own marital relationship with Emma was influencing his subject and producing what may be seen as a "Marriage Quartet".' See James Gibson, *Thomas Hardy: A Literary Life* (London: Macmillan, 1996), p. 124.

[18] The priestesses of this deity, Vestal Virgins, had to watch in turn, by day and night, the fire in the temple of Vesta on the state hearth. Their purity was all-important. Those who broke their vows of chastity were punished by death.

[19] The first edition of *The Golden Bough: A Study of Comparative Religion* appeared in two volumes in 1890 with a preface dated 8 March of that year. This first edition is the one Hardy read. On pages 63-4 of the Hardy notebook entitled 'Literary Notes II' is an entry headed '*The Golden Bough*. J. G. Frazer, M.A. vol. I (July. 7. 91)' which describes Frazer's book as 'a work on primitive superstitions & religion'. The entry then proceeds to summarize the contents of Volume I of the book, which Hardy had finished by that date. See *Literary Notebooks*, II, entry 1872.

correspondences. He sought to deepen its ethical complexity and aesthetic relevance to his modern theme of the 'march of mind'.[20]

Since *A Laodicean*'s artful use of Captain de Stancy as an Actaeon figure voyeuristically spying on the Diana-like Paula Power in her gymnasium, and the portrayal of a Dionysian William Dare, Hardy has been manipulating with increased sophistication mythological motifs to act as an ironic counterpoint to the dominant strand of his action. There is much evidence in the *Literary Notes* and the *Life* that Hardy monitored with avid curiosity erudite discussions of myth in the 1870s and 1880s.[21] He may have extracted a great deal of information from a lively 1885-86 debate in the pages of *The Nineteenth Century* journal between Max Müller and other anthropological luminaries on mythography.[22] Moreover, Hardy's reading, for example, of John Addington Symonds's *Studies of the Greek Poets* (1870)[23] alone would have acquainted him with most of the recent approaches to the investigation of ancient tales.[24] Although there is no evidence to suggest Hardy studied John Ruskin's chief work on mythology, *The Queen of the Air* (1869),[25] the *Literary Notebooks* indicates that he did read the second part at least of Walter Pater's impressionistic account of

---

[20] Alfred, Lord Tennyson, 'Locksley Hall' in *The Poems of Tennyson*, II, 128.

[21] Hardy knew Max Müller's work in the 1870s. See *Literary Notebooks*, I, entry 166; and *Literary Notebooks*, I, entry 578. On Hardy's familiarity with Müller's work see Michael Millgate, 'Hardy's Fiction: Some Comments on the Present State of Criticism', *English Literature in Transition* 14 (1971), 230-38.

[22] The essays are contained in volumes 18 and 19 of *The Nineteenth Century*: W. E. Gladstone, 'The Dawn of Creation and of Worship', 18 (1885), 698-714; T. H. Huxley, 'The Interpreters of Genesis and the Interpreters of Nature', 18 (1885), 849-60; Max Müller, 'Solar Myths', 18 (1885), 910-25; W. E. Gladstone, 'Proem to Genesis', 19 (1886), 1-21; Andrew Lang, 'Myths and Mythologists', 19 (1886), 46-60; T. H. Huxley, 'Mr Gladstone and Genesis', 19 (1886), 191-205; Henry Drummond, 'Mr Gladstone and Genesis', 19 (1886), 206-14. See *Literary Notebooks*, I, entries 1359 and 1361.

[23] John Addington Symonds, *Studies in the Greek Poets*, 2nd edn. 2 vols. (London: Smith, Elder, 1879). Hardy quotes extensively and with approval from Symonds. He took excerpts from the second series edition of the *Studies* (London, 1876). See *Literary Notebooks*, I, entry 615, which is a quotation from Symonds's discussion of Aeschylus. Hardy later came to know Symonds (1840-93) personally, and some of their correspondence is preserved.

[24] Symonds criticizes Max Müller's solar and linguistic theories, and more concisely, indicates the key flaws of other readings of mythic material: Euhemerism, George Grote's notion that myths are the products of irrational fancy; the Christian belief that myths are a debasement of untainted truth revealed to mankind by God; the interpretation of myths as parables conceived by priests and wise-men so as to communicate certain complex truths to the popular mind; the reduction of mythology to fetishism; and the idea of viewing myths as conscious poetry.

[25] John Ruskin, *The Queen of the Air: being a study of the Greek myths of cloud and storm* (Kent: George Allen, 1887).

'The Myth of Demeter and Persephone' (1876).[26] Both the title of *Tess*'s First Phase, 'The Maiden', suggesting Persephone's epithet, and Hardy's description of the Marlott festivities as a 'local Cerealia', referring to the Roman celebrations held in honour of Ceres during eight days in the month of April, alert us to a telling connection between Tess and the figures of Demeter and Persephone. Hardy may be in danger of deploying timeless archetypes that work to naturalize gender oppression, and he may lack a thoroughly defined sense of the political implications of classical reference in relation to the contemporary woman question; however, he establishes an ironic distance between reader and central protagonist. Although Marlott was once occupied by the myth-making Romans, Tess could not at this juncture know of any mythological precedent for her life. Hardy uses some of the emblems of Demeter and Persephone – flowers and a basket of fruit – to link his young heroine to the unified goddess. Tess's most unique feature is her 'flower-like mouth', and she carries a 'bunch of white flowers' (*Tess* 19) in her left hand during the Marlott procession. After visiting Alec d'Urberville she suddenly blushes at the spectacle of 'roses at her breast; roses in her hat; roses and strawberries in her basket to the brim' (*Tess* 47). In most accounts of the abduction of Persephone, including Walter Pater's, the divine maiden is picking roses as well as poppies when Hades or Pluto carries her off to the Underworld. Ovid, whom Hardy later draws upon to illustrate how Chaseborough 'metamorphosed itself thus madly' (*Tess* 67), portrays Ceres's daughter as 'Filling her basket, then the hollow of small breasts/With new-picked flowers'.[27] Hardy modifies this flower scene by having Alec take Tess to the 'fruit-garden' where he feeds her strawberries of the 'British Queen' variety and then adorns Tess's hat and basket of fruit with roses, giving her some also, 'to put in her bosom'. The 'British Queen' strawberries symbolically doom Tess to return near the end of the novel as Alec's Queen, his paid mistress, at the chic Sandbourne resort, recalling the pomegranate seeds that Hades tricks Persephone into eating to guarantee that she will return to the Underworld and rule as his 'Queen' for one-third of the year.

The Marlott club-walking implies that at crucial points in the narrative Tess, though standing on the threshold of 'rebirth', will never attain wholeness of being like the nature-goddess to whom she is compared. The

---

[26] Walter Pater, 'The Myth of Demeter and Persephone' in his *Greek Studies: A Series of Essays* (London: Macmillan, 1910), p. 93. Hardy's excerpt from Pater is taken from 'The Myth of Demeter and Persephone: II', *Fortnightly Review* 109 (1 January 1876), 263. See *Literary Notebooks*, I, entry 305. For Hardy's further reading in Pater, see *Literary Notebooks*, I, entries 1542, 1559, 1716.

[27] Ovid, *The Metamorphoses*, trans. Horace Gregory (New York: Mentor, 1964), p. 151. Hardy mentions reading 'some Horace and Ovid' about 1856. See *Life*, p. 28.

reunion of Demeter and Persephone contrasts with the stability that Tess never regains after the night of rape/seduction, when she is again wearing the white muslin gown of maidenhood displayed at the 'local Cerealia' (*Tess* 19), connecting this scene with the intricate pattern of sacrificial images which are present in the most vivid scenes in the novel. This event is rehearsed when Alec carries an apprehensive and frightened Tess – again dressed in white – off to his residence in a manner that grotesquely parodies Hades's seizing of the unwilling Persephone and bearing her away in his chariot to the Underworld. But instead of the Underworld god's 'golden car',[28] Alec ironically possesses a 'dog-cart' (*Tess* 57). And we are never permitted to forget the bitterly incongruous images of a Demeter who in the myth, once realizing that her daughter has been stolen, embarks on a frantic search and does everything in her power to rescue her, including laying waste the upper world which brings humanity to the verge of extinction, and Joan Durbeyfield who actively engineers the union between her daughter and the supposed relative of wealth. Like Pluto, whose name the Romans often translated into *Dis*, the Latin word for 'riches',[29] Alec has sufficient funds (derived from his father's commercial success in the industrialized North) to purchase his pleasure and capitalize on Tess's deep sense of obligation towards her impecunious family. As he drives the heroine downhill, the ground seems to open up like the chasm out of which Hades suddenly arose: 'The aspect of the straight road enlarged with their advance, the two banks dividing like a splitting stick' (*Tess* 57). Hardy stresses descent ('Down, down they sped, the wheels humming like a top'), and the name of Alec's country estate is appropriately 'The Slopes', whose incongruous amalgam of modern sterility and primitive fertility is its most troubling feature:

> [The house]...was of recent erection – indeed almost new – and of the same rich red colour that formed such a contrast with the evergreens of the lodge. Far behind the corner of the house – which rose like a geranium bloom against the subdued colours around – stretched the soft azure landscape of The Chase – a truly venerable tract of forest land; one of the few remaining woodlands in England of undoubted primaeval date, wherein Druidical mistletoe was still found on aged oaks, and where enormous yew-trees, not planted by the hand of man, grew as they had grown when they were pollarded for bows. All this sylvan antiquity however, though visible from The Slopes, was outside the immediate boundaries of the estate. (*Tess* 41)

---

[28] James Frazer, *The Golden Bough*, p. 406.
[29] See Carl Kerenyi, *Archetypal Images of Mother and Daughter*, trans. Ralph Manheim (Princeton: Princeton University Press, 1967), p. 30.

The sharply ironic contrast between the bright red newness of 'The Slopes' and the eerie prehistoric wilderness of The Chase[30] is underlined by the 'Druidical mistletoe...still found on aged oaks'. Hardy is referring to Pliny's famous description of the main rite of the Druids, quoted by Frazer in *The Golden Bough*.[31] Mistletoe was regarded as the semen of the gods:[32]

> From time immemorial the mistletoe has been the object of superstitious veneration in Europe. It was worshipped by the Druids, as we learn from a famous passage of Pliny...'The Druids...esteem nothing more sacred than the mistletoe and the tree on which it grows, provided only that the tree is an oak. But apart from this they choose oak-woods for their sacred groves and perform no sacred rites without oak-leaves; so that the very name of Druids may be regarded as a Greek appellation derived from their worship of the oak[33]

It is to The Chase that Alec takes Tess on the night he rapes/seduces her, a region whose 'primeval yews and oaks' (*Tess* 77) recalls the 'old oak copses and irregular belts of timber' (*Tess* 19) surrounding Marlott Green on which the club-walking is held.[34] The 'thick darkness' (*Tess* 76) that engulfs her on this night implies The Chase is Hardy's version of the Frazerian underworld, a 'gloomy subterranean realm',[35] to which Hades forcibly transports Persephone. The emptily hedonistic Alec, however, is no throwback to the complex Druidical rites analysed in *The Golden Bough*. He displays unfettered pagan sensualism without a modicum of pagan belief.

After her experience in The Chase, which Hardy portrays as a macabre parody of Hades/Pluto's abduction of 'the maiden', Tess is unable to reinvent herself in accordance with the seasonal cycle of dissolution and regeneration articulated by the Persephone myth. This failure to recreate

---

[30] Hardy's Chase is reminiscent of Keats's 'old oak forest', the prehistoric place of natural origins in the poem 'On Sitting Down to Read *King Lear* Once Again'. See *Keats: Complete Poetical Works*, ed. H. W. Garrod (Oxford: Oxford University Press, 1988), p. 380.

[31] D. H. Lawrence would also exploit Frazer's analysis of this ritual in the poem 'Under the Oak'. See *Complete Poems*, ed. with introd. Vivian de Sola Pinto and F. Warren Roberts (Harmondsworth, Middlesex: Penguin, 1993).

[32] Mistletoe is placed above the honeymoon bed at Wellbridge which is never slept in and later Tess contemplates suicide under mistletoe.

[33] James Frazer, *The Golden Bough*, p. 750.

[34] See Ellen Rooney, ' "A Little More Than Persuading": *Tess* and the subject of sexual violence', in *Rape and Representation*, ed. Lynn A. Higgins and Brenda R. Silver (New York: Columbia University Press, 1991), pp. 87-114.

[35] James Frazer, *The Golden Bough*, p. 406.

herself may result from the fact that she simply has the wrong audience for the presentation of a new identity. This notion harmonizes with Hardy's idea of theatricality and genre – Tess may be a poor judge of what 'genre' best 'fits' her new self-characterization and the 'unities' of her situation. The bewitching fascination the Persephone myth had for Hardy might be explained by the fact that it allowed for the notion of darkness and a period of desiccation as a prelude to gradual revival. Yet in Chapter 14, when Tess baptizes her illegitimate child with the help of her younger brothers and sisters, she does not discover within herself enough potency to prevent the death of her baby, who is born in the spring, the time when Persephone returns to Demeter, and is buried in August during the harvest, when the Romans commemorated Persephone's disappearance. Hardy develops a crucial ironic relation here. All happens as in the myth, yet it is all wrong: Alec is not Pluto and the late-Victorian belief system does not brook pagan fertility, quite the opposite in fact. Moreover, Hardy rearranges events: Tess's Kore in Spring is at Talbothays which offers only a heady illusion of rebirth; and her winter in Hades is at Flintcomb-Ash.

The girl-mother is reminiscent of Pater's Demeter 'our Lady of Sorrows, the *mater dolorosa* of the ancient world'.[36] Stately in her priestlike white nightgown (again invoking the garment an untarnished Tess wears at the Marlott club-walking), the protagonist assumes a magical prestige which late-Victorian bourgeois society would never allow its unmarried mothers.[37] Hardy freezes the scene in hypnotic specificity:

> Her figure looked singularly tall and imposing as she stood in her long white night-gown, a thick cable of twisted dark hair hanging straight down her back to her waist. The kindly dimness of the weak candle abstracted from her form and features the little blemishes which sunlight might have revealed – the stubble-scratches upon her wrists, and the weariness of her eyes – her high enthusiasm having a transfiguring effect upon the face which had been her undoing, showing it as a thing of immaculate beauty, with a touch of dignity which was almost regal. (*Tess* 99)

'The kindly dimness of the weak candle abstracted...the little blemishes' anticipates the sham transfiguration of Alec in his 'half-clerical' garb that abstracts 'the dandyism from his features' (*Tess* 297) during Tess's time at Flintcomb-Ash. As with the priest of nature, Giles Winterborne, seemingly

---

[36] Walter Pater, *Greek Studies*, p. 114.
[37] The role of a maternal figure is not new to Tess. In effect she is the only dependable parent in the Durbeyfield household and assumes her mother's responsibilities when Mrs Durbeyfield escapes to Rolliver's Inn.

rising out of the Hintock soil, the sun reflecting off his cider-making apparatus in *The Woodlanders* (156), Hardy makes us question whether we might be victims of a trick of light when Tess endeavours to save Sorrow. However, the heroine is not simply transported 'into spirituality, into saintly transfiguration',[38] for she is a very tangible presence: weary-eyed with stubble-scratched wrists. The 'things done' of this makeshift ritual are not as significant as the imperfect girl-mother at its centre, whose fervency fills the young children with awe. Tess refuses to let the outmoded moral scruples of patriarchal hegemony cast an oppressive shadow over her motherhood. In imitating a Christian rite she achieves an aura of sanctity, though not of Christian sanctity. To contend that Hardy draws her in an image of the 'immaculate' Virgin Mother seriously misreads her 'ecstasy of faith' and the ferocious irony at the expense of the sacrament of baptism with which the chapter closes.

> The ecstasy of faith almost apotheosized her; it set upon her face a glowing irradiation and brought a red spot into the middle of each cheek; while the miniature candle-flame inverted in her eye-pupils shone like a diamond. The children gazed up at her with more and more reverence, and no longer had a will for questioning. She did not look like Sissy to them now, but as a being large, towering and awful, a divine personage with whom they had nothing in common. (*Tess* 99-100)

Tess's spiritual regeneration is seen through the eyes of her dumbstruck younger brothers and sisters: 'She did not look like Sissy to them now'. To the breathlessly rapt children she assumes divine status, but as Hardy indicates, her 'ecstasy of faith' is not sufficient to apotheosize her given the prevailingly sombre and pensive mood of the scene. How can we put a more explicit analytical gloss on the nature of Tess's 'ecstasy'? To label her experience as unguarded rapture or a fundamental revelation of human individuality is inadequate. Walter Pater, in his 'Conclusion' to *The Renaissance: Studies in Art and Poetry* (1873), describes ecstasy as a moment of intoxication when the body and matter of the physical world coalesce. Tess's individual moment of transfiguration reveals a Paterian sense of quickened consciousness or a creative augmentation of the self. Hardy identifies a state of feeling within civilized identity so intense yet so fleeting and fugitive that the expressive effects of language can barely do it justice. At the height of her maternal anxiety Tess displays for one instant a

---

[38] Rosemarie Morgan, *Women and Sexuality in the Novels of Thomas Hardy* (London: Routledge, 1991), p. 102.

grace that is alien to the unforgiving, retributive Church imaged as consigning her illegitimate baby to the nethermost recess of hell. This dramatically stylized picture of the girl-mother is similar to Giles Winterborne's 'apotheosis' in that Hardy does not imply the development of a character's individual thought-patterns. Neither figure seems aware that they have been invested with a preternatural strength.

The elements of Paterian 'ecstasy' are also located in Hardy's depiction of the barn dance at Chaseborough, though in a markedly debased form. The time is a Saturday night in September, the month of the Eleusinian mysteries honouring Demeter and Persephone,[39] and the occasion is one of the weekly jaunts to the 'decayed market-town' (*Tess* 65). Hardy exploits the incongruity between his lax modern-day 'pilgrims' (*Tess* 65) who go to Chaseborough then spend Sunday 'sleeping off the dyspeptic effects of the curious compounds sold to them as beer' (*Tess* 65), and the aspirants of the Eleusinian mysteries, 'the most famous and solemn religious rites of ancient Greece'.[40] At Eleusis, Demeter disclosed to those who had been specially initiated the lessons of law and self-discipline, the incalculable benefits of agriculture and education, of maintaining an identity rooted in some fixed geographically and socially defined milieu.[41] Worshippers sought the promise of Demeter and Persephone that there would be springtime regeneration, the eternal return of life to earth in the new corn. Some of these religious observances are ironically echoed in Hardy's portrayal of the 'private little jig' at Chaseborough (*Tess* 66). The Trantridge farm workers use the agricultural festivities as an opportunity to 'drink hard' and dance. 'The choice spirit', says Hardy, 'who ruled The Slopes in that vicinity' (*Tess* 65) is Dionysus, who was celebrated in the Eleusinian mysteries not as ruler but as a divine child. The unearthly transfiguring effects of light which caused 'ideal and real' to 'clash' during the Marlott club-walking (*Tess* 19) are intensified here, yet another stubborn 'survival' of primitive fertility rituals:

> It was a windowless erection used for storage, and from the open
> door there floated into the obscurity a mist of yellow radiance, which

---

[39] 'The Eleusinian mysteries were celebrated in the month Boedromian (September-October), at the time of sowing'. See M. C. Howatson (gen. ed.), *The Oxford Companion to Classical Literature*, 2nd edn. (Oxford: Oxford University Press, 1989), p. 377.

[40] James Frazer, *The Golden Bough*, p. 408.

[41] See Frazer's description of the Thesmophoria rites at one of Demeter's festivals (*The Golden Bough*, p. 483). In ancient Greek a *thesmos* is a law or settled custom. During the annual autumn festival Demeter was honoured under the sobriquet Demeter Thesmophoros, or Demeter the Bearer of Laws. This implies that at one level the festival involved the cultivation of social habit consequent upon establishing secure, agrarian communities.

> at first Tess thought to be illuminated smoke. But on drawing nearer
> she perceived that it was a cloud of dust, lit by candles within the
> outhouse, whose beams upon the haze carried forward the outline of
> the doorway into the wide night of the garden. (*Tess* 66)

The border between the actual and the imaginary begins to dissolve:
'when [Tess] came close and looked in she beheld indistinct forms racing
up and down to the figure of the dance, the silence of their footfalls arising
from their being overshoe in "scroff" – that is to say the powdery residuum
from the storage of peat and other products, the stirring of which by their
turbulent feet created the nebulosity that involved the scene'. Hardy's
archly pedantic definition of 'scroff' implies that he is compiling a
Barnesian glossary of Dorset dialect. The thick, choking mist of pollen and
dust, linked with passion and destructive sexuality in the novel, shrouds the
Trantridge revellers from view. That the excitations and commotions of
feeling generated by the dance result in 'a sort of vegeto-human pollen'
(*Tess* 66), signals Hardy's ironic sense of the preposterous in this episode.
Under the influence of 'liquor' (*Tess* 67) and enlivened by the immediacy
of music as it dynamically associates bodies, the dancers feel a complete
oneness with nature; in the heady dreamlike atmosphere it appears as if
they have been transmuted into lustful classical demigods. By overtly
conceiving the dancers in terms of pagan mythology, Hardy accentuates the
sense of threat and barely suppressed chaos. Perhaps, like Tess, he is
fearful that any distinction between the 'creative' and the 'destructive',
between inspiration and dissipation, cannot be emphatically established.
That he simultaneously acknowledges the deep power and significance of
the communal occasion, yet distances himself from it reveals a grave
anxiety about, even alienation from, the incomplete view of nature afforded
here.

As in the Marlott club-walking (Chapter 2) and during the improvised
baptism (Chapter 14), Tess stands on the brink of being 'reborn'. However,
the orgiastic Chaseborough dance is a fertility ritual in which the morally
sensitive Tess cannot participate, and she resists the affective summons.
Although she is preternaturally responsive to music as a means of offering
sudden expansions of thought and sympathy, the Chaseborough episode
shows a hypnotized automatism taking over the dancers and yields no
positive unfolding of selfhood. Not only has Tess outgrown her mother's
peasant mentality, she is also unable to reconcile delirious immersion in the
weekend debauch with her overriding desire for ethical order. The dance
measure – infused with oppressive summer eroticism – agitates her, for the
scene is charged with a half-exhilarating, half-diabolic atmosphere, in
which possession and sexuality merge. As a youngster Hardy played the

fiddle at these kinds of country-dances,[42] often in company of his father as first violinist and his uncle as cellist. He witnessed how moderated movements kept in check by rhythmical restraint could suddenly descend into rowdy spontaneity.[43] Hardy implies that pagan joy has dwindled into reckless self-abandon:

> Through this floating fusty *debris* of peat and hay, mixed with the perspirations and warmth of the dancers, and forming together a sort of vegeto-human pollen, the muted fiddles feebly pushed their notes, in marked contrast to the spirit with which the measure was trodden out. They coughed as they danced, and laughed as they coughed. Of the rushing couples there could barely be discerned more than the high lights – the indistinctness shaping them to satyrs clasping nymphs – a multiplicity of Pans whirling a multiplicity of Syrinxes; Lotis attempting to elude Priapus, and always failing.
>
> At intervals a couple would approach the doorway for air, and the haze no longer veiling their features, the demigods resolved themselves into the homely personalities of her own next-door neighbours. Could Trantridge in two or three short hours have metamorphosed itself thus madly! (*Tess* 66-7)

On this night when the dancers assume the attributes of primitive gods, Tess is seduced/raped. In Greek mythology the water nymph, Syrinx, was pursued by the lascivious fertility god Pan, a creature with the horns, ears and legs of a goat; Syrinx could escape because the other gods, showing pity, turned her into a reed. Priapus, the god of animal and vegetable fertility, pursued Lotis, the daughter of the sea-god, but she also escaped by turning into a lotus flower. Tess does not elude her pursuer in The Chase. The apparent transformation of the reeling couples into 'satyrs clasping nymphs' suggests that 'levity' (*Tess* 66) and 'whorage' (*Tess* 70) are gradually eroding the time-honoured responsibilities of farm life. Unlike the 'local Cerealia' (*Tess* 19) once practised by Roman matrons who eschewed wine and sensual pleasure for several days, the second dance shows husbands and wives excitedly pursuing other drunken partners. The entire group of 'panting shapes' aspires to the only form of 'immortality'

---

[42] Robert Gittings, *Young Thomas Hardy* (Harmondsworth, Middlesex: Penguin, 1976), p. 58.

[43] Hardy's technical knowledge of folksong and the decaying Dorset working-class musical life in general made him better qualified to comment on traditional music than many Victorian folksong experts. See for example his letter of 1 September 1889 to J. J. Foster answering enquiries about a song. Hardy also published letters in such journals as *The English Folk Dance Society News* (e.g. Sept. 1926, pp. 384-5) and *The Journal of the English Folk Dance Society*.

left for them – to become 'demigods' through libertine surfeit. Tylor discussed dancing in relation to 'induced ecstasy' and 'demoniacal possession',[44] terms pertaining to Hardy's portrayal of the Chaseborough event when patterned simplicity gives way to dizzying activity. The effort to distinguish between human and nonhuman becomes futile: 'It was then that the ecstasy and the dream began, in which emotion was the matter of the universe, and matter but an adventitious intrusion likely to hinder you from spinning where you wanted to spin' (*Tess* 67).[45] The reader is engulfed by the revellers when Hardy shifts to the 'you' pronoun, literally bringing us down to earth with a comic collision that momentarily undercuts the disturbing strangeness of the weekly dance in which the process of possession transfigures its participants.

Hardy is careful to separate Tess's ecstatic state achieved when baptizing her child from its polluted counterpart induced by alcohol in her parents and fellow workers. The metamorphosis of the Chaseborough celebrants is, in reality, not from the human to the divine but from the human to the natural and amoral, a change strikingly imaged by the 'vegeto-human pollen' formed from the perspiration of the dancers and the dust of the shed. Only in the light of the lamp do the 'demigods' resolve themselves 'into the homely personalities' of Tess's 'next-door neighbours' (*Tess* 67). When a young man asks Tess to 'have a turn' with him, Hardy's tone and treatment modulates from the threatening to the exuberantly irreligious:

> 'Don't ye be nervous, my dear good soul!' expostulated between his coughs a young man with a wet face, and his straw hat so far back upon his head that the brim encircled it like the nimbus of a saint. 'What's yer hurry? To-morrow is Sunday, thank God, and we can sleep it off in church time. Now, have a turn with me?'
> (*Tess* 67)

The imagery of saints and halos that Hardy applies ironically to his strayed revellers on their trek homeward underlines how the Trantridge 'children of the open air' are like Tess's parents and their neighbours who evade the social 'muck and muddle' of life to seek 'beatitude' at Rolliver's tavern or

---

[44] E. B. Tylor, *Primitive Culture*, II, 420, 133.

[45] Compare this episode with the events described in Hardy's short story 'The Fiddler of the Reels'; or Dick Dewy's ecstatic perception of his cottage interior becoming 'like a picture in a dream' during the Christmas dance from *Under the Greenwood Tree*. Hardy's portrayal of the fiddlers in this episode, whose legs are 'firmly spread and eyes closed', heedless of 'the visible world' hints at the power of folk-music to express the demonic which becomes more pronounced during the Chaseborough scene.

The Pure Drop Inn.[46] They briefly attain a 'stage of mental comfort' in which 'their souls expanded beyond their skins, and spread their personalities warmly through the room' (*Tess* 30), while remaining careful to disguise their illegal drinking by repeating their 'Catechism' (*Tess* 32) about club-walking – one of the last threadbare links between Tess's ramshackle village and the nature-goddess Demeter.

That Tess is in search of a more advanced harmony analogous to that intimated by Pater becomes apparent in her refusal to be absorbed into the frenetic Chaseborough revel. The need for a purer context to enable 'rebirth' into a realm of enriched experience and multiplied consciousness is addressed in the Marlott harvesting (Chapter 14). Hardy again portrays 'survivals' of fertility myth from an unexpected angle; showing a similar resourcefulness with effects of mist and light, and a sense of suspended time and dance-like movement. But it is precisely these conditions of 'seeing' which leave the reader questioning the validity of the event as a renewed contact with mysterious, nonhuman forces. Chapter 14 opens with a depiction of a benevolent morning sun in August:

> The sun, on account of the mist, had a curious, sentient, personal look, demanding the masculine pronoun for its adequate expression. His present aspect, coupled with the lack of all human forms in the scene, explained the old-time heliolatries in a moment. One could feel that a saner religion had never prevailed under the sky. The luminary was a golden-haired, beaming, mild-eyed, godlike creature, gazing down in the vigour and intentness of youth upon an earth that was brimming with interest for him. (*Tess* 92)

The youthful sun-god overseeing the harvest establishes a picture of natural harmony and primal vitality. However, it is only because of the mist – a distorting medium that frequently induces moral and intellectual confusion in *Tess* (morning mist encourages Angel Clare's damaging illusions about the heroine in Chapter 20) – that the sun seems a benign deity, imbued with kindly human qualities. And the phrase 'one could feel that' implies a less than fully convinced interpreting observer. Hardy's attitude to the old 'heliolatries' is far from straightforward; to be in touch with primeval pagan meanings does not imply a more attractive way of life: people were once cruelly sacrificed to the sun, whose presence is aggressively tangible at one point: 'His light a little later broke through chinks of cottage shutters, throwing stripes like red-hot pokers upon

---

[46] See Denis W. Thomas, 'Drunkenness in Thomas Hardy's Novels', *College Language Association Journal* 28 (1984), 190-209.

cupboards' (*Tess* 92). Yet the sun presides over a community apparently close to the rhythms of fertility ritual: the long, rickety reaping-machine makes a ticking sound 'like the love-making of the grasshopper'; Tess and the other field-women show an intimate connection of human and natural processes; they are 'part and parcel of outdoor nature' (as the narrator says, 'A field-man is a personality afield; a field-woman is a portion of the field; she has somehow lost her own margin, imbibed the essence of her surrounding, and assimilated herself with it').[47] And the sun takes a personal interest in the dance-like motion of the workers who follow the pace of the reaping-machine and horses, contrasting with Flintcomb-Ash. However, the reminder that sun worship had its sacrificial aspect – sunlight imparts to the revolving Maltese cross of the reaping-machine 'a look of having been dipped in liquid fire' (*Tess* 92) – together with the brutal Marlott harvest-custom of killing small animals, ironically undercuts the quasi-idyllic elements of the scene:

> Rabbits, hares, snakes, rats, mice, retreated inwards as into a fastness, unaware of the ephemeral nature of their refuge, and of the doom that awaited them later in the day when, their covert shrinking to a more and more horrible narrowness, they were huddled together friends and foes, till the last few yards of upright wheat fell also under the teeth of the unerring reaper, and they were every one put to death by the sticks and stones of the harvesters. (*Tess* 93)[48]

In the opening paragraphs of Chapter 14, the harvest was presented as a mode of keeping man in touch with nature, thus drawing our attention to a reverence for order and unhurried rhythm, the involved patterning and choreography. Although 'oneness with nature is presented as a particularly female characteristic',[49] we are not invited to regard the goddess figure in Tess suckling her child during the meal-break:

---

[47] The name of Tess, a form of Theresa, is Greek for 'to glean' or 'to reap'. See R. N. G. Marken, ' "Sick for Home": The Theme of *Tess of the d'Urbervilles*', *English Studies in Canada* 4 (Fall 1978), 317-29 (see 320).

[48] Hardy's description bears a striking resemblance to an account of a Kentish practice from James Frazer's 'Notes on Harvest Customs' for the 1889 *Folk-Lore Journal*: 'as the reaping machine goes round and round the corn-field, the wild animals (hares, rabbits, &c.) retreat into the standing corn in the middle of the field, and when the last patch is to be cut down the reapers stand round it with sticks, ready to knock down and kill the animals when they dart out of the corn'. See J. G. Frazer, 'Notes on Harvest Customs', *Folk-Lore Journal* 7 (1889), 50.

[49] T. R. Wright, *Hardy and the Erotic* (London: Macmillan, 1989), p. 112.

The men who sat nearest considerately turned their faces towards the other end of the field, some of them beginning to smoke; one, with absent-minded fondness, regretfully stroking the jar that would no longer yield a stream...When the infant had taken its fill the young mother sat it upright in her lap, and looking into the far distance dandled it with a gloomy indifference that was almost dislike. (*Tess* 95)

'The worship of Demeter', says Pater, 'belongs to that older religion nearer to the earth' in which 'she is the goddess...at first, of the fertility of the earth in its wildness', and then later 'the goddess of agriculture, of the fertility of the earth when furthered by human skill'.[50] However, Hardy's tendency at this point is to demythologize and curb any expectation that Tess is now an earth-mother ensuring fertility for crops and man alike, for it is all a matter of perception.

The sophisticated scepticism and galling irony with which Hardy perceives 'survivals' have intensified significantly in the transition from *The Woodlanders* to *Tess*. Even the heroine's near-apotheosis when baptizing Sorrow is qualified by the shift in perspective and the venomous incongruities that expose the grave shortcomings of an Anglican Church whose agents fall short not only as priestly mediators between God and man but also as pastoral educators and spiritual guides. The Marlott vicar, for all his assurance to Tess that her baby will not suffer because of the improvised christening, refuses to give the child a Christian burial, although the self-appointed custodians of village respectability have more sway over his decision than either theological conviction or deference to Church hierarchy. The 'fragile soldier and servant' (*Tess* 100), a phrase ironically invoking the *miles christi*, is laid to rest 'at the cost of a shilling and a pint of beer to the sexton, in that shabby corner of God's allotment where He lets the nettles grow' (*Tess* 101). Hardy's 'humour' – if it can be called such at this stage of his novel-writing career – expresses unfeigned disgust at a social reality whose hypocritical and malicious pretences cause his witty effects to crumble amid the general confusion. But the most serious threat to any true discovery by excavation of deeper forces within Tess herself comes from Angel Clare when he appears as an exponent of the decorative rhetoric of 'Hellenic paganism'. Against the heroine's individual moment of transfiguration Hardy projects Clare's fatuous imaginings and nostalgic idealizations. The taint of trivializing dilettantism and romantic folly, infecting an already beleaguered Wessex through Fitzpiers's arrival at Little Hintock, is in *Tess* carried by the agnostic

---

[50] Walter Pater, *Greek Studies*, pp. 102, 103.

pseudo-intellectual Clare, whose visual strategies and recurrent posturing make it impossible profoundly to entertain traditional mythological representation as a means of invigorating a late-Victorian milieu.

Hardy tells us – and not without disparagement – that Clare is an 'advanced and well-meaning young man, a sample product of the last five-and-twenty years' (*Tess* 258). Given Angel is a 'sample product' of the last twenty-five years, we can view him as someone who has read, without fully comprehending, his Darwin and T. H. Huxley.[51] He bases his relationship with Tess on illusory neopaganism, and considering his rational mind has 'long discredited the old systems of mysticism', particularly Christian, he flirts with the notion 'that it might have resulted far better for mankind if Greece had been the source of the religion of modern civilisation, and not Palestine.'(*Tess* 161)[52] Nevertheless, this 'freethinker' who elevates J. S. Mill's 'intellectual liberty' (*Tess* 121) to the first article of his personal creed is ironically enslaved by the conventional morality of his father's Church, which he loves 'as one loves a parent' (*Tess* 120). Sharing Clym Yeobright's 'unconquerable...aversion to modern town-life' (*Tess* 121), this would-be scholar-gypsy expects he will become more closely attuned to the natural world at Talbothays. Clare's knowledge of classical Greece and his perception of the dairy as a lush pagan paradise replete with stereotypical pastoral presences like 'nymphs and swains' and 'Olympian shapes' allows Hardy to reintroduce the Demeter motif.

The satyrean qualities of Edred Fitzpiers and Alec d'Urberville contrast ironically with the sexual ineffectiveness and lack of animalism of Angel Clare. A complex dreamer and self-deluder, Clare is stunted, like Henry Knight and Sue Bridehead, by a highly evolved intellect that leads to ethical indecision and crippling hypersensitivity: what Arnold called 'this strange disease of modern life' with its 'heads o'ertaxed, and its palsied hearts'.[53] Hardy conveys a strong sense of Clare's moral idealism, if not of the appropriateness of his imaginative idealizing. He never permits the reader to forget, however, as Clare certainly does, that he see in nature what he wants and needs to perceive if he is to be temporarily liberated from the 'chronic melancholy' of his modern outlook. A well-bred and bookish intruder into the countryside, he is 'in the habit of neglecting the particulars of an outward scene for the general impression' (*Tess* 123). Whereas

---

[51] In Chapter 46 Tess repeats to Alec d'Urberville one of Angel's arguments, 'which might possibly have been paralleled in many a work of the pedigree ranging from the *Dictionnaire Philosophique* to Huxley's *Essays*' (*Tess* 312).
[52] Clare 'had persistently elevated Hellenic Paganism at the expense of Christianity' (*Tess* 329-330).
[53] Matthew Arnold, 'The Scholar-Gypsy', ll. 203, 205.

Fitzpiers revels in quoting Shelley, Clare actually shares physical traits with the Romantic poet. He is 'less Byronic than Shelleyan' (*Tess* 193): thin, delicate, light-haired, a sleepwalker and a Platonic idealist, 'looking for the ideal spiritual, not merely physical, relation with women'.[54] Clare neurotically denies the palpable reality of the female body; Alec and Fitzpiers often see little beyond it. D. H. Lawrence offers a judicious reading of Clare, whose spiritual violation of Tess inflicts arguably more damage than Alec's physical assault. Angel Clare has the very opposite qualities to those of Alec d'Urberville. Lawrence remarks how to the latter 'the female in himself is the only part of himself he will acknowledge: the body, the senses, that which he shares with the female. To Angel Clare, the female in himself is detestable, the body, the senses, that which he will share with a woman, is held degraded'.[55]

After her child's death, a dairymaid job at Talbothays in the verdant Blackmore Vale offers Tess a hallucinatory fantasy of rebirth, when she is stirred by the spring renewal and the 'forces of outdoor Nature' (*Tess* 109). In the sunless fog that precedes the dawn in Chapter 20, Clare deifies her. Again, Hardyan chiaroscuro becomes a distorting medium:

> The spectral, half-compounded, aqueous light which pervaded the open mead impressed them with a feeling of isolation, as if they were Adam and Eve. At this dim inceptive stage of the day Tess seemed to Clare to exhibit a dignified largeness both of disposition and physique, an almost regnant power – possibly because he knew that at that preternatural time hardly any woman so well-endowed in person as she was likely to be walking within the boundaries of his horizon...The mixed, singular, luminous gloom in which they walked along together to the spot where the cows lay, often made him think of the Resurrection-hour. He little thought that the Magdalen might be at his side. Whilst all the landscape was in neutral shade, his companion's face, which was the focus of his eyes, rising above the mist-stratum, seemed to have a sort of phosphorescence upon it. She looked ghostly, as if she were merely a soul at large...It was then...that she impressed him most deeply. She was no longer the milkmaid, but a visionary essence of woman – a whole sex condensed into one typical form. He called her Artemis, Demeter and other fanciful names, half-teasingly – which she did not like because she did not understand them. (*Tess* 134-5)

---

[54] Nancy Barrineau, 'Explanatory Notes' in *Tess of the d'Urbervilles*, ed. Juliet Grindle and Simon Gatrell (Oxford: The World's Classics, 1986), p. 397.
[55] D. H. Lawrence, *Study of Thomas Hardy*, p. 97.

Richard Carpenter writes, 'at Talbothays Hardy shows his heroine as sometimes much more impressive than a simple country lass ought by rights to be...In her naturalness, in her unsophisticated simplicity, and in her innocence...the peasant girl is at this point as complete an image of the archetypal earth-goddess as modern literature can show'.[56] His comments are misleading because it is not Hardy's sense of Tess that we receive at this moment but the impression attributed to Angel Clare. If 'the two lovers inhabit an Edenic world of unrestrained natural instincts',[57] it is one entirely of Clare's own creation. Clare is less interested in the actual, visible nature than in a mental representation of an idea of nature that shifts according to his moods and impulses. Hardy employs a double vision here: though the images mediated through Clare's perceiving consciousness are discredited, Tess is not. This could be an accurate vision of her, if only there were someone to see her accurately. The bitterest irony is that Angel completely falsifies and contaminates any glimpse of the natural. He converts the heroine's sensuous reality into the abstract essence of a tritely mythologized Nature. Into a traditionally Victorian framework of narrative omniscience, Hardy incorporates a device reminiscent of the Jamesian 'reflector'. Through Clare's erratic point of view, Hardy demonstrates, as he did when Grace Melbury transforms Winterborne into a fertility god in *The Woodlanders*, that the act of observation invests a power in the gazer to control and conceptualize what he/she sees. Angel, like Jude Fawley, is a 'lost man' who 'on visionary views would fancy feed,/Till his eye streamed with tears'.[58] Yet Hardy is scathing in his exposure of a streak of coarseness in Clare, who congratulates himself on walking with such a 'well-endowed' woman as Tess. Alec is not the only one who reduces the central protagonist to an abject and passive object, a mere source of erotic fascination.

Using the verbal and visual strategies of his modern bourgeois education, Clare remakes Tess into a specimen of pink-cheeked rustic maidenhood; he never lets her 'create an identity through differentiation on her terms'.[59] He enshrines Tess in his quasi-pagan pantheon as a 'fresh and virginal daughter of Nature', and yet selects her because she is more discerning and better schooled than the other milkmaids at Talbothays. Moreover, Hardy reveals how the young man's misconceptions thrive on tricks of light. He imposes a literary, counterfeit picture of unspoilt

---

[56] Richard Carpenter, *Thomas Hardy* (New York: Twayne, 1964), pp. 134-5.

[57] T. R. Wright, *Hardy and the Erotic*, p. 113.

[58] William Wordsworth, 'Lines: Left upon a Seat in a Yew-tree', ll. 44-6.

[59] Tom Lloyd, *Crises of Realism: Representing Experience in the British Novel, 1816-1910* (London: Associated University Presses, 1997), p. 145.

innocence and beauty on the protagonist (it is ironic that he calls her Artemis, the cold chaste goddess of the hunt, who slew with her arrows men who attempted to rape her). Demeter was also a goddess of chastity in some versions of the myth, but because of her ties with agriculture as a goddess of ripe grain, she was a fertility goddess too. Clare fancies that Tess combines the chastity of Artemis with the exuberant fruitfulness of a Demeter. This casual love-play stresses his confusion about how he should invent Tess. As the very embodiment of 'the great passionate pulse of existence' (*Tess* 161), she must be 'fresh and virginal', but without losing the productiveness of the fertility goddess, insofar as that is a real idea to him rather than the empty conceit of his educated type.

Clare imagines not the living heroine but an artificial image of divinity: essence overshadows existence in his distorted subjective perception. His injurious idealizing vision of Tess as nature-goddess is repudiated by the protagonist herself who does not comprehend the fanciful names:

> 'Call me Tess', she would say askance; and he did.
> Then it would grow lighter, and her features would become simply feminine; they had changed from those of a divinity who could confer bliss to those of a being who craved it. (*Tess* 135)

Clare shows no more belief in the pagan goddesses he conjures up than he does in anything else. However, because of Hardy's pessimistic attitude towards his own idiosyncratic mode of regard and chiaroscuro effects, he ensures that there is a thin line between Clare's imprisoning idealism and Tess's individual moment of transfiguration when baptizing her ailing child. We can compare 'the dignified largeness both of disposition and physique' which 'Tess seemed to Clare to exhibit' in the 'preternatural' early morning hours with the 'being large, towering and awful, a divine personage' with whom the Durbeyfield children 'had nothing in common' (*Tess* 100); the 'minute diamonds of moisture' which temporarily lend Tess an 'ethereal beauty' (*Tess* 134) with 'the miniature candle-flame inverted in her eye-pupils' that 'shone like a diamond' (*Tess* 99-100). Her 'seeming' to exhibit 'an almost regnant power' in Chapter 20, recalls the 'touch of dignity which was almost regal' (*Tess* 99). To Clare, 'Nature' is a brittle cultural construct; he consistently remakes Tess – he sees her with about as much pristine clarity as Jude Fawley does Christminster from the roof of the Brown House. At the time of her marriage to Clare, Hardy gives an account of Tess's sense of self:

> She knew that Angel was close to her; all the rest was a luminous mist. She was a sort of celestial person, who owed her being to

poetry; one of those classical divinities Clare was accustomed to talk
to her about when they took their walks together. (*Tess* 211)

On this special occasion, Tess thinks in a way that reveals the unmistakable
imprint of Clare's culture-bound metaphors and heedless glorifying. She
has internalized his attitude and becomes tarnished by it.

Clare abandons Tess after his appalled discovery that she is not as
chaste as Artemis after all, and makes possible her chance meeting with
Alec d'Urberville in winter at Flintcomb-Ash, when 'the low sun beamed'
in a village that is like 'a place of the dead'. The protagonist needs a second
to recover from the shock of comparing the sleazy arriviste and violent
sensualist she remembers with the dour evangelical preacher who now
approaches her. It is almost akin to a conjuring trick: 'To Tess's sense there
was, just at first, a ghastly *bizarrerie*, a grim incongruity, in the march of
these solemn words of Scripture out of such a mouth':

> It was less a reform than a transfiguration. The former curves of
> sensuousness were now modulated to lines of devotional passion.
> The lip-shapes that had meant seductiveness were now made to
> express supplication; the glow on the cheek that yesterday could be
> translated as riotousness was evangelized to-day into the splendour
> of pious rhetoric; animalism had become fanaticism; Paganism
> Paulinism. (*Tess* 297)

The word 'made' conveys the sheer effort of will required to produce so
extreme a change. But 'transfiguration', unlike its earlier occurrence to
imply Tess's multiplied consciousness during the improvised christening of
Sorrow, is used ironically in the passage to stress a bogus conversion
against which Alec's satyrean lineaments rebel. This 'grown' wheat cannot
be made 'wholesome' through Christian revelation. As Hardy's obsession
with alternative or competing perspective illustrates, the reader is unable
fully to trust a personal impression because no single way of seeing is
adequate in the mature fiction.

Tess's fraught encounter with the 'transfigured' Alec d'Urberville
occurs when she is a worker on the bleakly inhospitable Flintcomb-Ash
farm (the name suggesting burnt-out matter). Farmer Groby manages a
drab field that 'was a complexion, without features, as if a face from chin to
brow should be only an expanse of skin' (*Tess* 277). The simile here almost
matches one in two lines that Hardy recorded in his ' "1867" Notebook',
spoken by the sorrowing Demeter in Swinburne's poem, 'At Eleusis': 'All
fields are helpless in the sun, all trees/Stand as a man stripped out of all but

skin.'[60] The land around Flintcomb-Ash is imaged as a massive recumbent female, 'bosomed with semi-globular tumuli – as if Cybele the Many-breasted were supinely extended there' (*Tess* 273).[61] Walter Pater notes that Demeter 'was blended, or identified with the Rhea Cybele – the wilder earth-goddess of Phrygia'.[62] Given the hardened and unwelcoming surface of Flintcomb-Ash, it is apt that Cybele was thought to personify 'the earth in its primitive and savage state'.[63] The flints of the 'starve-acre place' (*Tess* 277) may have fertile 'phallic shapes' – perhaps a reminder that in what Frazer calls a 'ghastly rite', Cybele's priests castrated themselves in entering the service of the divinity – but the 'stubborn soil' thwarts any effort at cultivation. Upon this cheerless and deformed terrain, Tess struggles against harsh winter weather and the steam threshing-machine, whose engineer is portrayed thus:

> He was in the agricultural world, but not of it. He served fire and smoke...He travelled with his engine from farm to farm, from county to county, for as yet the steam threshing-machine was itinerant in this part of Wessex. He spoke in a strange northern accent, his thoughts being turned inwards upon himself...holding only strictly necessary intercourse with the natives, as if some ancient doom compelled him to wander here against his will in the service of his Plutonic master. (*Tess* 315-6)

The engineer, serving 'fire and smoke', has no feeling for the land; to him people are merely factors in the process of production. He is compared to a chthonic creature, a slave of Pluto Lord of the Dead. While Tess works on the machine she becomes, like Persephone in winter, literally separated from her mother, the earth. Since the effects of Alec and the threshing machine on Tess are virtually the same, reducing her towards a definition of herself as mere animal, Hardy transfers Pluto's epithet, the 'inexorable', from d'Urberville to the machine. With 'the inexorable wheels continuing

---

[60] Entry 82 from A. C. Swinburne, 'At Eleusis', ll. 43-44 in *Poems and Ballads*, first series, 5th edn. (London, 1873), p. 240 in 'The "1867" Notebook', *Literary Notebooks*, II, entry 82. The Demeter and Persephone myth is integral to Swinburne's mythic framework. Hardy quotes from Swinburne's work and alludes to it on numerous occasions throughout *Tess*. Bjork regards Swinburne as 'one of Hardy's earliest and strongest literary infatuations'. See *Literary Notebooks*, 'Annotations', I, entry 1288.

[61] This image recalls Hardy's description of Egdon in *The Mayor of Casterbridge* (330), whose tumuli 'jutted roundly into the sky from the uplands, as though they were the full breasts of Diana Multimammia supinely extended there'.

[62] Walter Pater, *Greek Studies*, p. 128.

[63] Felix Guirand (ed.), *The Larousse Encyclopedia of Mythology*, introd. Robert Graves (London: Paul Hamlyn, 1966), p. 173.

to spin', Tess unties the sheaves of corn sacred to Demeter to supply her 'Plutonic master'. Flintcomb-Ash, with its barren soil and machines that obliterate human identity, becomes for Tess 'pandaemonium' (*Tess* 324), the location of all demons and the capital of Hell in Milton's *Paradise Lost*. But she is a fertility figure who keeps her own productiveness alive amid the unrelieved desolation of the Flintcomb-Ash underworld, although the dramatic change in her physical appearance suggests otherwise: the way she mutilates her beauty and dresses to look older suggests a parallel with the grieving Demeter who alters her appearance at Eleusis to an old country hag, 'for a long time veiling her beauty under a worn countenance'.[64] But when Angel returns to claim Tess, the season is at best only a false spring: 'the so-called spring was but winter overlaid with a thin coat of greenness, and it was of a parcel with his expectations'.

Chapter 58, which describes Tess and Clare's impressions as they find themselves spending their honeymoon at Stonehenge, offers the final elaborate configuration of the Demeter motif. Tess approximates to a Persephone figure that simultaneously incorporates two warring states of nature: asexual (which stops her joining the Chaseborough dance) and sexual forces; the Christian and the pagan (her ancestor is called Pagan d'Urberville), the wantonly destructive[65] and the luxuriantly fecund. This combination is sacrificed at the ancient temple that recalls the Proserpine of Swinburne's *Poems and Ballads* (1866): a personification of nature as mortality and sleep. At sunrise Tess awakens to find herself surrounded on the altar stone by dark figures of the law who seem as if they are wearing ritual masks: 'in the growing light, their faces and hands...were silvered, the remainder of their figures dark' (*Tess* 381). Her execution by hanging marks the failure of a dignified conception of a natural divinity. That there is little hope of reconstruction is compounded by Hardy exploiting the staginess of Tess being apprehended in 'a place of cultural beginnings'[66] where people were sacrificed to the sun. Hardy follows Swinburne in denying the optimistic pattern of rebirth with its implication of an afterlife,

---

[64] Walter Pater, *Greek Studies*, p. 85.

[65] Tess's murder of Alec evokes contemporary socio-medical injunctions which warned of the perils of inexpressible female passion: '[i]n woman, the concentration of her feelings... adds to their intensity; and like a smouldering fire that has at last got vent, her passions, when no longer trammelled by conventional propriety, burst forth in unquenchable violence.' See J. G. Millingen, *Mind and Matter, Illustrated by Considerations on Heredity, Insanity, and the Influence of Temperament in the Development of the Passions* (London: H. Hurst, 1847), pp. 157-8.

[66] Kevin Z. Moore, *The Descent of the Imagination: The Decline of Postromantic Culture in the Later Novels of Thomas Hardy* (New York and London: New York University Press, 1990), p. 215.

which the Demeter and Persephone myth articulates. That he refuses to offer any compensating vision of redemption is underlined by the Henge, a forbidding image of stony circularity, an emblem of narrative closure. Despite the 'promise of a life to come'[67] implicit in the return of Persephone, Hardy is more interested in its tragic implications. Acceptance of a sacrificial communion and the attainment of new vitality will not work here. To Frazer it is 'one of the few myths in which the sunshine and clarity of the Greek genius are crossed by the shadow and mystery of death', and to Pater it shows 'that the "worship of sorrow" was not without its function in the Greek religion'.[68] At this mysterious site, Tess fully admits that the only certainty is death and oblivion: 'For there is no God found stronger than death; and death is a sleep'.[69] Clare cannot save Tess from her wish for 'the sleep eternal/In an eternal night'.[70] When she is hanged at Wintoncester, the earth is no longer under even the vestigial protection of non-Christian divinities, for Hardy's reference to the 'President of the Immortals' is cuttingly ironic. Clare professes how old faiths fallen into superstition must be demolished, but he cannot assemble any new myths to replace them.

Tess of the d'Urbervilles enacts the sacrifice of 'a goddess figure of immense stature'[71] in whom are found genuinely profound and mysterious forces, mediated and glimpsed on occasions that involve a process akin to transfiguration. Hardy's next published novel extends the fact that the only mythology available to fill the void once meaningfully occupied by classical stories is that of a soulless Christianity. The arrest of Tess at the pagan temple of Stonehenge, once home to a religion older than almost any other, implies the ruined character of the mythical past in a contemporary society moving unalterably towards spiritual suicide. This feeling is accentuated by the fact that Tess is sentenced in a court that is not even represented in the narrative.[72] The sacrifice of Tess Durbeyfield is seen not as a triumphant demonstration of a lingering pagan mythology, but as its

---

[67] Walter Pater, *Greek Studies*, p. 93.

[68] Ibid., p. 111.

[69] Algernon Charles Swinburne, 'Hymn to Proserpine', in *The Complete Works of Algernon Charles Swinburne*, ed. Sir Edmund Gosse and Thomas James Wise, 4 vols. (New York: Russell & Russell, 1968), I, 206.

[70] A. C. Swinburne, 'Hymn to Proserpine', *The Complete Works*, I, 207.

[71] Shirley A. Stave, *The Decline of the Goddess: Nature, Culture, and Women in Thomas Hardy's Fiction* (London: Greenwood Press, 1995), p. 101.

[72] See Beth Kalikoff, 'The Execution of Tess d'Urberville at Wintoncester', in *Executions and the British Experience from the Seventeenth to the Twentieth Century: A Collection of Essays*, ed. William B. Thesing (New York: McFarland & Co., 1990), pp. 111-21; Sarah Nicholson, 'The Woman Pays: Death and the Ambivalence of Providence in Hardy's Novels', *Literature and Theology* 16:1 (March 2002), 27-39.

deathstroke.[73] After the eponymous heroine there are no titans left to make any gesture of insurgency against the patriarchal Olympians in Wessex who ensnare her, only the shallow neo-pagan poses of Sue Bridehead. The foreboding conceit of Hardy's Henge, its shape rendering the black sky blacker, offers no hint of enlightened change for it has crumbled and fossilized into the Hebraic orthodoxies against which *Jude the Obscure* rails with unprecedented and despairing satire. The waving black flag that alerts all onlookers to Tess's death is ironically flying over Wintoncester, the original capital of Wessex. The most prominent features of the town reveal the incompatible forces which lead to Tess's execution, for Wintoncester is at once imaginative and rational, venerable and modish, hopefully idealistic and grimly historical. Cathedrals incongruously reside beside uninviting modern brick buildings, signifying how the past of romantic aspirations is petrified, swamped by more mundane constructions which are linear, lifeless and practical. Stonehenge and Wintoncester are primitive and modern versions of the same impulse to destroy. In the closing paragraphs Angel Clare is entrusted with the care of exactly what he deserves – the maiden Liza-Lu[74] (the mock paradise regained of a virginal Tess) – thus underscoring the angry sense of irrecoverable loss. The deliberately attenuated finale of Clare and Liza-Lu's miniature 'marriage' is a Hardyan jibe at the hackneyed romantic conclusion, a law of genre imposed by the lending libraries. However, the anticipated promise of fulfilment is shown in weak, naive figures wearily walking the last mile together.

Jude the Obscure (1895)

The ruling patriarchal elite, which executes Tess Durbeyfield is the very regime upheld by Christminster in *Jude the Obscure*. Hardy transmutes the tale of a neglected, sexually violated peasant girl into the tale of an orphaned boy of the rural working classes with an ardent love of learning, who becomes a victim of the lust of others as well as of his own. Hardy elaborates a frantic struggle between natural forces: the protagonist is pulled apart by the sexually charged Arabella Donn and the asexual Sue Bridehead, thus recalling the Fitzpiers/Winterborne and d'Urberville/Clare

---

[73] That Tess's execution occurs on a July morning may be mythically significant: Frazer notes that the pagan celebration of Lughnasa, a harvest festival in which the cutting of the grain is referred to metaphorically as the sacrifice of the Corn King, occurs in late July or early August.

[74] In the manuscript version of the novel, Tess is Liza-Lu's former name.

conflicts. However, a component essential to healthy living (such as inhabits Tess?) has vanished:

> High against the black sky the flash of a lamp would show crocketed pinnacles and indented battlements. Down obscure alleys, apparently never trodden now by the foot of man, and whose very existence seemed to be forgotten, there would jut into the path porticoes, oriels, doorways of enriched and florid middle-age design, their extinct air being accentuated by the rottenness of the stones. It seemed impossible that modern thought could house itself in such decrepit and superseded chambers. (*Jude* 79)[75]

Christianity, and the institutionalized form it takes in the city of Christminster (Oxford), is the 'survival' everywhere at issue in *Jude the Obscure*.[76] The naturally or artificially underlit scenes like the one above evoke the pervasive gloom of a religion that has usurped the sun- and earth-worship whose agent is vanquished in *Tess*. That *Jude* includes no mythical underpinning comparable to the divine tale of Demeter and Persephone is its central message. Christminster's Gothic styles of the past show it to be a fossilized relic of the Dark Ages: 'obscure' refers not only to Jude Fawley's social status, but also to the visual tone of the novel, thus affording a stark contrast to the intensity of sensuous experience in *Tess*'s many sunlit scenes. The rationalist historian Edward Gibbon (1737-94), one of the Oxonian phantoms Jude imagines walking the shadowy streets of the city (*Jude* 80), makes repeated use of the words 'obscure' and 'obscurity' when alluding to both Judaism and early Christianity in the fifteenth and sixteenth chapters of *The Decline and Fall*.[77] Hardy, after recording the disintegration of a vibrant pagan perspective in his previous published novel, now sifts through the repressive rubble of late-Victorian England under the perpetual twilight of Christminster. He captures the stagnant medievalism of this city by repeatedly stressing the deprivation of visual sensation among its 'rotten' buildings and 'wasting walls' (*Jude* 337). That it seems impossible 'modern thought' could house itself in such 'decrepit and superseded chambers' implies how a sense of monstrous incongruity

---

[75] Thomas Hardy, *Jude the Obscure*, ed. with introd. Patricia Ingham (Oxford: The World's Classics, 1985). Hereafter referred to as *Jude*.

[76] Hardy was in the city of Oxford when *Jude* was being planned and drafted in 1892, and again in 1893.

[77] Christianity 'gently insinuated itself into the minds of men, grew up in silence and obscurity, derived new vigour from opposition, and finally erected the triumphant banner of the Cross on the ruins of the Capitol'. See Edward Gibbon, *The Decline and Fall of the Roman Empire*, introd. Hugh Trevor-Roper, 3 vols. (London: Everyman, 1993), I, 487.

has replaced *A Laodicean*'s ebullient assurance. Incongruities now serve Hardy's polemical purpose as an outlet for disruptive feeling and disgust, for *Jude* was 'a sensationally outspoken novel for its time'.[78] His social concern, which desired the 'break up' of 'the present pernicious conventions in respect of women, customs, religion',[79] is at its most belligerent. We are never able to forget the pressures against which Hardy's once buoyant and impish artistic repertoire becomes ineffectual: the gossips who object to an unmarried pregnant woman (Sue)[80] engraving the Ten Commandments, an outmoded but still constricting Christian code that shatters an individual's concept of self, so that the body and senses are reviled as gross and animal. Both Sue and Arabella Donn are ultimately portrayed as two poles of one dismantled feminine sexuality, whose union (briefly embodied by Tess) can no longer be achieved in an orthodox culture.

Hardy's searing vision of late-Victorian Oxford reveals that this 'most Christian city in the country' (*Jude* 95) is moribund matter that cuts us off not from the past, but from the present; it signifies 'inert, crystallised opinion – hard as a rock – which the vast body of men have vested interests in preserving'.[81] Sue Bridehead regards the city as 'full of fetichists and ghost-seers': an august seat of English 'high' culture, with its 'barbarous customs and superstitions' (*Jude* 226) ironically epitomizing a lower stage of cultural evolution. Although Hardy calls Christminster 'extinct' (*Jude* 79), this daunting citadel of medieval privilege and intellectual irrelevance is nevertheless poisoning the modern moment and conditioning the future. Sue proclaims defiantly that: 'The mediaevalism of Christminster must go, be sloughed off, or Christminster itself will have to go.' (*Jude* 155) But *Jude* reveals Hardy's agonized recognition that this 'survival' cannot be magisterially swept aside.[82] In previous novels Hardy enjoys the bizarre position these remnants hold in an ostensibly rational, proudly progressive society. But the persistence of Christminster long after the circumstances in which it originated has much more disturbing implications. Unlike those

---

[78] James Gibson, *Thomas Hardy: A Literary Life* (London: Macmillan, 1996), p. 131.

[79] Hardy's letter to the Fawcett Society (30 November 1906). Quoted in Rosemary Sumner, *Thomas Hardy: Psychological Novelist* (London: Macmillan, 1981), p. 190.

[80] Sue is one of Tess Durbeyfield's earlier names in the manuscript.

[81] Thomas Hardy, *Life*, p. 284. See also Timothy Hands, 'Jude in Oxford', *Thomas Hardy Journal* 11:3 (October 1995), 61-5.

[82] Given the extent of Hardy's knowledge of Percy Shelley, he might have had in mind how the Romantic poet believed Oxford should be lost if the 'World's New Age' was to be inaugurated. In a further irony, Shelley had been expelled from Oxford in 1811 for writing 'The Necessity of Atheism' – the very necessity which lies behind Jude and Sue's alienation from the more self-consciously genteel portion of the Wessex community.

earlier 'survivals' that function as records of oppression, Casterbridge's Roman amphitheatre and Stonehenge, Hardy's university city is still operational. And he knows that the need 'to locate a more fulfilling existence outside custom and convention'[83] is stymied by a stultifying Church of England ethos that must everywhere deny it. This sense of crisis is illuminated by Swinburne's 'Hymn to Proserpine', from which Sue actually quotes (*Jude* 97):

> Thou hast conquered, O pale Galilean:
> The world has grown grey from thy breath![84]

Christminster, an 'ancient medieval pile' whose 'dark corners...no lamplight reached' (*Jude* 79), is a world 'grown grey' from the 'breath' of Swinburne's 'pale Galilean', Jesus. Tess Durbeyfield, Hardy's dignified conception of a nature-goddess is in *Jude* superseded by the life-denying force of Christ. Hardy acknowledges in often harrowing detail that the pointless sobriety of Hebraism has not only neutered pagan culture, but effaced it altogether. *Jude*'s epigraph, 'The Letter Killeth' (2 Corinthians 3:6), refers to the letter of Scriptural law whose deformative effects are exposed throughout the novel. A return to what Sue calls 'Greek joyousness', a vital secular future free from 'what twenty-five centuries have taught the race since their time' (*Jude* 312) is impossible. All that remains is her clandestine homage not so much to the defeated classical culture itself as to Swinburnian neo-paganism. In her defiantly agnostic phase, Sue purchases naked figurines of Venus and Apollo from an itinerant hawker and furtively smuggles them into her lodgings, arranging them on each side of the Crucifix, telling her Anglo-Catholic landlady that the pagan statuettes are Saints Mary Magdalene and Peter.[85] This is not 'religious syncretism'[86] but the trivializing dilettantism already apparent in Angel Clare's pretentious gestures and glib rhetoric. Swinburne is a favourite author for Sue because, Hardy implies, she thinks of him as crusading for a renewal of a pagan erotic religious impulse commemorating forces close to nature, such as the love-goddess Venus, or Demeter and her

---

[83] Elizabeth Langland, 'Becoming a Man in *Jude the Obscure*', in Margaret G. Higonnet (ed.), *The Sense of Sex: Feminist Perspectives on Hardy* (Urbana and Chicago: University of Illinois Press, 1993), p. 39.

[84] Sue also quotes Swinburne's 'Hymn to Proserpine' (*Jude* 155): 'O ghastly glories of saints, dead limbs of gibbeted Gods!'

[85] Like Peter, Sue eventually repudiates her new testaments of love and, like Magdalene, will end her days as a repentant whore.

[86] Robert Fraser (ed.), *Sir James Frazer and the Literary Imagination: Essays in Affinity and Influence* (London: Macmillan, 1990), p. v.

daughter Proserpine. But the human energies these deities represent have no place in the unreal city of Christminster. Moreover, Sue vehemently opposes the sexual experience that would logically accompany her philosophy. As her surname implies and Lawrence explains in his *Study of Thomas Hardy* (1914), the bride in this 'fine-nerved, sensitive girl' is fatally constrained by the head.

Hardy's agitated awareness of the indestructibility of the pale Galilean's Christminster stronghold is underlined by numerous allusions to a Biblical mythology which has marginalized the classical pagan tales, and whose traces were acutely felt in earlier novels. Critics have been puzzled by the apparent contradiction of Hardy, for whom Christianity had lost almost all rational justification, repeatedly invoking a biblical source. But he does so in a way that disdainfully strips it of its sanctified authority. The Christian myth and its consolations are shown as completely irrelevant to Jude's plight. Although Hardy affected dismay at the fierce controversy aroused by *Jude* – 'you can imagine my surprise at the *Guardian* saying that everything sacred is brought into contempt...in the novel'[87] – the *Guardian* was closer to the truth than many contemporary reviews. Hardy provides an almost blasphemous retelling of Christ-like suffering through his apocryphal 'gospel' of an obscure Jude of modern town life, a kind of ordinary brother to Jesus (as the martyred Saint Jude was often thought to be). Saint Jude is the patron of lost causes and Matthew Arnold described Oxford as 'the home of lost causes' (*Jude* 82).[88] Jude's life is thus a folly (a Fawley[89] in Hardy's pun on the surname), because he never actually corresponds to anything or anyone, though he supposes he does.

Hardy's self-lacerating wit is everywhere explicit in the way his non-hero excludes rational perception in order to pursue an imagined earthly paradise of intellectual and religious fulfilment that shimmers in the distance. But the 'city of light' (*Jude* 21) of his 'first ecstasy' (*Jude* 26) which seems engulfed by a beatific haze,[90] is on closer inspection full of

---

[87] Thomas Hardy, *Collected Letters*, II, 98.

[88] Jude is in some sense ironically linked with the hero of Arnold's *The Scholar Gypsy* whose narrator (positioned on a hill-top) lets his eye, like Jude's from the heights of the Brown House, travel 'down to Oxford's towers' (l. 30).

[89] In 1892 Hardy had been investigating his family records, and his researches had taken him to Great Fawley in Berkshire – the place where his grandmother Mary Head, had been born.

[90] Jude's distant prospect of Christminster recalls the young idealist Gareth's first distant vision of Camelot in Tennyson's *Idylls of the King*. See *The Poems of Tennyson*, III, 287:

> At times the summit of the high city flashed;
> At times the spires and turrets half-way down
> Pricked through the mist.   (ll. 210-12)

mouldering 'historical documents' (*Jude* 84). Jude mistakes the glow of real decay for that of imagined energy. In this savage alternative 'gospel', Hardy depicts the Cross as an invincible and disheartening force, recalling Swinburne's 'Before a Crucifix' from *Songs before Sunrise* (1871), in which the poet pleads, 'set not thine hand unto' the 'Worm-eaten...cross': 'Let not thy tree of freedom be/Regrafted from that rotting tree'. The 'rotting tree' is the centrepiece of a religion that celebrates only death, cancelling out any pagan glimpses of Eleusinian regeneration. Jude and Sue first meet in Christminster, 'at the cross in the pavement which marked the spot of the martyrdoms'; and Jude begins his 'ministry' at Melchester at the age of thirty, 'an age which much attracted him as being that of his exemplar when he first began to teach in Galilee' (*Jude* 134). Jude's casual exclamation to Sue at the time of their elopement, 'There, dear; don't mind! Crucify me, if you will!' (253), implies his future course.[91] That he undergoes a mundane 'crucifixion' is reinforced when he and Sue arrive at Christminster again on Remembrance Day in the novel's final section. The parallel between Commemoration Week at Oxford and the week of the Passover is made evident when Sue speaks of coming up to 'Jerusalem' to see the 'festival', and describes 'leaving Kennetbridge for this place' as 'like coming from Caiaphas to Pilate' (*Jude* 348). Caiaphas, the Jewish high priest, handed Jesus over to Pilate, the Roman Governor who had him crucified.

Jude's callow hopes of succeeding in the 'Holy Jerusalem' (*Jude* 16) of Christminster are fuelled by an orthodox faith very much in the Augustinian conservative tradition. He goes through what Sue calls specifically a 'Tractarian stage' against which she herself has rebelled, aping Swinburne's heterodox Hellenism. As Hardy said in a letter to William Archer (2nd January 1896), the central characters are not merely 'puppets invented to express my personal views in their talk'[92] but carefully conceived products and hapless victims of 'Oxford' culture. Among the 'ghostly presences' Jude imagines walking the streets of Christminster soon after his arrival, three have special significance:

> among...the most real to Jude Fawley were the founders of the religious school called Tractarian; the well-known three, the enthusiast, the poet, and the formularist, the echoes of whose teachings had influenced him even in his obscure home. (*Jude* 80)

---

[91] The reductive parallels between Jude and Jesus Christ recur. See pp. 93, 109, 127, 134, 253, 348, 373.

[92] Thomas Hardy, *Collected Letters*, II, 104.

The 'well-known three' are John Henry Newman (1801-90), John Keble (1792-1866)[93] and Edward Pusey (1800-82).[94] Jude is at first inspired no less strongly than these men by devotion to the historical tradition of Christian religion, an ascetic and unworldly vision that he and they found in the Church Fathers.[95] The 'Oxford Movement', which prospered from the late 1830s until the mid-1840s, was led by a group of young Oxford-trained theologians who hoped to regenerate the Church of England.[96] In a series of pamphlets titled *Tracts for the Times* (1833-41), they argued the continuity of Anglicanism with Roman Catholicism.[97] These pamphlets also attacked doctrinal laxity and called for a swift return to traditional forms of worship. Hardy clearly has the Tractarians in mind when describing Jude's wish to join that stifling semi-monastic university community from which the poet Clough finally escaped. The theological atmosphere of the university in the aftermath of the 'Oxford Movement' also became increasingly repellent to free-thinking Swinburne.[98] Hardy exposes the dogmatisms and absurdities of a deeply conservative religious crusade that has cut off spirit and passion from holistic living. Jude's adherence to the exacting moral standards of a don preparing to take orders collapses as inevitably as biological imperatives are revealed. Eventually,

---

[93] John Keble's volume of poems, *The Christian Year*, first published in 1827, went through over ninety editions by the close of the nineteenth century. It was avidly read by followers of the Tractarians.

[94] See Patrick R. O'Malley, 'Oxford's Ghosts: *Jude the Obscure* and the End of the Gothic', *Modern Fiction Studies* 46:3 (Fall 2000), 646-71.

[95] Jan Jedrzejewski shows that Hardy, like Jude, imagined going to university and being ordained. Hardy's own early religious experience has typically been portrayed as moderately strict and consistently High Church, with regular attendance at the Tractarian services at Stinsford. However, the situation was more complex as Hardy attended Nonconformist schools where he witnessed the burning of the Pope and Cardinal Wiseman in effigy during the 'Papal Aggression' of 1850, and his home religious life could be characterized as undogmatic. Jedrzejewski persuasively records Hardy's growing ambivalence towards and ultimate repudiation of Anglo-Catholicism during the late 1860s and 1870s. See *Thomas Hardy and the Church* (London: Macmillan, 1996).

[96] On 'The Oxford Movement' see Owen Chadwick, *The Victorian Church*, 2 vols. (London: Adam & Charles Black, 1966), I, sections 1 and 3; Yngve Brilioth, *The Anglican Revival: Studies in the Oxford Movement* (London: Longmans, Green, 1925); S. L. Ollard, *A Short History of the Oxford Movement* (London: Mowbray, 1915); Raymond Chapman, *Faith and Revolt: Studies in the Literary Influence of the Oxford Movement* (London: Weidenfeld & Nicolson, 1970).

[97] The influence of Tractarian thinking could be felt more strongly at Oxford than perhaps anywhere. Keble College was founded in 1866.

[98] Swinburne went up to Balliol College, Oxford in January 1856, but left in 1860 without taking a degree. He wrote later: 'My Oxonian career culminated in total and scandalous failure.' Quoted in Philip Henderson, *Swinburne: The Portrait of a Poet* (London: Routledge & Kegan Paul, 1974), p. 44.

he realizes that his Tracts and Church Fathers are themselves 'survivals', fatal to the best human instincts, and fit only for the fire: 'Paley, Pusey, Newman, and the rest had gone to ashes' (*Jude* 229).

The 'Oxford Movement' was an effort to bring certain rituals (including auricular confession, veneration of saints, theologies of the Real Presence of Christ at the Eucharist and of apostolic succession, and such symbols as the crucifix, candles and colourful ecclesiastical vestments) back into Anglican religious practice. Explicitly Catholic styles of church architecture and liturgy were perceived as important links not only with a pre-Reformation church, but also with that of Saint Augustine. The result was not merely a new antiquarian interest in church history, but also an active campaign to 'restore' Gothic and Renaissance churches. In *Contrasts* (1836), Pugin declared

> There is no need of visiting the distant shores of Greece and Egypt to make discoveries in art. England abounds in hidden and unknown antiquities of surpassing interest. What madness, then, while neglecting our own religious...types of architecture and art, to worship at the revived shrines of ancient corruption, and profane the temple of a crucified Redeemer by the architecture and emblems of heathen Gods.[99]

Jude sets about restoring the temples of 'a crucified Redeemer' after the humiliating collapse of his intellectual objectives. Initially fascinated by the iconography of Romanist Catholicism, he plans to be a renewer of religion, but only as an ecclesiastical stonemason, making aesthetic forgeries of lost originals and repairing the very walls that exclude him. Religious life becomes to Jude an architectural fossil, for Christminster is vestigial, not vital. Like the wilful obscurantism of the 'Oxford Movement' itself, the city is 'as dead as a fern-leaf in a lump of coal' for 'other developments were shaping in the world around [Jude] in which Gothic architecture and

---

[99] A. W. N. Pugin, *Contrasts*, introd. H. R. Hitchcock (New York: Humanities Press, 1969), pp. 17-18. Interestingly, in 1880, polemicist James Bateman situated Catholic architecture at the core of his tirade against the seductive idolatry of Romanism; of Roman Catholic cathedrals, he contended: 'None can deny their powers of fascination. They are masterpieces of art, and miracles of beauty. They exercise an almost irresistible charm over the cultivated mind. Yet heathen temples did the same! And what after all is Romish Christianity but a "baptised Paganism", in which the old demi-gods are superseded by modern "saints", and the worship of Diana replaced by the cultus of the Virgin!' See James Bateman, *The Church Association: Its Policy and Prospects*, 3rd edn. (London: Ridgway, 1880), p. 56.

its associations had no place' (*Jude* 85).[100] The emblem of the fern-leaf in the coal signifies the lost vibrancy of an older age and reveals how the organic has literally turned to stone over time.

Hardy, with ferocious irony, shows Jude, who once dreamed of scaling the venerable branches of a 'tree of knowledge' (*Jude* 21) in this 'living city' (*Jude* 99), locating instead a sepulchral place of disease and decay, a 'Graveyard of Dead Creeds',[101] whose oriels and hidden pathways evoke the mazes of monasteries and fortresses that imprison the protagonists in Anne Radcliffe's fiction. Even the names of Christminster colleges – 'Rubric' and 'Sarcophagus' crusted with 'four centuries of gloom' and 'bigotry' (*Jude* 351) – are symbolically apt. This scalding portrayal of the Christminster cadaver is reminiscent of 'The Century's corpse outleant' of 'The Darkling Thrush': a century replete with cultural aspirations that have buttressed rather than interrogated the prevailing ethos.[102] Jude's appointed task reflects this: as an artisan-copier he must invest shards and splinters of the medieval past with an artificial life, each feature as unsightly and petrified as the grinning gargoyles on the college buildings. Hardy wrote in his Preface to the 1895 edition of *A Pair of Blue Eyes* that 'to restore the grey carcases of a mediaevalism whose spirit had fled seemed a not less incongruous act than to set about renovating the adjoining crags themselves.'[103] The irony is that Jude's trade binds him to Oxford's churches and graveyards: to maintaining precisely that medievalizing Catholicism which blights his academic plans and threatens the tranquillity of his domestic life with Sue.

The persistence of the Christminster 'survival' is given a more devastating impact because the search for a more rewarding mode of existence founded on the presence of folklore 'survivals' is futile in *Jude*. Indeed, Hardy travesties Tylor's doctrine by introducing the 'itinerant

---

[100] In a letter to *The Times*, 7 October 1914, Hardy commented that Gothic architecture has been 'a dead art for the last three hundred years, in spite of the imitations broadcast over the land'.

[101] Hardy's 'The Graveyard of Dead Creeds' is contained in the *Human Shows* volume. See *Complete Poems*, pp. 724-5.

[102] Hardy's depiction of a moribund Christminster recalls the poet Samuel Rogers's response to Italy:

> this land of shadows, where we live
> More in past time than present, where the ground,
> League beyond league, like one great cemetery,
> Is covered o'er with mouldering monuments.

See Samuel Rogers, *The Poetical Works of Samuel Rogers*, with a memoir by Edward Bell (London: E. Moxon, 1891), pp. 296-7.

[103] Thomas Hardy, *A Pair of Blue Eyes*, p. 3.

quack-doctor' Vilbert: 'Cottagers formed his only patients, and his Wessex-wide repute was among them alone...He was, in fact, a survival' (*Jude* 22). Although Phillotson pursues his 'grand hobby' of writing *The Roman Antiquities of Wessex* (which is never completed), the local traditions that function as a storehouse of anthropological curiosities in previous novels have become almost as 'extinct' (*Jude* 79) as Christminster's crumbling masonry. Hardy's delineation of the ancient thatched-cottage hamlet of Marygreen village bears this out: 'Old as it was...the well-shaft was probably the only relic of the local history that remained absolutely unchanged' (*Jude* 6). Other roots deep down into village life have nearly disappeared. While the university city is choked with the malign residue of a medieval past, Marygreen boasts very little past at all. Kevin Moore remarks that Jude begins life in culture 'by rejecting his natural Wessex home; thus he alienates himself from...folk tradition'.[104] But the uncompromising severity of Hardy's treatment reveals that Marygreen, unlike Marlott in *Tess* that still possesses some threadbare remnants of bygone days, has no folk tradition for the protagonist to disavow.

For Tylor and other 'representative men'[105] in comparative evolutionary anthropology, their discipline could not have developed without the tireless collection and meticulous study of folklore. 'On the whole, till now', wrote Andrew Lang in 1891, 'the folk have prolonged the ancient life, as it was in customs and belief long before Homer sang, long before the Hebrew legislation was codified and promulgated.'[106] But the demolished cottages, felled trees and 'obliterated graves' (*Jude* 6) of Marygreen attest the extinction not only of a historical past replete with anthropological data but also the intensely personal past of its inhabitants. The poem 'On an Invitation to Visit the United States' indicates why Hardy cherished England over America, because time had left very distinctive marks upon its landscape, which was 'scored with prints of perished hands'.[107] In a notebook entry Hardy described 'Nature' as a 'book which has in every page important meanings'.[108] *Jude* shows the impossibility of deducing who has 'traversed the fields' (*Woodlanders* 94), because the earth's document has been erased. The young Jude is as free of 'association' with regional history as the rooks he is supposed to be scaring away from Farmer Troutham's farm. Whereas Clym Yeobright in *The Return of the Native*

[104] Kevin Z. Moore, *The Descent of the Imagination: Post-Romantic Culture in the Later Novels of Thomas Hardy* (New York: New York University Press, 1993), p. 226.
[105] Anon., 'Primitive Man: Tylor and Lubbock', *Quarterly Review* 137 (July 1874), 40-77.
[106] Andrew Lang, 'Presidential Address', *The International Folk-Lore Congress 1891*, p. 7.
[107] Thomas Hardy, *Complete Poems*, p. 110.
[108] Thomas Hardy, *Literary Notebooks*, I, entry 114.

regards the Egdon tumuli as curious memorials of an inscrutably remote race, Marygreen's surroundings show a drained and barren milieu only vaguely connected with human life. Like Flintcomb-Ash before it, Marygreen is situated on high chalkland that rises steeply out of the surrounding valleys and reflects the repetitive drudgery of rural labour. The totally functional aspect of the area is accentuated by Hardy's offhand, parched prose, which contrasts with the richly evocative rendering of Blackmore Vale in *Tess*, with its Turneresque flourishes of colour and sunlight:

> The fresh harrow-lines seemed to stretch like the channellings in a piece of new corduroy, lending a meanly utilitarian air to the expanse, taking away its gradations, and depriving it of all history beyond that of the few recent months, though to every clod and stone there really attached associations enough and to spare – echoes of songs from ancient harvest-days, of spoken words, and of sturdy deeds. Every inch of ground had been the site, first or last of energy, gaiety, horse-play, bickerings, weariness...in that ancient cornfield many a man had made love-promises to a woman at whose voice he trembled by the next seed-time after fulfilling them in the church adjoining. (*Jude* 8-9)

Hardy stresses low-keyed, muted colours like brown to evoke the bleak inescapable dreariness of the field's deep concave. The 'harrow-lines' dominating this arable land should show 'history' as a palimpsest, but only the most recent 'layer' holds any significance for the characters who see it. This area is robbed of anthropological value (folksongs from 'ancient harvest-days', dialect words of especial interest, remnants of pagan fertility rites) by the very activity that describes it in human terms: tilling the earth. The constantly altering face of the fields has swept away centuries of peasant lore that Frazerians often explained as withered remains of ancient mythology. In Charles Warne's antiquarian study *Ancient Dorset* (1872), the 'ruthless necessities of agriculture' are already a cause for deep concern: 'no extenuation can be admitted for the act of those who, in disregard of all remonstrance, and apparently actuated by mercenary motives, permit the encroachments of agriculture to obliterate from the face of the soil the vestiges of ancient occupancy'.[109]

---

[109] Charles Warne, *Ancient Dorset: The Celtic, Roman, Saxon, and Danish Antiquities of the County, including the Early Coinage. Also an Introduction to the Ethnology of Dorset, and other Archaeological Notices of the County, by William Wake Smart* (Bournemouth: D. Sydenham, 1872), p. iii.

The fate of Marygreen's original church is of a piece with the destruction of 'old association' in the vicinity: it 'had been taken down and either cracked up into heaps of road-metal in the lane, or utilized as pig-sty walls, garden-seats, guard-stones to fences' (*Jude* 6). The summary revitalization of the church's stones and timber as 'pig-sty walls' (the profane uses to which consecrated building materials are put) again shows how Hardy's creative energies are now firmly grounded in a sense of monstrous, rather than boisterous, incongruity. *Jude* abounds with many similar 'pig' allusions to suggest symbolically the predominance, whether in Marygreen or Christminster, of values unrelieved by any trace of true human spirituality. Such references – from Hardy's awareness of the Gadarene swine[110] to the untidy pork-butcher's shop where Arabella recaptures Jude – become a bizarre substitute for the folklore 'survivals' whose obliteration is borne out by Marygreen's featureless condition. Arabella Donn, the daughter of a pig-farmer, first gains Jude's attention by pelting him on the cheek with 'a piece of flesh' that Hardy – ridiculing the customary euphemistic circumlocutions used by his bourgeois reviewers – decorously calls 'the characteristic part of a barrow-pig' (*Jude* 35). The youthful Jude, an aspiring university don driving his drab bakery cart around the countryside(!), receives a blunt summons from another type of Don(n) – Arabella, who sees in him a sexual conquest and a means thereby of gaining a safe, respectable marriage. At the moment he is struck by the penis of a castrated boar, he is taking mental inventory of his reading in the classics (a bizarrely comic collision of the carnal and ethereal). This 'low' missile, which shatters briefly Jude's delusive dreams of 'high' culture, is the prelude to Abby's strategy (perhaps parodic of Circe's enchantments in Homer's *Odyssey*) of distracting him from Christminster Abbey where he pictures himself as a bishop with an income of £5,000 a year.

Arabella Donn is no more a figure of healthy sexuality than Sue Bridehead. Arabella is a crass materialist, 'a complete and substantial female animal' (*Jude* 36), whose piggishness links her with the 'unclean animal' of Mosaic law. Margaret Oliphant, in her virulent review of *Jude* for *Blackwood's Magazine* in January 1896, described her as 'a human pig, like the beast whom in a horrible scene she and her husband kill'.[111] Oliphant is referring to the pig-sticking which Hardy invites us to see as a macabre parody of primitive sacrifice, instances of which dominate the

---

[110] Gadarene is mentioned in the Bible only in connection with one incident: the miracle concerning the legion of demons who were allowed to enter the herd of swine. See Matthew 8:25; Mark 5:1; Luke 8:26.

[111] See R. G. Cox (ed.), *Thomas Hardy: The Critical Heritage* (London: Routledge & Kegan Paul, 1970), p. 258.

pages of *The Golden Bough*. The pig, particularly the sow, was once considered a chthonic animal, the 'uterine animal of the earth'.[112] Frazer writes in relation 'to the corn-goddess Demeter':

> remembering that in European folk-lore the pig is a common embodiment of the corn-spirit, we may now ask whether the pig, which was so closely associated with Demeter, may not have been originally the goddess herself in animal form? The pig was sacred to her; in art she was portrayed carrying or accompanied by a pig; and the pig was regularly sacrificed in her mysteries[113]

'Pherrephata', one of the many variants of Persephone's name, means 'killer of suckling pigs', associating her with the pigs sacrificed during the Eleusinian Mysteries and other ceremonies consecrated to the Mother.[114] However, Jude's reluctant slaughter of the pig reveals an unbridgeable gulf between an ancient ceremonial treating the animal as sacred and the modern-day equivalent in which it is regarded as 'an inferior species' (*Jude* 124). The exercise is little more than a meaningless infliction of suffering from which other creatures recoil: 'A robin peered down at the preparations from the nearest tree, and, not liking the sinister look of the scene, flew away, though hungry' (*Jude* 63). Hardy continues, 'By this time Arabella had joined her husband, and Jude, rope in hand, got into the sty, and noosed the affrighted animal, who, beginning with a squeak of surprise, rose to repeated cries of rage.' (*Jude* 63) The 'squeak' – ordinarily the sound of a mouse – seems a sufficiently whimsical detail to undercut the reader's initial discomfort.[115] Yet it is Hardy's swift alternations between threat and amusement, horror and farce (even the combination of such extremes so that we cannot respond to either one alone) upon which the disturbing impact of the pig-killing relies.[116] This epitomizes the highly complex challenge of the incongruous in *Jude*, erupting at oddly dangerous and perplexing moments.

A *Laodicean*'s amusing flourishes offer relief by diverting energy from unpleasant emotion, but this is something that *Jude* resolutely refuses to do.

---

[112] Carl Kerenyi, 'Kore', in C. G. Jung and Carl Kerenyi, *Essays on a Science of Mythology: The Myth of the Divine Child and the Mysteries of Eleusis* (Princeton: Princeton University Press, 1969), p. 119.

[113] James Frazer, *The Golden Bough*, p. 483.

[114] The pig became the emblem of Eleusis, stamped on all Eleusinian coins.

[115] John Fletcher in his 'To the Reader' from *The Faithful Shepherdess* (c.1608-10), described the genre of tragicomedy as 'mirth and killing'.

[116] Walter Kerr's comment on black comedy is relevant to this scene: 'the laughter that greets black comedy is sporadic, uncertain, ill-at-ease'. See *Tragedy and Comedy* (New York: Simon & Shuster, 1967), p. 176.

After Arabella and her husband bind the pig down its note 'changed its quality. It was not now rage, but the cry of despair; long-drawn, slow and hopeless' (*Jude* 63). As in most of *Jude*'s 'black farce' episodes, our emotional and intellectual reactions become tangled (life is simultaneously perceived as ridiculous and deadly serious), and this in turn undermines any sense of a minutely ordered, familiar universe. After keeping the reader uneasily suspended between what is funny and what is frightening as an aghast, feckless Jude almost botches the killing, Hardy ends the scene by showing the squalid, undignified facts of the betrayed animal's death. The post-*Laodicean* fiction has been inexorably moving towards this crisis-point at which Hardy, trapped by anxiety, finds it impossible to respond with buoyantly witty effects to a fundamental lack of coherence in a supposedly 'Christian' society.

> However unworkmanlike the deed, it had been mercifully done. The blood flowed out in a torrent instead of in the trickling stream she had desired. The dying animal's cry assumed its third and final tone, the shriek of agony; his glazing eyes riveting themselves on Arabella with the eloquently keen reproach of a creature recognizing at last the treachery of those who had seemed his only friends. (*Jude* 64)

The red and white imagery that dominates *Tess* (Alec's blood spreading like a stain across the Sandbourne ceiling) is given a gruesome reprise in the depiction of the bled pig dying in the snow. Jude's flounderings here reveal to his wife and reader alike how inadequate to the unattractive tasks of 'real' life he is. The act impinges on him not as a farmer's matter-of-fact chore, but as a sickening series of physical phenomena from which he cannot, for all his nausea, escape. Hardy consciously presents the pig stripped of any reference to Eleusis, and its slaughter underlines his central theme of paganism's defeat by a 'Christian' ethos which has bleached all mystery out of the 'Mysteries'.

From the moment Jude's lofty daydreams are interrupted by the flying pig's-pizzle, it becomes clear that his Christminster brand of religiosity cannot empower him because it fails to brook the biological imperatives which are equally necessary for healthy human living. Hardy plays this tragic situation as frenetic black farce when Jude is initiated into a life of deforming excess after the crash of his ambitions. This is conveyed by Jude's drunken recitation of the Creed in Latin at a seedy backstreet tavern.

> The barmaid concocted the mixture with the bearing of a person compelled to live among animals of an inferior species, and the glass

was handed across to Jude, who, having drunk the contents, stood up
and began rhetorically, without hesitation:
'Credo in unum Deum, Patrem omnipotentem, Factorem coeli et
terrae, visibilium omnium et invisibilium.'
'Good, Excellent Latin!' cried one of the undergraduates, who,
however, had not the slightest conception of a single word. (*Jude*
124)

Hardy's anti-Christian satire achieves increasingly harsh results: he
cheapens the solemn and sober facts of Anglican ceremonial with a
malevolent glee. 'Somebody threw down threepence, the glass was handed,
Jude stretched out his arm for it without looking, and having swallowed the
liquor went on in a moment in a revived voice, raising it as he neared the
end with the manner of a priest leading a congregation' (*Jude* 124-5).
Hardy's iconoclasm explores, as it did during the pig-killing, the geography
of that ill-defined border-zone separating humour from the grotesque. The
image of Jude, the pseudo-priest, 'leading' his 'congregation' of topers,
prostitutes and dissipated undergraduates in the cheerless Christminster pub
reflects the truculent spirit of incongruity which seeks to offend and
disorientate, rather than mollify and win over, the readership. Through this
episode Hardy implies there is nothing in the 'Christian' city which could
evoke the spiritual, mystical or awesome nature of existence. When Jude
meets Abby again after her return from Australia he discovers her working
as a barmaid-priestess dispensing the sacrament and absolution in a tavern
with a bar composed of confessional booths or 'compartments' (*Jude* 186).
The aggressive juxtaposition of opposing extremes (the exalted and the
profane) recalls Hardy's image of Marygreen's time-crusted church
summarily dismantled and converted into 'pig-sty walls' (*Jude* 6). But this
blackest of late-Victorian comedies does not enable Hardy himself to stand
apart from the 'fossil' of Christminster at which he laughs so bitterly.
Jude's bizarre performance at the pub reveals not the triumphant expression
of a luminous spirit in a desiccated society, but an unsettling outlet for
impotent rage as the 'Tutor of St. Slums' declaims to Tinker Taylor, Bower
o' Bliss and the rural underclass whose lives the Christminster grandees do
not even acknowledge.
That the form of the novel itself bears wildly contrasting generic effects
implies how Hardy's witty resources, once so bracing and flamboyant in *A
Laodicean*, evaporate under the sheer weight of a social despair he is
unable to counteract. Despite an increasingly bellicose polemical energy in
his fiction after *Two on a Tower*, Hardy finally recognizes that, despite his
best inflammatory efforts, the late-Victorian ethos upheld by the
Christminster 'survival' ratifies the status quo instead of challenging it with

any political passion aimed at amelioration. This crushing awareness lies behind Jude's extraordinary comedy of crisis that also imbues Phillotson's brawl. James Gibson's assertion that 'many find the book too gloomy to read',[117] overlooks the effect this riotous situation has on the reading experience. Hardy fashions the initial conflict between Shaston town council ('the respectable inhabitants and well-to-do fellow-natives of the town [who] were against Phillotson to a man'), and a motley 'group of itinerants, who frequented the numerous fairs and markets held up and down Wessex during the summer and autumn months' (*Jude* 260). These curious 'itinerants' belong to what Henry Mayhew calls in *London Labour and the London Poor* (1861-62) 'rural nomads...that large class who live by either selling, showing, or doing something through the country'. Indeed the entire episode slyly invokes Mayhew's subdivision of mankind into 'the wanderers and the settlers' borrowed from James Cowles Prichard's taxonomic anthropology in *Researches into the Physical History of Mankind* (1836).[118] Mayhew explains

> Of the thousand millions of human beings that are said to constitute the population of the entire globe, there are – socially, morally, and perhaps even physically considered – but two distinct and broadly marked races, viz., the wanderers and the settlers – the vagabond and the citizen – the nomadic and the civilized tribes.[119]

Phillotson's 'dozen or more champions' who 'rose up in his defence as from the ground' mischievously implies that they are similar to brave Arthurian knights of chivalric romance, appearing almost by magic to safeguard his honour. Unfortunately, these 'champions' inhabit the louche late-Victorian underclass of 'nomadic tribes' such as 'pedlars, showmen, harvest-men', whose manners and mores so enthralled Mayhew. Hardy exploits with malevolent relish the incongruity of Phillotson, a staid middle-aged pedant, winning the belligerent sympathies of 'two cheapjacks, a shooting-gallery proprietor and the ladies who loaded the guns, a pair of boxing masters, a steam-roundabout manager, two travelling broommakers, who called themselves widows, a gingerbread-stall keeper...and a 'test-your-strength' man' (*Jude* 260). His reference to the 'gingerbread-stall keeper' anticipates Sue's later occupation selling 'Christminster cakes' at Kennetbridge. It is an index of how the image of the fair in Hardy's fiction, formerly transgressive and inextricably intertwined with heretical fertility

---

[117] James Gibson, *Thomas Hardy: A Literary Life* (London: Macmillan, 1996), p. 131

[118] James Cowles Prichard (1786-1848) was one of the earliest British anthropologists.

[119] Henry Mayhew, *London Labour and the London Poor* (London: Constable, 1968), p. 1.

in *The Mayor of Casterbridge*, has degenerated into pathetic travesty since Jude and Sue choose these occasions to display their edible miniatures of a pernicious 'survival'.[120]

> This generous phalanx of supporters and a few others of independent judgement whose own domestic experiences had not been without vicissitude came up and warmly shook hands with Phillotson; after which they expressed their thoughts so strongly to the meeting that issue was joined, the result being a general skuffle, wherein...a church-warden was dealt such a topper with the map of Palestine that his head went right through Samaria, and many black eyes and bleeding noses were given, one of which, to everybody's horror, was the venerable incumbent's, owing to the zeal of an emancipated chimney-sweep, who took the side of Phillotson's party. When Phillotson saw the blood running down the rector's face he deplored almost in groans the untoward and degrading circumstances, regretted that he had not resigned when called upon, and went home so ill that next morning he could not leave his bed. (*Jude* 260-61)

Hardy extends his anti-Christian satire by using the rural nomads which Mayhew typified in racial and cultural terms no different from those applied to African 'primitives'; they were 'distinguished for their repugnance to continuous labour – for their disregard of female honour – their love of cruelty – their pugnacity – and their utter want of religion'.[121] Hardy's tone is effortlessly insouciant as the earnest public enquiry dedicated to upholding fine Anglican principles in the province descends into 'a general scuffle'. This Fieldingesque passage shows Hardy in boisterously comic mood, but the next paragraph disconcertingly shifts the focus from the uproar of the committee-room to Phillotson's silent bedchamber as he experiences a mid-life crisis: the 'melancholy event was the beginning of a serious illness for him; and he lay in his lonely bed in the pathetic state of mind of a middle-aged man who perceives at length that his life, intellectual and domestic, is tending to failure and gloom' (*Jude* 261). As in the closing chapters of *The Woodlanders* where Marty South's requiem for Winterborne jars with old Melbury's absurdly anti-climactic quest for his daughter, Hardy's agonized perception of a time hopelessly out of joint is enacted in his conscious yoking together of disparate literary

---

[120] For the Great Wessex Agricultural Show at Stoke-Barehills, Jude makes a model of Cardinal College.

[121] Quoted in Eileen Yeo, 'Mayhew as a Social Investigator', in E. P. Thompson and E. Yeo (eds.), *The Unknown Mayhew. Selections from the Morning Chronicle, 1849-50* (Harmondsworth, Middlesex: Penguin, 1984), pp. 86-7.

genres without attempting to reconcile them. The passage describing the scuffle is Hardy in nonchalantly comic mood, whose élan derives from viewing clerical authority as a matter of social convention rather than one of uncritical acceptance (a chimney-sweep gives the rector a bloody nose). Moreover, the church-warden is dealt such a 'topper' that his head 'went right through Samaria' – referring to the name of the Northern Israelite capital and the territory surrounding it. Hardy compares the clerisy that denounces Phillotson to 'Samaritans': a conservative group within the spectrum of Judaism who distrusted anything that smacked of innovation or modernizing, and observed the Sabbath with extreme strictness.

Hardy uses the disruptive presence of a decadent underclass at a meeting presided over by churchmen to attack the flagrant hypocrisy of middle-class mores. But this intemperate celebration of anti-Establishment animus cannot be sustained. *A Laodicean*'s occasions of lighthearted joviality comprise a formidable mechanism which enables Hardy to transcend an apprehension of social stagnation, but *Jude*'s droll moments articulate instead paralysis, confinement and diminishing possibilities. This receives its most unnerving expression with the arrival of Little Father Time.

> He was Age masquerading as Juvenility, and doing it so badly that his real self showed through crevices. A ground swell from ancient years of night seemed now and then to lift the child in this his morning-life, when his face took a back view over some great Atlantic of time, and appeared not to care about what it saw. (*Jude* 290)

Given that the Wessex of *Jude* contains almost no folkloric 'survivals' (highlighted by the effacement of Marygreen's 'historical records'), it is as if Hardy needs to compensate for that absence of a long temporal perspective by introducing an agent of dislocation and erasure whose 'face took a back view over some great Atlantic of time'. Many scholars deplore the violent incongruity of this figure in a novel largely presented in terms of verisimilitude. He is at once 'Arabella's boy' (realistic) and 'Age masquerading as Juvenility' (symbolizing what is unknown to the conscious mind). But this disturbing collision of disparate literary modes expresses Hardy's pervasive sense of things falling apart, piquant wit sliding into torment, the very form of the novel itself giving way under pressure from modern expressionist techniques which deal in the abstract and the indeterminate.

Although commentators persist in labelling Little Father Time an awkward violation of the canons of Victorian realism, Hardy takes great pains to make this character psychologically credible, a product of his circumstances rather than an inert, highly stylized figure.[122] He has grown up to feel totally unwanted and he is frightened by Jude's inability to secure lodgings for the family at Christminster (an ironic reference to Mary and Joseph at Bethlehem?). Looking to Sue for reassurance he finds only rejection. Her self-pitying statements to him in the Mildew Lane garret drive the already morbid child to despair, turning him into a murderer and a suicide. Though the child is firmly established as historically recognizable, Hardy invites other more symbolic/allegorical readings, for the name of Little Father Time links him with the Christian emblem of 'grim reaper with hourglass and scythe'. The sight of a hanged Father Time flanked by his two half-siblings shows Hardy at his most savage, travestying the slaughter of the innocents[123] and the Biblical Crucifixion. We are reminded again of the Passion, when Jude first accepts Sue's bereavement, alluding to the account of Christ's death in Mark 15:35: 'Then let the veil of our temple be rent in twain from this hour' (*Jude* 373).

Father Time is also moulded by Hardy's sustained interest in classical drama. The scrupulous pursuit of symmetry in the novel implies obsessive alertness to the potentialities of this ancient art-form. Sue remarks soon after the arrival of Father Time in England, 'It makes me feel as if a tragic doom overhung our family, as it did the house of Atreus' (*Jude* 297). The house of Atreus was said in Greek legend to be cursed. Its disasters afford the foundation for Aeschylus's trilogy *Oresteia*. And Jude quotes from *Agamemnon* in the aftermath of the child's suicide and murder – 'Nothing can be done...Things are as they are, and will be brought to their destined issue' (*Jude* 358). Jude and Sue, by comparing their plight to Greek drama, view themselves as tragic culture-heroes, doomed to error all the way. Hardy discredits their pretensions to this august stature. This is revealed when Jude tries to commit suicide at the end of Book I. He walks into the middle of a frozen pond hoping the ice will give way underneath him, but it refuses to break even after he jumps on it! He 'supposed he was not a sufficiently dignified person for suicide' (*Jude* 70). Little Father Time's murderous remedy for unwanted births shows him as the *deus ex machina* in a Greek tragedy played as hectic black farce amid the hidebound Hebraism of Oxford. Christine Brooke-Rose calls Jude's quotation from

---

[122] Havelock Ellis, in an 1896 article on *Jude the Obscure*, praised the novel as an exemplar of realist modernism in which Hardy displayed a verisimilitude to the experiences of general humanity.

[123] See Jeremiah 2:34 and 19:4.

Agamemnon, 'abysmally bathetic and irrelevant',[124] yet she misses a crucial double irony. Hardy would like to shore up these eloquent Greek fragments against ruin but in the nightmare world of Christminster such allusions strike a consistently false note. *Jude* is Hardy's Waste Land without Eliot's hope. The ghastly hollowness of such quotations imbues the 'strange and consummate horror' of the infanticide (*Jude* 356). When Jude and Sue discover their dead children hanging on the back of a door, organ-music is playing at a nearby college chapel. Jude recognizes it as the anthem from the seventy-third Psalm, 'Truly God is loving unto Israel' (*Jude* 356)! Such Grand Guignol especially outraged Hardy's late-Victorian readers, and Martin Seymour-Smith asks whether it strains 'the fabric of the book'.[125] This is precisely the effect Hardy desires. It is owing to the brutal therapy of Time that Jude fully awakens from his enthralment to dreams of 'high' Christminster culture into prosaic concrete history, the Arnoldian 'Iron Time' stripped of ameliorating vision.

The catastrophe caused by Little Father Time, and the unqualified suffering of Sue and Jude in the closing chapters, mark what Irwin and Gregor call 'the outermost reach of Hardy's art'.[126] But the Remembrance Day celebration which Jude hears on his deathbed reveals Hardy's creative resources adopting the most extreme effects: comedy at the end of its tether.[127] What Deborah Collins calls Hardy's 'perverse pleasure' in watching his protagonists 'fragment'[128] cannot be assessed as a brave or empowering response to the sickness confronting him but is in itself a symptom of the general malaise. Hardy savours the powerlessness of the eponymous non-hero who is 'half-elevated' on his bed: an unpleasantly mocking irony and a last sign of the illusory position he held in life. Jude's self-administered last rites, in which he seems to efface himself, subsuming his own first person 'I' under that of Job, is juxtaposed with the explosion of colour and jubilation outside. The carnivalesque 'hurrahs' of 'the many and strong' resounding throughout Christminster – abrupt interruptions which almost drown out his dying curse from Job – ironically evoke the cheers which greet Tennyson's Sir Galahad as he enters the 'Heavenly Jerusalem'. The youthful Jude calls Christminster a 'Heavenly Jerusalem' (*Jude* 16) before the sickening material features of the real city disabuse

---

[124] Christine Brooke-Rose, 'Ill Wit and Sick Tragedy: *Jude the Obscure*' in Lance St. John Butler (ed.), *Alternative Hardy* (London: Macmillan, 1994), p. 28.

[125] Martin Seymour-Smith, *Hardy* (London: Bloomsbury, 1995), p. 528.

[126] Michael Irwin and Ian Gregor, 'Either Side of Wessex' in Lance St. John Butler (ed.), *Thomas Hardy after Fifty Years* (London: Macmillan, 1977), p. 115.

[127] The phrase is partly borrowed from H. G. Wells's *Mind at the End of its Tether*.

[128] Deborah L. Collins, *Thomas Hardy and His God: A Liturgy of Unbelief* (London: Macmillan, 1993), p. 99.

him of his ideals. The triumph of Galahad's epic quest contrasts with the dismal collapse of Jude's ambitions, for he is no patrician like the Arthurian knight, nor is he ever entitled to a place at an ancient university like Tennyson.[129] As in the pig-killing episode which shows the romantic and the drab colliding to create effects of considerable unease, Hardy selects ironic deflation and grotesque incongruity not as a coping device in a tense situation, but to aggravate the bleakness of the general prospect. The wandering Jude, who once had visions of a Promised Land, ends up amid the vividly realized squalor of Christminster's Mildew Lane where the facts of alcohol abuse and pneumonia alone prevail.[130]

> [S]houts and hurrahs came from somewhere in the direction of the river.
> 'Ah-yes! The Remembrance games,' he murmured. 'And I here. And Sue defiled!'
> The hurrahs were repeated, drowning the faint organ notes. Jude's face changed more: he whispered slowly, his parched lips scarcely moving:
> *'Let the day perish wherein I was born, and the night in which it was said, There is a man child conceived.'*
> ('Hurrah!')
> *'Let that day be darkness; let not God regard it from above, neither let the light shine upon it. Lo, let that night be solitary, let no joyful voice come therein.'*
> ('Hurrah!')
> (*Jude* 426)

Jude's bookish quotation from Job is an attempt to award himself a sonorous 'high tragedy' finale. Frank Giordano observes, 'there is an unmistakable sense in which Jude's suicide is heroic'.[131] But Hardy debunks his protagonist's strivings after 'heroic' status with chilling ironic insistence. The cheers and laughter of the Christminster crowds act as a macabre counterpoint and make a nonsense out of Jude's murmured words. Hardy's witty effects are now ruined at root. His desperation is manifest in the Remembrance Day procession when a cab-driver viciously kicks his horse in the belly 'at college gates in the most religious and educational city in the world' (*Jude* 346). While Jude lies on his deathbed meditating on how his pathetically ludicrous fantasies have fallen victim to 'Time, in

---

[129] Tennyson attended Trinity College, Cambridge.

[130] See Norman Vance, 'Secular Apocalyptic and Thomas Hardy', *History of European Ideas* 26:3-4 (2002), 201-10.

[131] Frank. R. Giordano Jr., *'I'd Have My Life Unbe': Thomas Hardy's self-destructive characters* (Alabama: University of Alabama Press, 1984), p. 129.

his own gray style',[132] Arabella is affecting a hearty availability to secure a new mate for herself. And there is no grandiose ending for the impetuous maverick Sue, who inveighed against the absurdly prescriptive ideologies of bourgeois femininity.[133] Forsaking her sceptical rationality for the punishing asceticism of the Judaic-Christian sackcloth, she returns to a legal husband who physically repels her, and yields to the marital attentions she thinks will expiate her aberrant indulgence with Jude, mortifying 'the terrible flesh – the curse of Adam'.[134] Hardy elaborates the stark irony of a once 'freethinking' New Woman wearily capitulating to the ceaseless excoration of a religious mania that the physician Henry Maudsley would have termed a 'reversion to the old belief of savages'.[135] The approved acts of penance, far from being hallmarks of a proud 'Christian' community, are an atavistic throwback to a superstitious and barbaric past.

What Christminster finally epitomizes and instructs is for Jude the very antithesis of a shining earthly paradise. The eerily empty Gothic milieu of this decrepit city evokes Conrad's London, 'a cruel devourer of the world's light',[136] an energy sink absorbing vitality around it, swallowing lives. Hardy's adventures in time and in tone end with the portrayal of a deadening 'survival', that cannot be ousted by a more humane and charitable social order. His almost autistic isolation and cultural despair at the institutionalized structures that define and limit human choice imbue his

---

[132] Percy Bysshe Shelley, 'Epipsychidion', (l. 55) in *Shelley: Selected Poetry, Prose and Letters*, ed. A. S. B. Glover (London: Nonesuch Press, 1951), p. 530.

[133] See Roxanne Jurta, ' "Not-So-New Sue": The Myth of *Jude the Obscure* as a New Woman Novel', *Journal of the Eighteen Nineties Society* 26 (1999), 13-21; Shanta Dutta, 'Sue's "Obscure" Sisters', *Thomas Hardy Journal* 12:2 (May 1996), 48-59; Martin Wilson, ' "Lovely Conundrum" and Locus for Conflict: The Figure of Sue Bridehead in Hardy's *Jude the Obscure*', *Thomas Hardy Journal* 11:3 (October 1995), 90-101.

[134] On Sue's pathology of nervous disintegration in relation to 'aberrant sexuality' and nineteenth-century medical science see Cynthia Eagle Russett, *Sexual Science: The Victorian Construction of Womanhood* (Cambridge, Mass.: Harvard University Press, 1989); Lawrence Rothfield, *Vital Signs: Medical Realism in Nineteenth-Century Fiction* (Princeton: Princeton University Press, 1992); Lynda Nead, *Myths of Sexuality: Representations of Women in Victorian Britain* (Oxford: Blackwell, 1988); Frank Mort, *Dangerous Sexualities: Medico-Moral Politics in England Since 1830* (London: Routledge & Kegan Paul, 1987); Athena Vrettos, *Somatic Fictions: Imagining Illness in Victorian Culture* (Stanford: Stanford University Press, 1995); Jil Larson, 'Sexual Ethics in Fiction by Thomas Hardy and the New Woman Writers' in Alice Jenkins and Juliet John (eds.), *Rereading Victorian Fiction* (London: Macmillan, 2000), pp. 159-72. Martin Wilson, ' "Lovely Conundrum" and Locus for Conflict: The Figure of Sue Bridehead in Hardy's *Jude the Obscure*', *Thomas Hardy Journal* 11:3 (October 1995), 90-101.

[135] Henry Maudsley, *Natural Causes and Supernatural Seemings* (London: Kegan Paul, Trench, 1886), p. 161.

[136] Joseph Conrad, *The Secret Agent: A Simple Tale*, ed. Bruce Harkness and S. W. Reid (Cambridge: Cambridge University Press, 1990), p. 12.

attacks on 'terrible, dogmatic ecclesiasticism – Christianity so called (but really Paulinism plus idolatry) – on morals and true religion'.[137] That the pale Galilean's city is all-conquering can be seen in the way Christian mythology has banished any allusion to the immemorial pagan culture whose agent is executed at the end of *Tess*. Hardy's majestic conception of a nature-goddess will not leave any sustaining inheritance to the next generation. He can only grieve like Swinburne for those classical deities 'whom Christmas overthrew'[138] and left to gather dust in the Elgin Room of the British Museum. The unique alchemy of Hardy's art, which could recast traumatic circumstances into a piquant positive, vanishes along with the faint echoes of pagan myth. He can no longer defuse the fact that in *Jude* a pioneering modernity of outlook and sincere human feeling are continually subject to crushing extinction on the part of social custom.[139] Instead, he furnishes a whispered prayer for annihilation, approaching the raw realities of Christminster with self-lacerating wit. The devastating discoveries made in *Jude the Obscure* ensure that Hardy's efforts to address the intractable clash of interests between humankind's higher cerebral activity and the biological imperatives Darwin attributed to a 'past and lower state of civilisation',[140] end on a note of utter blankness.

---

[137] Thomas Hardy, *Collected Letters*, II, 143.

[138] Thomas Hardy, 'Christmas in the Elgin Room', *Complete Poems*, p. 928.

[139] On Jude and Sue's failure to 'lay out, and live by, a new set of ground rules designed to free them from what they see as the intellectually and spiritually repressive constraints of social and biological expectation', see Jane Wood, *Passion and Pathology in Victorian Fiction* (Oxford: Oxford University Press, 2001), pp. 163-214.

[140] Charles Darwin, *The Descent of Man, and Selection in Relation to Sex* (1871), 2nd edn. (London: John Murray, 1883), p. 564.

Chapter 7

A Bizarre Farewell to Fiction?

The Well-Beloved (1892/97)

Perhaps no other Wessex novel has engendered so much critical confusion as *The Well-Beloved*, a black farce serialized in *The Illustrated London News* from 1 October to 17 December 1892, and radically revised for publication in volume form in March 1897. D. H. Lawrence's impatient dismissal of what is technically Hardy's final published novel as 'fatuity'[1] gives some indication of its anomalous and testing qualities. Hardy himself recognized the extent to which the story strays from the realistic ethic of the Victorian novel and its mimetic techniques. In his Preface to the volume in the 1912 edition, he believed *The Well-Beloved* differed 'from all or most others of the series in that the interest aimed as is of an ideal or subjective nature'. H. M. Daleski typifies recent Hardy scholars when he remarks on *The Well-Beloved*: 'It is a light – and slight – fantasy' which 'has none of the novelist's customary brilliance and depth and certainly does not engage his obsessions. I think *Jude the Obscure* should continue to be seen as Hardy's final statement in the novel.'[2] *The Well-Beloved*'s fabular structure can be seen as a reaction to *Jude*'s rigorous concentration on the unrelieved intractability of loss, by creating a different and maybe protective tone. Yet in *The Well-Beloved*'s alternative endings Hardy not only reflects on many of his preceding novels but also administers the last rites to his extraordinary fiction-writing career. His 1892 conclusion explodes a theme that increasingly dominates his work from *The Woodlanders* onwards: the disastrous results of misperception, which thrives on tricks of light. The 1897 version closes with an unsparingly bitter comment on Hardy's ardent anthropological interest in measuring current social developments against the mental and physical heirlooms of village

---

[1] D. H. Lawrence, *Study of Thomas Hardy*, p. 93.
[2] H. M. Daleski, *Thomas Hardy and Paradoxes of Love* (Columbia and London: University of Missouri Press, 1997), p. 187. See also Richard Carpenter, *Thomas Hardy*, pp. 67-8; Martin Seymour-Smith, *Hardy*, p. 594. For a more sympathetic account see Patricia Ingham, 'Provisional Narratives: Hardy's Final Trilogy' in Lance St. John Butler (ed.), *Alternative Hardy* (London: Macmillan, 1991).

tradition, that 'vast mass of unwritten folk-lore, local chronicle, local topography, and nomenclature' which 'has nearly sunk, into eternal oblivion'.[3]

Hardy's central protagonist Jocelyn Pierston (Pearston in the 1892 text)[4] is a sculptor who, like his creator, has moved from relatively modest origins in southwest England to become an acclaimed and affluent member of polite metropolitan society. Pierston's endeavour to capture in stone an immaculate female form makes him a descendant of all the naive 'fantasts' and frustrated idealists who populate the psychic terrain of the later fiction.[5] Pierston believes the 'female' is a worthy object of, but cannot ever create, great art. His chronic inability (or refusal) to recognize 'the reality of any world outside himself'[6] links him with the 'unpractical lofty-notioned dreamer' Edred Fitzpiers (*Woodlanders* 172), who much prefers 'the ideal world to the real' (*Woodlanders* 87) in order to practise his self-serving aestheticism of erotic indulgence. Angel Clare, though not hedonistic like Fitzpiers, is a variation on this type; as is Jude Fawley, who regards the epicene Sue Bridehead as 'an ideal character, about whose form he [begins] to weave curious and fantastic day-dreams' (*Jude* 90). Angel Clare exacts a particular kind of perfection from the woman of his choice, and to serve this demand he transforms the felt potency of ancient divinities (such as Artemis and Demeter) into a superficial intellectual concept.[7] Pierston is an exaggerated parody of Clare and uses a poeticizing tendency to convert any trace of carnal passion into sterile neo-pagan rhetoric: 'Sometimes at night he dreamt that [the Well-Beloved] was "the wile-weaving Daughter of high Zeus" in person, bent on tormenting him for his sins against her beauty in his art – the implacable Aphrodite herself' (1897 *WB* 184-5).[8] He also speculates whether the 'love-queen of his isle' may actually be the Old Testament fertility goddess 'Ashtaroth' (see Judges 2:13), or the Norse

---

[3] Michael Millgate (ed.), *Thomas Hardy's Public Voice*, pp. 181-5. This quotation is taken from Hardy's 1902 contribution to H. Rider Haggard's 'Dorsetshire' chapter of his *Rural England: Being an Account of Agricultural and Social Researches Carried Out in the Years 1901 & 1902*, 2 vols. (London: Longmans, Green, 1902).

[4] All references are to Thomas Hardy, *'The Pursuit of the Well-Beloved' and 'The Well-Beloved'*, ed. with introd. Patricia Ingham (Harmondsworth, Middlesex: Penguin, 1997). Hereafter referred to as *WB*.

[5] For further discussion of these 'fantasts' see Andrew Radford, '"Fallen Angel": Hardy's Critique of Shelley in the Final Wessex Novels', *Thomas Hardy Yearbook* 29 (2000), 51-63.

[6] Ian Gregor, *The Great Web*, p. 151.

[7] An earlier title for *Tess of the d'Urbervilles* was 'Too Late Beloved'.

[8] Michael Millgate contends that Pierston's 'repeated invocations of Aphrodite under names so various' implies 'a possible influence from [Hardy's] recent reading of Frazer's *The Golden Bough*'. See Michael Millgate, *Thomas Hardy: His Career as a Novelist* (London: Bodley Head, 1971), p. 293.

'Freyja' (1897 *WB* 276): deities linked with the cosmic generative force pervading all nature.

The Well-Beloved records the irreversible atrophy of belief in elemental natural energies to replenish late-Victorian culture. Hardy's anguished perception of this fact prompted D. H. Lawrence, in his March 1913 review of *Georgian Poetry, 1911-1912*, to situate his literary precursor, almost venomously, among the *fin-de-siècle* 'nihilists, the intellectual, hopeless people' who epitomize 'a dream of demolition'[9] from which his own generation must awaken. Pearston's destructive fictions about women are fuelled by the meaningless abstractions of metaphysics, which effectively distance experience and reveal an unacknowledged desire for mastery over the seductive specimens who embody his mysterious pagan muse. He withdraws into an intensely private domain of reminiscence, repetition and adjournment as if this were an insurance against the ineluctable movement towards mortality.[10] In both versions of *The Well-Beloved*, the hero's deeply introverted sexuality and failure to distinguish between the actual and imaginary, the profound and the inconsequential, lead to frequent embarrassment. Pierston's sacrifice in gratification of the sensual appetite that preserves Fitzpiers and destroys d'Urberville, has tragicomic results. When 'the outer brightness' is brought to bear on Pearston's narrow, infatuated viewpoint in the 1892 version, the outcome transcends impish wit:

> 'Nurse,' [Pearston] said. 'Let me see you. Why do you always keep behind my head?'
> She went to the window, through which the light had only been allowed even now to enter between the blinds. Reaching it, she pulled the blind up a little way, till the outer brightness fell full upon her. An unexpected shock was the result. The face which had been stamped on his mind-sight by the voice, the face of Marcia forty years ago, vanished utterly. In its place was a wrinkled crone, with a pointed chin, her figure bowed, her hair as white as snow. To this the once handsome face had been brought by the raspings, chisellings, stewings, bakings, and freezings of forty years. The Juno of that day was the Witch of Endor of this.
> He must have shuddered at the discovery of what time had done, possibly have uttered a slight gasp; at all events, she knew in some

---

[9] D. H. Lawrence, 'Georgian Poetry: 1911-1912' in *Phoenix: The Posthumous Papers of D. H. Lawrence*, ed. with introd. Edward D. Macdonald (London: Heinemann, 1961), p. 250.
[10] As Annette Federico observes, Pierston is 'an ascetic aesthete: there is a prudishness to his passion'. See *Masculine Identity in Hardy and Gissing* (London and Toronto: Associated University Presses, 1991), p. 82.

way of the shock of his sensitiveness that her skeleton-figure caused
him. (1892 *WB* 167-8)

Like Wordsworth's hopeless dreamer, Pearston has until now resisted
forfeiting control over the suspension of history and let his romantic
idealizing fancies 'fade into the light of common day'.[11] When disabused of
his 'visions' he tries 'to tear open his wound, and bring eternal night upon
this lurid awakening' (1892 *WB* 168). The 'stress of seeing clearly' (1892
WB 167) is too much for Pearston to bear after spending his entire life
chasing the chimerical incarnations of solitary desire. 'Hardy's novels'
according to Penelope Vigar, are 'best understood if they are seen as
narrative pictures' employing 'techniques comparable with those of the
painter – chiaroscuro, perspective, effects of distancing and balance'.[12] But
Pearston and his creator learn that the always fraught if bracing (and in the
mature fiction increasingly hazardous) game of indulging unexpected
visual impressions and painterly effects of light, has collapsed. Hardy's
1892 conclusion is both a gloriously extravagant and barbed appreciation of
this fact.

After a botched attempt at drowning himself in a small skiff headed
into the turbulent currents of the Race, Pearston awakens to find himself in
bed at his lodgings in East Wake and to discover that his wife Marcia, now
'a wrinkled crone' in the morning rays, has returned after forty years. His
temporarily impaired sight after the Race debacle was caused by crashing
into the side of a lightship (1892 *WB* 164)![13] Hardy exploits with wrenching
black humour the incongruity for Pearston between the imperious and
radiant 'Juno' he remembers and the crumpled 'Witch of Endor' now
confronting him without the benefit of cosmetic aids. Pearston's response
to finding himself permanently yoked to a Marcia grown cadaverous and
old shows callous insensitivity. This deliberately enfeebled finale reveals
unfeigned contempt for a serial audience in the serial itself by debunking
the expected happy ending to Pearston's unrelenting pursuit of the ideal
feminine in art.

His wife passed by the mantelpiece, over which hung an enlarged
photograph of Avice, that he had brought thither when he left the

---

[11] William Wordsworth, 'Intimations of Immortality', (5.76).

[12] Penelope Vigar, *The Novels of Thomas Hardy: Illusion and Reality* (University of
London: Athlone Press, 1974), p. 15.

[13] Pearston has no more aptitude for suicide than Jude Fawley, who tries to secure for
himself a tragic finale by jumping repeatedly on the ice in the middle of a large pond. The
ice cracks, but he does not sink. He concludes that he is 'not a sufficiently dignified person
for suicide' (*Jude* 70) and goes home.

other house, as the single object which he cared to bring. The
contrast of the ancient Marcia's aspect, both with this portrait and
with her own fine former self, brought into his brain a sudden sense
of the grotesqueness of things...An irresistible fit of laughter, so
violent as to be an agony, seized upon him, and started in him with
such momentum that he could not stop it. He laughed and laughed,
till he was almost too weak to draw breath.

Marcia hobbled up, frightened. 'What's the matter?' she asked;
and, turning to a second nurse, 'He is weak – hysterical.'

'O – no, no! I – I – it is too droll – this ending to my would-be
romantic history!' Ho-ho-ho! (1892 *WB* 168)

Pearston notices on the mantelpiece his enlarged photograph of Avice the
third, whom he had recently married.[14] The frozen moment of a photograph
in which Avice's vivacious and youthful beauty is preserved forever
clashes with the physical decay of his other wife Marcia, whose face bears
the 'raspings' and 'chisellings' of time when she pulls back the curtains.

The edgy uncertainty of what will happen after Pearston's hysterical
laughter when he sees the aged Marcia is compounded by the immediately
following 'Ho-ho-ho!' from the Hardyan narrator himself. His response
implies that there can be no sane reaction to the extreme folly of Pearston's
artistic quest other than by exercising derisive humour. This is a highly
disconcerting commentary from a presence that has hitherto kept a wry,
measured detachment from the quixotic hero. Pearston's perception of the
ludicrous is problematic because it offers us no sense of purgative or
cathartic release. His ghastly and uninhibited laughter, 'so violent as to be
an agony', is a desperate last resort; he sees no other way of coping with
the brutal ironies visited upon him in this severely diminished present
which is little more than an unresounding interval between life and death.
Hardy illustrates with amused savagery how the man who has disavowed
his past enthralment to the successive embodiments of an imaginary ideal
has to confront a world now bleached of human value. This conclusion,
which consigns Pearston to a limbo of lost joy, remains one of the most
powerfully disturbing moments in Hardy's fiction, and belies the critical
charge that *The Well-Beloved* is merely delicate or contrived whimsy.

---

[14] In revising the serial version, Hardy radically reshaped the plot by eliminating his
protagonist's two marriages – the early marriage to Marcia Bencomb, and the marriage to
Avice III at the end of the story, thus freeing the novel from scathing attacks on the legal
institution of marriage. See A. A. M. Bulaila, ' "The Clay but not the Potter": Love and
Marriage in *The Well-Beloved*', *Thomas Hardy Journal* 9:2 (May 1993), 61-71; Ralph W.
V. Elliot, 'The Infatuated Artist: Thomas Hardy and *The Well-Beloved*', *Thomas Hardy
Journal* 3:2 (May 1987), 20-33.

In the last chapter of the 1897 text Pierston is a bachelor who accommodates himself to the mediocre and marries the decrepit and impoverished Marcia out of pity (now by a farcical chance confined to a wheelchair for the nuptials). Hardy again ridicules the romantic love plot with its wedding-bells finale: a law of genre imposed by the periodical press that encourages progressive narratives of healthy self-fulfilment. The anticipated promise of hope is snidely reproduced in a marriage of elderly nonsexual convenience. With his unflinching acceptance of his own limitations, Pierston enjoys a placidity that he has never felt before, but at the cost of losing all gifts as an artist:

> His business was, among kindred undertakings which followed the extinction of the Well-Beloved and other ideals, to advance a scheme for the closing of the old natural fountains in the Street of Wells, because of their own possible contamination, and supplying the townlet with water from pipes, a scheme that was carried out at his expense, as is well known. He was also engaged in acquiring some old moss-grown, mullioned Elizabethan cottages, for the purpose of pulling them down because they were damp; which he afterwards did, and built new ones with hollow walls, and full of ventilators.
>
> At present he is sometimes mentioned as 'the late Mr. Pierston' by gourd-like young art-critics and journalists; and his productions are alluded to as those of a man not without genius, whose powers were insufficiently recognized in his lifetime. (1897 *WB* 336)

Roy Morrell undervalues the sad images of emasculation and surrender when he remarks of this revised ending that Pierston and Marcia 'face their ugliness and their infirmities and other realities of life and time; and, for Pierston anyway, life is for the first time truly satisfying'.[15] Hardy unsettles our sentimental expectations by showing marriage as a dispiritingly bleak arrangement induced only by the worldly-minded pragmatism that now governs Pierston's retirement. The wry Hardyan narrator, who in the 1897 text sedulously maintains his distance from the action, describes how Pierston, having willed the 'extinction' of his erotic and aesthetic impulses, occupies himself with philanthropic schemes. The mournful sobriety of this 1897 ending, making Pierston's lack of self-awareness far more explicit, is in its own way as stark as the finale of Hardy's previous published novel, in which the self-scourging narrator lampoons the bathetic hopelessness of Jude's academic plans. Pierston shows less rational understanding of the nature of things than when he was driven by his elusive 'one shape of many

---

[15] Roy Morrell, *Thomas Hardy: The Will and the Way* (Kuala Lumpur: University of Malaya Press, 1968), p. 119.

names'. Angel Clare is compelled to adjust his imprisoning idealism to the exigencies of the present, and to accept that he cannot recreate others just to suit his preconceptions. Pierston, the most perverse of Hardy's lovers, reveals a catastrophic inability to fully acknowledge that, for love to flourish, tangible external reality must sooner or later disperse the impalpable ether of a visionary world.

Pierston's serious illness in the 1897 version[16] prior to his undertaking sweeping social reforms, parodies a stock device in Victorian fiction: to be virtually on one's deathbed traditionally affords an opportunity for frank self-assessment. Hardy explodes this plot-cliché by showing that the curing of Pierston's genealogical obsession entails his abject decline as a sculptor. Thus the hero's cry of relief, 'Thank Heaven I am old at last. The curse is removed' contains heavy narratorial irony. That he should sometimes be referred to 'by young art-critics and journalists' as 'the late Mr Pierston' also veils a symbolic truth. The basic and interlinked components of his temperament – the responsiveness to vague but deep impressions generated in moments of self-absorption, and the capacity to sculpt works of art – are dead. Recent scholars have argued that this resolution is oblique autobiography in which Hardy performs 'a Prospero-like burning of his books'.[17] But Hardy was not ready to be shelved as an unremarkable has-been by middlebrow magazine reviewers: the close of his novel-writing career also heralded the beginning of a long and distinguished career as a poet.

The 1897 conclusion is notable for its mordant treatment of the social concern that lends *The Woodlanders*, *Tess* and *Jude* an especially stringent and pugnacious tone. In all particulars the protection of the island's traditional integrity would normally be the ideal promoted by Hardy, whose General Preface to the 1912 Wessex Edition affirms his antiquarian efforts 'to preserve' a 'fairly true record' of a disappearing life.[18] E. B. Tylor urged his peers to locate those 'peoples in the world, among whom a prompt and minute investigation would save some fast vanishing memory of their social laws and customs'.[19] But Pierston's transformation is so extreme that

---

[16] Pierston falls ill with a fever after attending Avice II's funeral in the drenching rain.

[17] Michael Millgate, *Biography*, p. 284. See also J. B. Bullen, 'Hardy's *The Well-Beloved*, Sex, and Theories of Germ Plasm', in Phillip V. Mallett and Ronald P. Draper (eds.), *A Spacious Vision: Essays on Hardy* (Newmill: Patten Press, 1994), p. 79.

[18] See also Hardy's Prefatory Note to the *Life*, justifying the inclusion of '[s]ome incidents of his country experiences' which 'may be considered as trivial', on the grounds that 'they embody customs and manners of old West-of-England life that have now entirely passed away' (3-4).

[19] E. B. Tylor, 'On a Method of Investigating the Development of Institutions; Applied to Laws of Marriage and Descent', p. 269.

he becomes an unapologetic destroyer of historic beauty instead of its custodian. He shows none of the typical antiquarian's 'respect...towards the monuments and relics of the ages upon which the civil and social institutions of to-day are in great measure founded'.[20] Hardy's natural imaginative habit was to view such vestiges as capsules of the past, transmitting the climate of a lost locality. Pierston, once so alert to the bittersweet intensities of memory on the peninsula where he was born and bred, now becomes the ruthless instrument of its 'modernisation', razing the anachronistic landmarks, such as 'moss-grown, mullioned Elizabethan cottages'.[21] Perry Meisel misconstrues the philosophy of these 'improvements' by remarking that Pierston 'is at last successful in marrying and in performing practical services to his native community'.[22] This reading ignores the fact that the solitary dreamer can no longer dream; he applies himself instead to the dreariest utilitarian projects – 'the kind of figure, with a proper sense of *richesse oblige*, that Hardy may have felt some pressure from his Dorchester fellow-townsmen to become'.[23]

Two of the social schemes Pierston undertakes after abandoning sculpture are specified in some detail, and Hardy does not select these examples at random. The symbolism – blocking 'the old natural fountains' and constructing new cottages with 'hollow walls' – summarizes and judges, unflinchingly, the epilogue to the protagonist's idiosyncratic career. Pierston, a man who once sought and welcomed reveries, with a relish for being knocked out of kilter by the fitful promptings of a romantic past, is now a 'hollow' man whose former 'ever-bubbling spring' (1897 *WB* 248) of inspiration has evaporated. The replacement of 'the old natural fountains' with piped water implies that he never comprehended the deeper springs of his own curious temperament and finally eradicates them altogether. Although the insidious process of technological and social growth – heralded by a more enterprising generation among whose agents may be included Paula Power, George Somerset and Donald Farfrae in earlier novels – has yet to infiltrate the homely rurality of Pierston's birthplace, future developments are even here unavoidable. We are given repeated reminders of the proximity of the railway and of the larger, more

---

[20] Anon., 'Recent discoveries in Art and Archaeology in Rome', *Quarterly Review* 144 (July 1877), 46.

[21] Hardy writes in *The Woodlanders* how 'old association' provides 'an almost exhaustive biographical or historical acquaintance with every object, animate and inanimate, within the observer's horizon' (95).

[22] Perry Meisel, *Thomas Hardy: The Return of the Repressed* (New Haven, Conn. and London: Yale University Press, 1972), p. 163.

[23] Norman Page, 'Introduction', *The Well-Beloved*, The Everyman Edition (London: Everyman, 1997), xxix.

modish milieu into which the Isle will be absorbed: opulent hotels, elegant artist studios and chic purpose-built flats served by lifts. There is a grimly enjoyed irony in Pierston acting as 'obliterator of historic records' like the anonymous neo-Gothic renovator who dismantles Marygreen's quaint hump-backed church in *Jude the Obscure*. One of the peninsula's most visionary scions becomes the proponent of a bland, uninspiring modernism: the disease of practical but jaded change generated from within. According to Hardy in his essay 'The Dorsetshire Labourer' (1883), it is in the seclusion of rural Dorsetshire that 'happiness will find her last refuge on earth'.[24] Pierston's aesthetic vandalism, Hardy implies, will be a deathstroke to the 'happiness' of the inbred and curiously isolated Slingers population. The Hardyan narrator, who in *Jude* directs his humanitarian zeal to myriad social injustices, now wearily accepts the imminence of cultural dissolution.

Pierston's aggressively practical projects are so devastating because in the 1897 *Well-Beloved* Hardy expands our sense of the Isle as an environment replete with precious anthropological data. In striking contrast to Pierston's drastic demolition work in the 1897 conclusion is Hardy's prefatory celebration of the 'peninsula carved by Time out of a single stone', 'the home' of a 'well-nigh distinct people', with its 'strange beliefs and singular customs' bearing the stamp of 'centuries immemorial' (1897 *WB* 3).[25] Michael Irwin explains that in *The Well-Beloved* Hardy portrays 'a specialized landscape of an uncharacteristic kind...the Isle of Slingers features but a single clump of trees, and seems virtually devoid of animal, bird or insect life'.[26] This offers only a partial impression of the island setting and most particularly of the rocky formation of which it is composed. The soaring 'infinitely stratified walls of oolite' extend upward from the non-human world and supply an august record of the passing of geological time and then, when carved into building material, of historical time: 'Norman, Anglian, Roman, Balearic-British'. Moreover, the Isle's topography and exceptional social fabric, and its historically altering relationship to the mainland are drawn with antiquarian gusto in the 1897 version. Pierston's renovations endanger a district crowned by landmarks of its Celtic and Roman forbears. The Isle is 'the last local stronghold of

---

[24] Thomas Hardy, *Personal Writings*, p. 169.

[25] Though Hardy's Preface reveals an awareness of Victorian geology, it also invites us to consider the link between the Isle as a natural piece of sculpture and Jocelyn Pierston's art, in which his *ideal* visions are transformed into sculpture using the *material* of his quarryman father's Portland stone.

[26] Michael Irwin, *Reading Hardy's Landscapes* (London: Macmillan, 2000), p. 132. See also Ralph Pite, *Hardy's Geography: Wessex and the Regional Novel* (New York: Palgrave, 2002).

the Pagan divinities, where Pagan customs lingered yet, Christianity had established itself precariously at best' (1897 *WB* 186). Additional sentences elaborate this long temporal perspective where recollection fades into the persistence of outmoded tradition and primitive myth, lending new prominence to the genealogy that the sculptor shares with all three Avice Caros, and the intertwining of his destiny with the superstition of 'handfesting': the ratification of betrothal by sexual relations before marriage – a widespread tradition of which Hardy himself may have been a product. This indigenous custom antedates Christianity itself, for Pierston could never marry a 'kimberlin' or a stranger from the mainland. To the reviewer for the *Athenaeum* (10 April 1897), although the island custom was 'doubtless interesting from an anthropological point of view', it had 'no influence on the action of the story, and need not have been alluded to'.[27] But the portrayal of 'handfesting' implicitly defies what Hardy saw as the fetid, repressive covenant of modern marriage by disclosing a more archaic alternative that is basically a series of quasi-incestuous couplings.[28]

Hardy's depiction of 'handfesting' signals an astute awareness of what James Frazer perceived as the 'truth' that 'to this day the peasant remains a pagan and savage at heart'; that his civilization 'is merely a thin veneer which the hard knocks of life soon abrade, exposing the solid core of paganism and savagery below'.[29] Frazer's terms are evocative because Hardy's time-voyages in the 1897 *Well-Beloved* enact a movement downwards and backwards into the obscure primitive layers underlying the crust of late-Victorian culture, weighing the minutiae of social circumstance against the buried life of subterranean experience. In his *Observations on Popular Antiquities* (1774), John Brand explained that 'Handefasting' still existed on nineteenth-century Portland, the peninsula off the Wessex coast to which Hardy's Isle of Slingers closely corresponds. Brand writes: 'I have been more than once assured from credible authority on Portland Island, that something very like it is still practised there very generally, where the inhabitants seldom or never intermarry with any one on the main-land'.[30] To employ the term J. F. McLennan coined in his *Primitive Marriage* (1865), Pierston's island community is 'endogamous'. McLennan discusses tribes in which all the members are 'of the same blood, or feigning themselves to be so'; where there is 'Connubium between members of the tribe' and where marriage outside the tribe is

---

[27] R. G. Cox, *Thomas Hardy: The Critical Heritage*, p. 318.
[28] See T. O'Toole, 'Genealogy and Narrative Jamming in Hardy's *The Well-Beloved*', *Narrative* 1:3 (October 1993), 207-22.
[29] Quoted in Robert Ackerman, *J. G. Frazer: His Life and Work*, p. 252.
[30] John Brand, *Observations on Popular Antiquities*, II, 87-8.

prohibited and receives draconian punishment.[31] For Tylor, reassessing his 'old friend' McLennan's theories in the 1880s, endogamy was 'a policy of isolation, cutting off a horde or village, even from the parent-stock whence it separated, if only a generation of two back'.[32] Sir John Lubbock, writing in the third edition of his *The Origin of Civilization*, commented that endogamy seems 'to have arisen from a feeling of race-pride, and a disdain of surrounding tribes'.[33]

Hardy evokes a 'survival' of the endogamous system in *The Well-Beloved*, because 'no islander had ever been known to break' the 'compact' of 'the primitive betrothal' (1897 *WB* 233). Pierston is unable to love a woman other than of 'the island race', thus Hardy fortifies, as J. B. Bullen contends, 'the sense of anthropological determinism by suggesting that not merely custom, but genetic propensity is responsible for the endogamy of the small family groups in this community'.[34] By alerting us to Pierston's 'altruism' in the 1897 finale – which will efface the scattered fragments of a mysterious past from the Isle of Slingers – Hardy sourly dismantles his own self-appointed role as the anthropologist of Wessex. In her examination of the story-telling faculty in the Wessex novels Barbara Hardy argues:

> Instead of collecting folk-tales and fairy-tales, as scholars do, [Hardy] uses the novel for archaeology and anthropology, as he looks at past and present by creating storytellers who look at past and present. The communal storytelling is less conspicuous than other rural arts and crafts, like the church music, the mummers' play, the maypole ritual, Harvest festival and the Christmas dancing, because it is more integral and common. And also because it is still part of a live culture.[35]

By showing Pierston's stern repudiation not only of his personal past but also the compelling history enshrined in the physical antiquities of his island sanctuary, Hardy makes his final desolate statement on a once 'live'

---

[31] J. F. McLennan, *Primitive Marriage*, p. 22.

[32] E. B. Tylor, 'On a Method of Investigating the Development of Institutions; Applied to Laws of Marriage and Descent', pp. 265, 267.

[33] Sir John Lubbock, *The Origin of Civilisation*, 2nd edn., p. 136. Quoted in John F. McLennan, *Studies in Ancient History* (London: Bernard Quaritch, 1876), xii.

[34] J. B. Bullen, 'Hardy's *The Well-Beloved*, Sex, and Theories of Germ Plasm', in P. V. Mallett and R. P. Draper (eds.), *A Spacious Vision: Essays on Hardy* (Newmill: Patten Press, 1994), p. 81.

[35] Barbara Hardy, *Thomas Hardy: Imagining Imagination in Hardy's Poetry and Fiction* (London and New Brunswick, NJ: Athlone Press, 2000), p. 23.

folk-culture that has become a mausoleum to the memory of a ruined world.

Hardy's abandonment of novel-writing in favour of poetry was not simply a result of the violent controversy aroused by his 1890s fiction. Hardy did not tremble at the frown of Mrs Grundy; he fully expected accusations of 'indecent directness'[36] given his readiness to dispute those rules about marriage and sexual passion which had come to define the boundaries of normality. Behind Hardy's indignation at the journalists who found his subject matter in *The Well-Beloved* unseemly – 'That a fanciful, tragi-comic half allegorical tale of a poor visionary pursuing a Vision should be stigmatized as sexual and disgusting is I think a piece of mendacity hard to beat in the annals of the press'[37] – was a seditious delight in teasing a bigoted and privileged literary establishment. *The Well-Beloved's* multiple endings signal Hardy's bullish refusal to palliate his critics and produce anodyne art for a tender middle-class readership. That both versions of the text conclude so awkwardly, mocking 'the regulation finish that "they married and were happy ever after" ',[38] attests Hardy's veiled malice in irony against the philistinism of institutionalized 'household reading'. While Pierston's pre-eminence as an artist is never proclaimed, he strives like his creator to pursue novelty of expression in the face of sharply defined, rigidly enforced conventions.[39] James Joyce argued in his 1900 essay entitled 'Ibsen's New Drama' that Hardy was among those nineteenth-century authors who had failed to extend the methods of narrative prose fiction. However, the revised *Well-Beloved*, published in the year of Victoria's Diamond Jubilee, reveals a verbal texture which has few precedents in the Victorian novel. That pathos, tragedy and the ludicrous co-exist so curiously in this story guarantees its continuing status as a notoriously odd generic experiment in the Hardy canon. Even the vituperative critic in *The World*, who saw the story as a lamentable illustration of Hardy's 'sex-mania', sarcastically acknowledged its wilful eccentricity: 'It may be fairly admitted that in the whole range of fiction from the days of the Greek author of *The Wonders of Thule* down to Mr. Hardy himself, there is nothing at all approximating to the plot of *The Well-*

---

[36] T.R. Wright, *Hardy and the Erotic*, p. 108.

[37] Thomas Hardy, *Collected Letters* II, 154.

[38] Thomas Hardy, *Personal Writings*, p. 128.

[39] Pierston's consultation of his friend the painter Alfred Somers is important here (1897 *WB* 34). That Somers, a prosperous member of the London glitterati, has a studio at 'Mellstock Gardens' (Mellstock is the fictional name for Hardy's birthplace at Higher Bockhampton) implies Hardy is offering an acerbic portrait of the type of artist he might have become: vapid, morally unimpeachable, slavishly following the latest trends.

Beloved'.[40] After fracturing the prevailing notions about fiction set by the bourgeois serial market in *The Well-Beloved*, there was nowhere left for Hardy to go except into the realm of poetry.

---

[40] *The World*, 24 March 1897, p. 13.

Bibliography

Primary Sources

Hardy, Thomas. *'A Changed Man', 'The Waiting Supper' and other Tales*. London: Macmillan, 1962.

————. *The Collected Letters of Thomas Hardy*, ed. Richard L. Purdy and Michael Millgate, 7 vols. Oxford: Clarendon Press, 1978-88.

————. *The Complete Poems of Thomas Hardy*, The New Wessex Edition, ed. James Gibson. London: Macmillan, 1976.

————. *Desperate Remedies*, The New Wessex Edition, ed. with introd. C. J. P. Beatty. London: Macmillan, 1986.

————. *The Distracted Preacher and other Tales*, ed. with introd. Susan Hill. Harmondsworth, Middlesex: Penguin, 1986.

————. *Far from the Madding Crowd*, ed. with introd. Suzanne B. Falck-Yi. Oxford: The World's Classics, 1993.

————. *A Group of Noble Dames*. Dover: Allan Sutton, 1993.

————. *The Hand of Ethelberta*, The New Wessex Edition, ed. with introd. Robert Gittings. London: Macmillan, 1975.

————. *Jude the Obscure*, ed. with introd. Patricia Ingham. Oxford: The World's Classics, 1985.

————. *A Laodicean*, ed. with introd. Jane Gatewood. Oxford: The World's Classics, 1991.

————. *The Life and Work of Thomas Hardy by Thomas Hardy*, ed. Michael Millgate. London: Macmillan, 1984.

————. *Life's Little Ironies*, ed. with introd. Alan Manford. Oxford: The World's Classics, 1996.

————. *The Literary Notebooks of Thomas Hardy*, ed. Lennart A. Björk, 2 vols. London: Macmillan, 1985.

————. *The Mayor of Casterbridge*, ed. with introd. Dale Kramer. Oxford: The World's Classics, 1987.

————. *One Rare Fair Woman: Thomas Hardy's Letters to Florence Henniker, 1893-1922*, ed. Evelyn Hardy and F. B. Pinion. London: Macmillan, 1972.

————. *A Pair of Blue Eyes*, ed. with introd. Roger Ebbatson. Harmondsworth, Middlesex: Penguin, 1985.

————. *The Personal Notebooks of Thomas Hardy*, ed. Richard H. Taylor. London: Macmillan, 1978.

————. *'The Pursuit of the Well-Beloved' and 'The Well-Beloved'*, ed. with introd. Patricia Ingham. Harmondsworth, Middlesex: Penguin, 1997.

——. *The Return of the Native*, ed. with introd. Simon Gatrell. Oxford: The World's Classics, 1986.

——. *The Short Stories of Thomas Hardy*. London: Macmillan, 1928.

——. *Tess of the d'Urbervilles*, ed. with introd. Juliet Grindle and Simon Gatrell. Oxford: The World's Classics, 1988.

——. *Thomas Hardy's Personal Writings: Prefaces, Literary Opinions, Reminiscences*, ed. Harold Orel. London: Macmillan, 1967.

——. *Thomas Hardy's Public Voice. The Essays, Speeches, and Miscellaneous Prose*, ed. Michael Millgate. Oxford: Clarendon Press, 2001.

——. *The Trumpet-Major and Robert His Brother*, ed. with introd. Roger Ebbatson. Harmondsworth, Middlesex: Penguin, 1986.

——. *Two on a Tower*, ed. with introd. Sulieman M. Ahmad. Oxford: The World's Classics, 1993.

——. *Under the Greenwood Tree*, ed. with introd. Simon Gatrell. Oxford: The World's Classics, 1985.

——. *Wessex Tales*, ed. with introd. Kathryn R. King. Oxford: The World's Classics, 1991.

——. *The Woodlanders*, ed. with introd. Dale Kramer. Oxford: The World's Classics, 1986.

Secondary Sources
(The Sciences of Humankind 1750-1930)

Anon. 'Darwin's *Origin of Species*', *Quarterly Review* 108 (1860), 254-67.

Anon. 'Debased Hellenism and the New Renaissance', *Church Quarterly Review* 10 (1880), 99-121.

Anon. 'Dimensions of the gigantic figure cut in a mountain in Dorsetshire', *Gentleman's Magazine* 34 (July 1764), 335-6.

Anon. 'Dr. Buckland's *Bridgewater Treatise*', *Quarterly Review* 56 (April 1836), 31-64.

Anon. 'The *Encyclopaedia Britannica*', *Quarterly Review* 70 (June 1842), 44-72.

Anon. 'Ethnology, or the Science of Races', *Quarterly Review* 88 (October 1848), 429-87.

Anon. 'Fergusson's *Handbook of Architecture*', *Edinburgh Review* 105 (January 1857), 112-41.

Anon. 'Hamilton &c. on Architecture', *Quarterly Review* 58 (February 1837), 61-82.

Anon. 'Hope's *History of Architecture*', *Quarterly Review* 53 (April 1835), 338-71.

Anon. 'Introduction', *Archaeologia Cantiana: Being Transactions of Kent Archaeological Society* 1 (1858), 1-22.

Anon. 'Introduction', *Archaeological Journal* 6 (1849), 1-12.

Anon. 'The London and North-Western Railway', *Quarterly Review* 84 (December 1848), 1-65.

Anon. 'Lyell – on *Life and its Successive Development*', *Quarterly Review* 89 (September 1851), 412-51.

Anon. 'Lyell's *Principles of Geology*', *Quarterly Review* 53 (April 1835), 406-48.

Anon. 'Murchison's *Silurian System*', *Quarterly Review* 64 (June 1839), 102-20.

Anon. 'Old English Domestic Architecture', *Quarterly Review* 45 (July 1831), 471-504.

Anon. 'On the History and Prospects of Antiquarianism in England', *Edinburgh Review* 86 (October 1847), 307-28.

Anon. 'The Organic World now in Progress', *Quarterly Review* 47 (March 1832), 103-32.

Anon. 'Popular Science', *Quarterly Review* 84 (March 1849), 307-44.

Anon. 'Primitive Man: Tylor and Lubbock', *Quarterly Review* 137 (July 1874), 40-77.

Anon. 'Principles of Gothic Architecture', *Quarterly Review* 69 (December 1841), 111-49.

Anon. 'Recent discoveries in Art and Archaeology in Rome', *Quarterly Review* 144 (July 1877), 46-81.

Anon. 'Schliemann's *Mycenae*', *Quarterly Review* 145 (January 1878), 62-93.

Anon. 'The Science of Electricity as applied in Peace and War', *Quarterly Review* 144 (July 1877), 138-79.

Anon. 'Scientific Lectures – their Use and Abuse', *Quarterly Review* 145 (January 1878), 35-61.

Anon. 'Sir John Herschel's *Astronomical Observations at the Cape of Good Hope*', *Quarterly Review* 85 (June 1849), 1-31.

Anon. 'The Society of Antiquaries Defended', *Gentleman's Magazine* (November 1829), 417-26.

Anon. 'The State of English Architecture', *Quarterly Review* 132 (January 1872), 295-335.

Anon. 'Stonehenge', *Quarterly Review* 108 (1860), 200-25.

Anon. 'Tylor on *Primitive Culture*', *Edinburgh Review* 135 (January 1872), 89-90.

Adams, W. H. Davenport. *Life in the Primeval World*. London: Nelson, 1872.

Anderson, John. *The Course of Creation*. 1850; Cincinnati: Moore, Anderson, Wilstach & Keys, 1853.

————. 'The Antiquity of Man', *British and Foreign Evangelical Review* 16 (1867), 383-400.

————. 'Human Remains in Superficial Drift', *Annual Report of the British Association for the Advancement of Science* 29 (1859). Contents summarized in *Athenaeum*, October 1, 1859.

————. 'The Antiquity of Man', *Quarterly Review* 37 (1863), 410-41.

————. 'The Antiquity of Man', *Westminster Review* 79 (1863), 272-91.

Ansted, David T. *Geological Gossip*. London: Routledge, 1860.

————. 'The Testimony of Geology to the Age of the Human Race', *National Review* 10 (1860), 279-312.

Argyll, Duke of . 'Opening Address', *Proceedings of the Royal Society of Edinburgh* 4 (1862), 362-70.

——————. *Primeval Man*. New York: George Routledge & Sons, 1869.

Babington, Churchill. *Introductory Lecture on the Study of Archaeology Delivered before the University of Cambridge*. Cambridge: Dayton & Bell, 1865.

Bain, Alexander. *Mind and Body; the Theories of Their Relation*. London: Henry S. King, 1873.

Barnes, William, 'A British Earthwork', *Proceedings of the Dorset Natural History and Antiquarian Field Club* 1 (1876), 94-6.

——————. 'Notes on the History of Shaftesbury', *Proceedings of the Dorset Natural History and Antiquarian Field Club* 3 (1878), 27-33.

——————. 'Notes on the so called Roman Roads', *Proceedings of the Dorset Natural History and Antiquarian Field Club* 5 (1880), 69-80.

Bateman, James. *The Church Association: Its Policy and Prospects*. 3rd edn. London: Ridgway, 1880.

Bonney, T. G. 'Stone Circles and Megalithic Remains' in George Laurence Gomme (ed.), *The Gentleman's Magazine Library: A Classified Collection of the Chief Contents of 'The Gentleman's Magazine' from 1731-1868. Archaeology: Part II*. London: Elliot Stock, 1886.

Borlase, William Copeland. 'Account of the Exploration of Tumuli at Trevalga, in the parish of St. Coulomb Minor, Cornwall', *Archaeologia* 24 (1873), 422-7.

Brabrook, Edward W. 'Memorial on the Death of Queen Victoria', *Folk-Lore* 12 (1901), 98.

Brand, John. *Observations on the Popular Antiquities of Great Britain: chiefly illustrating the Origin of our Vulgar and Provincial Customs, Ceremonies, and Superstitions*, rev. with introd. Sir Henry Ellis, 3 vols. 1848-49; New York: AMS Press, 1970.

Brockie, William. 'More Flint Implements', *Athenaeum* (December 17, 1859), 815.

Bruce, John C. 'The Practical Advantages Accruing from the Study of Archaeology', *Archaeological Journal* 14 (1857), 1-7.

Buckland, William. *Geology and Mineralogy Considered with Reference to Natural Theology*, 2nd edn., 2 vols. London: Routledge, 1858.

Burne, Charlotte. 'The Collection of English Folk-Lore', *Folklore* 1 (1890), 318-22.

Caird, Edward. *The Evolution of Religion. The Gifford Lectures delivered before the University of St. Andrews in Sessions 1890-91 and 1891-2*, 2 vols. Glasgow: James Maclehose & Sons, 1893.

Carnarvon, Earl of. 'The Archaeology of Berkshire', *Journal of the British Archaeological Association* 15 (1860), 1-25.

Carter, Robert Brudenell. *On the Pathology and Treatment of Hysteria*. London: John Churchill, 1853.

Chambers, Robert (ed.). *The Book of Days. A Miscellany of Popular Antiquities in connection with the Calendar including Anecdote, Biography & History, Curiosities of Literature and Oddities of Human Life and Character*, 2 vols. London and Edinburgh: W. & R. Chambers, 1869.

Clodd, Edward. *The Childhood of the World. A Simple Account of Man in Early Times*. London and New York: Macmillan, 1873.

————. *Memories.* London: Chapman & Hall, 1916.

————. *Myths and Dreams.* London: Chatto & Windus, 1885.

————. 'Primitive Man on his Own Origin', *Quarterly Review* 215 (1911), 97-118.

Coleridge, Hartley. 'On the Poetical Use of the Heathen Mythology', *London Magazine* 5 (1822), 115-30.

Colvin, Sidney. 'Restoration and Anti-Restoration', *Nineteenth Century* 2 (1877), 442-67.

Conynham, A. 'Presidential Address', *Journal of the British Archaeological Association* 5 (1849), 285-8.

Cook, Stanley A. 'Israel and Totemism', *Jewish Quarterly Review* 14 (1902), 413-48.

Cooke, William. *The Fallacies of the Alleged Antiquity of Man Proved.* London: Hamilton, Adams, 1872.

Croker, Dillon. 'On the Advantages of the Study of Archaeology', *Journal of the British Archaeological Association* 5 (1849), 288-9.

Darwin, Charles. *The Autobiography of Charles Darwin*, ed. Nora Barlow. London: Collins, 1958.

————. *The Descent of Man, and Selection in Relation to Sex.* 1871. 2nd edn. London: John Murray, 1883.

————. *The Origin of Species by Means of Natural Selection of The Preservation of Favoured Races in the Struggle for Life*, ed. J. W. Burrow. Harmondsworth, Middlesex: Penguin, 1985.

Davenport Adams, W. H. *Life in the Primeval World (founded on Meunier's 'Les Animaux D'Autrefois.').* London: T. Nelson & Sons, 1872.

Dawkins, William Boyd. 'The Antiquity of Man', *British Quarterly Review* 58 (1874), 342-67.

————. *Cave Hunting.* London: Macmillan, 1874.

————. *Early Man in Britain.* London: Macmillan, 1880.

Dawson, J. W. *Fossil Man and Their Modern Representatives*, 3rd edn. London: Hodder & Stoughton, 1887.

————. 'Primitive Man and Revelation', *Journal of the Transactions of the Victoria Institute* 8 (1874-75), 59-63.

————. *The Story of the Earth and Man.* London: Hodder & Stoughton, 1873.

Deane, George. 'Modern Scientific Inquiry and Religious Thought', *British Quarterly Review* 59 (1874), 34-54.

De la Beche, Henry T. *The Geological Observer*, 2nd edn. London: Longman, 1853.

Donaldson, Thomas Leverton. *Preliminary discourses pronounced before the University College of London, upon the commencement of a series of lectures, on Architecture, 17 October, 1842.* London: J. Smith, 1842.

Dowse, Thomas Stretch. *On Brain and Nerve Exhaustion (Neurasthenia), and on the Nervous Sequelæ of Influenza.* London: Ballière, Tindall and Cox, 1894.

D'Oyly, C. J. 'Man in Creation', *Contemporary Review* 8 (1868), 550-68.

Drummond, Henry. 'Mr Gladstone and Genesis', *Nineteenth Century* 19 (1886), 206-14.

Duncan, Isabella. *Pre-Adamite Man*, 2nd edn. London: Saunders, Otley, 1860.

[Eastlake, E.]. 'Photography', *Quarterly Review* 101 (April 1857), 442-68.

Evans, John. 'The Abbeville Human Jaw', *Athenaeum* (June 6, 1863), 747-78.

――――. 'Account of Some Further Discoveries of Flint Implements in the Drift on the Continent and in England', *Archaeologia* 39 (1862), 57-84.

――――. *The Ancient Stone Implements, Weapons, and Ornaments of Great Britain.* New York: Appleton, 1872.

Falconer, Hugh. 'Falconer on the Reputed Fossil Man of Abbeville', *Anthropological Review* 1 (1863), 177-9.

Farrer, James A. *Primitive Manners and Customs.* London: Chatto & Windus, 1879.

Fergusson, James. *History of the Modern Styles of Architecture: being a sequel to the Handbook of Architecture.* London: John Murray, 1862.

――――. 'Non-Historic Times', *Quarterly Review* 128 (1870), 432-73.

[Forbes, J. D.]. 'Lyell on the Antiquity of Man', *Edinburgh Review* 118 (1863), 255-302.

――――. 'On the Antiquity of Man', *Good Words* 5 (1864), 253-8, 432-40.

Fosbroke, Thomas Dudley. *Encyclopaedia of Antiquities: and elements of archaeology, classical and medieval*, 2 vols. London: T. Tegg & Sons, 1843.

Foster, J. J. 'Dorset Folk-Lore', *Folk-Lore Journal* 6 (1888), 115-19.

Fowle, T. W. 'The Place of Conscience in Evolution', *Nineteenth Century* 4 (1878), 1-18.

Frazer, Sir James George. *The Golden Bough: A Study in Magic and Religion*, ed. with introd. Robert Fraser. Oxford: The World's Classics, 1994.

――――. 'Notes on Harvest Customs', *Folk-Lore Journal* 7 (1889), 48-52.

――――. *Psyche's Task and the Scope of Social Anthropology.* London: Macmillan, 1913.

――――. *Totemism and Exogamy: A Treatise on Certain Early Forms of Superstition and Society*, 4 vols. London: Macmillan, 1910.

Freeman, Edward A. 'The Mythical and Romantic Elements in Early English History', *Fortnightly Review* 4 (1866), 636-48

Geikie, Archibald.'Anniversary Address', *Proceedings of the Geological Society of London* 47 (1891), 48-62.

Gill, W. A. 'The Origin and Interpretation of Myths', *Macmillan's Magazine* 56 (1887), 118-29.

Gladstone, W. E. 'Dawn of Creation and of Worship', *Nineteenth Century* 18 (1885), 698-714.

――――. 'Free Trade, Railways, and Commerce', *Nineteenth Century* 7 (January-June 1880), 367-88.

――――. 'Proem to Genesis', *Nineteenth Century* 19 (1886), 1-21.

Gomme, George Laurence. *Folklore as an Historical Science.* London: Methuen & Co., 1908.

Gorilla [Phillip Egerton]. 'Monkeyana', *Punch* (May 18, 1861), 206.

Greenwell, William. 'Notices of the Examination of Ancient Grave-Hills in the North Riding of Yorkshire', *Archaeological Journal* 22 (1865), 97-117, 241-65.

Grote, George. 'Grecian Legends and Early History', *Westminster Review* 39 (1846), 165-80.

Hardwick, Charles. *Traditions, Superstitions, and Folk-Lore (chiefly Lancashire and the North of England): Their affinity to others in widely-distributed localities: Their Eastern Origin and Mythical Significance.* London: Simpkin, Marshall & Co., 1872; repr. Manchester, England: E. J. Morten, 1973.

Harrison, J. E. *Prolegomena to the Study of Greek Religion.* Cambridge: Cambridge University Press, 1903.

————. *Themis.* Cambridge: Cambridge University Press, 1912.

Hartland, Sidney (ed.). *County Folk-Lore, Printed Extracts: Gloucestershire*, vol. 1. London: David Nutt, 1895.

————. *The Myth of Perseus*, 2 vols. London: Grimm Library, 1894.

————. 'The Science of Folk-Lore', *Folk-Lore Journal* 3 (1885), 13-28.

Haughton, Samuel. 'The History of the Earth and Its Inhabitants', *Dublin University Magazine* 58 (1861), 105-13.

Henslow, John S. 'Celts in the Drift', *Athenaeum* (November 19, 1859), 668.

Hewlett, Henry Gay. 'The Rationale of Mythology', *Cornhill Magazine* 35 (1877), 405-20.

Hodgson, John. 'On the Study of Antiquities', *Archaeologia Aeliana: or, Miscellaneous Tracts, relating to Antiquity* 1 (1822), i-xix.

[Holland, Henry]. 'Man and Nature', *Edinburgh Review* 120 (1864), 464-500.

Hone, William. *The Every-Day Book and Table Book or, Everlasting Calendar of Popular Amusements, Sports, Pastimes, Ceremonies, Manners, Customs, and Events incident to each of the Three Hundred and Sixty-five Days, in Past and Present Times*, 3 vols. London: T. Tegg & Son, 1835.

Hopkins, William. 'Address of the President', *Quarterly Journal of the Geological Society of London* 8 (1852), xxiv-lxxx.

Horner, Leonard. 'Address of the President', *Quarterly Journal of the Geological Society of London* 3 (1847), xxii-xc.

Hutchins, John. *The History and Antiquities of Dorset (Interspersed with some remarkable particulars of natural history; and adorned with a correct map of the county, and views of antiquities, seats of the nobility and gentry)* 3rd edn. corrected by William Shipp and James Whitworth Hodson, 4 vols. Westminster: John Bowyer Nichols & Sons, 1861.

Hutchinson, William. *A View of Northumberland, with an excursion to the Abbey of Mailcross in Scotland. (Ancient customs which prevail in the county of Northumberland, etc.).* 2 vols. Newcastle: W. Charnley, 1778.

Huxley, T. H. 'The Interpreters of Genesis and the Interpreters of Nature', *Nineteenth Century* 18 (1885), 849-60.

————. 'Mr. Gladstone and Genesis', *Nineteenth Century* 19 (1886), 191-205.

————. 'On the Method of Zadig', in *Science and Hebrew Tradition.* London: Macmillan, 1901.

Jacobs, Joseph and Alfred Nutt (ed.). *The International Folk-Lore Congress 1891. Papers and Transactions.* London: David Nutt, 1892.

Jevons, F. B. *An Introduction to the History of Religion*. London: Methuen, 1896.

Jewitt, Llewellyn. *Grave Mounds and Their Contents: A Manual of Archaeology*. London: Groombridge, 1870.

Keary, C. F. (ed.). *The Dawn of History: An Introduction to Pre-historic Study*. London: Mozley & Smith, 1878.

————. *Outlines of Primitive Belief among the Indo-European Races*. London: Mozley & Smith, 1882.

————. 'Some Phases of Early Religious Development', *Nineteenth Century* 4 (1878), 355-71.

Kemble, J. M. 'On the Utility of Antiquarian Collections in Relation to the Prehistoric Annals of the Different Countries of Europe', *Proceedings of the Royal Irish Academy* 6 (1857), 462-80.

Lang, Andrew. *Custom and Myth*. London: Longmans & Co., 1884.

————. 'The Golden Bough', *Fortnightly Review* 69 (1901), 235-48.

————. *John Knox and the Reformation*. London: Longmans & Co., 1905.

————. *The Making of Religion*. London: Longmans & Co., 1898.

————. *Myth, Ritual and Religion*, 2 vols. London: Longmans & Co., 1887.

————. 'Myths and Mythologists', *Nineteenth Century* 19 (1886), 46-60.

————. 'Preface' to *The Folk-Lore Record*. London: Nichols & Sons, 1879.

————. *The Secret of the Totem*. London: Longmans & Co., 1905.

Lewes, G. H. *The Physiology of Common Life*, 2 vols. Edinburgh: Blackwood, 1859-60.

Lewis, William Bevan. *A Textbook of Mental Diseases*. London: Charles Griffin, 1889.

Lubbock, John. 'Address Delivered to the Section of "Primeval Antiquities" at the London Meeting of the Archaeological Institute, July, 1866', *Archaeological Journal* 23 (1867), 190-209.

————. *The Origin of Civilisation and the Primitive Condition of Man. The Mental and Social Condition of Savages*, 2nd edn., with additions. London: Longmans, Green, & Co., 1870.

————. *Pre-historic Times as illustrated by Ancient Remains and the Manners and Customs of Modern Savages*, 4th edn. London: Frederic Norgate, 1878.

Lyell, Charles. *Geological Evidences of the Antiquity of Man*. London: John Murray, 1863.

————. *The Principles of Geology, Being an Attempt to Explain the Former Changes of the Earth's Surface, by Reference to Causes now in Operation*, 3 vols. London: John Murray, 1830-33.

Lyell, Katherine M. *Life and Letters of Sir Charles Lyell*, 2 vols. London: John Murray, 1881.

Lysons, Samuel. *Our British Ancestors: Who and What Were They? An Inquiry*. Oxford and London: John Henry & James Parker, 1865.

Lytton, Lord. 'Inaugural Address at the St. Albans Congress', *Journal of the British Archaeological Association* 26 (1870), 1-33.

Mansel-Pleydell, John Clavel, 'Presidential Addresses', *Proceedings of the Dorset Natural History and Antiquarian Field Club* 1 (1876), 1-14; 3 (1878), 1-19; 7 (1882), 23-7; 12 (1887), 1-15; 13 (1888), 1-29; 14 (1889), 1-28.

Mantell, Gideon. 'Illustrations of the Connexion between Archaeology and Geology', *Edinburgh New Philosophical Journal* 50 (1851), 235-54.

—————. *The Medals of Creation; or, First Lessons in Geology, and in the Study of Organic Remains*, 2 vols. London: Henry G. Bohn, 1844.

—————. *The Wonders of Geology; or, A Familiar Exposition of Geological Phenomena*, 2 vols. London: Henry G. Bohn, 1848.

Marett, R. R. 'From Spell to Prayer', *Folk-Lore* 15 (1904), 132-65.

—————. 'The Interpretation of Survivals', *Quarterly Review* 231 (1919), 445-61.

—————. 'The Psychology of Culture Contact, Presidential Address to the Folklore Society', *Folklore* 28 (1917), 1-18.

Maudsley, Henry. *Natural Causes and Supernatural Seemings*. London: Kegan Paul, Trench, 1886.

McLennan, John Ferguson. 'Bride-Catching', *Argosy* 2 (1886), 37-45.

—————. *Primitive Marriage: An Inquiry into the Origin of the Form of Capture in Marriage Ceremonies*, ed. with introd. Peter Rivière. Chicago: Chicago University Press, 1970.

—————. *Studies in Ancient History*. London: Bernard Quaritch, 1876.

—————. 'The Worship of Animals and Plants. Part 1', *Fortnightly Review* 6 (1869), 407-27.

Millingen, J. G. *Mind and Matter, Illustrated by Considerations on Heredity, Insanity, and the Influence of Temperament in the Development of the Passions*. London: H. Hurst, 1847.

Milner, John. 'Barrows in Dorsetshire' in George Laurence Gomme (ed.). *The Gentleman's Magazine Library: A Classified Collection of the Chief Contents of 'The Gentleman's Magazine' from 1731-1868. Archaeology: Part I*. London: Elliot Stock, 1886.

Moore, J. Scott. *Pre-Glacial Man and Geological Chronology*. Dublin: Hodges, Smith, & Foster, 1868.

Müller, Max. *Lectures on the Science of Language (delivered at the Royal Institution of Great Britain in April, May, & June, 1861)*, 3rd edn. London: Longman, Green, Longman, & Roberts, 1862.

—————. 'Solar Myths', *Nineteenth Century* 18 (1885), 910-25.

Murchison, Charles. 'Editor's Note', in *Paleontological Memoirs and Notes of Hugh Falconer*, 2 vols. London: Hardwicke, 1868.

Newton, Charles. 'On the Study of Archaeology', *Archaeological Journal* 8 (1850), 1-26.

Nicholson, John. *Folk Lore of East Yorkshire*. London: Hull, Driffield, 1890.

Northampton, Marquis of. 'Inaugural Address', *Archaeological Journal* 2 (1846), 302-3.

Northcote, Stafford H. 'Inaugural Address at the Exeter Congress', *Journal of the British Archaeological Association* 18 (1862), 1-21.

Oldfield, Edmund. 'Introductory Address', *Archaeological Journal* 10 (1852), 1-6.

Ordish, T. F. 'Folk Drama', *Folk-Lore* 2 (1891), 314-35.

————. 'English Folk Drama', *Folk-Lore* 4 (1893), 149-75.

Owen, Richard. *Paleontology*. Edinburgh: Adam & Charles Black, 1860.

Pattison, S. R. *New Facts and Old Records: A Plea for Genesis*. London: Jackson, 1868(?).

Pengelly, William. *An Introductory Address Delivered before the Torquay Natural History Society at the Commencement of the Lecture Session, December 7, 1863*. London: Simpkin & Marshall, 1864.

Pettigrew, T. J. 'On the Antiquities of the Isle of Wight', *Journal of the British Archaeological Association* 11 (1855), 177-93.

————. 'On the Study of Archaeology and the Objects of the British Archaeological Association', *Journal of the British Archaeological Association* 6 (1850), 163-76.

Phillips, John. *Life on Earth*. London: Macmillan, 1860.

[Phillips, John]. 'Review of *Geological Evidences of the Antiquity of Man*, by Charles Lyell', *Quarterly Review* 114 (1863), 369-417.

Pitt-Rivers, Augustus Lane Fox. *Address by Lt.-General A. H. L. F. Pitt-Rivers at the opening of The Dorset County Museum, 1884*. Dorchester: The Friary Press, 1984.

————. 'An Examination into the Character and Probable Origins of the Hill Forts of Sussex', *Archaeologia* 42 (1868), 27-52; 53-76.

Pote, B. E. 'Ancient Figurative Language: Creuzer and Knight', *Foreign Quarterly Review* 23 (1839), 30-46.

Pugin, Augustus Welby Northmore. *Contrasts: or A Parallel between the Noble Edifices of the Middle Ages, and Corresponding Buildings of the Present Day; shewing the Present Decay of Taste*, introd. H. R. Hitchcock. New York: Humanities Press, 1969.

Read, Henry Darwin. 'The Reputed Traces of Primeval Man', *Blackwood's Magazine* 88 (1860), 422-38.

Reader, John. 'Review of *Geological Gossip*, by D. T. Ansted', *British Quarterly Review* 32 (1860), 258-9.

Reinach, Salomon. 'The Growth of Mythological Study', *Quarterly Review* 215 (1911), 423-41.

Roberts, George, 'The Fossil Finder of Lyme Regis', *Chambers Journal of Popular Literature*, vol. 7 (1857), 382-4.

Sayce, A. H. *The Principles of Comparative Philology*. London: Trubner & Co., 1875.

Sedgwick, Adam. 'Address of the President', *Proceedings of the Geological Society of London* 1 (1820), 281-316.

[Smith, William H.]. 'Wilson's *Prehistoric Man*', *Blackwood's Magazine* 93 (1863), 525-44.

Smith, William Robertson. *Kinship and Marriage in Ancient Arabia*. Cambridge: Cambridge University Press, 1895.

————. *The Religion of the Semites*. Edinburgh: A. & C. Black, 1889.

Spencer, Herbert. *Social Statics, Abridged and Revised, together with The Man versus the State.* London: Williams & Norgate, 1892.

—————. *The Principles of Psychology.* London: Longman & Co., 1855.

Stanley, William Owen. 'On the Remains of Ancient Circular Habitations in Holyhead Island, with Notes on Associated Relics by Albert Way', *Archaeological Journal* 24 (1867), 229-64.

Stothard, Charles Alfred. *The Monumental Effigies of Great Britain, selected from our cathedrals and churches, for the purpose of bringing together, and preserving correct representations of the best historical illustrations extant, from the Norman Conquest to the reign of Henry the Eighth,* ed. Alfred John Kempe. London, 1833. New edn. with additions by John Hewitt. London: Chatto & Windus, 1876.

Strutt, Joseph. *The Sports and Pastimes of the People of England. Including the Rural and Domestic Recreations, May Games, Mummeries, Shows, Processions, Pageants, and Pompous Spectacles, from the Earliest Period to the Present Time.* New edn. with index William Hone. London: T. Tegg & Son, 1838.

Swayne, G. C. 'The Value and Charm of Antiquarian Study', *Antiquary* 1 (1880), 3-5.

Symonds, John Addington. *Essays: Speculative and Suggestive,* 2 vols. London: Chapman & Hall, 1890.

—————. *Studies of the Greek Poets,* 2nd edn. 2 vols. London: Smith, Elder, 1879.

Taylor, John. 'The Hand of Man in Kirkdale Cavern', *Macmillan's Magazine* 6 (1862), 386-98.

Thoms, William John. *Choice Notes from 'Notes and Queries'. Folk Lore.* London: Bell & Daldy, 1859.

Tomline, George. 'Inaugural Address at the Suffolk Congress', *Journal of the British Archaeological Association* 21 (1865), 1-4.

Tylor, Alfred. 'On the Discovery of Supposed Human Remains in the Tool-Bearing Drift of Moulin-Quignon', *Anthropological Review* 1 (1863), 166-8.

Tylor, E. B. 'Anniversary Address', *Journal of the Anthropological Institute* 9 (1880), 443-58.

—————. *Anthropology: An Introduction to the Study of Man and Civilization.* London: Macmillan, 1881.

—————. 'The Condition of Prehistoric Races, as inferred from observation of Modern Tribes', *Transactions of the International Congress of Prehistoric Archaeology* (1869), 11-25.

—————. 'Discovery of a Celtic Kitchen-Refuse-Heap at Normanby in Cleveland', *Gentleman's Magazine* 16 (1864), 162-7.

—————. 'English Dictionaries', *Quarterly Review* 135 (1873), 445-81.

—————. 'Lake Dwellings', *Quarterly Review* 125 (1868), 418-40.

—————. 'Maine's Village Communities', *Quarterly Review* 131 (1871), 176-89.

—————. 'The Matriarchal Family System', *Nineteenth Century* 40 (1896), 81-96.

—————. 'On a Method of Investigating the Development of Institutions; Applied to Laws of Marriage and Descent', *Journal of the Anthropological Institute* 18 (November 1888), 245-72.

————. 'On the Origin of Language', *Fortnightly Review* 4 (1866), 544-59.

————. 'On the Tasmanians as Representatives of Palaeolithic Man', *Journal of the Anthropological Institute* 23 (1893), 141-52.

————. *Primitive Culture: Researches into the Development of Mythology, Philosophy, Religion, Art, and Custom*, 4th edn. 2 vols. London: John Murray, 1903.

————. 'The Religion of Savages', *Fortnightly Review* 6 (1866), 71-86.

————. 'Remarks on Totemism, with Especial Reference to Some Modern Theories Respecting It', *Journal of the Anthropological Institute* 28 (1898), 138-48.

————. *Researches into the Early History of Mankind and the Development of Civilization*. London: John Murray, 1865.

————. 'Review of *The Lake Dwellings of Switzerland and other parts of Europe* by Ferdinand Keller', *Fortnightly Review* 6 (1866), 765-8.

————. 'Review of Lubbock's *Prehistoric Times*', *Nature* 1 (1869), 103.

————. 'Review of Max Müller's *Chips from a German Workshop*', *Fortnightly Review* 3 (1868), 225-8.

————. 'Review of *A Memoir of Baron Bunsen*', *Fortnightly Review* 3 (1868), 715-18.

————. 'Review of *Memorials of Service in India, from the correspondence of the late Major Samuel Charters Macpherson*', *Fortnightly Review* 4 (1866), 639-40.

————. 'The Science of Language', *Quarterly Review* 119 (1866), 394-435.

————. 'South-Sea Island Mythology', *Quarterly Review* 142 (1876), 232-51.

————. 'The Study of Customs', *Macmillan's Magazine* 46 (1882), 73-86.

————. 'T. H. Huxley as Anthropologist', *Fortnightly Review* 58 (1894), 310-11.

————. 'Wild Men and Beast-Children', *Anthropological Review* 1 (1863), 21-32.

————. 'William von Humboldt', *Quarterly Review* 124 (1868), 504-24.

Udal, John Symonds. 'Christmas Mummers in Dorsetshire', *Folk-Lore Record* 3: 1 (1880), 87-116.

————. *Dorsetshire Folk-Lore (with a Fore-Say by William Barnes)*. 1922; repr. St. Peter Port, Guernsey: Toucan Press, 1970.

Vines, H. *A Brief Sketch of the Rise and Progress of Photography, with Particular Reference to the Practice of Daguerreotype*. Bristol, 1852.

Vivian, Edward. 'On the Earliest Traces of Human Remains in Kent's Cavern', *Annual Report of the British Association for the Advancement of Science* 26 (1856), 119-23.

Walford, Edward. 'Preface', *Antiquary* 1 (1880), i-iv.

Wallace, Alfred Russell. 'The Origin of the Human Races and the Antiquity of Man Deduced from the Theory of Natural Selection', *Anthropological Review* 2 (1864), clviii-clxx.

————. 'The Origin of Species and Genera', *Nineteenth Century* 7 (January-June 1880), 93-107.

Warne, Charles. *Ancient Dorset: The Celtic, Roman, Saxon, and Danish Antiquities of the County, including The Early Coinage. Also An Introduction to the Ethnology of Dorset, and other Archaeological Notices of the County, by William Wake Smart*. Bournemouth: D. Sydenham, 1872.

——. *Celtic Tumuli of Dorset: An Account of Personal and other Researches in the Sepulchral Mounds of the Durotriges*. London: T. Tegg & Sons, 1866.

Way, Albert. 'Introduction', *Archaeological Journal* 1 (1844), 1-6.

[Wedgwood, Julia]. 'Sir Charles Lyell on the Antiquity of Man', *Macmillan's Magazine* 7 (1863), 476-87.

[Westmacott, Richard]. 'Introduction', *Archaeological Journal* 7 (1850), 1-7.

White, Malcolm. 'Does Scripture Settle the Antiquity of Man?', *British and Foreign Evangelical Review* 21 (1869), 128-37.

[Wood, H. H]. 'Lake Dwellings of Switzerland', *Contemporary Review* 4 (1867), 380-94.

Wright, Thomas. 'On the Progress and Present Condition of Archaeological Science', *Journal of the British Archaeological Association* 22 (1866), 64-84.

Wrottesley, Lord. 'Presidential Address', *Annual Report of the British Association for the Advancement of Science* 30 (1860), lv-lxxv.

Young, John R. *Modern Scepticism in Relation to Modern Science*. London: Saunders, Otley, 1865.

York, Archbishop of. 'Inaugural Address to the Annual Meeting of the Royal Archaeological Institute', *Archaeological Journal* 24 (1867), 83-91.

Thomas Hardy Scholarship and other Secondary Sources

Abercrombie, Lascelles. *Thomas Hardy: A Critical Study*. London: Secker, 1912.

Abrams, M. C. (gen. ed.). *The Norton Anthology of English Literature*, 2 vols. New York and London: W. W. Norton & Company, 1986.

Ackerman, Robert. 'Frazer on Myth and Ritual', *Journal of the History of Ideas* 36 (1975), 115-34.

——. *J. G. Frazer: His Life and Work*. Cambridge: Cambridge University Press, 1987.

Adams, James Eli. 'Women Red in Tooth and Claw: Nature and the Feminine in Tennyson and Darwin', *Victorian Studies* 33 (1989), 7-27.

Adamson, Jane. '*Tess of the d'Urbervilles*: Time and Its Shapings', *Critical Review* 26 (1984), 18-36.

Albritton, Claude C. *The Abyss of Time: Changing Conceptions of the Earth's Antiquity since the Sixteenth Century*. San Francisco: Freeman Cooper, 1980.

Alden, Patricia. *Social Mobility in the English Bildungsroman*. Ann Arbor, Michigan: UMI Research Press, 1986.

——. *Writers, Readers, and Occasions: Selected Essays on Victorian Literature and Life*. Columbus: Ohio State University Press, 1989.

Alexander, B. J. 'Criticism of Thomas Hardy's Novels: A Selected Checklist', *Studies in the Novel* 4 (1972), 630-54.

Allingham, Philip V. 'Robert Barnes' Illustrations for Thomas Hardy's *The Mayor of Casterbridge* as Serialised in *The Graphic*', *Victorian Periodicals* 28:1 (Spring 1995), 27-39.

Anderson, Carol Reed. 'Time, Space, and Perspective in Thomas Hardy', *Nineteenth Century Fiction* 9 (1954), 192-209.

Anderson, Wayne C. 'The Rhetoric of Silence in Hardy's Fiction', *Studies in the Novel* 17 (1985), 53-68.

Archer, William. *Real Conversations.* London: Heinemann, 1904.

Arnold, Matthew. *The Poems of Matthew Arnold*, ed. Kenneth Allot. London: Longmans, 1965.

Auerbach, Nina. 'The Rise of the Fallen Woman', *Nineteenth-Century Fiction* 35 (1980), 29-52.

Babb, Howard. 'Setting and Theme in *Far from the Madding Crowd*', *Journal of English Literary History* 30 (1963), 147-61.

Bacon, Francis. *Essays.* London and New York: Oxford University Press, 1921.

Bailey, J. O. *Poetry of Thomas Hardy: A Handbook and Commentary.* Chapel Hill, North Carolina: University of North Carolina Press, 1970.

—————. *Thomas Hardy and the Cosmic Mind: a New Reading of 'The Dynasts'.* Chapel Hill, North Carolina: University of North Carolina Press, 1956.

Barbon, Jim. 'Star-Crossed Love: The Gravity of Science in Thomas Hardy's *Two on a Tower*', *Victorian Newsletter* 94 (Fall 1998), 27-32.

Barnes, William. *Poems of Rural Life in the Dorset Dialect.* London: Kegan Paul, Trench & Co, 1888.

Barrell, John. 'Geographies of Hardy's Wessex', *Journal of Historical Geography* 8 (1982), 347-61.

Barzun, Jacques. 'Truth and Poetry in Thomas Hardy', *Southern Review* 6 (1940), 179-92.

—————. *Selected Poems of William Barnes, Chosen and Edited by Thomas Hardy.* London: Macmillan, 1980.

Basalla, George, William Coleman and Robert H. Kargon (eds.). *Victorian Science: A Self-Portrait from the Presidential Addresses to the British Association for the Advancement of Science.* New York: Anchor Books, 1970.

Basham, Diana. '*Jude the Obscure* and *Idylls of the King*', *Thomas Hardy Society Review* I, 10 (1984), 311-16.

Bayley, John. *An Essay on Hardy.* Cambridge: Cambridge University Press, 1978.

Beach, Joseph Warren. *The Technique of Thomas Hardy.* New York: Russell & Russell, 1962.

Beatty, C. J. P. 'An Architectural Anomaly in *Jude the Obscure*', *Thomas Hardy Society Review* I, 10 (1984), 310-11.

—————. *The Architectural Notebook of Thomas Hardy.* Dorset: Dorset Natural History and Archaeological Society, 1966.

Beebe, Maurice, Bonnie Culotta and Erin Marcus. 'Criticism of Thomas Hardy: A Selected Checklist', *Modern Fiction Studies* 6 (1960), 258-79.

Beer, Gillian. *Darwin's Plots: Evolutionary Narrative in Darwin, George Eliot and Nineteenth Century Fiction.* London: Routledge & Kegan Paul, 1983.

—————. *Open Fields: Science in Cultural Encounter*. Oxford: Clarendon Press, 1996.

Benson, Michael. 'Moving Bodies in Hardy and Beckett', *Essays in Criticism* 34 (1984), 229-43.

Benvenuto, Richard. 'Another Look at the Other Eustacia', *Novel* 4 (1970), 77-9.

—————. 'Modes of Perception: The Will to Live in *Jude the Obscure*', *Studies in the Novel* 2 (1970), 31-41.

—————. '*The Return of the Native* as a Tragedy in Six Books', *Nineteenth Century Fiction* 26 (1971), 83-93.

Berger, John. *Ways of Seeing*. New York: Viking, 1973.

Berger, Sheila. *Thomas Hardy and Visual Structures: Framing, Disruption, Process*. New York and London: New York University Press, 1990.

Bettey, J. H. *Dorset*. City and County Histories, gen. ed. Lionel Munby. London: David & Charles, 1974.

—————. *Rural Life in Wessex 1500-1900*. Guernsey: Alan Sutton, 1987.

Björk, Lennart A. (ed.) *The Literary Notes of Thomas Hardy*. Goteborg, Sweden: Acta Universitatis Gothoburgensis, 1974.

Blagg, T. F. C. 'The Cult and Sanctuary of Diana Nemorensis', in *Pagan Gods and Shrines of the Roman Empire*, ed. Martin Henig and Anthony King. Oxford: Oxford University Committee for Archaeology, 1986.

Bloom, Harold. *Thomas Hardy. Modern Critical Views*. New York: Chelsea House, 1987.

—————. *Thomas Hardy's 'Jude the Obscure'. Modern Critical Interpretations*. New York: Chelsea House, 1987.

—————. *Thomas Hardy's 'The Mayor of Casterbridge'. Modern Critical Interpretations*. New York: Chelsea House, 1988.

—————. *Thomas Hardy's 'The Return of the Native'. Modern Critical Interpretations*. New York: Chelsea House, 1987.

Blunden, Edmund. *Thomas Hardy*. London: Macmillan, 1967.

Blythe, Ronald. *Characters and Their Landscapes*. San Diego: Harcourt, 1983.

—————. 'Introduction' to Thomas Hardy, *A Pair of Blue Eyes*, The New Wessex Edition. London: Macmillan, 1976.

Boumelha, Penny. *Thomas Hardy and Women: Sexual Ideology and Narrative Form*. Brighton: Harvester, 1982.

Bowden, Mark. *Pitt Rivers*. Cambridge: Cambridge University Press, 1991.

Bowler, Peter J. *Fossils and Progress: Palaeontology and the Idea of Progressive Evolution in the Nineteenth Century*. New York: Science History, 1976.

—————. *The Invention of Progress: The Victorians and the Past*. Oxford: Basil Blackwell, 1990.

Bradbury, Malcolm. *The Modern British Novel*. Harmondsworth, Middlesex: Penguin, 1994.

Brasnett, Hugh. *Thomas Hardy: a Pictorial Guide*. Romney Marsh: John Waite, 1984.

Brick, Allen. 'Paradise and Consciousness in Hardy's *Tess*', *Nineteenth Century Fiction* 17 (1962), 115-34.

Brilioth, Yngve. *The Anglican Revival: Studies in the Oxford Movement.* London: Longmans, Green, 1925.

Brody, Alan. *The English Mummers and their Plays.* Philadelphia: University of Pennsylvania Press, 1970.

Brooke, John Hedley. *Science and Religion: Some Historical Perspectives.* Cambridge: Cambridge University Press, 1991.

Brooke-Rose, Christine. 'Ill Wit and Sick Tragedy: *Jude the Obscure*', in Lance St. John Butler (ed.), *Alternative Hardy.* London: Macmillan, 1994.

Brooks, Jean R. *Thomas Hardy: The Poetic Structure.* London: Elek, 1971.

Brown, Douglas. *Thomas Hardy.* London: Longmans, 1961.

————. *Thomas Hardy: 'The Mayor of Casterbridge'.* London: Edward Arnold, 1962.

Buckler, William E. *The Poetry of Thomas Hardy: a Study in Art and Ideas.* New York: New York University Press, 1983.

————. 'Thomas Hardy's Sense of Self: The Poet behind the Autobiographer in *The Life of Thomas Hardy*', *Prose Studies* 3 (1980), 69-86.

————. 'Victorian Modernism: the Arnold-Hardy Succession', *Browning Institute Studies* 11 (1983), 9-21.

Buckley, Jerome Hamilton. *The Triumph of Time. A Study of the Victorian Concepts of Time, History, Progress and Decadence.* Cambridge, Mass.: Harvard University Press, 1966.

————, (ed.). *The Worlds of Victorian Fiction.* Cambridge, Mass.: Harvard University Press, 1975.

Bulaila, A. A. M. ' "The Clay but not the Potter": Love and Marriage in *The Well-Beloved*', *Thomas Hardy Journal* 9:2 (May 1993), 61-71.

————. '*Desperate Remedies*: Not Just a Minor Novel', *Thomas Hardy Journal* 14:1 (February 1998), 65-74.

Bullen, J. B. *The Expressive Eye: Fiction and Perception in the Work of Thomas Hardy.* Oxford: Clarendon Press, 1986.

————. 'Thomas Hardy, Sex and Theories of the Germ Plasm', in Phillip V. Mallett and Ronald P. Draper (eds.), *A Spacious Vision: Essays on Hardy.* Newmill: Patten Press, 1994.

Burrow, J. W. *Evolution and Society.* Cambridge: Cambridge University Press, 1966.

————. *A Liberal Descent: Victorian Historians and the English Past.* Cambridge: Cambridge University Press, 1981.

————. 'The Uses of Philology in Victorian England', in Robert Robson (ed.), *Ideas and Institutions of Victorian Britain.* London: Barnes & Noble, 1967.

Burstein, Janet. 'The Journey Beyond Myth in *Jude the Obscure*', *Texas Studies in Literature and Language* 15 (1972), 499-515.

Butler, Lance St. John (ed.). *Alternative Hardy.* London: Macmillan, 1991.

————. *Thomas Hardy.* Cambridge: Cambridge University Press, 1978.

———— (ed.). *Thomas Hardy after Fifty Years.* London: Macmillan, 1977.

Butts, Mary. *The Crystal Cabinet: my childhood at Salterns.* Boston: Beacon Press, 1988.

Byron, Lord George Gordon. *Don Juan*, ed. E. Steffan and T.G. Steffan. Harmondsworth, Middlesex: Penguin, 1996.

Cadbury, Deborah. *The Dinosaur Hunters. A Story of Scientific Rivalry And the Discovery of the Prehistoric World*. London: Fourth Estate, 2001.

Cambridge, O. P. 'In Memoriam Rev. William Barnes, B.D.', *Proceedings of the Dorset Natural History and Antiquarian Field Club* 8 (1887), i-xix.

Carpenter, Richard. 'Hardy's "Gurgoyles" ', *Modern Fiction Studies* 6 (1960), 223-32.

————. 'The Mirror and the Sword: Imagery in *Far from the Madding Crowd*', *Nineteenth Century Fiction* 18 (1964), 331-45.

————. *The Neglected Hardy: Thomas Hardy's Lesser Novels*. London: Macmillan, 1981.

————. *Thomas Hardy*. New York: Twayne, 1964.

————. 'Thomas Hardy and the Old Masters', *Boston University Studies in English* 5 (1961), 18-28.

Casagrande, Peter J. *Hardy's Influence on the Modern Novel*. London: Macmillan, 1988.

————. 'Hardy's Wordsworth: A Record and a Commentary', *English Literature in Transition* 20 (1977), 210-37.

————. *Unity in Hardy's Novels. 'Repetitive Symmetries'*. London: Macmillan, 1982.

Cecil, Lord David. *Hardy the Novelist*. Indianapolis: Bobbs-Merrill, 1946.

Chadwick, Owen. *The Victorian Church*, 2 vols. London: Adams & Charles Black, 1966.

Chambers, E. K. *The Medieval Stage*, 2 vols. Oxford: Oxford University Press, 1903.

————. *The English Folk Play*. Oxford: Clarendon Press, 1917.

Chandler, Alice. *A Dream of Order: The Medieval Ideal in Nineteenth-Century Literature*. Lincoln: University of Nebraska Press, 1970.

Chapman, Raymond. ' "Arguing About the Eastward Position": Thomas Hardy and Puseyism', *Nineteenth Century Literature* 42 (1987), 275-94.

————. *Faith and Revolt: Studies in the Literary Influence of the Oxford Movement*. London: Weidenfeld & Nicolson, 1970.

Chase, Mary Ellen. *Thomas Hardy from Serial to Novel*. Minneapolis: University of Minnesota Press, 1927.

Chedzoy, Alan. *William Barnes: A Life of the Dorset Poet*. Wimborne, Dorset: Dovecote Press, 1985.

Chevenix-Trench, R. 'Dorset Under Arms in 1803', *Proceedings of the Dorset Natural History and Archaeological Society* 90 (1969), 303-12.

Chew, Samuel. *Thomas Hardy: Poet and Novelist*. New York: Russell & Russell, 1964.

Child, Harold H. *Thomas Hardy*. London: Nisbet, 1916.

Christie, John and Sally Shuttleworth (eds.). *Nature Transfigured: Science and Literature 1700-1900*. Manchester: Manchester University Press, 1989.

Clapp-Intyre, Alisa. *Angelic Airs, Subversive Songs: Music as Social Discourse in the Victorian Novel.* Athens, Ohio: Ohio University Press, 2002.

Claridge, Laura. 'Tess: A Less than Pure Woman Ambivalently Presented', *Texas Studies in Literature and Language* 28 (1986), 324-38.

Clark, Kenneth. *The Gothic Revival: An Essay in the History of Taste.* London: Murray, 1928.

Clarke, Basil F. L. *Church Builders of the Nineteenth Century: A Study of the Gothic Revival in England.* Newton Abbot: David & Charles, 1969.

Clarke, Robert W. 'Hardy's Farmer Boldwood: Shadow of a Magnitude', *West Virginia University Philological Papers* 17 (1970), 45-56.

Clifford, Emma. 'The Child: the Circus: and *Jude the Obscure*', *Cambridge Journal* 7 (1954), 531-46.

————.'The Impressionistic View of History in *The Dynasts*', *Modern Language Quarterly* 22 (1961), 21-31.

Clive, John. *Not by Fact Alone: Essays on the Writing and Reading of History.* London: Collins, Harvill, 1989.

Cockburn, John Alexander. *Introduction to Thomas Hardy: the Artist, the Man, and the Disciple of Destiny.* London: Grant Richards, 1921.

Cohen, Sandy. 'Blind Clym, Unchristian Christian and the Redness of the Reddleman: Character Correspondences in *The Return of the Native*', *Thomas Hardy Year Book* 11 (1984), 49-55.

Collins, Deborah L. *Thomas Hardy and his God: A Liturgy of Unbelief.* London: Macmillan, 1990.

Collins, Wilkie. *Basil*, ed. Dorothy Goldman. Oxford: Oxford University Press, 1990.

Conrad, Joseph. *The Secret Agent: A Simple Tale.* Ed. Bruce Harkness and S. W. Reid. Cambridge: Cambridge University Press, 1990.

Cook, Stanley Arthur. *The Study of Religions.* London: Adam & Charles Black, 1914.

Cosslett, Tess. *The 'Scientific Movement' and Victorian Literature.* Sussex: Harvester Press, 1982.

Cox, Richard (ed.). *Sexuality and Victorian Literature.* Knoxville, Tenn.: University of Tennessee Press, 1984.

Cox, R. G. (ed.). *Thomas Hardy: The Critical Heritage.* London: Routledge & Kegan Paul, 1970.

Cronin, Meoghan Byrne. ' "As a Diamond Kills an Opal": Charm and Countercharm in Thomas Hardy's *A Pair of Blue Eyes*', *Victorians Institute Journal* 26 (1998), 121-47.

Crosby, Christina. *Victorians and 'The Woman Question'.* New York and London: Routledge, 1991.

Cullen-Brown, Joanna (ed.). *Figures in a Wessex Landscape: Thomas Hardy's Picture of English Country Life.* London: Allison & Busby, 1987.

Culler, A. Dwight. *The Victorian Mirror of History.* New Haven: Yale University Press, 1986.

Cunliff, John W. *English Literature during the Last Half Century.* New York: Macmillan, 1940.

Cunningham, A. R. 'The "New Woman Fiction" of the 1890s', *Victorian Studies* 17 (1973), 177-86.

Cunningham, Gail. *The New Woman and the Victorian Novel.* London: Macmillan, 1978.

Dale, Peter Alan. *In Pursuit of a Scientific Culture: Science, Art and Society in the Victorian Age.* Madison: University of Wisconsin Press, 1989

——————. 'Thomas Hardy and the best consummation possible', in John Christie and Sally Shuttleworth (eds.), *Nature Transfigured: Science and Literature, 1700-1900.* Manchester and New York: Manchester University Press, 1989.

Daleski, H. M. *Thomas Hardy and the Paradoxes of Love.* Columbia and London: University of Missouri Press, 1997.

Dalziel, Pamela. 'Anxieties of Representation: The Serial Illustrations to Hardy's *The Return of the Native*', *Nineteenth Century Literature* 51 (1996), 84-110.

Danby, John F. '*Under the Greenwood Tree*', *Critical Quarterly* 1 (1959), 5-13.

Daniel, Glyn and Colin Renfrew. *The Idea of Prehistory.* Edinburgh: Edinburgh University Press, 1988.

Daniel, Samuel. '*Poems' and 'A Defence of Ryme*', ed. Arthur Colby Sprague. Chicago and London: University of Chicago Press, 1965.

Dave, J. C. *The Human Predicament in Hardy's Novels.* London: Macmillan, 1985.

Davidson, Arnold E. 'On Reading *The Well-Beloved* as a Parable of Art', *Thomas Hardy Yearbook* 14 (1987), 14-17.

Davie, Donald. *Thomas Hardy and British Poetry.* New York: Oxford University Press, 1972.

Davis, Lloyd (ed.). *Virginal Sexuality and Textuality in Victorian Literature.* Albany, New York: State University of New York Press, 1993.

Davis, W. Eugene and Helmut E. Gerber (eds.). *Thomas Hardy: an Annotated Bibliography of Writings about Him*, vol. II: *1970-1978 and Supplement for 1871-1969.* Dekalb, Illinois: Northern Illinois University Press, 1983.

De Quincey, Thomas. *Confessions of an English Opium-Eater and Other Writings*, ed. with introd. Grevel Lindop. Oxford: The World's Classics, 1996.

Deacon, Lois and Terry Coleman. *Providence and Mr. Hardy.* London: Hutchinson, 1966.

Dean, Dennis R. *Gideon Mantell and the Discovery of Dinosaurs.* Cambridge: Cambridge University Press, 1999.

Dean, Susan. *Hardy's Poetic Vision in 'The Dynasts': The Diorama of a Dream.* Princeton: Princeton University Press, 1977.

Deen, Leonard W. 'Heroism and Pathos in Hardy's *Return of the Native*', *Nineteenth Century Fiction* 15 (1960), 207-19.

DeLaura, David J. 'The "Ache of Modernism" in Hardy's Later Novels', *English Literary History* 34 (1967), 380-99.

Dellamora, Richard. *A Study of Masculine Desire.* Chapel Hill: University of North Carolina Press, 1989.

Dellheim, Charles. *The Face of the Past: The Preservation of the Medieval Inheritance in Victorian England.* Cambridge: Cambridge University Press, 1982.

Desmond, Adrian. *Archetypes and Ancestors: Palaeontology in Victorian London, 1850-75.* Chicago: University of Chicago Press, 1982.

——————. *The Hot-Blooded Dinosaurs: A Revolution in Palaeontology.* London: Blond & Briggs, 1975.

Dickens, Charles. 'Associations of Childhood', *All the Year Round* (30 June 1860), 274-8.

——————. *Barnaby Rudge,* ed. with introd. Gordon Spence. Harmondsworth, Middlesex: Penguin, 1986.

——————. *Dombey and Son,* ed. with introd. Alan Horsman. Oxford: Clarendon Press, 1974.

——————. *Uncollected Writings from Household Words,* ed. Harry Stone, 2 vols. Bloomington, Indiana: University of Indiana Press, 1968.

Dike, D. A. 'A Modern Oedipus: *The Mayor of Casterbridge*', *Essays in Criticism* 2 (1952), 169-79.

Dobree, Bonamy, *The Lamp and the Lute: Studies in Six Modern Authors.* Oxford: Clarendon Press, 1929.

Dorson, Richard. *The British Folklorists. A History.* London: Routledge & Kegan Paul, 1968.

—————— (ed.), *Peasant Customs and Savage Myths. Selections from the British Folklorists,* 2 vols. Chicago: University of Chicago Press, 1968.

Downie, R. Angus. *Frazer and the Golden Bough.* London: Victor Gollancz, 1970.

Drabble, Margaret (ed.). *The Genius of Thomas Hardy.* London: Weidenfeld & Nicolson, 1976.

Draffan, Robert A. 'Hardy's *Under the Greenwood Tree*', *English* 22 (1973), 55-60.

Draper, Ronald (ed.) *Thomas Hardy: The Tragic Novels.* London: Macmillan, 1986.

—————— and Phillip V. Mallett (eds.). *A Spacious Vision: Essays on Hardy.* Newmill: Patten Press, 1994.

Drinka, George Frederick. *The Birth of Neurosis: Myth, Malady, and the Victorians.* New York: Simon & Shuster, 1984.

Duffin, Henry Charles. *Thomas Hardy: A Study of the Wessex Novels, the Poems, and 'The Dynasts'.* Manchester: Manchester University Press, 1967.

Dugdale, Giles. *William Barnes of Dorset.* London: Edward Arnold, 1953.

Dunbabin, J. P. D. *Rural Discontent in Nineteenth Century Britain.* London: Faber & Faber, 1974.

Durden, Mark. 'Ritual and Deception: Photography and Thomas Hardy', *Journal of European Studies*, 30:1 (March 2000), 57-69.

Dutta, Shanta. *Ambivalence in Hardy: A Study of His Attitude to Women.* London: Macmillan, 2000.

——————. 'Sue's "Obscure" Sisters', *Thomas Hardy Journal* 12:2 (May 1996), 60-71.

Eagleton, Terry. 'Introduction', to Thomas Hardy, *Jude the Obscure*, The New Wessex Edition. London: Macmillan, 1986.

——————. 'Thomas Hardy: Nature as Language', *Critical Quarterly* 13 (1971), 155-62.

Eastman, D. 'Time and Propriety in *Far from the Madding Crowd*', *Interpretations* 10 (1978), 20-33.

Ebbatson, Roger. *The Evolutionary Self: Hardy, Forster, Lawrence*. Sussex: Harvester Press, 1982.

——. *Hardy: The Margin of the Unexpressed*. Sheffield: Sheffield Academic Press, 1993.

Edwards, Duane D. '*The Mayor of Casterbridge* as Aeschylean Tragedy', *Studies in the Novel* 4 (1972), 608-18.

Eggenschwiler, David. 'Eustacia Vye, Queen of Night and Courtly Pretender', *Nineteenth Century Fiction* 25 (1970-71), 444-54.

Eliot, George. *Daniel Deronda*, ed. Terence Cave. Harmondsworth, Middlesex: Penguin, 1995.

——. 'The Influence of Rationalism: Lecky's History', in *Impressions of Theophrastus Such: Essays and Leaves from a Note-book*. Edinburgh and London: William Blackwood & Sons, 1901.

Elliot, Albert Pettingrew. *Fatalism in the Works of Thomas Hardy*. New York: Russell & Russell, 1966.

Elliott, Ralph W. V. 'The Infatuated Artist: Thomas Hardy and *The Well-Beloved*', *Thomas Hardy Journal* 3:2 (May 1987), 20-33.

——. *Thomas Hardy's English*. Oxford and London: Basil Blackwell & Andre Deutsch, 1984.

Elsbree, Langdon. 'Tess and the Local Cerealia', *Philological Quarterly* 45 (October 1961), 606-8.

Emerson, Ralph Waldo, *The Collected Works of Ralph Waldo Emerson*, 4 vols. Cambridge, Mass.: Harvard University Press, 1971-87.

Enstice, Andrew. *Thomas Hardy: Landscapes of the Mind*. London: Macmillan, 1979.

Epstein, Leonora. 'Sale and Sacrament: The Wife Auction in *The Mayor of Casterbridge*', *English Language Notes* 24:4 (June 1987), 50-56.

Evans, Robert. 'The Other Eustacia', *Novel* 1 (1968), 251-9.

Fayen, George. '*The Woodlanders:* Inwardness and Memory', *Studies in English Literature* 1 (1965), 81-100.

Federico, Annette. *Masculine Identity in Hardy and Gissing*. London and Toronto: Associated University Presses, 1991.

Feldman, Burton and Robert D. Richardson (eds.). *The Rise of Modern Mythography 1680-1860*. Bloomington, Indiana: Indiana University Press, 1972.

Fernando, Lloyd. 'Thomas Hardy's Rhetoric of Painting', *Review of English Literature* 6 (1965), 62-73.

Firor, Ruth. *Folkways in Thomas Hardy*. Philadelphia: University of Pennsylvania Press, 1931.

Fischler, Alexander. 'An Affinity for Birds: Kindness in Hardy's *Jude the Obscure*', *Studies in the Novel* 13 (1981), 250-65.

——. 'Gins and Spirits: The Letter's Edge in *Jude the Obscure*', *Studies in the Novel* 16 (1984), 1-19.

————. 'Theatrical Techniques in Thomas Hardy's Short Stories', *Studies in Short Fiction* 3 (1966), 435-45.

Fisher, Joe. *Hidden Hardy*. London: Macmillan, 1992.

Fletcher, Geoffrey. *Popular Art in England*. London: Harrap, 1962.

Fletcher, Ian (ed.). *Decadence and the 1890s*. London: Edward Arnold, 1979.

Forsyth, R. A. 'The Conserving Myth of William Barnes', *Victorian Studies* 6 (1963), 325-40.

Fortey, Richard. *Trilobite! Eyewitness to Evolution*. London: Flamingo, 2001.

Fraser, Robert. *The Making of 'The Golden Bough': The Origins and Growth of an Argument*. London: Macmillan, 1990.

————(ed.). *Sir James Frazer and the Literary Imagination: Essays in Affinity and Influence*. London: Macmillan, 1990.

Freeman, Janet. 'Ways of Looking at Tess', *Studies in Philology* 79 (1982), 311-23.

Freud, Sigmund. *Totem and Taboo. Some Points of Agreement between the Mental Lives of Savages and Neurotics*, trans. James Strachey. London: Routledge & Kegan Paul, 1950.

Froude, James Anthony. *Thomas Carlyle: a History of his Life in London, 1834-1881*, 2 vols. London: Longmans, Green, & Co., 1884.

Gallop, Jane. *Feminism and Psychoanalysis: The Daughter's Seduction*. London: Macmillan, 1982.

Garlock, David. 'Entangled Genders: Plasticity, Indeterminacy, and Constructs of Sexuality in Darwin and Hardy', *Dickens Studies Annual* 27 (1998), 287-305.

Garson, Marjorie. *Hardy's Fables of Integrity: Woman, Body, Text*. Oxford: Clarendon Press, 1991.

Geoffrey of Monmouth. *The History of the Kings of Britain*, trans. with introd. Lewis Thorpe. Harmondsworth, Middlesex: Penguin, 1966.

Gibbon, Edward. *The Decline and Fall of the Roman Empire*, introd. Hugh Trevor-Roper, 3 vols. London: Everyman, 1993.

Gibson, James. *Thomas Hardy: A Literary Life*. London: Macmillan, 1996.

Gilmour, Robin. *The Victorian Period: The Intellectual and Cultural Context of English Literature, 1830-1890*. Harlow, Essex: Longman, 1994.

Giordano, Frank R., Jr. *'I'd Have My Life Unbe': Thomas Hardy's Self-Destructive Characters*. Alabama: University of Alabama Press, 1984.

Girouard, Mark. *Life in the English Country House: A Social and Architectural History*. Harmondsworth, Middlesex: Penguin, 1980.

————. *The Return to Camelot: Chivalry and the English Gentleman*. New Haven and London: Yale University Press, 1981.

Gittings, Robert. *The Older Hardy*. Harmondsworth, Middlesex: Penguin, 1976.

————. *Young Thomas Hardy*. Harmondsworth, Middlesex: Penguin, 1986.

Goetz, W. R. 'The Felicity and Infelicity of Marriage in *Jude the Obscure*', *Nineteenth Century Fiction* 38 (1983), 189-213.

Goode, John. *Thomas Hardy: The Offensive Truth*. Oxford: Basil Blackwell, 1988.

Goodheart, Eugene. 'Thomas Hardy and the Lyrical Novel', *Nineteenth Century Fiction* 12 (1957), 215-25.

Green, Laura Morgan. *Educating Women: Cultural Conflict and Victorian Literature.* Athens, Georgia: Ohio University Press, 2001.

Gregor, Ian. *The Great Web: The Form of Hardy's Major Fiction.* London: Faber & Faber, 1974.

──────. 'Introduction' to Thomas Hardy, *The Mayor of Casterbridge*, The New Wessex Edition. London: Macmillan, 1975.

Grimsditch, Herbert Bothwick. *Characters and Environment in the Novels of Thomas Hardy.* New York: Haskell House, 1966.

Gross, John. *The Rise and Fall of the Man of Letters: Aspects of English Literary Life Since 1800.* New York: Macmillan, 1969.

Groube, L. M. and M. C. Bowden. *The Archaeology of Rural Dorset: Past, Present and Future.* Dorset Natural History and Archaeological Society Monograph Series No. 4. Dorchester, Dorset: Friary Press, 1980.

Grundy, Joan. *Hardy and the Sister Arts.* Great Britain: Harper & Row Publishers Inc., 1979.

Guerard, Albert J. (ed.). *Hardy: A Collection of Critical Essays.* Englewood Cliffs, New Jersey: Prentice-Hall, 1963.

──────. *Thomas Hardy: The Novels and Stories.* Cambridge, Mass.: Harvard University Press, 1964.

Guirand, Felix (ed.). *The Larousse Encyclopedia of Mythology*, introd. Robert Graves. London: Paul Hamlyn, 1966.

Hagan, John. 'A Note on the Significance of Diggory Venn', *Nineteenth Century Fiction* 16 (1961-62), 147-55.

Halperin, John. *Egoism and Self-Discovery in the Victorian Novel.* New York: Burt Franklin, 1974.

──────. 'Leslie Stephen, Thomas Hardy, and *A Pair of Blue Eyes*', *Modern Language Review* 75 (1980), 738-45.

Hands, Timothy. ' "A Bewildered Child and his Conjurors": Hardy and the Ideas of his Time', in Lance St. John Butler (ed.). *New Perspectives on Thomas Hardy.* London: Macmillan, 1993.

──────. 'Jude in Oxford', *Thomas Hardy Journal* 11:3 (October 1995), 61-5.

──────. *Thomas Hardy: Distracted Preacher? Hardy's Religious Biography and Its Influence on his Novels.* London: Macmillan, 1989.

Hardy, Barbara. 'Introduction' to Thomas Hardy, *A Laodicean.* The New Wessex Edition. London: Macmillan, 1976.

──────. *Thomas Hardy: Imagining Imagination in Hardy's Poetry and Fiction.* London: New Brunswick, New Jersey: Athlone Press, 2000.

Hardy, Evelyn. 'Thomas Hardy and Turner – "The Painter's Eye" ', *London Magazine* 15 (1975), 17-27.

Hardy, Florence Emily. *The Early Life of Thomas Hardy 1840-1891.* London: Macmillan, 1928.

──────. *The Later Years of Thomas Hardy 1892-1928.* London: Macmillan, 1930.

Hardy, Thomas. *The Well-Beloved.* The Everyman Edition. Ed. Norman Page. London: Everyman, 1997.

Harris, Nicola. 'An Impure Woman: The Tragic Paradox and Tess as Totem', *Thomas Hardy Yearbook* 26 (1998), 18-21.

──────. ' "The "Petrified Eye": Fixed Moments and the Visible Narrative in *A Pair of Blue Eyes* (1873)', *Thomas Hardy Yearbook* 31 (2001), 17-33.

Harrisson, Frederic. 'A Few Words about the Nineteenth Century', in *The Choice of Books*. London: Macmillan, 1907.

Harvey, John. *Victorian Novelists and their Illustrators*. New York: New York University Press, 1971.

Hassett, Michael E. 'Compromised Romanticism in *Jude the Obscure*', *Nineteenth Century Fiction* 25 (1971), 432-43.

Hawkins, Desmond. *Concerning Agnes: Thomas Hardy's 'Good Little Pupil'*. Gloucester: Alan Sutton, 1982.

──────. *Thomas Hardy*. London: Macmillan, 1950.

──────. *Thomas Hardy. Novelist and Poet*. Newton Abbot, Devon: David & Charles, 1976.

Hawthorne, Nathaniel. *The House of the Seven Gables; A Romance*. New York: New American Library, 1961.

Hayes, Elizabeth T. (ed.). *Images of Persephone: Feminist Readings in Western Literature*. Miami: University Press of Florida, 1992.

Hayles, N. Katherine. *Chaos and Order: Complex Dynamics in Literature and Science*. Chicago and London: University of Chicago Press, 1991.

Heilman, Robert B. 'Hardy's *Mayor* and the Problem of Invention', *Criticism* 5 (1963), 199-213.

──────. 'Hardy's Sue Bridehead', *Nineteenth Century Fiction* 20 (1966), 307-23.

Henderson, Philip. *Swinburne: The Portrait of a Poet*. London: Routledge & Kegan Paul, 1974.

Henisch, Bridget Ann. *Fast and Feast: Food in Medieval Society*. University Park and London: Pennsylvania University Press, 1990.

Herbert, Lucille. 'Hardy's Views in *Tess of the d'Urbervilles*', *Journal of English Literary History* 37 (1970), 77-94.

Hersey, George L. *High Victorian Gothic: A Study in Associationism*. Baltimore: Johns Hopkins University Press, 1972.

Higgins, Lynne A. and Brenda R. Silver (ed.). *Rape and Representation*. USA: Columbia University Press, 1991.

Hodgen, Margaret T. *The Doctrine of Survivals: A Chapter in the History of Scientific Method in the Study of Man*. London: Allenson, 1936.

Hofling, Charles F. 'Thomas Hardy and the Mayor of Casterbridge', *Comprehensive Psychiatry* 9 (1968), 428-39.

Holland, Clive. *Thomas Hardy, OM*. London: Jenkins, 1933.

Hornback, Bert C. *The Metaphor of Chance: Vision and Technique in the Works of Thomas Hardy*. Athens, Georgia: Ohio University Press, 1971.

Horne, Lewis B. 'The Darkening Sun of Tess Durbeyfield', *Texas Studies in Literature and Language* 13 (1971), 299-311.

Horwath, William Frank. 'The Ache of Modernism: Thomas Hardy, Time and the Modern Novel', Unpublished Dissertation. University of Michigan, 1970.

Howatson, M. C. (gen. ed.). *The Oxford Companion to Classical Literature*, 2nd edn. Oxford: Oxford University Press, 1989.

Howe, Irving. *Thomas Hardy*. London: Macmillan, 1967.

Hughes, John. *'Ecstatic Sound': Music and Individuality in the Work of Thomas Hardy*. Aldershot: Ashgate, 2001.

Hugman, Bruce. *Hardy: 'Tess of the d'Urbervilles'*. London: Edward Arnold, 1970.

Humm, Maggie. 'Gender and Narrative in Thomas Hardy', *Thomas Hardy Yearbook* 11 (1984), 41-8.

Ingham, Patricia. 'The Evolution of *Jude the Obscure*', *Review of English Studies* 27 (1976), 27-37, 159-69.

————. 'Hardy and *The Wonders of Geology*', *Review of English Studies* 31 (1980), 59-64.

Irwin, Michael. *Reading Hardy's Landscapes*. London: Macmillan, 2000.

———— and Ian Gregor, 'Either Side of Wessex', in Lance St. John Butler (ed.), *Thomas Hardy after Fifty Years*. London: Macmillan, 1977.

Jackson, Arlene M. 'The Evolutionary Aspect of Hardy's Modern Men', *Revue Belge de Philologie et D'Histoire* 56 (1978), 641-9.

————. *Illustrations and the Novels of Thomas Hardy*. Totowa, New Jersey: Rowman & Littlefield, 1981.

Jackson-Houlston, C. M. *Ballads, Songs and Snatches: The Appropriation of Folk Song and Popular Culture in British Nineteenth-century Realist Prose*. Aldershot: Ashgate, 1999.

Jacobus, Mary. 'Hardy's Magian Retrospect', *Essays in Criticism* 32 (1982), 258-79.

————. 'Sue the Obscure', *Essays in Criticism* 25 (1975), 304-28.

————. 'Tess's Purity', *Essays in Criticism* 26 (1976), 318-38.

Jann, Rosemary. 'Hardy's Rustics and the Construction of Class', *Victorian Literature and Culture* 28:2 (2000), 411-25.

Jedrzejewski, Jan. *Thomas Hardy and the Church*. London: Macmillan, 1996.

Jeffries, Richard. *Hodge and his Masters*. London: Smith, Elder & Co., 1880.

Jenkins, Alice and Juliet John (eds.). *Rereading Victorian Fiction*. London: Macmillan, 2000.

Jenkyns, Richard. *The Victorians and Ancient Greece*. Oxford: Basil Blackwell, 1980.

Johnson, Bruce. *True Correspondence: A Phenomenology of Thomas Hardy's Novels*. Tallahassee, Florida: University Press of Florida, 1983.

Johnson, Lionel. *The Art of Thomas Hardy*, 1894; rev. edn., New York: Dodd, Mead, 1923.

Jones, Lawrence O. 'Imitation and Expression in Thomas Hardy's Theory of Fiction', *Studies in the Novel* 7 (1975), 507-25.

————. 'Thomas Hardy and the Cliff without a Name', in *Geography and Literature: A Meeting of the Disciplines*, ed. William E. Mallory and Paul Simpson-Housley. Syracuse, New York: Syracuse University Press, 1987.

Jordan, Mary Ellen. 'Thomas Hardy's *The Return of the Native*: Clym Yeobright and Melancholia', *American Imago* 39 (1982), 101-18.

Jurta, Roxanne. ' "Not-So-New Sue": The Myth of *Jude the Obscure* as a New Woman Novel', *Journal of the Eighteen Nineties Society* 26 (1999), 13-21.

Karl, Frederick R. '*The Mayor of Casterbridge*: A New Fiction Defined: 1960', *Modern Fiction Studies* 21 (1975), 405-28.

Kaufman, Robert F. *The Relationship Between Illustration and Text in the Novels of Dickens, Thackeray, Trollope and Hardy*. Unpublished dissertation. New York University, 1974.

Kay-Robinson, Denys. *Hardy's Wessex Reappraised*. Newton Abbot: David & Charles, 1972.

Keating, Peter (ed.). *Into Unknown England 1866-1913: Selections from the Social Explorers*. Manchester: Manchester University Press, 1981.

Keats, John. *Keats: Complete Poetical* Works, ed. H. W. Garrod. Oxford: Oxford University Press, 1988.

Kerenyi, Carl. *Archetypal Images of Mother and Daughter*, trans. Ralph Manheim. Princeton: Princeton University Press, 1967.

————. 'Kore', in C. G. Jung and Carl Kerenyi, *Essays on a Science of Mythology: The Myth of the Divine Child and the Mysteries of Eleusis*. Princeton: Princeton University Press, 1969.

Kerr, Barbara. *Bound to the Soil: A Social History of Dorset 1750-1918*. Wakefield: EP Publishing, 1975.

Kerr, Walter. Tragedy and Comedy. New York: Simon & Shuster, 1967.

Kiely, Robert. 'Vision and Viewpoint in *The Mayor of Casterbridge*', *Nineteenth Century Fiction* 23 (1968), 189-200.

Killham, John. *Tennyson and 'The Princess': Reflections of an Age*. London: Athlone Press, 1958.

Kirk, Geoffrey. *Myth: Its Meaning and Function in Ancient and Other Cultures*. Cambridge: Cambridge University Press, 1970.

Kissane, James. 'Victorian Mythology', *Victorian Studies* 6 (September 1962), 1-28.

Knoepflmacher, U. C. and G. B. Tennyson (eds.). *Nature and the Victorian Imagination*. Berkeley, California: University of California Press, 1977.

Kozicki, Henry. 'Myths of Redemption in Hardy's *Tess of the d'Urbervilles*', *Papers on Language and Literature* 10 (1974), 150-58.

Kramer, Dale (ed.). *The Cambridge Companion to Thomas Hardy*. Cambridge: Cambridge University Press, 1999.

———— (ed.). *Critical Approaches to the Fiction of Thomas Hardy*. London: Macmillan, 1979.

————. *Thomas Hardy: The Forms of Tragedy*. Detroit: Wayne State University Press, 1975.

Krasner, James. *The Entangled Eye: Visual Perception and the Representation of Nature in Post-Darwinian Narrative*. Oxford: Oxford University Press, 1992.

Kucich, John. *Repression in Victorian Fiction*. Berkeley, Los Angeles: University of California Press, 1987.

Kuklick, Henrika. *The Savage Within: the Social History of British Anthropology, 1885-1945*. Cambridge: Cambridge University Press, 1991.

Kuper, Adam. *The Invention of Primitive Society: Transformations of an Illusion*. London: Routledge, 1999.

Laird, John Tudor. 'New Light on the Evolution of *Tess of the d'Urbervilles*', *Review of English Studies* 31 (1980), 414-35.

————. *The Shaping of 'Tess of the d'Urbervilles'*. Oxford: Oxford University Press, 1975.

Land, Stephen K. *Thomas Hardy: The Architecture of Fiction*. New York: AMS Press, 1993.

Landes, David S. *Revolution in Time: Clocks and the Making of the Modern World*. Cambridge, Mass.: Harvard University Press, 1983.

Lang, William D. 'Mary Anning and the Pioneer Geologists of Lyme', *Proceedings of the Dorset Natural History and Archaeological Society*, 60 (1939), 142-64.

Langbaum, Robert. *Thomas Hardy in Our Time*. London: Macmillan, 1995.

Lange, Roderyk. *The Nature of Dance: An Anthropological Perspective*. London: Macdonald & Evans, 1975.

Langland, Elizabeth. 'Becoming a Man in *Jude the Obscure*', in Margaret G. Higonnet (ed.), *The Sense of Sex: Feminist Perspectives on Hardy*. Urbana and Chicago: University of Illinois Press, 1993.

————. 'A Perspective of One's Own: Thomas Hardy and the Elusive Sue Bridehead', *Studies in the Novel* 12 (1980), 12-28.

Law, Jules David. 'Sleeping Figures: Hardy, History and the Gendered Body', *English Literary History* 65:1 (Spring 1998), 223-57.

Lawrence, D. H. *Complete Poems*, ed. with introd. Vivian de Sola Pinto and F. Warren Roberts. Harmondsworth, Middlesex: Penguin, 1993.

————. *Kangaroo*. Harmondsworth, Middlesex: Penguin, 1997.

————. *Phoenix: The Posthumous Papers of D. H. Lawrence*, ed. with introd. Edward D. McDonald. London: Heinemann, 1936.

————. *The Rainbow*, ed. Mark Kinkead-Weekes. Cambridge: Cambridge University Press, 1989.

————. *Study of Thomas Hardy and Other Essays*, ed. Bruce Steele. Cambridge: Cambridge University Press, 1986.

Learner, Lawrence. *Thomas Hardy's 'The Mayor of Casterbridge': Tragedy or Social History*. London: Sussex University Press, 1975.

Leavis, L. R. 'The Late Nineteenth Century Novel and the Change Towards the Sexual – Gissing, Hardy and Lawrence', *English Studies* 64 (1985), 36-47.

Leopold, Joan. *Culture in Comparative and Evolutionary Perspective: E. B. Tylor and the Making of 'Primitive Culture'*. Berlin: Dietrich Reimer Verlag, 1980.

Levine, George. *Darwin and the Novelists: Patterns of Science in Victorian Fiction*. Cambridge, Mass.: Harvard University Press, 1988.

Levine, Philippa A. *The Amateur and the Professional: Antiquarians, Archaeologists and Historians*. Cambridge: Cambridge University Press, 1986.

Lewin, Roger. *Bones of Contention: Controversies in the Search for Human Origins.* New York: Touchstone-Simon & Schuster, 1988.

Lewis, Bernard. *History: Remembered, Recovered, Invented.* Princeton: Princeton University Press, 1976.

Lindberg, David C. and Ronald L. Numbers (eds.). *God and Nature: Historical Essays on the Encounter between Christianity and Science.* Berkeley and Los Angeles: University of California Press, 1986.

Lloyd, Tom. *Crises of Realism: Representing Experience in the British Novel, 1816-1910.* London: Associated University Presses, 1997.

Lock, Charles. 'Hardy and the Railway', *Essays in Criticism*, 50:1 (January 2000), 44-66.

Lodge, David. 'Introduction' to Thomas Hardy, *The Woodlanders*, The New Wessex Edition. London: Macmillan, 1976.

————. *The Language of Fiction: Essays in Criticism and Verbal Analysis of the English Novel.* London: Routledge & Kegan Paul, 1966.

————. 'Thomas Hardy and Cinematographic Form', *Novel* 7 (1974), 246-54.

MacLeod, Roy. *The 'Creed of Science' in Victorian England.* Aldershot: Ashgate, 1997.

MacNeice, Louis. *The Collected Poems of Louis MacNeice*, ed. E. R. Dodds. London: Faber & Faber, 1966.

Malcolmson, Robert W. *Popular Recreations in English Society, 1700-1850.* Cambridge: Cambridge University Press, 1973.

Marken, R. N. G. ' "Sick for Home": The Theme of *Tess of the d'Urbervilles*', *English Studies in Canada* 4 (Fall 1978), 317-29.

Marples, Morris. *White Horses and other Hill Figures.* Gloucester: Allan Sutton, 1981.

Marsden, Barry M. *The Early Barrow Diggers.* New Jersey: Noyes Press, 1974.

————. *Pioneers of Prehistory: Leaders and Landmarks in English Archaeology (1500-1900).* Ormskirk, Lancashire: Hesketh, 1983.

Marsden, Kenneth. *The Poems of Thomas Hardy.* London: Athlone Press, 1969.

Martin, Bruce K. 'Whatever Happened to Eustacia Vye?', *Studies in the Novel* 4 (1972), 619-27.

Martin, Robert Bernard. *Tennyson: The Unquiet Heart.* Oxford: Clarendon Press, 1980.

May, Charles E. '*Far from the Madding Crowd* and *The Woodlanders*: Hardy's Grotesque Pastorals', *English Literature in Transition* 17 (1974), 147-58.

————. 'Thomas Hardy and the Poetry of the Absurd', *Texas Studies in Literature and Language* 12 (1970), 63-73.

Mayhew, Thomas. *London Labour and the London Poor.* London: Constable, 1968.

Maynard, John. *Victorian Discourses on Sexuality and Religion.* Cambridge: Cambridge University Press, 1993.

Mayo, Robert. *The English Novel in the Magazines, 1740-1815.* Chicago: Northwestern University Press, 1962.

McBride, Mary. 'The Influence of *On Liberty* on Thomas Hardy's *The Mayor of Casterbridge*', *Mill Newsletter* 19:1 (1984), 12-17.

McCann, Eleanor. 'Blind Will or Blind Hero: Philosophy and Myth in Hardy's *The Return of the Native*', *Criticism* 3 (1961), 140-57.

McDowell, Arthur S. *Thomas Hardy: a Critical Study*. London: Faber & Faber, 1931.

McDowell, Frederick P. W. 'Hardy's "Seemings or Personal Impressions"; The Symbolic Use of Image and Content in *Jude the Obscure*', *Modern Fiction Studies* 6 (1960), 233-50.

Meisel, Perry. *Thomas Hardy: The Return of the Repressed*. New Haven and London: Yale University Press, 1972.

Merivale, Patricia. *Pan the Goat-God: His Myth in Modern Times*. Cambridge, Mass.: Harvard University Press, 1969.

Merrill, Lynn. *The Romance of Victorian Natural History*. Oxford: Oxford University Press, 1989.

Michell, John. *Megalithomania: Artists, Antiquarians, and Archaeologists at the Old Stone Monuments*. London: Thames & Hudson, 1982.

Miller, J. Hillis. 'Introduction' to Thomas Hardy, *The Well-Beloved*. The New Wessex Edition. London: Macmillan, 1976.

──────. *Thomas Hardy: Distance and Desire*. Cambridge, Mass.: Harvard University Press, 1970.

Millgate, Michael. 'Hardy's Fiction: Some Comments on the Present State of Criticism', *English Literature in Transition* 14 (1971), 230-38.

──────. *Thomas Hardy: A Biography*. Oxford: Clarendon Press, 1982.

──────. *Thomas Hardy: His Career as a Novelist*. London: Bodley Head, 1975.

──────. 'Thomas Hardy', in *Victorian Fiction: A Second Guide to Research*, ed. George H. Ford. New York: Modern Language Association of America, 1978.

Mingay, G. E. *Rural Life in Victorian England*. London: Heinemann, 1977.

Moore, Kevin Z. *The Descent of the Imagination: Post-Romantic Culture in the Later Novels of Thomas Hardy*. New York: New York University Press, 1993.

Morgan, Charles. *The House of Macmillan*. New York: Macmillan, 1944.

Morgan, Rosemarie. *Cancelled Words: Rediscovering Thomas Hardy*. London: Routledge, 1995.

──────. *Women and Sexuality in the Novels of Thomas Hardy*. London: Routledge, 1991.

Morgan, Thais E. (ed.). *Victorian Sages and Cultural Discourse: Renegotiating Gender and Power*. New Brunswick: Rutgers University Press, 1990.

Morgan, William. 'The Novel as Risk and Compromise, Poetry as Safe Haven: Hardy and the Victorian Reading Public', *Victorian Newsletter* 69 (1986), 1-3.

Morrell, Roy. *Thomas Hardy: The Will and the Way*. Kuala Lumpur: University of Malaya Press, 1968.

Mort, Frank. *Dangerous Sexualities: Medico-Moral Politics in England Since 1830*. London: Routledge & Kegan Paul, 1987.

Murfin, Ross C. *Swinburne, Hardy, Lawrence and the Burden of Belief*. Chicago and London: University of Chicago Press, 1978.

Murphy, Patricia. *Time is of the Essence: Temporality, Gender and the New Woman.* Albany, New York: State University of New York Press, 2001.

Nead, Lynda. *Myths of Sexuality: Representations of Women in Victorian Britain.* Oxford: Blackwell, 1988.

Nelson, Harland S. 'Stagg's Gardens: The Railway Through Dickens's World', *Dickens Studies Annual* 3 (1980), 41-53.

Newberry, George. *Index to 'Proceedings of the Dorset Natural History & Archaeological Society', Volumes 1-110, 1876-1988.* Bridport: Dorset Natural History & Archaeological Society, 1989.

Nicholson, Sarah. 'The Woman Pays: Death and the Ambivalence of Providence in Hardy's Novels', *Literature and Theology* 16:1 (March 2002), 27-39.

Nickel, Doug. 'The Camera and other Drawing Machines', in *British Photography in the Nineteenth Century*, ed. Mike Weaver. Cambridge: Cambridge University Press, 1982.

Ollard, S. L. *A Short History of the Oxford Movement.* London: Mowbray, 1915.

O'Malley, Patrick R. 'Oxford's Ghosts: *Jude the Obscure* and the End of the Gothic', *Modern Fiction Studies*, 46:3 (Fall 2000), 646-71.

Orel, Harold. *The Final Years of Thomas Hardy, 1912-1938.* London: Macmillan, 1976.

————. *Thomas Hardy's Epic Drama: A Study of 'The Dynasts'.* New York: Greenwood, 1969.

Osawa, Mamoru, Yoshinoshin Goto, Takashi Iijima, J. O. Bailey, Roy Morrell, Frank Pinion and Harold Orel (eds.). *A Thomas Hardy Dictionary*, revised by Saburo Minakawa and Michio Yoshikawa. Tokyo: Meicho-Fukyu-Kai, 1984.

O'Toole, Tess. 'Genealogy and Narrative Jamming in Hardy's *The Well-Beloved*', *Narrative* 1:3 (October 1993), 207-22.

Ovid, *The Metamorphoses*, trans. Horace Gregory. New York: Mentor, 1964.

Page, Norman. 'Hardy's Pictorial Art in *The Mayor of Casterbridge*', *Etudes Anglaises* 25 (1972), 486-92.

———— *Thomas Hardy.* London: Routledge & Kegan Paul, 1976.

———— (ed.). *Thomas Hardy Annual: No. 1.* London: Macmillan, 1982.

———— (ed.). *Thomas Hardy Annual: No. 2.* London: Macmillan, 1983.

———— (ed.). *Thomas Hardy Annual: No. 3.* London: Macmillan, 1984.

———— (ed.). *Thomas Hardy Annual: No. 4.* London: Macmillan, 1985.

———— (ed.). *Thomas Hardy Annual: No. 5.* London: Macmillan, 1986.

Paris, Bernard J. 'A Confusion of Many Standards: Conflicting Value Systems in *Tess of the d'Urbervilles*', *Nineteenth Century Fiction* 24 (1969), 57-79.

Pater, Walter. *Greek Studies: A Series of Essays.* London: Macmillan, 1910.

————. *The Renaissance: Studies in Art and Poetry*, ed. with introd. Adam Phillips. Oxford: The World's Classics, 1986.

Paterson, John. 'An Attempt at Grand Tragedy', in R. P. Draper (ed.). *Hardy: The Tragic Novels.* London: Macmillan, 1975.

————. 'The Genesis of *Jude the Obscure*', *Studies in Philology* 57 (1960), 87-98.

—————. *The Making of 'The Return of the Native'*, Berkeley, California: University of California Press, 1960.

—————. 'The Mayor of Casterbridge as Tragedy', *Victorian Studies* 3 (1959), 151-72.

—————. 'The Return of the Native as an Antichristian Document', *Nineteenth Century Fiction* 14 (1959), 111-27.

Patmore, Coventry. 'William Barnes: the Dorsetshire Poet', *Macmillan's Magazine* 6 (1862), 153-60.

Paulin, Tom. *Thomas Hardy: The Poetry of Perception.* London: Macmillan, 1975.

Payne, Christiana. *Toil and Plenty: Images of the Agricultural Landscape in England, 1780-1890.* New Haven: Yale University Press, 1993.

Peck, John. 'Hardy and Joyce: A Basis for Comparison', *Ariel,* 12 (1981), 71-85.

—————. 'Hardy's *The Woodlanders*: The Too Transparent Web', *English Literature in Transition* 24 (1981), 147-54.

Peckham, Morse. *Victorian Revolutionaries: Speculations on Some Heroes of a Culture Crisis.* New York: George Braziller, 1970.

Penn, K. J. *Historic Towns in Dorset.* Dorset Natural History and Archaeological Society Monograph Series No.1. Dorchester, Dorset: Friary Press, 1980.

Pettit, Charles P. C. *A Catalogue of the Works of Thomas Hardy in Dorchester Reference Library.* Dorchester: Dorset County Library, 1984.

—————— (ed.). *New Perspectives on Thomas Hardy.* London: Macmillan, 1994.

Phillips, Patricia. *The Scientific Lady: A Social History of Women's Scientific Interests, 1520- 1918.* New York: St. Martin's Press, 1990.

Pickrel, Paul. '*Jude the Obscure* and the Fall of Phaeton', *Hudson Review* 39 (1988), 231-50.

Pinion, F. B. (ed.). *Budmouth Essays on Thomas Hardy: Papers Presented at the 1975 Summer School.* Dorchester, Dorset: Thomas Hardy Society, 1976.

—————— (ed.). *A Hardy Companion: A Guide to the Works of Thomas Hardy and Their Background.* London: Macmillan, 1968.

—————. 'Introduction' to Thomas Hardy, *Two on a Tower.* The New Wessex Edition. London: Macmillan, 1976.

—————. *Thomas Hardy: Art and Thought.* London: Macmillan, 1977.

—————— (ed.). *A Thomas Hardy Dictionary.* London: Macmillan, 1973.

—————. *Thomas Hardy: His Life and Friends.* London: Macmillan, 1995.

Pite, Ralph. *Hardy's Geography: Wessex and the Regional Novel.* New York: Palgrave, 2002.

Poole, Adrian. ' "Men's Words" and Hardy's Women', *Essays in Criticism* 31 (1981), 328-45.

Powys, John Cowper. *Maiden Castle.* Harmondsworth, Middlesex; Penguin, 1976.

Purdy, Richard Little. *Thomas Hardy: A Biographical Study.* Oxford: Clarendon Press, 1968.

Rabbetts, John. *From Hardy to Faulkner: Wessex to Yoknapatawpha.* New York: St. Martin's Press, 1989.

Radford, Andrew. ' "Fallen Angel": Hardy's Critique of Shelley in the Final Wessex Novels', *Thomas Hardy Yearbook* 29 (2000), 51-63.

──────. 'Thomas Hardy's "Fiddler of the Reels" and musical folklore', *Thomas Hardy Journal* 15:2 (May 1999), 72-81.

Radford, Jean (ed.). *The Progress of Romance: The Politics of Popular Fiction.* London: Methuen, 1986.

Raine, Craig. 'Conscious Artistry in *The Mayor of Casterbridge*', in Charles P. C. Pettit (ed.), *New Perspectives on Thomas Hardy.* London: Macmillan, 1994.

Ray, Gordon N. *The Illustrator and the Book in England from 1790-1914.* New York: Pierpont Morgan Library, 1976.

Richards, Mary C. 'Thomas Hardy's Ironic Vision', *Nineteenth Century Fiction* 3 (1949), 265-79.

──────. 'Thomas Hardy's Ironic Vision', *Nineteenth Century Fiction* 4 (1949), 21-35.

Rimmer, Mary. 'Club Laws: Chess and the Construction of Gender in *A Pair of Blue Eyes*', in Margaret R. Higonnet (ed.), *The Sense of Sex: Feminist Perspectives on Hardy.* Urbana and Chicago: University of Illinois press, 1993.

Risquelme, Jean-Paul. *The Modernity of Thomas Hardy's Poetry.* Cambridge: Cambridge University Press, 1999.

Rogers, Kathleen. 'Women in Thomas Hardy', *Centennial Review* 19 (1975), 249-58.

Rogers, Samuel. *The Poetical Works of Samuel Rogers*, with a memoir by Edward Bell. London: E. Moxon, 1891.

Rothfield, Lawrence. *Vital Signs: Medical Realism in Nineteenth-Century Fiction.* Princeton, NJ: Princeton University Press, 1992.

Ruskin, John. *The Queen of the Air: being a study of the Greek myths of cloud and storm.* Kent: George Allen, 1887.

──────. *The Works of John Ruskin*, ed. E. T. Cook and Alexander Wedderburn, 39 vols. London: George Allen, 1903-12.

Russett, Cynthia Eagle. *Sexual Science: The Victorian Construction of Womenhood.* Cambridge, Mass.: Harvard University Press, 1989.

Saintsbury, George. 'The Early Development of Hardy's *Far from the Madding Crowd*', *Texas Studies in Language and Literature* 9 (1968), 415-28.

Schneidau, Herbert N. *Waking Giants: The Presence of the Past in Modernism.* Oxford: Oxford University Press, 1991.

Schweik, Robert C. 'Character and Fate in Hardy's *The Mayor of Casterbridge*', *Nineteenth Century Fiction* 21 (1966), 249-62.

──────. 'Moral Perspectives in *Tess of the d'Urbervilles*', *College English* 24 (1962), 14-18.

Scott, James E. 'Spectacle and Symbol in Thomas Hardy's Fiction', *Philosophical Quarterly* 44 (1965), 527-44.

──────.'Thomas Hardy's Use of the Gothic: An Examination of Five Representative Works', *Nineteenth Century Fiction* 17 (1963), 363-80.

Seymour-Smith, Martin. *Hardy.* London: Bloomsbury, 1995.

Shelley, Percy Bysshe. *Shelley: Selected Poetry, Prose and Letters*, ed. A. S. B. Glover. London: Nonesuch Press, 1951.

Sherren, Wilkinson. *The Wessex of Romance*. London: Chapman, 1902.

Shutt, Nicola. 'Nobody's Child: The Theme of Illegitimacy in the Novels of Charles Dickens, George Eliot and Wilkie Collins'. Unpublished D.Phil. dissertation. University of York, 1991.

Shuttleworth, Sally. *Charlotte Bronte and Victorian Psychology*. Cambridge: Cambridge University Press, 1996.

————. *George Eliot and Nineteenth-Century Science: The Make-Believe of a Beginning*. New York: Cambridge University Press, 1984.

Silverman, Kaja. 'History, Figuration and Female Subjectivity in *Tess of the d'Urbervilles*', *Novel* 18 (1984), 5-28.

Simmons, James C. *The Novelist as Historian: Essays on the Victorian Historical Novel*. The Hague: Mouton Press, 1973.

Sinnema, Peter W. *The Dynamics of the Printed Page: Representing the Nation in the 'Illustrated London News', 1842-1892*. Aldershot: Ashgate, 1998.

Slack, Robert C. 'The Text of Hardy's *Jude the Obscure*', *Nineteenth Century Fiction* 11 (1957), 261-75.

Slade, Tony. 'Leslie Stephen and *Far from the Madding Crowd*', *Thomas Hardy Journal* I:2 (1985), 31-40.

Small, Helen. *Love's Madness: Medicine, the Novel, and Female Insanity 1800-1865*. Oxford: Clarendon Press, 1996.

Smart, Alistair. 'Pictorial Images in the Novels of Thomas Hardy', *Review of English Studies* 12 (1961), 262-80.

Smith, Lindsay. *The Politics of Focus: Women, Children and Nineteenth-Century Photography*. Manchester: Manchester University Press, 1998.

Snell, K. D. M. *Annals of the Labouring Poor: Social Change and Agrarian England, 1660-1900*. Cambridge: Cambridge University Press, 1985.

Somerville, Alexander. *The Whistler at the Plough; containing travels, statistics, and descriptions of scenery and agricultural customs in most parts of England; with letters from Ireland: also 'Free trade and the League', a biographic history*, 3 vols. Manchester: J. Marshall, 1852.

Southerington, F. R. *Hardy's Vision of Man*. London: Chatto & Windus, 1971.

Springer, Marlene. *Hardy's Use of Allusion*. London: Macmillan, 1983.

Squillace, Robert. 'Hardy's Mummers', *Nineteenth Century Literature* 41 (1986), 172-89.

Squires, Michael. *The Pastoral Novel: Studies in George Eliot, Thomas Hardy, and D. H. Lawrence*. Charlottesville: University Press of Virginia, 1974.

Starzyk, Lawrence J. 'Hardy's *The Mayor of Casterbridge*: The Antitraditional Basis of Tragedy', *Studies in the Novel* 4 (1972), 592-607.

Stave, Shirley A. *The Decline of the Goddess: Nature, Culture and Women in Thomas Hardy's Fiction*. Westport, Conn.: Greenwood Press, 1995.

Steel, Gayla R. *Sexual Tyranny in Wessex*. New York: Peter Long Publishing Inc., 1993.

Steig, Michael. 'Fantasy and Mimesis in Literary Character: Shelley, Hardy, and Lawrence', *English Studies in Canada* 1 (1975), 160-71.

————. 'The Problems of Literary Values in Two Early Hardy Novels', *Texas Studies in Language and Literature* 12 (1970), 55-62.

————.'Sue Bridehead', *Novel* 1 (1968), 260-66.

Stephen, Leslie. 'A Bad Five Minutes In The Alps', in *Essays on Freethinking and Plainspeaking*. London: Longmans, Green & Co., 1873.

————. Letter to Thomas Hardy, 17 February 1874. Hardy Memorial Collection, Dorset County Museum.

———— and Sidney Lee (eds.). *The Dictionary of National Biography, From the Earliest Times to 1900*, vol. 12. London: Oxford University Press, 1921-22.

Stewart, J. I. M. *Thomas Hardy: A Critical Biography*. London: Longmans, 1971.

Stocking Jr., George W. *Race, Culture, and Evolution*. New York: Free Press, 1968.

————. *Functionalism Historicized: Essays in British Social Anthropology*. History of Anthropology, no. 2. Wisconsin: University of Wisconsin Press, 1984.

————. *Victorian Anthropology*. New York: Free Press, 1987.

Sumner, Rosemary. ' "The adventure to the unknown": Hardy, Lawrence and developments in the Novel', in Phillip V. Mallett and Ronald P. Draper (eds.), *A Spacious Vision: Essays on Hardy*. Newmill: Patten Press, 1994.

————. *A Route to Modernism: Hardy, Lawrence, Woolf*. London: Macmillan, 2000.

————. *Thomas Hardy: Psychological Novelist*. London: Macmillan, 1981.

Swinburne, Algernon Charles. *The Complete Works of Algernon Charles Swinburne*, ed. Sir Edmund Gosse and Thomas James Wise, 4 vols. New York: Russell & Russell, 1968.

Sylvia, Richard D. 'Hardy's Feminism: Apollonian Myth and *Two on a Tower*', *Thomas Hardy Journal* 12:2 (May 1996), 48-59.

————. 'Thomas Hardy's *Desperate Remedies*: "All My Sin Has Been Because I Love You So" ', *Colby Quarterly* 35:2 (June 1999), 102-16.

Tanner, Tony. 'Colour and Movement in Hardy's *Tess of the d'Urbervilles*', *Critical Quarterly* 10 (1968), 219-39.

Tennyson, Alfred Lord. *The Poems of Tennyson*, ed. Christopher Ricks, 3 vols. Harlow, Essex: Longman, 1987.

Thackeray, William Makepeace. 'The Roundabout Papers No. 8', *Cornhill Magazine* 2 (1860), 501-12.

Thesing, William B. (ed.). *Executions and the British Experience from the Seventeenth to the Twentieth Century: A Collection of Essays*. New York: McFarland & Co., 1990.

Thomas, Denis. 'Drunkenness in Thomas Hardy's Novels', *College Language Association Journal* 28 (1984), 190-209.

Thomas, Jane. *Thomas Hardy, Femininity and Dissent: Reassessing the 'Minor' Novels*. London: Macmillan, 1999.

Thompson, Charlotte. 'Language and the Shape of Reality in *Tess of the d'Urbervilles*', *Journal of English Literary History* 50 (1983), 729-62.

Thurley, Geoffrey. *The Psychology of Hardy's Novels: The Nervous and the Statuesque*. St. Lucia, Queensland: University of Queensland Press, 1975.

Tiddy, R. J. E. *The Mummers' Play*. Oxford: Clarendon Press, 1923; repr. Chicheley: Paul P. B. Minet, 1972.

Tobin, Thomas J. 'Women as Others in *The Mayor of Casterbridge*', *McNeese Review* 36 (1998), 19-26.

Torrens, Hugh. 'Mary Anning of Lyme; the greatest fossilist the world ever knew', *British Journal of the History of Science*, 28 (1995), 257-84.

Toth, Tobor. ' "Did They Sacrifice to God Here?" "No, I Believe to the Sun" ', *British and American Studies* 4:1 (1999), 15-22.

Turner, Frank M. *Between Science and Religion: The Reaction to Scientific Naturalism in Late Victorian England*. New Haven: Yale University Press, 1974.

Tuttleton, James W. *Vital Signs: Essays on American Literature and Criticism*. Chicago: Ivan R. Dee, 1996.

Unwin, Rayner. *The Rural Muse: Studies in the peasant poetry of England*. London: George Allen & Unwin, 1954.

Urwin, G. G. *'The Mayor of Casterbridge'*. Oxford: Basil Blackwell, 1964.

Vance, Norman. 'Secular Apocalyptic and Thomas Hardy', *History of European Ideas* 26:3-4 (2000), 201-10.

Van Ghent, Dorothy. 'On *Tess of the d'Urbervilles*', in *The English Novel: Form and Function*. New York: Holt, Rinehart & Winston, 1953.

Van Keuren, David K. 'Museums and Ideology: Augustus Pitt-Rivers, Anthropological Museums, and Social Change in Later Victorian Britain', *Victorian Studies* 28 (1984), 171-89.

Vickery, John B. *The Literary Impact of 'The Golden Bough'*. Princeton, New Jersey: Princeton University Press, 1973.

————. *Myth and Literature: Contemporary Theory and Practice*. Lincoln, Nebraska: University of Nebraska Press, 1966.

Vigar, Penelope. *The Novels of Thomas Hardy: Illusion and Reality*. University of London: Athlone Press, 1974.

Virgil. *The Aeneid*, trans. C. Day Lewis. Oxford: The World's Classics, 1986.

Vrettos, Athena. *Somatic Fictions: Imagining Illness in Victorian Culture*. Stanford: Stanford University Press, 1995.

Walters, Usha. *The Poetry of Thomas Hardy's Novels*. Saltzburg: Institut fur Anglistik und Americanistik, 1980.

Weatherby, H. L. 'Two Hardys', *Sewanee Review* 92 (1984), 162-71.

Weaver, Mike (ed.). *British Photography in the Nineteenth Century*. Cambridge: Cambridge University Press, 1989.

Weber, Carl. *Hardy of Wessex: His Life and Literary Career*. London: Routledge & Kegan Paul, 1965.

Webster, Harvey Curtis. *On a Darkling Plain*. Chicago: University of Chicago Press, 1947.

Welsh, Alexander. 'Realism as a Practical and Cosmic Joke', *Novel* 9 (1975), 23-39.

Wheeler, R. E. M. *Maiden Castle, Dorset*. Report of the Research Committee of the Society of Antiquaries of London, No. 12. Oxford: Society of Antiquaries, 1943.

White, James F. *The Cambridge Movement: The Ecclesiologists and the Gothic Revival*. Cambridge: Cambridge University Press, 1962.

White, R. J. *Thomas Hardy and History*. London: Macmillan, 1974.

Wickens, Glen. 'Hardy and the Aesthetic Mythographers: The Myth of Demeter and Persephone in *Tess of the d'Urbervilles*', *University of Toronto Quarterly* 53:1 (Fall 1983), 85-106.

Widdowson, Peter. *Hardy in History: A Study in Literary Sociology*. London: Routledge, 1989.

—————.' "Moments of Vision": Postmodernising *Tess of the d'Urbervilles;* or *Tess of the d'Urbervilles* Faithfully Presented', in Charles P. C. Pettit (ed.), *New Perspectives on Thomas Hardy*. London: Macmillan, 1994.

Williams, Merryn. *A Preface to Hardy*. London and New York: Longman, 1976.

—————. *Thomas Hardy and Rural England*. London: Macmillan, 1972.

Williams, Raymond. *The Country and the City*. London: Chatto & Windus, 1973.

Willis, Delta. *The Hominid Gang: Behind the Scenes in the Search for Human Origins*. New York: Viking, 1989.

Wilson, Martin. ' "Lovely Conundrum" and Locus for Conflict: The Figure of Sue Bridehead in Hardy's *Jude the Obscure*', *Thomas Hardy Journal* 11:3 (October 1995), 90-101.

Wing, George. '*Edwin Drood* and *Desperate Remedies*: Prototypes of Detective Fiction in 1870', *Studies in English Literature* 13 (1973), 667-87.

—————. *Hardy*. Edinburgh and London: Oliver & Boyd, 1963.

Winter, Michael. 'A Note towards an Historical and Class Analysis of Thomas Hardy's Novels', *Literature and History* 6 (1980), 174-81.

Wolff, Robert Lee. *Gains and Losses: Novels of Faith and Doubt in Victorian England*. New York: Garland, 1977.

Wong, Nancy Ting-Man. 'Human Time in the Wessex Novels', Unpublished dissertation. University of Pittsburgh, 1973.

Wood, Jane. *Passion and Pathology in Victorian Fiction*. Oxford: Oxford University Press, 2001

Wordsworth, William. *The Prelude: A Parallel Text*, ed. J. C. Maxwell. Harmondsworth, Middlesex: Penguin, 1986.

Wotton, George. *Thomas Hardy: Towards a Materialist Criticism*. Dublin: Gill & Macmillan, 1985.

Wright, Austin (ed.). *Victorian Literature: Modern Essays in Criticism*. New York: Oxford University Press, 1966.

Wright, R. J. *Thomas Hardy and History*. London: Macmillan, 1974.

Wright, T. R. *Hardy and the Erotic*. London: Macmillan, 1989.

Wright, Walter F. *The Shaping of 'The Dynasts'*. Lincoln: University of Nebraska Press, 1967.

Yeazell, Ruth Bernard (ed.). *Sex, Politics and Science in the Nineteenth-Century Novel: Selected Papers from the English Institute, 1983-84*. Baltimore: Johns Hopkins University Press, 1986.

Yeo, Eileen. *The Contest for Social Science: Relations and Representations of Gender and Class*. London: Rivers Oram, 1996
————. 'Mayhew as a Social Investigator', in E. P. Thompson and E. Yeo (eds.), *The Unknown Mayhew. Selections from the Morning Chronicle, 1849-50* Harmondsworth, Middlesex: Penguin, 1984.
Yoder, Albert C. 'Concepts of Mythology in Victorian England', Unpublished Ph.D. dissertation. Florida State University, 1971.
Young, Robert M. *Darwin's Metaphor*. Cambridge: Cambridge University Press, 1985.
Zietlow, Paul. *Moments of Vision: The Poetry of Thomas Hardy*. Cambridge, Mass.: Harvard University Press, 1974.

Index